2017 SUPPLEMENT TO

AMERICAN CRIMINAL PROCEDURE

CASES AND COMMENTARY

Tenth Edition

■ ■ ■

Stephen A. Saltzburg

Wallace and Beverley Woodbury University Professor,
The George Washington University School of Law

Daniel J. Capra

Philip D. Reed Professor of Law,
Fordham University School of Law

AMERICAN CASEBOOK SERIES®

WEST
ACADEMIC
PUBLISHING

American Casebook Series is a trademark registered in the U.S. Patent and Trademark Office.

© 2014–2016 LEG, Inc. d/b/a West Academic
© 2017 LEG, Inc. d/b/a West Academic
     444 Cedar Street, Suite 700
     St. Paul, MN 55101
     1-877-888-1330

West, West Academic Publishing, and West Academic are trademarks of West Publishing Corporation, used under license.

Printed in the United States of America

ISBN: 978-1-68328-779-7

TABLE OF CONTENTS

TABLE OF CASES

The principal cases are in bold type.

———————

2017 SUPPLEMENT TO

AMERICAN CRIMINAL PROCEDURE

CASES AND COMMENTARY

Tenth Edition

CHAPTER 1

BASIC PRINCIPLES

■ ■ ■

II. TWO SPECIAL ASPECTS OF CONSTITUTIONAL LAW: THE INCORPORATION DOCTRINE AND RETROACTIVE APPLICATION OF CONSTITUTIONAL DECISIONS

B. RETROACTIVITY

3.   Current Supreme Court Approach to Retroactivity

Page 28. Add at the bottom of the page:

Substantive Changes Are Fully Retroactive Under Teague v. Lane: Welch v. United States

In Welch v. United States, 136 S.Ct. 1257 (2016), the Supreme Court considered the retroactive effect of a previous decision in which it held that a sentencing provision in a federal criminal statute was void for vagueness. (The decision was Johnson v. United States, 135 S.Ct. 2551 (2015), invalidating the "residual clause" of the Armed Career Criminal Act under which defendants could be sentenced to 15 years to life in prison.) Welch was convicted in a federal court and sentenced under the statute's "residual clause," and after the Supreme Court decided *Johnson*, he sought habeas relief. Welch argued that the new decision should be given full retroactive effect, because it was on a question of "substantive" law and essentially held that the defendant's conduct could not be sentenced under the statutory provision. The Supreme Court agreed with Welsh in an opinion by Justice Kennedy, and remanded the case for resentencing. Justice Kennedy provided the following analysis of how the *Johnson* decision required retroactive application even to cases on collateral review, under the exception provided in *Teague*:

> The normal framework for determining whether a new rule applies to cases on collateral review stems from the plurality opinion in Teague v. Lane, 489 U.S. 288 (1989). * * * The parties here assume that the *Teague* framework applies in a federal collateral challenge to a federal conviction as it does in a federal collateral challenge to a state conviction, and we proceed on that assumption.

1

Under *Teague*, as a general matter, new constitutional rules of criminal procedure will not be applicable to those cases which have become final before the new rules are announced. *Teague* and its progeny recognize two categories of decisions that fall outside this general bar on retroactivity for procedural rules. First, new substantive rules generally apply retroactively. Second, new "watershed rules of criminal procedure," which are procedural rules "implicating the fundamental fairness and accuracy of the criminal proceeding," will also have retroactive effect.

* * *

A rule is substantive rather than procedural if it alters the range of conduct or the class of persons that the law punishes. This includes decisions that narrow the scope of a criminal statute by interpreting its terms, as well as constitutional determinations that place particular conduct or persons covered by the statute beyond the State's power to punish. Procedural rules, by contrast, regulate only the manner of determining the defendant's culpability. Such rules alter the range of permissible methods for determining whether a defendant's conduct is punishable. They do not produce a class of persons convicted of conduct the law does not make criminal, but merely raise the possibility that someone convicted with use of the invalidated procedure might have been acquitted otherwise.

Under this framework, the rule announced in *Johnson* is substantive. By striking down the [statutory provision] as void for vagueness, *Johnson* changed the substantive reach of the Armed Career Criminal Act, altering the range of conduct or the class of persons that the Act punishes. Before *Johnson*, the Act applied to any person who possessed a firearm after three violent felony convictions, even if one or more of those convictions fell under only the residual clause. An offender in that situation faced 15 years to life in prison. After *Johnson*, the same person engaging in the same conduct is no longer subject to the Act and faces at most 10 years in prison. The residual clause is invalid under *Johnson*, so it can no longer mandate or authorize any sentence. *Johnson* establishes, in other words, that even the use of impeccable factfinding procedures could not legitimate a sentence based on that clause. It follows that *Johnson* is a substantive decision.

By the same logic, *Johnson* is not a procedural decision. *Johnson* had nothing to do with the range of permissible methods a court might use to determine whether a defendant should be sentenced under the Armed Career Criminal Act. It did not, for example, allocate decisionmaking authority between judge and jury or regulate the evidence that the court could consider in making its decision. * * *

Johnson affected the reach of the underlying statute rather than the judicial procedures by which the statute is applied. *Johnson* is thus a substantive decision and so has retroactive effect under *Teague* in cases on collateral review.

Justice Thomas dissented in *Welch.*

Retroactive Application of Substantive Rules Is Required by the Constitution: Montgomery v. Louisiana

As discussed in Chapter 11 of the Text, the Supreme Court in Miller v. Alabama, 132 S.Ct. 2455 (2012), held that the Eighth Amendment bars the government from imposing a sentence of life imprisonment without parole on a juvenile convicted of homicide, absent consideration of the juvenile's special circumstances in light of the principles and purposes of juvenile sentencing. In Montgomery v. Louisiana, 136 S.Ct. 718 (2016), the Court considered whether *Miller* must be applied retroactively to defendants whose convictions were final when *Miller* was decided. In an opinion written by Justice Kennedy, the Court decided that *Miller* was a substantive decision, and thus fit within the exception provided by *Teague v. Lane* to the general rule that new rules are not applicable to finalized convictions. The complicating factor was that Montgomery sought relief by way of a post-conviction claim in a state court collateral proceeding, arguing that the *state* court was required to apply *Miller* retroactively; and Louisiana argued that *Teague* was an application of habeas corpus principles that did not bind the states. Justice Kennedy sided with Montgomery, concluding that *Teague's* exception for full retroactivity of substantive decisions was required by the Constitution. He explained as follows:

> The Court now holds that when a new substantive rule of constitutional law controls the outcome of a case, the Constitution requires state collateral review courts to give retroactive effect to that rule. *Teague's* conclusion establishing the retroactivity of new substantive rules is best understood as resting upon constitutional premises. That constitutional command is, like all federal law, binding on state courts. This holding is limited to *Teague's* first exception for substantive rules; the constitutional status of *Teague's* exception for watershed rules of procedure need not be addressed here.

> This Court's precedents addressing the nature of substantive rules, their differences from procedural rules, and their history of retroactive application establish that the Constitution requires substantive rules to have retroactive effect regardless of when a conviction became final.

> The category of substantive rules discussed in Teague originated in Justice Harlan's approach to retroactivity. *Teague* adopted that

reasoning. Justice Harlan defined substantive constitutional rules as "those that place, as a matter of constitutional interpretation, certain kinds of primary, private individual conduct beyond the power of the criminal law-making authority to proscribe." * * *

Substantive rules, then, set forth categorical constitutional guarantees that place certain criminal laws and punishments altogether beyond the State's power to impose. It follows that when a State enforces a proscription or penalty barred by the Constitution, the resulting conviction or sentence is, by definition, unlawful. Procedural rules, in contrast, are designed to enhance the accuracy of a conviction or sentence by regulating the manner of determining the defendant's culpability. Those rules merely raise the possibility that someone convicted with use of the invalidated procedure might have been acquitted otherwise. Even where procedural error has infected a trial, the resulting conviction or sentence may still be accurate; and, by extension, the defendant's continued confinement may still be lawful. For this reason, a trial conducted under a procedure found to be unconstitutional in a later case does not, as a general matter, have the automatic consequence of invalidating a defendant's conviction or sentence.

The same possibility of a valid result does not exist where a substantive rule has eliminated a State's power to proscribe the defendant's conduct or impose a given punishment. Even the use of impeccable factfinding procedures could not legitimate a verdict where the conduct being penalized is constitutionally immune from punishment. Nor could the use of flawless sentencing procedures legitimate a punishment where the Constitution immunizes the defendant from the sentence imposed. No circumstances call more for the invocation of a rule of complete retroactivity.

By holding that new substantive rules are, indeed, retroactive, *Teague* continued a long tradition of giving retroactive effect to constitutional rights that go beyond procedural guarantees. * * *

* * * There is no grandfather clause that permits States to enforce punishments the Constitution forbids. To conclude otherwise would undercut the Constitution's substantive guarantees. * * * If a State may not constitutionally insist that a prisoner remain in jail on federal habeas review, it may not constitutionally insist on the same result in its own postconviction proceedings. Under the Supremacy Clause of the Constitution, state collateral review courts have no greater power than federal habeas courts to mandate that a prisoner continue to suffer punishment barred by the Constitution. * * * Where state collateral review proceedings permit prisoners to challenge the lawfulness of their confinement, States cannot refuse to give

retroactive effect to a substantive constitutional right that determines the outcome of that challenge.

As a final point, it must be noted that the retroactive application of substantive rules does not implicate a State's weighty interests in ensuring the finality of convictions and sentences. *Teague* warned against the intrusiveness of "continually forc[ing] the States to marshal resources in order to keep in prison defendants whose trials and appeals conformed to then-existing constitutional standards." This concern has no application in the realm of substantive rules, for no resources marshaled by a State could preserve a conviction or sentence that the Constitution deprives the State of power to impose.

Justice Kennedy further found that the rule in *Miller* was in fact substantive:

The Court now holds that *Miller* announced a substantive rule of constitutional law. The conclusion that *Miller* states a substantive rule comports with the principles that informed *Teague*. *Teague* sought to balance the important goals of finality and comity with the liberty interests of those imprisoned pursuant to rules later deemed unconstitutional. *Miller*'s conclusion that the sentence of life without parole is disproportionate for the vast majority of juvenile offenders raises a grave risk that many are being held in violation of the Constitution.

Justice Scalia, joined by Justices Thomas and Alito, dissented in *Montgomery*. He first argued that *Teague's* exception for substantive rules does not bind the states. He declared as follows:

Neither *Teague* nor its exceptions are constitutionally compelled. Unlike today's majority, the *Teague*-era Court understood that cases on collateral review are fundamentally different from those pending on direct review because of considerations of finality in the judicial process. * * * A state court need only apply the law as it existed at the time a defendant's conviction and sentence became final. And once final, a new rule cannot reopen a door already closed. Any relief a prisoner might receive in a state court after finality is a matter of grace, not constitutional prescription.

* * *

Teague's central purpose was to do away with the old regime's tendency to "*continually* force the States to marshal resources in order to keep in prison defendants whose trials and appeals conformed to then-existing constitutional standards." Today's holding thwarts that purpose with a vengeance. Our ever-evolving Constitution changes the rules of "cruel and unusual punishments" every few years. * * * Justice Harlan noted the diminishing force of finality (and hence the equitable propriety—not the constitutional requirement—of disregarding it) when the law punishes nonpunishable *conduct*. But one cannot imagine a clearer frustration of the sensible policy of *Teague* when the ever-moving target of impermissible *punishments* is at issue. Today's holding not only forecloses Congress from eliminating this expansion of *Teague* in federal courts, but also foists this distortion upon the States.

Justice Scalia further concluded that *Miller* was a procedural rule, not a substantive one, because it did not completely bar imposition of life imprisonment but rather required the state to undertake procedures before doing so. He explained as follows:

> The majority * * * insists that *Miller* barred life-without-parole sentences "for all but the rarest of juvenile offenders, those whose crimes reflect permanent incorrigibility. * * * " The problem is that *Miller* stated, quite clearly, precisely the opposite: "Our decision does not categorically bar a penalty for a class of offenders or type of crime * * *. Instead, it mandates only that a sentencer *follow a certain process*—considering an offender's youth and attendant characteristics—before imposing a particular penalty." 132 S.Ct., at 2471 (emphasis added).

Justice Thomas wrote a separate dissent in *Montgomery*. He stated that the majority's opinion "repudiates established principles of finality. It finds no support in the Constitution's text, and cannot be reconciled with our Nation's tradition of considering the availability of postconviction remedies a matter about which the Constitution has nothing to say."

Justice Thomas noted, however, that the States "have a modest path to lessen the burdens that today's decision will inflict on their courts. States can stop entertaining claims alleging that this Court's Eighth Amendment decisions invalidated a sentence, and leave federal habeas courts to shoulder the burden of adjudicating such claims in the first instance. Whatever the desirability of that choice, it is one the Constitution allows States to make."

CHAPTER 2

SEARCHES AND SEIZURES OF PERSONS AND THINGS

■ ■ ■

II. THRESHOLD REQUIREMENTS FOR FOURTH AMENDMENT PROTECTIONS: WHAT IS A "SEARCH"? WHAT IS A "SEIZURE"?

B. THE RETURN OF THE TRESPASS ANALYSIS

Page 56. After the section on *"Pervasive, Prolonged Surveillance After Jones"*, **add the following headnote:**

Use of Tracking Devices for Civil-Based Purposes: Grady v. North Carolina

In Grady v. North Carolina, 135 S.Ct. 1368 (2015) (per curiam), Grady claimed that a state court order requiring him to enroll in a satellite-based monitoring system as a recidivist sex-offender—wearing tracking devices at all times for the rest of his life—constituted an illegal search in violation of the Fourth Amendment. Grady relied on *United States v. Jones* (Text, page 45). The state argued that the monitoring was a civil program so that *Jones* was inapposite, but the Court rejected this argument. The Court stated that "the government's purpose in collecting information does not control whether the method of collection constitutes a search." It reasoned that "[t]he state's program is plainly designed to obtain information . . . by physically intruding on a subject's body," which effects a Fourth Amendment search. The Court did "not decide the ultimate question of the program's constitutionality" and remanded for the state courts to make a determination as to the reasonableness of the intrusion.

IV. OBTAINING A SEARCH WARRANT: CONSTITUTIONAL PREREQUISITES

A. DEMONSTRATING PROBABLE CAUSE

5. Quantity of Information Required for Probable Cause

Page 147. Add the following headnote at the end of the section:

Legalized Marijuana and Probable Cause

With medical marijuana being legalized in a number of jurisdictions and marijuana sales being authorized by a few states, officers seeking search warrants for marijuana in those states might have to show probable cause that the marijuana that is the subject of the warrant is not lawfully possessed. In Commonwealth v. Canning, 471 Mass. 341, 28 N.E.3d 1156 (Mass.2015), for example, the Massachusetts Supreme Judicial Court held that enactment of a medical marijuana law means that state law enforcement officers seeking a warrant to search for evidence of a marijuana manufacturing operation must show probable cause that the suspects are not permitted by law to grow marijuana.

It should be noted though, that the fact that states may legalize possession or sale of marijuana under some circumstances does not limit the authority of federal officers to seek warrants. So, even though a state can bar its own officers from seeking warrants to search for marijuana that is lawfully possessed or sold under state law, federal officers can freely seek warrants as long as they have probable cause that suspects are violating federal law.

V. TO APPLY OR NOT APPLY THE WARRANT CLAUSE

A. ARRESTS IN PUBLIC AND IN THE HOME

3. The Constitutional Rule: Arrests in Public

Page 200. After the first full paragraph, add the following:

Can Reasonable Force Be Found Excessive Due to a Prior Fourth Amendment Violation? County of Los Angeles v. Mendez

What if police employ reasonable force, but only after they had already committed a different Fourth Amendment violation? For example, what if officers illegally enter a home and when they enter they see the homeowner raise a gun at them and prepare to shoot? In response to that action, the officers shoot the homeowner. Assume the shooting was found reasonable.

Does it become unreasonable because of the illegal entry? That was the question addressed by the Supreme Court in County of Los Angeles v. Mendez, 137 S.Ct. 1539 (2017), in which the plaintiffs were shot by police who entered the premises illegally, but were shot only after one of the plaintiffs was found holding a gun. The Ninth Circuit held that the officers' use of force, though reasonable under the immediate circumstances, was as a matter of law unreasonable because the plaintiff's taking up a gun was "provoked" by the illegal entry. The Supreme Court, in a unanimous opinion by Justice Alito, rejected the Ninth Circuit's analysis and found that an otherwise reasonable use of force could not be found unreasonable on the basis of a prior illegality. The Court reasoned as follows:

> Our case law sets forth a settled and exclusive framework for analyzing whether the force used in making a seizure complies with the Fourth Amendment. See *Graham,* 490 U.S., at 395. As in other areas of our Fourth Amendment jurisprudence, determining whether the force used to effect a particular seizure is reasonable requires balancing of the individual's Fourth Amendment interests against the relevant government interests. * * *

> The reasonableness of the use of force is evaluated under an objective inquiry that pays careful attention to the facts and circumstances of each particular case. And the reasonableness of a particular use of force must be judged from the perspective of a reasonable officer on the scene, rather than with the 20/20 vision of hindsight. Excessive force claims are evaluated for objective reasonableness based upon the information the officers had when the conduct occurred. That inquiry is dispositive: When an officer carries out a seizure that is reasonable, taking into account all relevant circumstances, there is no valid excessive force claim.

> The basic problem with the provocation rule is that it fails to stop there. Instead, the rule provides a novel and unsupported path to liability in cases in which the use of force was reasonable. Specifically, it instructs courts to look back in time to see if there was a *different* Fourth Amendment violation that is somehow tied to the eventual use of force. That distinct violation, rather than the forceful seizure itself, may then serve as the foundation of the plaintiff's excessive force claim.

> This approach mistakenly conflates distinct Fourth Amendment claims. Contrary to this approach, the objective reasonableness analysis must be conducted separately for each search or seizure that is alleged to be unconstitutional. An excessive force claim is a claim that a law enforcement officer carried out an unreasonable seizure through a use of force that was not justified under the relevant circumstances. It is not a claim that an officer used reasonable force

after committing a distinct Fourth Amendment violation such as an unreasonable entry.

By conflating excessive force claims with other Fourth Amendment claims, the provocation rule permits excessive force claims that cannot succeed on their own terms. That is precisely how the rule operated in this case. The District Court found (and the Ninth Circuit did not dispute) that the use of force by the deputies was reasonable under *Graham*. However, respondents were still able to recover damages because the deputies committed a separate constitutional violation (the warrantless entry into the shack) that in some sense set the table for the use of force. That is wrong. *The framework for analyzing excessive force claims is set out in Graham. If there is no excessive force claim under Graham,* there is no excessive force claim at all. To the extent that a plaintiff has other Fourth Amendment claims, they should be analyzed separately.

Justice Alito emphasized, however, that the plaintiffs might still recover if they could show that the illegal entry proximately caused their injuries. He explained as follows:

The provocation rule may be motivated by the notion that it is important to hold law enforcement officers liable for the foreseeable consequences of all of their constitutional torts. However, there is no need to distort the excessive force inquiry in order to accomplish this objective. To the contrary, both parties accept the principle that plaintiffs can—subject to qualified immunity—generally recover damages that are proximately caused by any Fourth Amendment violation. Thus, there is no need to dress up every Fourth Amendment claim as an excessive force claim. For example, if the plaintiffs in this case cannot recover on their excessive force claim, that will not foreclose recovery for injuries proximately caused *by the warrantless entry*. The harm proximately caused by these two torts may overlap, but the two claims should not be confused.

Justice Alito concluded that on remand, "the court should revisit the question whether proximate cause permits respondents to recover damages for their shooting injuries based on the deputies' failure to secure a warrant at the outset." He stated that "[p]roper analysis of this proximate cause question require[s] consideration of the foreseeability or the scope of the risk created by the predicate conduct, and require[s] the court to conclude that there was some direct relation between the injury asserted and the injurious conduct alleged." In other words, was it reasonably foreseeable that in entering the premises without a warrant, the officers would encounter someone with a gun in his hands?

Page 200. At the end of the *Note on the Use of Excessive Force in Making an Arrest* (after the discussion of *Scott v. Harris*) add the following case:

PLUMHOFF V. RICKART

United States Supreme Court, 2014.
134 S.Ct. 2012.

JUSTICE ALITO delivered the opinion of the Court.[*]

The courts below denied qualified immunity for police officers who shot the driver of a fleeing vehicle to put an end to a dangerous car chase. We reverse and hold that the officers did not violate the Fourth Amendment. In the alternative, we conclude that the officers were entitled to qualified immunity because they violated no clearly established law.

I

A

Because this case arises from the denial of the officers' motion for summary judgment, we view the facts in the light most favorable to the nonmoving party, the daughter of the driver who attempted to flee. Near midnight on July 18, 2004, Lieutenant Joseph Forthman of the West Memphis, Arkansas, Police Department pulled over a white Honda Accord because the car had only one operating headlight. Donald Rickard was the driver of the Accord, and Kelly Allen was in the passenger seat. Forthman noticed an indentation, "roughly the size of a head or a basketball" in the windshield of the car. He asked Rickard if he had been drinking, and Rickard responded that he had not. Because Rickard failed to produce his driver's license upon request and appeared nervous, Forthman asked him to step out of the car. Rather than comply with Forthman's request, Rickard sped away.

Forthman gave chase and was soon joined by five other police cruisers driven by Sergeant Vance Plumhoff and Officers Jimmy Evans, Lance Ellis, Troy Galtelli, and John Gardner. The officers pursued Rickard east on Interstate 40 toward Memphis, Tennessee. While on I-40, they attempted to stop Rickard using a "rolling roadblock," but they were unsuccessful. The District Court described the vehicles as "swerving through traffic at high speeds," and respondent does not dispute that the cars attained speeds over 100 miles per hour. During the chase, Rickard and the officers passed more than two dozen vehicles.

Rickard eventually exited I-40 in Memphis, and shortly afterward he made "a quick right turn," causing contact to occur between his car and

---

[*]   JUSTICE GINSBURG joins the judgment and Parts I, II, and III-C of this opinion. JUSTICE BREYER joins this opinion except as to Part IIIB-2.

Evans' cruiser. As a result of that contact, Rickard's car spun out into a parking lot and collided with Plumhoff's cruiser. Now in danger of being cornered, Rickard put his car into reverse "in an attempt to escape." As he did so, Evans and Plumhoff got out of their cruisers and approached Rickard's car, and Evans, gun in hand, pounded on the passenger-side window. At that point, Rickard's car made contact with yet another police cruiser. Rickard's tires started spinning, and his car "was rocking back and forth," indicating that Rickard was using the accelerator even though his bumper was flush against a police cruiser. At that point, Plumhoff fired three shots into Rickard's car. Rickard then "reversed in a 180 degree arc" and maneuvered onto another street, forcing Ellis to step to his right to avoid the vehicle. As Rickard continued fleeing down that street, Gardner and Galtelli fired 12 shots toward Rickard's car, bringing the total number of shots fired during this incident to 15. Rickard then lost control of the car and crashed into a building. Rickard and Allen both died from some combination of gunshot wounds and injuries suffered in the crash that ended the chase.

B

Respondent, Rickard's surviving daughter, filed this action under 42 U.S.C. § 1983, against the six individual police officers and the mayor and chief of police of West Memphis. She alleged that the officers used excessive force in violation of the Fourth and Fourteenth Amendments.

The officers moved for summary judgment based on qualified immunity, but the District Court denied that motion, holding that the officers' conduct violated the Fourth Amendment and was contrary to law that was clearly established at the time in question. [The Court of Appeals affirmed.]

II

[The Court holds that the Court of Appeals properly exercised jurisdiction, because the trial court's determination was a final order.]

III

A

Petitioners contend that the decision of the Court of Appeals is wrong for two separate reasons. They maintain that they did not violate Rickard's Fourth Amendment rights and that, in any event, their conduct did not violate any Fourth Amendment rule that was clearly established at the time of the events in question. When confronted with such arguments, we held in Saucier v. Katz, 533 U.S. 194, 200 (2001), that "the first inquiry must be whether a constitutional right would have been violated on the facts alleged." Only after deciding that question, we concluded, may an appellate court turn to the question whether the right at issue was clearly established at the relevant time.

* * *

B

A claim that law-enforcement officers used excessive force to effect a seizure is governed by the Fourth Amendment's "reasonableness" standard. See Graham v. Connor, 490 U.S. 386 (1989); Tennessee v. Garner, 471 U.S. 1 (1985). In *Graham,* we held that determining the objective reasonableness of a particular seizure under the Fourth Amendment "requires a careful balancing of the nature and quality of the intrusion on the individual's Fourth Amendment interests against the countervailing governmental interests at stake." The inquiry requires analyzing the totality of the circumstances.

We analyze this question from the perspective of a reasonable officer on the scene, rather than with the 20/20 vision of hindsight. We thus allow for the fact that police officers are often forced to make split-second judgments—in circumstances that are tense, uncertain, and rapidly evolving—about the amount of force that is necessary in a particular situation.

In this case, respondent advances two main Fourth Amendment arguments. First, she contends that the Fourth Amendment did not allow petitioners to use deadly force to terminate the chase. Second, she argues that the "degree of force was excessive," that is, that even if the officers were permitted to fire their weapons, they went too far when they fired as many rounds as they did. We address each issue in turn.

1

In Scott v. Harris, 550 U.S. 372 (2007), we considered a claim that a police officer violated the Fourth Amendment when he terminated a high-speed car chase by using a technique that placed a "fleeing motorist at risk of serious injury or death." The record in that case contained a videotape of the chase, and we found that the events recorded on the tape justified the officer's conduct. We wrote as follows: * * *

> "[R]espondent's vehicle rac[ed] down narrow, two-lane roads in the dead of night at speeds that are shockingly fast. We see it swerve around more than a dozen other cars, cross the double-yellow line, and force cars traveling in both directions to their respective shoulders to avoid being hit. We see it run multiple red lights and travel for considerable periods of time in the occasional center left-turn-only lane, chased by numerous police cars forced to engage in the same hazardous maneuvers just to keep up."

In light of those facts, we thought it was quite clear that the police officer did not violate the Fourth Amendment. We held that a "police officer's attempt to terminate a dangerous high-speed car chase that threatens the lives of innocent bystanders does not violate the Fourth

Amendment, even when it places the fleeing motorist at risk of serious injury or death."[3]

We see no basis for reaching a different conclusion here. * * * Under the circumstances at the moment when the shots were fired, all that a reasonable police officer could have concluded was that Rickard was intent on resuming his flight and that, if he was allowed to do so, he would once again pose a deadly threat for others on the road. Rickard's conduct even after the shots were fired—as noted, he managed to drive away despite the efforts of the police to block his path—underscores the point.

In light of the circumstances we have discussed, it is beyond serious dispute that Rickard's flight posed a grave public safety risk, and here, as in *Scott*, the police acted reasonably in using deadly force to end that risk.

2

We now consider respondent's contention that, even if the use of deadly force was permissible, petitioners acted unreasonably in firing a total of 15 shots. We reject that argument. It stands to reason that, if police officers are justified in firing at a suspect in order to end a severe threat to public safety, the officers need not stop shooting until the threat has ended. As petitioners noted below, "if lethal force is justified, officers are taught to keep shooting until the threat is over."

* * * This would be a different case if petitioners had initiated a second round of shots after an initial round had clearly incapacitated Rickard and had ended any threat of continued flight, or if Rickard had clearly given himself up. But that is not what happened.

In arguing that too many shots were fired, respondent relies in part on the presence of Kelly Allen in the front seat of the car, but we do not think that this factor changes the calculus. Our cases make it clear that Fourth Amendment rights are personal rights which may not be vicariously asserted. The question before us is whether petitioners violated Rickard's Fourth Amendment rights, not Allen's. * * * After all, it was Rickard who put Allen in danger by fleeing and refusing to end the chase, and it would be perverse if his disregard for Allen's safety worked to his benefit.

C

We have held that petitioners' conduct did not violate the Fourth Amendment, but even if that were not the case, petitioners would still be entitled to summary judgment based on qualified immunity.

---

[3] In holding that petitioners' conduct violated the Fourth Amendment, the District Court relied on reasoning that is irreconcilable with our decision in *Scott*. The District Court held that the danger presented by a high-speed chase cannot justify the use of deadly force because that danger was caused by the officers' decision to continue the chase. In *Scott*, however, we declined to "lay down a rule requiring the police to allow fleeing suspects to get away whenever they drive so recklessly that they put other people's lives in danger," concluding that the Constitution "assuredly does not impose this invitation to impunity-earned-by-recklessness."

An official sued under § 1983 is entitled to qualified immunity unless it is shown that the official violated a statutory or constitutional right that was " 'clearly established' " at the time of the challenged conduct. * * * We think our decision in Brosseau v. Haugen, 543 U.S. 194 (2004) (*per curiam*) squarely demonstrates that no clearly established law precluded petitioners' conduct at the time in question. In *Brosseau,* we held that a police officer did not violate clearly established law when she fired at a fleeing vehicle to prevent possible harm to other officers on foot who she believed were in the immediate area, occupied vehicles in the driver's path and any other citizens who might be in the area. After surveying lower court decisions regarding the reasonableness of lethal force as a response to vehicular flight, we observed that this is an area "in which the result depends very much on the facts of each case" and * * * held that *Garner* and *Graham,* which are "cast at a high level of generality," did not clearly establish that the officer's decision was unreasonable.

Brosseau makes plain that as of February 21, 1999—the date of the events at issue in that case—it was not clearly established that it was unconstitutional to shoot a fleeing driver to protect those whom his flight might endanger.

* * *

Under the circumstances present in this case, we hold that the Fourth Amendment did not prohibit petitioners from using the deadly force that they employed to terminate the dangerous car chase that Rickard precipitated. In the alternative, we note that petitioners are entitled to qualified immunity for the conduct at issue because they violated no clearly established law.

The judgment of the Court of Appeals is reversed, and the case is remanded for further proceedings consistent with this opinion.

More on Excessive Force and High-Speed Chases: Mullenix v. Luna

In Mullenix v. Luna, 136 S.Ct. 305 (2015), a per curiam opinion, the Court held that the lower courts erred in denying qualified immunity to a police officer who fired six shots at a fleeing vehicle and killed the driver. The driver fled from another officer who approached him to execute an arrest warrant. The deceased led the police on an 18 minute chase at speeds between 85 and 110 miles per hour; during the chase he called the police, claiming to have a gun and threatening to shoot at police officers if they continued to pursue him. The Court cited Brosseau v. Haugen, 543 U.S. 194 (2004) (per curiam) for the proposition that qualified immunity must be assessed by looking to the specific facts confronting an officer, and not at a higher level of generality. The Court noted that the lower court had held that Mullenix violated the clearly established rule that a police officer may not "use deadly force against a fleeing felon who does not pose a sufficient threat of harm to the officer or others." The correct inquiry, the Court explained, "was whether it was clearly established that the Fourth Amendment prohibited the officer's conduct in the situation she confronted: whether to shoot a disturbed felon, set on avoiding capture through vehicular flight, when persons in the immediate area are at risk from that flight." The Court found that it was certainly a matter of debate as to whether the officer acted unreasonably given the circumstances presented.

Justice Scalia concurred in the judgment and argued that the case did not involve the application of deadly force in effecting an arrest, because the shooting officer's goal was to stop the car by destroying the engine. He described this as a risky enterprise but argued that the question was whether it was reasonable to undertake it in light of the risk to the driver.

Justice Sotomayor was the sole dissenter. She argued that the clearly established legal question was whether there was a governmental interest in shooting at the car rather than waiting for it to run over spike strips which had been planted in the road, and that the majority pointed to no such interest. The majority responded that spike strips present dangers of their own; that the shooter feared the driver might shoot at or run over the officers manning the spike strips; and that the spike strips might not work.

4.   Protections Against Erroneous Warrantless Arrests

Page 203. At the end of the section, add the following:

Continued Pretrial Detention of the Basis of False Evidence: Manuel v. City of Joliet

The Court in Manuel v. City of Joliet, 137 S.Ct. 911 (2016), reviewed a claim that Manuel was detained for trial on the basis of manufactured evidence. He received a prompt post-arrest hearing, and the judge found probable cause—but on the basis of false evidence manufactured by the officer-defendants. The question for the Court was whether the continued pretrial detention was covered by the Fourth Amendment. The Court, in an opinion by Justice Kagan for six justices, relied on *Gerstein* and held that the Fourth Amendment applied to the post-hearing, pretrial detention. Justice Kagan stated that "[l]egal process did not expunge Manuel's Fourth Amendment claim because the process he received failed to establish what that Amendment makes essential for pretrial detention— probable cause to believe that he committed a crime." Justice Alito, joined by Justice Thomas, dissented, arguing that once the judicial process has begun, relief from a wrongful detention must be found in the Due Process Clause, not the Fourth Amendment.

B. STOP AND FRISK

3. Grounds for a Stop: Reasonable Suspicion

a. *Source of Information*

Page 263. Add this new case to the end of the headnote titled "*J.L. and a Tip About Reckless Driving*":

In the following case, the Court upholds a stop on the basis of an anonymous tip about reckless driving—but not on the rationale that the lower courts had used in similar cases, as discussed in the Casebook.

NAVARETTE V. CALIFORNIA

Supreme Court of the United States, 2014.
134 S.Ct. 1683.

JUSTICE THOMAS delivered the opinion of the Court.

After a 911 caller reported that a vehicle had run her off the road, a police officer located the vehicle she identified during the call and executed a traffic stop. We hold that the stop complied with the Fourth Amendment because, under the totality of the circumstances, the officer had reasonable suspicion that the driver was intoxicated.

* * *

On August 23, 2008, a Mendocino County 911 dispatch team for the California Highway Patrol (CHP) received a call from another CHP dispatcher in neighboring Humboldt County. The Humboldt County dispatcher relayed a tip from a 911 caller, which the Mendocino County team recorded as follows: "Showing southbound Highway 1 at mile marker 88, Silver Ford 150 pickup. Plate of 8-David-94925. Ran the reporting party off the roadway and was last seen approximately five [minutes] ago." The Mendocino County team then broadcast that information to CHP officers at 3:47 p.m.

A CHP officer heading northbound toward the reported vehicle responded to the broadcast. At 4:00 p.m., the officer passed the truck near mile marker 69. At about 4:05 p.m., after making a U-turn, he pulled the truck over. A second officer, who had separately responded to the broadcast, also arrived on the scene. As the two officers approached the truck, they smelled marijuana. A search of the truck bed revealed 30 pounds of marijuana. The officers arrested the driver, petitioner Lorenzo Prado Navarette, and the passenger, petitioner Josè Prado Navarette.

Petitioners moved to suppress the evidence, arguing that the traffic stop violated the Fourth Amendment because the officer lacked reasonable suspicion of criminal activity. Both the magistrate who presided over the suppression hearing and the Superior Court disagreed.[1] Petitioners pleaded guilty to transporting marijuana and were sentenced to 90 days in jail plus three years of probation.

The California Court of Appeal affirmed, concluding that the officer had reasonable suspicion to conduct an investigative stop. The court reasoned that the content of the tip indicated that it came from an eyewitness victim of reckless driving, and that the officer's corroboration of the truck's description, location, and direction established that the tip was reliable enough to justify a traffic stop. Finally, the court concluded that the caller reported driving that was sufficiently dangerous to merit an investigative stop without waiting for the officer to observe additional reckless driving himself. The California Supreme Court denied review. We granted certiorari and now affirm.

* * *

The Fourth Amendment permits brief investigative stops—such as the traffic stop in this case—when a law enforcement officer has "a particularized and objective basis for suspecting the particular person stopped of criminal activity." The "reasonable suspicion" necessary to justify such a stop "is dependent upon both the content of information possessed by police and its degree of reliability." Alabama v. White, 496 U.S. 325 (1990). The standard takes into account "the totality of the circumstances—the whole picture." Although a mere "hunch" does not create reasonable suspicion, the level of suspicion the standard requires is considerably less than proof of wrongdoing by a preponderance of the evidence, and obviously less than is necessary for probable cause.

* * *

These principles apply with full force to investigative stops based on information from anonymous tips. We have firmly rejected the argument "that reasonable cause for a[n investigative stop] can only be based on the officer's personal observation, rather than on information supplied by another person." Adams v. Williams, 407 U.S. 143, 147 (1972). Of course, an anonymous tip alone seldom demonstrates the informant's basis of knowledge or veracity. That is because "ordinary citizens generally do not provide extensive recitations of the basis of their everyday observations," and an anonymous tipster's veracity is "by hypothesis largely unknown, and unknowable." *White, supra.* But under appropriate circumstances, an anonymous tip can demonstrate "sufficient indicia of reliability to provide reasonable suspicion to make [an] investigatory stop." *Id.*

---

[1]   At the suppression hearing, counsel for petitioners did not dispute that the reporting party identified herself by name in the 911 call recording. Because neither the caller nor the Humboldt County dispatcher who received the call was present at the hearing, however, the prosecution did not introduce the recording into evidence. The prosecution proceeded to treat the tip as anonymous, and the lower courts followed suit.

Our decisions in Alabama v. White and Florida v. J. L. are useful guides. In *White*, an anonymous tipster told the police that a woman would drive from a particular apartment building to a particular motel in a brown Plymouth station wagon with a broken right tail light. The tipster further asserted that the woman would be transporting cocaine. After confirming the innocent details, officers stopped the station wagon as it neared the motel and found cocaine in the vehicle. We held that the officers' corroboration of certain details made the anonymous tip sufficiently reliable to create reasonable suspicion of criminal activity. By accurately predicting future behavior, the tipster demonstrated "a special familiarity with respondent's affairs," which in turn implied that the tipster had "access to reliable information about that individual's illegal activities." We also recognized that an informant who is proved to tell the truth about some things is more likely to tell the truth about other things, "including the claim that the object of the tip is engaged in criminal activity."

In *J. L.*, by contrast, we determined that no reasonable suspicion arose from a bare-bones tip that a young black male in a plaid shirt standing at a bus stop was carrying a gun. The tipster did not explain how he knew about the gun, nor did he suggest that he had any special familiarity with the young man's affairs. As a result, police had no basis for believing "that the tipster ha[d] knowledge of concealed criminal activity." Furthermore, the tip included no predictions of future behavior that could be corroborated to assess the tipster's credibility. We accordingly concluded that the tip was insufficiently reliable to justify a stop and frisk.

* * *

The initial question in this case is whether the 911 call was sufficiently reliable to credit the allegation that petitioners' truck "ran the [caller] off the roadway." Even assuming for present purposes that the 911 call was anonymous, we conclude that the call bore adequate indicia of reliability for the officer to credit the caller's account. The officer was therefore justified in proceeding from the premise that the truck had, in fact, caused the caller's car to be dangerously diverted from the highway.

By reporting that she had been run off the road by a specific vehicle— a silver Ford F-150 pickup, license plate 8D94925—the caller necessarily claimed eyewitness knowledge of the alleged dangerous driving. That basis of knowledge lends significant support to the tip's reliability. [Citing *Gates* and *Spinelli*]. This is in contrast to *J. L.*, where the tip provided no basis for concluding that the tipster had actually seen the gun. Even in *White*, where we upheld the stop, there was scant evidence that the tipster had actually observed cocaine in the station wagon. We called *White* a " 'close case' " because "[k]nowledge about a person's future movements indicates some familiarity with that person's affairs, but having such knowledge does not necessarily imply that the informant knows, in particular, whether that person is carrying hidden contraband." A driver's claim that another vehicle ran her off the road, however, necessarily implies that the informant knows the other car was driven dangerously.

There is also reason to think that the 911 caller in this case was telling the truth. Police confirmed the truck's location near mile marker 69 (roughly 19 highway miles south of the location reported in the 911 call) at 4:00 p.m. (roughly 18 minutes after the 911 call). That timeline of events suggests that the caller reported the incident soon after she was run off the road. That sort of contemporaneous report has long been treated as especially reliable. In evidence law, we generally credit the proposition that statements about an event and made soon after perceiving that event are especially trustworthy because "substantial contemporaneity of event and statement negate the likelihood of deliberate or conscious misrepresentation." Advisory Committee's Notes on Fed. Rule Evid. 803(1) (describing the rationale for the hearsay exception for "present sense impressions"). A similar rationale applies to a "statement relating to a startling event"—such as getting run off the road—"made while the declarant was under the stress of excitement that it caused." Fed. Rule Evid. 803(2) (hearsay exception for "excited utterances"). Unsurprisingly, 911 calls that would otherwise be inadmissible hearsay have often been admitted on those grounds. * * * There was no indication that the tip in *J. L.* (or even in *White*) was contemporaneous with the observation of criminal activity or made under the stress of excitement caused by a startling event, but those considerations weigh in favor of the caller's veracity here.

Another indicator of veracity is the caller's use of the 911 emergency system. A 911 call has some features that allow for identifying and tracing callers, and thus provide some safeguards against making false reports with immunity. As this case illustrates, 911 calls can be recorded, which provides victims with an opportunity to identify the false tipster's voice and subject him to prosecution * * *. The 911 system also permits law enforcement to verify important information about the caller. In 1998, the Federal Communications Commission (FCC) began to require cellular carriers to relay the caller's phone number to 911 dispatchers. Beginning in 2001, carriers have been required to identify the caller's geographic location with increasing specificity. And although callers may ordinarily block call recipients from obtaining their identifying information, FCC regulations exempt 911 calls from that privilege. None of this is to suggest that tips in 911 calls are *per se* reliable. Given the foregoing technological and regulatory developments, however, a reasonable officer could conclude that a false tipster would think twice before using such a system. The caller's use of the 911 system is therefore one of the relevant circumstances that, taken together, justified the officer's reliance on the information reported in the 911 call.

* * *

Even a reliable tip will justify an investigative stop only if it creates reasonable suspicion that "criminal activity may be afoot." We must therefore determine whether the 911 caller's report of being run off the roadway created reasonable suspicion of an ongoing crime such as drunk driving as opposed to an isolated episode of past recklessness. We conclude that the behavior alleged by the 911 caller, viewed from the standpoint of an objectively reasonable police officer, amounts to reasonable suspicion of drunk driving. The stop was therefore proper.[2]

Reasonable suspicion depends on "the factual and practical considerations of everyday life on which reasonable and prudent men, not legal technicians, act." Under that commonsense approach, we can appropriately recognize certain driving behaviors as sound indicia of drunk driving. * * * Indeed, the accumulated experience of thousands of officers suggests that these sorts of erratic behaviors are strongly correlated with drunk driving. Of course, not all traffic infractions imply intoxication. Unconfirmed reports of driving without a seatbelt or slightly over the speed limit, for example, are so tenuously connected to drunk driving that a stop on those grounds alone would be constitutionally suspect. But a reliable tip alleging the dangerous behaviors discussed above generally would justify a traffic stop on suspicion of drunk driving.

The 911 caller in this case reported more than a minor traffic infraction and more than a conclusory allegation of drunk or reckless driving. Instead, she alleged a specific and dangerous result of the driver's conduct: running another car off the highway. That conduct bears too great a resemblance to paradigmatic manifestations of drunk driving to be dismissed as an isolated example of recklessness. Running another vehicle off the road suggests lane-positioning problems, decreased vigilance, impaired judgment, or some combination of those recognized drunk driving cues. And the experience of many officers suggests that a driver who almost strikes a vehicle or another object—the exact scenario that ordinarily causes running another vehicle off the roadway—is likely intoxicated. As a result, we cannot say that the officer acted unreasonably under these circumstances in stopping a driver whose alleged conduct was a significant indicator of drunk driving.

Petitioners' attempts to second-guess the officer's reasonable suspicion of drunk driving are unavailing. It is true that the reported behavior might also be explained by, for example, a driver responding to "an unruly child or other distraction." But we have consistently recognized that reasonable

---

[2]   Because we conclude that the 911 call created reasonable suspicion of an ongoing crime, we need not address under what circumstances a stop is justified by the need to investigate completed criminal activity. *Cf.* United States v. Hensley, 469 U.S. 221, 229 (1985).

suspicion "need not rule out the possibility of innocent conduct." United States v. Arvizu, 534 U.S. 266, 277 (2002).

Nor did the absence of additional suspicious conduct, after the vehicle was first spotted by an officer, dispel the reasonable suspicion of drunk driving. It is hardly surprising that the appearance of a marked police car would inspire more careful driving for a time. Extended observation of an allegedly drunk driver might eventually dispel a reasonable suspicion of intoxication, but the 5-minute period in this case hardly sufficed in that regard. Of course, an officer who already has such a reasonable suspicion need not surveil a vehicle at length in order to personally observe suspicious driving. Once reasonable suspicion of drunk driving arises, "the reasonableness of the officer's decision to stop a suspect does not turn on the availability of less intrusive investigatory techniques." United States v. Sokolow, 490 U.S., at 11 (1989). This would be a particularly inappropriate context to depart from that settled rule, because allowing a drunk driver a second chance for dangerous conduct could have disastrous consequences.

* * *

Like *White*, this is a "close case." As in that case, the indicia of the 911 caller's reliability here are stronger than those in *J. L.*, where we held that a bare-bones tip was unreliable. Although the indicia present here are different from those we found sufficient in *White*, there is more than one way to demonstrate "a particularized and objective basis for suspecting the particular person stopped of criminal activity." Under the totality of the circumstances, we find the indicia of reliability in this case sufficient to provide the officer with reasonable suspicion that the driver of the reported vehicle had run another vehicle off the road. That made it reasonable under the circumstances for the officer to execute a traffic stop. We accordingly affirm.

JUSTICE SCALIA, with whom JUSTICE GINSBURG, JUSTICE SOTOMAYOR, and JUSTICE KAGAN join, dissenting.

The California Court of Appeal in this case relied on jurisprudence from the California Supreme Court (adopted as well by other courts) to the effect that "an anonymous and uncorroborated tip regarding a possibly intoxicated highway driver" provides without more the reasonable suspicion necessary to justify a stop. Today's opinion does not explicitly adopt such a departure from our normal Fourth Amendment requirement that anonymous tips must be corroborated; it purports to adhere to our prior cases, such as Florida v. J. L and Alabama v. White. Be not deceived.

Law enforcement agencies follow closely our judgments on matters such as this, and they will identify at once our new rule: So long as the caller identifies where the car is, anonymous claims of a single instance of possibly careless or reckless driving, called in to 911, will support a traffic stop. This is not my concept, and I am sure would not be the Framers', of a people secure from unreasonable searches and seizures. I would reverse the judgment of the Court of Appeal of California.

* * *

The California Highway Patrol in this case knew nothing about the tipster on whose word—and that alone—they seized Lorenzo and Josè Prado Navarette. They did not know her name. They did not know her phone number or address. They did not even know where she called from (she may have dialed in from a neighboring county).

The tipster said the truck had "[run her] off the roadway," but the police had no reason to credit that charge and many reasons to doubt it, beginning with the peculiar fact that the accusation was anonymous. Eliminating accountability is ordinarily the very purpose of anonymity. The unnamed tipster "can lie with impunity," *J. L., supra*, at 275 (KENNEDY, J., concurring). Anonymity is especially suspicious with respect to the call that is the subject of the present case. When does a victim complain to the police about an arguably criminal act (running the victim off the road) without giving his identity, so that he can accuse and testify when the culprit is caught?

The question before us, the Court agrees, is whether the "content of information possessed by police and its degree of reliability" gave the officers reasonable suspicion that the driver of the truck (Lorenzo) was committing an ongoing crime. When the only source of the government's information is an informant's tip, we ask whether the tip bears sufficient "indicia of reliability" to establish "a particularized and objective basis for suspecting the particular person stopped of criminal activity."

The most extreme case, before this one, in which an anonymous tip was found to meet this standard was *White*. There the reliability of the tip was established by the fact that it predicted the target's behavior in the finest detail—a detail that could be known only by someone familiar with the target's business: She would, the tipster said, leave a particular apartment building, get into a brown Plymouth station wagon with a broken right tail light, and drive immediately to a particular motel. Very few persons would have such intimate knowledge, and hence knowledge of the unobservable fact that the woman was carrying unlawful drugs was plausible. Here the Court makes a big deal of the fact that the tipster was dead right about the fact that a silver Ford F-150 truck (license plate 8D94925) was traveling south on Highway 1 somewhere near mile marker 88. But everyone in the world who saw the car would have that knowledge, and anyone who wanted the car stopped would have to provide that information. Unlike the situation in *White*, that generally available knowledge in no way makes it plausible that the tipster saw the car run someone off the road.

The Court says that "[b]y reporting that she had been run off the road by a specific vehicle ... the caller necessarily claimed eyewitness knowledge." So what? The issue is not how she claimed to know, but whether what she claimed to know was true. The claim to "eyewitness knowledge" of being run off the road supports *not at all* its veracity; nor does the amazing, mystifying prediction (so far short of what existed in *White*) that the petitioners' truck *would be heading south on Highway 1.*

The Court finds "reason to think" that the informant "was telling the truth" in the fact that police observation confirmed that the truck had been driving near the spot at which, and at the approximate time at which, the tipster alleged she had been run off the road. According to the Court, the statement therefore qualifies as a "present sense impression" or "excited utterance," kinds of hearsay that the law deems categorically admissible given their low likelihood of reflecting "deliberate or conscious misrepresentation." So, the Court says, we can fairly suppose that the accusation was true.

No, we cannot. To begin with, it is questionable whether either the "present sense impression" or the "excited utterance" exception to the hearsay rule applies here. The classic "present sense impression" is the recounting of an event that is occurring before the declarant's eyes, as the declarant is speaking ("I am watching the Hindenburg explode!"). And the classic "excited utterance" is a statement elicited, almost involuntarily, by the shock of what the declarant is immediately witnessing ("My God, those people will be killed!"). It is the immediacy that gives the statement some credibility; the declarant has not had time to dissemble or embellish. There is no such immediacy here. The declarant had time to observe the license number of the offending vehicle, 8D94925 (a difficult task if she was forced off the road and the vehicle was speeding away), to bring her car to a halt, to copy down the observed license number (presumably), and (if she was using her own cell phone) to dial a call to the police from the stopped car. Plenty of time to dissemble or embellish.

Moreover, even assuming that less than true immediacy will suffice for these hearsay exceptions to apply, the tipster's statement would run into additional barriers to admissibility and acceptance. According to the very Advisory Committee's Notes from which the Court quotes, cases addressing an unidentified declarant's present sense impression "indicate hesitancy in upholding the statement alone as sufficient" proof of the reported event. For excited utterances as well, the "knotty theoretical" question of statement-alone admissibility persists—seemingly even when the declarant is known. * * * It is even unsettled whether excited utterances of an unknown declarant are *ever* admissible. A leading treatise reports that "the courts have been reluctant to admit such statements, principally because of uncertainty that foundational requirements, including the impact of the event on the declarant, have been satisfied." In sum, it is unlikely that the law of evidence would deem the mystery caller in this case "especially trustworthy."

Finally, and least tenably, the Court says that another "indicator of veracity" is the anonymous tipster's mere "use of the 911 emergency system." Because, you see, recent "technological and regulatory developments" suggest that the identities of unnamed 911 callers are increasingly less likely to remain unknown. Indeed, the systems are able to identify "the caller's geographic location with increasing specificity." * * * But assuming the Court is right about the ease of identifying 911 callers, it proves absolutely nothing in the present case unless the anonymous caller was *aware* of that fact. It is the tipster's *belief* in anonymity, not its *reality*, that will control his behavior. There is no reason to believe that your average anonymous 911 tipster is aware that 911 callers are readily identifiable.[2]

* * *

All that has been said up to now assumes that the anonymous caller made, at least in effect, an accusation of drunken driving. But in fact she did not. She said that the petitioners' truck "[r]an [me] off the roadway." That neither asserts that the driver was drunk nor even raises the *likelihood* that the driver was drunk. The most it conveys is that the truck did some apparently nontypical thing that forced the tipster off the roadway, whether partly or fully, temporarily or permanently. Who really knows what (if anything) happened? The truck might have swerved to avoid an animal, a pothole, or a jaywalking pedestrian.

But let us assume the worst of the many possibilities: that it was a careless, reckless, or even intentional maneuver that forced the tipster off the road. Lorenzo might have been distracted by his use of a hands-free cell phone, or distracted by an intense sports argument with Josè. Or, indeed, he might have intentionally forced the tipster off the road because of some personal animus, or hostility to her "Make Love, Not War" bumper sticker. I fail to see how reasonable suspicion of a *discrete instance* of irregular or hazardous driving generates a reasonable suspicion of *ongoing intoxicated driving*. What proportion of the hundreds of thousands—perhaps millions—of careless, reckless, or intentional traffic violations committed each day is attributable to drunken drivers? I say 0.1 percent. I have no basis for that except my own guesswork. But unless the Court has some basis in reality to believe that the proportion is many orders of magnitude

---

[2]   The Court's discussion of reliable 911 traceability has so little relevance to the present case that one must surmise it has been included merely to assure officers in the future that anonymous 911 accusations—even untraced ones—are not as suspect (and hence as unreliable) as other anonymous accusations. That is unfortunate.

above that—say 1 in 10 or at least 1 in 20—it has no grounds for its unsupported assertion that the tipster's report in this case gave rise to a *reasonable suspicion* of drunken driving.

Bear in mind that that is the only basis for the stop that has been asserted in this litigation. The stop required suspicion of an ongoing crime, not merely suspicion of having run someone off the road earlier. And driving while being a careless or reckless person, unlike driving while being a drunk person, is not an ongoing crime. In other words, in order to stop the petitioners the officers here not only had to assume without basis the accuracy of the anonymous accusation but also had to posit an unlikely reason (drunkenness) for the accused behavior.

In sum, at the moment the police spotted the truck, it was more than merely "*possible*" that the petitioners were not committing an ongoing traffic crime. It was overwhelmingly likely that they were not.

* * *

It gets worse. Not only, it turns out, did the police have no good reason *at first* to believe that Lorenzo was driving drunk, they had very good reason *at last* to know that he was not. The Court concludes that the tip, plus confirmation of the truck's location, produced reasonable suspicion that the truck not only had been *but still was* barreling dangerously and drunkenly down Highway 1. In fact, alas, it was not, and the officers knew it. They followed the truck for five minutes, presumably to see if it was being operated recklessly. And *that* was good police work. While the anonymous tip was not enough to support a stop for drunken driving under Terry v. Ohio, it was surely enough to counsel observation of the truck to see if it was driven by a drunken driver. But the pesky little detail left out of the Court's reasonable-suspicion equation is that, for the five minutes that the truck was being followed (five minutes is a *long* time), Lorenzo's driving was irreproachable. Had the officers witnessed the petitioners violate a single traffic law, they would have had cause to stop the truck, Whren v. United States, 517 U.S. 806, 810, and this case would not be before us. And not only was the driving *irreproachable*, but the State offers no evidence to suggest that the petitioners even did anything *suspicious*, such as suddenly slowing down, pulling off to the side of the road, or turning somewhere to see whether they were being followed. Consequently, the tip's suggestion of ongoing drunken driving (if it could be deemed to suggest that) not only went uncorroborated; it was affirmatively undermined.

A hypothetical variation on the facts of this case illustrates the point. Suppose an anonymous tipster reports that, while following near mile marker 88 a silver Ford F-150, license plate 8D949925, traveling southbound on Highway 1, she saw in the truck's open cab several five-foot-tall stacks of what was unmistakably baled cannabis. Two minutes later, a highway patrolman spots the truck exactly where the tip suggested it would be, begins following it, but sees nothing in the truck's cab. It is not enough to say that the officer's observation merely failed to corroborate the tipster's accusation. It is more precise to say that the officer's observation *discredited* the informant's accusation: The crime was supposedly occurring (and would continue to occur) in plain view, but the police saw nothing. Similarly, here, the crime supposedly suggested by the tip was ongoing intoxicated driving, the hallmarks of which are many, readily identifiable, and difficult to conceal. That the officers witnessed nary a minor traffic violation nor any other "sound indici[um] of drunk driving" strongly suggests that the suspected crime was *not* occurring after all. The tip's implication of continuing criminality, already weak, grew even weaker.

Resisting this line of reasoning, the Court curiously asserts that, since drunk drivers who see marked squad cars in their rearview mirrors may evade detection simply by driving "more careful[ly]," the "absence of additional suspicious conduct" is "hardly surprising" and thus largely irrelevant. Whether a drunk driver drives drunkenly, the Court seems to think, is up to him. That is not how I understand the influence of alcohol. I subscribe to the more traditional view that the dangers of intoxicated driving are the intoxicant's impairing effects on the body—effects that no mere act of the will can resist. Consistent with this view, I take it as a fundamental premise of our intoxicated-driving laws that a driver soused enough to swerve once can be expected to swerve again—and soon. If he does not, and if the only evidence of his first episode of irregular driving is a mere inference from an uncorroborated, vague, and nameless tip, then the Fourth Amendment requires that he be left alone.

* * *

The Court's opinion serves up a freedom-destroying cocktail consisting of two parts patent falsity: (1) that anonymous 911 reports of traffic violations are reliable so long as they correctly identify a car and its location, and (2) that a single instance of careless or reckless driving necessarily supports a reasonable suspicion of drunkenness. All the malevolent 911 caller need do is assert a traffic violation, and the targeted car will be stopped, forcibly if necessary, by the police. If the driver turns out not to be drunk (which will almost always be the case), the caller need fear no consequences, even if 911 knows his identity. After all, he never alleged drunkenness, but merely called in a traffic violation—and on that point his word is as good as his victim's.

Drunken driving is a serious matter, but so is the loss of our freedom to come and go as we please without police interference. To prevent and detect murder we do not allow searches without probable cause or targeted *Terry* stops without reasonable suspicion. We should not do so for drunken driving either. After today's opinion all of us on the road, and not just drug dealers, are at risk of having our freedom of movement curtailed on suspicion of drunkenness, based upon a phone tip, true or false, of a single instance of careless driving. I respectfully dissent.

Page 280. At the end of the page, after the section on quantum of reasonable suspicion, add the following new section:

c.   *Can a Mistake of Law Give Rise to Reasonable Suspicion? Heien v. North Carolina*

Like probable cause, the reasonable suspicion standard allows an officer to make reasonable mistakes of fact. For example, an officer might stop a suspect walking late at night because he has white powder all over his clothes. If it turns out that the guy is coming home from his job at the bakery, the officer has made a mistake but it is a reasonable one—the fact that the officer ends up being mistaken is of no moment so long as that mistake was reasonable. But does the same hold for a mistake of law? The Supreme Court addressed this question in the following case.

HEIEN v. NORTH CAROLINA
Supreme Court of the United States, 2014.
135 S.Ct. 530.

CHIEF JUSTICE ROBERTS delivered the opinion of the Court.

The Fourth Amendment prohibits "unreasonable searches and seizures." Under this standard, a search or seizure may be permissible even though the justification for the action includes a reasonable factual mistake. An officer might, for example, stop a motorist for traveling alone in a high-occupancy vehicle lane, only to discover upon approaching the car that two children are slumped over asleep in the back seat. The driver has not violated the law, but neither has the officer violated the Fourth Amendment.

But what if the police officer's reasonable mistake is not one of fact but of law? In this case, an officer stopped a vehicle because one of its two brake lights was out, but a court later determined that a single working brake light was all the law required. The question presented is whether such a mistake of law can nonetheless give rise to the reasonable suspicion necessary to uphold the seizure under the Fourth Amendment. We hold that it can. Because the officer's mistake about the brake-light law was reasonable, the stop in this case was lawful under the Fourth Amendment.

I

On the morning of April 29, 2009, Sergeant Matt Darisse of the Surry County Sheriff's Department sat in his patrol car near Dobson, North

Carolina, observing northbound traffic on Interstate 77. Shortly before 8 a.m., a Ford Escort passed by. Darisse thought the driver looked "very stiff and nervous," so he pulled onto the interstate and began following the Escort. A few miles down the road, the Escort braked as it approached a slower vehicle, but only the left brake light came on. Noting the faulty right brake light, Darisse activated his vehicle's lights and pulled the Escort over.

Two men were in the car: Maynor Javier Vasquez sat behind the wheel, and petitioner Nicholas Brady Heien lay across the rear seat. Sergeant Darisse explained to Vasquez that as long as his license and registration checked out, he would receive only a warning ticket for the broken brake light. A records check revealed no problems with the documents, and Darisse gave Vasquez the warning ticket. But Darisse had become suspicious during the course of the stop—Vasquez appeared nervous, Heien remained lying down the entire time, and the two gave inconsistent answers about their destination. Darisse asked Vasquez if he would be willing to answer some questions. Vasquez assented, and Darisse asked whether the men were transporting various types of contraband. Told no, Darisse asked whether he could search the Escort. Vasquez said he had no objection, but told Darisse he should ask Heien, because Heien owned the car. Heien gave his consent, and Darisse, aided by a fellow officer who had since arrived, began a thorough search of the vehicle. In the side compartment of a duffle bag, Darisse found a sandwich bag containing cocaine. The officers arrested both men.

The State charged Heien with attempted trafficking in cocaine. Heien moved to suppress the evidence seized from the car, contending that the stop and search had violated the Fourth Amendment of the United States Constitution. After a hearing at which both officers testified and the State played a video recording of the stop, the trial court denied the suppression motion, concluding that the faulty brake light had given Sergeant Darisse reasonable suspicion to initiate the stop, and that Heien's subsequent consent to the search was valid. Heien pleaded guilty but reserved his right to appeal the suppression decision.

The North Carolina Court of Appeals reversed. The initial stop was not valid, the court held, because driving with only one working brake light was not actually a violation of North Carolina law. The relevant provision of the vehicle code provides that a car must be

> "equipped with a stop lamp on the rear of the vehicle. The stop lamp shall display a red or amber light visible from a distance of not less than 100 feet to the rear in normal sunlight, and shall be actuated upon application of the service (foot) brake. The stop lamp may be incorporated into a unit with one or more other rear lamps." N.C. Gen. Stat. Ann. § 20–129(g) (2007).

Focusing on the statute's references to "a stop lamp" and "[t]he stop lamp" in the singular, the court concluded that a vehicle is required to have only one working brake light—which Heien's vehicle indisputably did. The justification for the stop was therefore "objectively unreasonable," and the stop violated the Fourth Amendment

The State appealed, and the North Carolina Supreme Court reversed. [That court] assumed for purposes of its decision that the faulty brake light was not a violation. But the court concluded that, for several reasons, Sergeant Darisse could have reasonably, even if mistakenly, read the vehicle code to require that both brake lights be in good working order. Most notably, a nearby code provision requires that "all originally equipped rear lamps" be functional. Because Sergeant Darisse's mistaken understanding of the vehicle code was reasonable, the stop was valid. * * * We granted certiorari.

II

* * *

A traffic stop for a suspected violation of law is a "seizure" of the occupants of the vehicle and therefore must be conducted in accordance with the Fourth Amendment. All parties agree that to justify this type of seizure, officers need only "reasonable suspicion"—that is, "a particularized and objective basis for suspecting the particular person stopped" of breaking the law. The question here is whether reasonable suspicion can rest on a mistaken understanding of the scope of a legal prohibition. We hold that it can.

As the text indicates and we have repeatedly affirmed, the ultimate touchstone of the Fourth Amendment is reasonableness. To be reasonable is not to be perfect * * * . We have recognized that searches and seizures based on mistakes of fact can be reasonable. The warrantless search of a home, for instance, is reasonable if undertaken with the consent of a resident, and remains lawful when officers obtain the consent of someone who reasonably appears to be but is not in fact a resident. See Illinois v. Rodriguez, 497 U.S. 177, 183–186 (1990). By the same token, if officers with probable cause to arrest a suspect mistakenly arrest an individual matching the suspect's description, neither the seizure nor an accompanying search of the arrestee would be unlawful. See Hill v. California, 401 U.S. 797, 802–805 (1971). The limit is that "the mistakes must be those of reasonable men."

But reasonable men make mistakes of law, too, and such mistakes are no less compatible with the concept of reasonable suspicion. Reasonable suspicion arises from the combination of an officer's understanding of the facts and his understanding of the relevant law. The officer may be reasonably mistaken on either ground. Whether the facts turn out to be not what was thought, or the law turns out to be not what was thought, the result is the same: the facts are outside the scope of the law. There is no reason, under the text of the Fourth Amendment or our precedents, why this same result should be acceptable when reached by way of a reasonable mistake of fact, but not when reached by way of a similarly reasonable mistake of law.

The dissent counters that our cases discussing probable cause and reasonable suspicion, most notably *Ornelas* v. *United States*, 517 U.S. 690, 696–697 (1996), have contained "scarcely a peep" about mistakes of law. It would have been surprising, of course, if they had, since none of those cases involved a mistake of law.

Although such recent cases did not address mistakes of law, older precedents did. In fact, cases dating back two centuries support treating legal and factual errors alike in this context. Customs statutes enacted by Congress not long after the founding authorized courts to issue certificates indemnifying customs officers against damages suits premised on unlawful seizures. Courts were to issue such certificates on a showing that the officer had "reasonable cause"—a synonym for "probable cause"—for the challenged seizure. United States v. Riddle, 9 U.S. 311 (1809). In United States v. Riddle, a customs officer seized goods on the ground that the English shipper had violated the customs laws by preparing an invoice that undervalued the merchandise, even though the American consignee declared the true value to the customs collector. Chief Justice Marshall held that there had been no violation of the customs law because, whatever the shipper's intention, the consignee had not actually attempted to defraud the Government. Nevertheless, because "the construction of the law was liable to some question," he affirmed the issuance of a certificate of probable cause: "A doubt as to the true construction of the *law* is as reasonable a cause for seizure as a doubt respecting the fact."

This holding—that reasonable mistakes of law, like those of fact, would justify certificates of probable cause—was reiterated in a number of 19th-century decisions. By the Civil War, there had been "numerous cases in which [a] captured vessel was in no fault, and had not, under a true construction of the law, presented even ground of suspicion, and yet the captor was exonerated because he acted under an honest mistake of the law." The La Manche, 14 F. Cas. 965, 972, F. Cas. No. 8004 (No. 8,004) (D Mass. 1863).

Riddle and its progeny are not directly on point. Chief Justice Marshall was not construing the Fourth Amendment, and a certificate of probable cause functioned much like a modern-day finding of qualified immunity, which depends on an inquiry distinct from whether an officer has committed a constitutional violation. But Chief Justice Marshall was nevertheless explaining the concept of probable cause, which, he noted elsewhere, "in all cases of seizure, has a fixed and well known meaning. It imports a seizure made under circumstances which warrant suspicion." Locke v. United States, 11 U.S. 339, 7 Cranch 339 (1813). * * *

The contrary conclusion would be hard to reconcile with a much more recent precedent. In Michigan v. DeFillippo, 443 U.S. 31 (1979), we addressed the validity of an arrest made under a criminal law later declared unconstitutional. A Detroit ordinance that authorized police officers to stop and question individuals suspected of criminal activity also made it an offense for such an individual "to refuse to identify himself and produce evidence of his identity." Detroit police officers sent to investigate a report of public intoxication arrested Gary DeFillippo after he failed to identify himself. A search incident to arrest uncovered drugs, and DeFillippo was charged with possession of a controlled substance. The Michigan Court of Appeals ordered the suppression of the drugs, concluding that the identification ordinance was unconstitutionally vague and that DeFillippo's arrest was therefore invalid.

Accepting the unconstitutionality of the ordinance as a given, we nonetheless reversed. At the time the officers arrested DeFillippo, we explained, "there was no controlling precedent that this ordinance was or was not constitutional, and hence the conduct observed violated a presumptively valid ordinance." Acknowledging that the outcome might have been different had the ordinance been "grossly and flagrantly unconstitutional," we concluded that under the circumstances "there was abundant probable cause to satisfy the constitutional prerequisite for an arrest."

The officers were wrong in concluding that DeFillippo was guilty of a criminal offense when he declined to identify himself. That a court only *later* declared the ordinance unconstitutional does not change the fact that DeFillippo's conduct was lawful when the officers observed it. But the officers' assumption that the law was valid was reasonable, and their observations gave them "abundant probable cause" to arrest DeFillippo. Although DeFillippo could not be prosecuted under the identification ordinance, the search that turned up the drugs was constitutional.

Heien struggles to recast *DeFillippo* as a case solely about the exclusionary rule, not the Fourth Amendment itself. In his view, the officers' mistake of law resulted in a violation the Fourth Amendment, but suppression of the drugs was not the proper remedy. We did say in a footnote that suppression of the evidence found on *DeFillippo* would serve none of the purposes of the exclusionary rule. But that literally marginal discussion does not displace our express holding that the arrest was constitutionally valid because the officers had probable cause. * * *

Heien * * * contends that the reasons the Fourth Amendment allows some errors of fact do not extend to errors of law. Officers in the field must make factual assessments on the fly, Heien notes, and so deserve a margin of error. In Heien's view, no such margin is appropriate for questions of law: The statute here either requires one working brake light or two, and the answer does not turn on anything "an officer might suddenly confront in the field." But Heien's point does not consider the reality that an officer may "suddenly confront" a situation in the field as to which the application of a statute is unclear—however clear it may later become. A law prohibiting "vehicles" in the park either covers Segways or not, but an officer will nevertheless have to make a quick decision on the law the first time one whizzes by.

Contrary to the suggestion of Heien and *amici*, our decision does not discourage officers from learning the law. The Fourth Amendment tolerates only *reasonable* mistakes, and those mistakes—whether of fact or of law—must be *objectively* reasonable. We do not examine the subjective understanding of the particular officer involved. Cf. Whren v. United States, 517 U.S. 806, 813 (1996). And the inquiry is not as forgiving as the one employed in the distinct context of deciding whether an officer is entitled to qualified immunity for a constitutional or statutory violation. Thus, an officer can gain no Fourth Amendment advantage through a sloppy study of the laws he is duty-bound to enforce.

Finally, Heien and *amici* point to the well-known maxim, "Ignorance of the law is no excuse," and contend that it is fundamentally unfair to let police officers get away with mistakes of law when the citizenry is accorded no such leeway. Though this argument has a certain rhetorical appeal, it misconceives the implication of the maxim. The true symmetry is this: Just as an individual generally cannot escape criminal liability based on a mistaken understanding of the law, so too the government cannot impose criminal liability based on a mistaken understanding of the law. If the law required two working brake lights, Heien could not escape a ticket by claiming he reasonably thought he needed only one; if the law required only one, Sergeant Darisse could not issue a valid ticket by claiming he reasonably thought drivers needed two. But just because mistakes of law cannot justify either the imposition or the avoidance of criminal liability, it does not follow that they cannot justify an investigatory stop. And Heien is not appealing a brake-light ticket; he is appealing a cocaine-trafficking conviction as to which there is no asserted mistake of fact or law.

III

Here we have little difficulty concluding that the officer's error of law was reasonable. Although the North Carolina statute at issue refers to "a stop lamp," suggesting the need for only a single working brake light, it also provides that "[t]he stop lamp may be incorporated into a unit with one or more *other* rear lamps." N.C. Gen. Stat. Ann. § 20–129(g) (emphasis added). The use of "other" suggests to the everyday reader of English that a "stop lamp" is a type of "rear lamp." And another subsection of the same provision requires that vehicles "have all originally equipped rear lamps or the equivalent in good working order," § 20–129(d), arguably indicating that if a vehicle has multiple "stop lamp[s]," all must be functional.

The North Carolina Court of Appeals concluded that the "rear lamps" discussed in subsection (d) do not include brake lights, but, given the "other," it would at least have been reasonable to think they did. Both the majority and the dissent in the North Carolina Supreme Court so concluded, and we agree. This "stop lamp" provision, moreover, had never been previously construed by North Carolina's appellate courts. It was thus objectively reasonable for an officer in Sergeant Darisse's position to think that Heien's faulty right brake light was a violation of North Carolina law. And because the mistake of law was reasonable, there was reasonable suspicion justifying the stop.

The judgment of the Supreme Court of North Carolina is

Affirmed.

JUSTICE KAGAN, with whom JUSTICE GINSBURG joins, concurring.

I concur in full in the Court's opinion, which explains why certain mistakes of law can support the reasonable suspicion needed to stop a vehicle under the Fourth Amendment. In doing so, the Court correctly emphasizes that the "Fourth Amendment tolerates only . . . *objectively* reasonable" mistakes of law. And the Court makes clear that the inquiry into whether an officer's mistake of law counts as objectively reasonable "is not as forgiving as the one employed in the distinct context of deciding whether an officer is entitled to qualified immunity." I write separately to elaborate briefly on those important limitations.

First, an officer's "subjective understanding" is irrelevant: As the Court notes, "[w]e do not examine" it at all. That means the government cannot defend an officer's mistaken legal interpretation on the ground that the officer was unaware of or untrained in the law. And it means that * * * an officer's reliance on an incorrect memo or training program from the police department makes no difference to the analysis. Those considerations pertain to the officer's subjective understanding of the law and thus cannot help to justify a seizure.

Second, the inquiry the Court permits today is more demanding than the one courts undertake before awarding qualified immunity. Our modern qualified immunity doctrine protects "all but the plainly incompetent or those who knowingly violate the law." * * *

A court tasked with deciding whether an officer's mistake of law can support a seizure thus faces a straightforward question of statutory construction. If the statute is genuinely ambiguous, such that overturning the officer's judgment requires hard interpretive work, then the officer has made a reasonable mistake. But if not, not. As the Solicitor General made the point at oral argument, the statute must pose a "really difficult" or "very hard question of statutory interpretation." And indeed, both North Carolina and the Solicitor General agreed that such cases will be "exceedingly rare."

The Court's analysis of Sergeant Darisse's interpretation of the North Carolina law at issue here appropriately reflects these principles. * * *

JUSTICE SOTOMAYOR, dissenting.

* * *

I would hold that determining whether a search or seizure is reasonable requires evaluating an officer's understanding of the facts against the actual state of the law. I would accordingly reverse the judgment of the North Carolina Supreme Court, and I respectfully dissent from the Court's contrary holding.

I

[W]hen we have talked about the leeway that officers have in making probable-cause determinations, we have focused on their assessments of facts. We have conceded that an arresting officer's state of mind does not factor into the probable-cause inquiry, "except for *the facts* that he knows." Devenpeck v. Alford, 543 U.S. 146, 153 (2004) (emphasis added). And we have said that, to satisfy the reasonableness requirement, "what is generally demanded of the many *factual determinations* that must regularly be made by agents of the government . . . is not that they always be correct, but that they always be reasonable." Illinois v. Rodriguez, 497 U.S. 177, 185 (1990) (emphasis added). There is scarcely a peep in these cases to suggest that an officer's understanding or conception of anything other than the facts is relevant.

This framing of the reasonableness inquiry has not only been focused on officers' understanding of the facts, it has been justified in large part based on the recognition that officers are generally in a superior position, relative to courts, to evaluate those facts and their significance as they unfold. * * *

The same cannot be said about legal exegesis. After all, the meaning of the law is not probabilistic in the same way that factual determinations are. Rather, "the notion that the law is definite and knowable" sits at the foundation of our legal system. And it is courts, not officers, that are in the best position to interpret the laws.

Both our enunciation of the reasonableness inquiry and our justification for it thus have always turned on an officer's factual conclusions and an officer's expertise with respect to those factual conclusions. Neither has hinted at taking into account an officer's understanding of the law, reasonable or otherwise.

II

Departing from this tradition means further eroding the Fourth Amendment's protection of civil liberties in a context where that protection has already been worn down. Traffic stops like those at issue here can be "annoying, frightening, and perhaps humiliating." We have nevertheless held that an officer's subjective motivations do not render a traffic stop unlawful. Whren v. United States, 517 U.S. 806 (1996). But we assumed in *Whren* that when an officer acts on pretext, at least that pretext would be the violation of an actual law. Giving officers license to effect seizures so long as they can attach to their reasonable view of the facts some reasonable legal interpretation (or misinterpretation) that suggests a law has been violated significantly expands this authority. One wonders how a citizen seeking to be law-abiding and to structure his or her behavior to avoid these invasive, frightening, and humiliating encounters could do so.

In addition to these human consequences—including those for communities and for their relationships with the police—permitting mistakes of law to justify seizures has the perverse effect of preventing or delaying the clarification of the law. Under such an approach, courts need not interpret statutory language but can instead simply decide whether an officer's interpretation was reasonable. * * * This result is bad for citizens, who need to know their rights and responsibilities, and it is bad for police, who would benefit from clearer direction.

Of course, if the law enforcement system could not function without permitting mistakes of law to justify seizures, one could at least argue that permitting as much is a necessary evil. But I have not seen any persuasive argument that law enforcement will be unduly hampered by a rule that precludes consideration of mistakes of law in the reasonableness inquiry. After all, there is no indication that excluding an officer's mistake of law from the reasonableness inquiry has created a problem for law enforcement in the overwhelming number of Circuits which have adopted that approach. If an officer makes a stop in good faith but it turns out that, as in this case, the officer was wrong about what the law proscribed or required, I know of no penalty that the officer would suffer. Moreover, such an officer would likely have a defense to any civil suit on the basis of qualified immunity.

Nor will it often be the case that any evidence that may be seized during the stop will be suppressed, thanks to the exception to the exclusionary rule for good-faith police errors. * * *

In short, there is nothing in our case law requiring us to hold that a reasonable mistake of law can justify a seizure under the Fourth

Amendment, and quite a bit suggesting just the opposite. I also see nothing to be gained from such a holding, and much to be lost.

III

* * *

On the practical side, the Court primarily contends that an officer may confront "a situation in the field as to which the application of a statute is unclear." One is left to wonder, however, why an innocent citizen should be made to shoulder the burden of being seized whenever the law may be susceptible to an interpretive question. * * *

While I appreciate that the Court has endeavored to set some bounds on the types of mistakes of law that it thinks will qualify as reasonable, and while I think that the set of reasonable mistakes of law ought to be narrowly circumscribed if they are to be countenanced at all, I am not at all convinced that the Court has done so in a clear way. It seems to me that the difference between qualified immunity's reasonableness standard—which the Court insists without elaboration does not apply here—and the Court's conception of reasonableness in this context—which remains undefined—will prove murky in application. I fear the Court's unwillingness to sketch a fuller view of what makes a mistake of law reasonable only presages the likely difficulty that courts will have applying the Court's decision in this case.

* * *

To my mind, the more administrable approach—and the one more consistent with our precedents and principles—would be to hold that an officer's mistake of law, no matter how reasonable, cannot support the individualized suspicion necessary to justify a seizure under the Fourth Amendment. I respectfully dissent.

5. **Brief and Limited Detentions: The Line Between "Stop" and "Arrest"**

    e. *Investigation of Matters Other than the Reasonable Suspicion That Supported the Stop: Stop After a Stop*

Page 294. Add the following new case at the bottom of the page:

RODRIGUEZ v. UNITED STATES

Supreme Court of the United States, 2015.
135 S.Ct. 1609.

JUSTICE GINSBURG delivered the opinion of the Court.

In Illinois v. Caballes, 543 U.S. 405 (2005), this Court held that a dog sniff conducted during a lawful traffic stop does not violate the Fourth

Amendment's proscription of unreasonable seizures. This case presents the question whether the Fourth Amendment tolerates a dog sniff conducted after completion of a traffic stop. We hold that a police stop exceeding the time needed to handle the matter for which the stop was made violates the Constitution's shield against unreasonable seizures. A seizure justified only by a police-observed traffic violation, therefore, becomes unlawful if it is prolonged beyond the time reasonably required to complete the mission of issuing a ticket for the violation. The Court so recognized in *Caballes*, and we adhere to the line drawn in that decision.

I

Just after midnight on March 27, 2012, police officer Morgan Struble observed a Mercury Mountaineer veer slowly onto the shoulder of Nebraska State Highway 275 for one or two seconds and then jerk back onto the road. Nebraska law prohibits driving on highway shoulders, and on that basis, Struble pulled the Mountaineer over at 12:06 a.m. Struble is a K-9 officer with the Valley Police Department in Nebraska, and his dog Floyd was in his patrol car that night. Two men were in the Mountaineer: the driver, Dennys Rodriguez, and a front-seat passenger, Scott Pollman.

Struble approached the Mountaineer on the passenger's side. After Rodriguez identified himself, Struble asked him why he had driven onto the shoulder. Rodriguez replied that he had swerved to avoid a pothole. Struble then gathered Rodriguez's license, registration, and proof of insurance, and asked Rodriguez to accompany him to the patrol car. Rodriguez asked if he was required to do so, and Struble answered that he was not. Rodriguez decided to wait in his own vehicle.

After running a records check on Rodriguez, Struble returned to the Mountaineer. Struble asked passenger Pollman for his driver's license and began to question him about where the two men were coming from and where they were going. Pollman replied that they had traveled to Omaha, Nebraska, to look at a Ford Mustang that was for sale and that they were returning to Norfolk, Nebraska. Struble returned again to his patrol car, where he completed a records check on Pollman, and called for a second officer. Struble then began writing a warning ticket for Rodriguez for driving on the shoulder of the road.

Struble returned to Rodriguez's vehicle a third time to issue the written warning. By 12:27 or 12:28 a.m., Struble had finished explaining the warning to Rodriguez, and had given back to Rodriguez and Pollman the documents obtained from them. As Struble later testified, at that point, Rodriguez and Pollman "had all their documents back and a copy of the written warning. I got all the reason[s] for the stop out of the way[,] . . . took care of all the business."

Nevertheless, Struble did not consider Rodriguez "free to leave." Although justification for the traffic stop was "out of the way," Struble asked for permission to walk his dog around Rodriguez's vehicle. Rodriguez said no. Struble then instructed Rodriguez to turn off the ignition, exit the vehicle, and stand in front of the patrol car to wait for the second officer. Rodriguez complied. At 12:33 a.m., a deputy sheriff arrived. Struble retrieved his dog and led him twice around the Mountaineer. The dog alerted to the presence of drugs halfway through Struble's second pass. All told, seven or eight minutes had elapsed from the time Struble issued the written warning until the dog indicated the presence of drugs. A search of the vehicle revealed a large bag of methamphetamine.

Rodriguez was indicted in the United States District Court for the District of Nebraska on one count of possession with intent to distribute 50 grams or more of methamphetamine. He moved to suppress the evidence seized from his car on the ground, among others, that Struble had prolonged the traffic stop without reasonable suspicion in order to conduct the dog sniff.

After receiving evidence, a Magistrate Judge recommended that the motion be denied. The Magistrate Judge found no probable cause to search the vehicle independent of the dog alert. He further found that no reasonable suspicion supported the detention once Struble issued the written warning. He concluded, however, that under Eighth Circuit precedent, extension of the stop by "seven to eight minutes" for the dog sniff was only a *de minimis* intrusion on Rodriguez's Fourth Amendment rights and was therefore permissible.

The District Court adopted the Magistrate Judge's factual findings and legal conclusions and denied Rodriguez's motion to suppress. The court noted that, in the Eighth Circuit, "dog sniffs that occur within a short time following the completion of a traffic stop are not constitutionally prohibited if they constitute only de minimis intrusions." The court thus agreed with the Magistrate Judge that the "7 to 10 minutes" added to the stop by the dog sniff "was not of constitutional significance." Impelled by that decision, Rodriguez entered a conditional guilty plea and was sentenced to five years in prison.

The Eighth Circuit affirmed. The "seven- or eight-minute delay" in this case, the opinion noted, resembled delays that the court had previously ranked as permissible. The Court of Appeals thus ruled that the delay here constituted an acceptable "*de minimis* intrusion on Rodriguez's personal liberty." Given that ruling, the court declined to reach the question whether Struble had reasonable suspicion to continue Rodriguez's detention after issuing the written warning.

We granted certiorari to resolve a division among lower courts on the question whether police routinely may extend an otherwise-completed traffic stop, absent reasonable suspicion, in order to conduct a dog sniff. * * *

II

A seizure for a traffic violation justifies a police investigation of that violation. "[A] relatively brief encounter," a routine traffic stop is "more analogous to a so-called '*Terry* stop' . . . than to a formal arrest." *Knowles v. Iowa,* 525 U.S. 113, 117 (1998). Like a *Terry* stop, the tolerable duration of police inquiries in the traffic-stop context is determined by the seizure's "mission"—to address the traffic violation that warranted the stop, and attend to related safety concerns. Because addressing the infraction is the purpose of the stop, it may last no longer than is necessary to effectuate that purpose. Authority for the seizure thus ends when tasks tied to the traffic infraction are—or reasonably should have been—completed.

Our decision[ ] in *Caballes* * * * heed[s] these constraints. [W]e concluded that the Fourth Amendment tolerated certain unrelated investigations that did not lengthen the roadside detention. * * * An officer, in other words, may conduct certain unrelated checks during an otherwise lawful traffic stop. But * * * he may not do so in a way that prolongs the stop, absent the reasonable suspicion ordinarily demanded to justify detaining an individual. * * *

Beyond determining whether to issue a traffic ticket, an officer's mission includes "ordinary inquiries incident to [the traffic] stop." *Caballes,* 543 U.S., at 408. Typically such inquiries involve checking the driver's license, determining whether there are outstanding warrants against the driver, and inspecting the automobile's registration and proof of insurance. These checks serve the same objective as enforcement of the traffic code: ensuring that vehicles on the road are operated safely and responsibly. A dog sniff, by contrast, is a measure aimed at "detect[ing] evidence of ordinary criminal wrongdoing." Indianapolis v. Edmond, 531 U.S. 32, 40–41 (2000). Candidly, the Government acknowledged at oral argument that a dog sniff, unlike the routine measures just mentioned, is not an ordinary incident of a traffic stop. Lacking the same close connection to roadway safety as the ordinary inquiries, a dog sniff is not fairly characterized as part of the officer's traffic mission.

In advancing its *de minimis* rule, the Eighth Circuit relied heavily on our decision in Pennsylvania v. Mimms, 434 U.S. 106 (1977) (*per curiam*). In *Mimms*, we reasoned that the government's "legitimate and weighty" interest in officer safety outweighs the "*de minimis*" additional intrusion of requiring a driver, already lawfully stopped, to exit the vehicle. The Eighth Circuit, echoed in Justice Thomas's dissent, believed that the imposition here similarly could be offset by the Government's "strong interest in interdicting the flow of illegal drugs along the nation's highways."

Unlike a general interest in criminal enforcement, however, the government's officer safety interest stems from the mission of the stop itself. Traffic stops are especially fraught with danger to police officers, so an officer may need to take certain negligibly burdensome precautions in order to complete his mission safely. On-scene investigation into other crimes, however, detours from that mission. So too do safety precautions taken in order to facilitate such detours. Thus, even assuming that the imposition here was no more intrusive than the exit order in *Mimms*, the dog sniff could not be justified on the same basis. Highway and officer safety are interests different in kind from the Government's endeavor to detect crime in general or drug trafficking in particular.

The Government argues that an officer may "incremental[ly]" prolong a stop to conduct a dog sniff so long as the officer is reasonably diligent in pursuing the traffic-related purpose of the stop, and the overall duration of the stop remains reasonable in relation to the duration of other traffic stops involving similar circumstances. The Government's argument, in effect, is that by completing all traffic-related tasks expeditiously, an officer can earn bonus time to pursue an unrelated criminal investigation. The reasonableness of a seizure, however, depends on what the police in fact do. In this regard, the Government acknowledges that "an officer always has to be reasonably diligent." How could diligence be gauged other than by noting what the officer actually did and how he did it? If an officer can complete traffic-based inquiries expeditiously, then that is the amount of "time reasonably required to complete [the stop's] mission." As we said in *Caballes* and reiterate today, a traffic stop "prolonged beyond" that point is "unlawful." The critical question, then, is not whether the dog sniff occurs before or after the officer issues a ticket, as Justice Alito supposes, but whether conducting the sniff "prolongs"—*i.e.,* adds time to—"the stop."

III

The Magistrate Judge found that detention for the dog sniff in this case was not independently supported by individualized suspicion, and the District Court adopted the Magistrate Judge's findings. The Court of Appeals, however, did not review that determination. * * * The question whether reasonable suspicion of criminal activity justified detaining Rodriguez beyond completion of the traffic infraction investigation, therefore, remains open for Eighth Circuit consideration on remand.

* * *

For the reasons stated, the judgment of the United States Court of Appeals for the Eighth Circuit is vacated, and the case is remanded for further proceedings consistent with this opinion.

It is so ordered.

JUSTICE KENNEDY, dissenting.

My join in JUSTICE THOMAS' dissenting opinion does not extend to Part III. Although the issue discussed in that Part was argued here, the

Court of Appeals has not addressed that aspect of the case in any detail. In my view the better course would be to allow that court to do so in the first instance.

JUSTICE THOMAS, with whom JUSTICE ALITO joins, and with whom JUSTICE KENNEDY joins as to all but Part III, dissenting.

Ten years ago, we explained that "conducting a dog sniff [does] not change the character of a traffic stop that is lawful at its inception and otherwise executed in a reasonable manner." Illinois v. Caballes, 543 U.S. 405, 408 (2005). The only question here is whether an officer executed a stop in a reasonable manner when he waited to conduct a dog sniff until after he had given the driver a written warning and a backup unit had arrived, bringing the overall duration of the stop to 29 minutes. Because the stop was reasonably executed, no Fourth Amendment violation occurred. The Court's holding to the contrary cannot be reconciled with our decision in *Caballes* or a number of common police practices. It was also unnecessary, as the officer possessed reasonable suspicion to continue to hold the driver to conduct the dog sniff. I respectfully dissent.

I

* * *

Because Rodriguez does not dispute that Officer Struble had probable cause to stop him, the only question is whether the stop was otherwise executed in a reasonable manner. I easily conclude that it was. Approximately 29 minutes passed from the time Officer Struble stopped Rodriguez until his narcotics-detection dog alerted to the presence of drugs. That amount of time is hardly out of the ordinary for a traffic stop by a single officer of a vehicle containing multiple occupants even when no dog sniff is involved. During that time, Officer Struble conducted the ordinary activities of a traffic stop—he approached the vehicle, questioned Rodriguez about the observed violation, asked Pollman about their travel plans, ran serial warrant checks on Rodriguez and Pollman, and issued a written warning to Rodriguez. And when he decided to conduct a dog sniff, he took the precaution of calling for backup out of concern for his safety.

As *Caballes* makes clear, the fact that Officer Struble waited until after he gave Rodriguez the warning to conduct the dog sniff does not alter this analysis. Because "the use of a well-trained narcotics-detection dog . . . generally does not implicate legitimate privacy interests," "conducting a dog sniff would not change the character of a traffic stop that is lawful at its inception and otherwise executed in a reasonable manner." The stop here was "lawful at its inception and otherwise executed in a reasonable manner." As in *Caballes*, "conducting a dog sniff [did] not change the character of [the] traffic stop," and thus no Fourth Amendment violation occurred.

II

Rather than adhere to the reasonableness requirement that we have repeatedly characterized as the "touchstone of the Fourth Amendment," the majority constructed a test of its own that is inconsistent with our precedents.

A

* * * The majority's rule * * * imposes a one-way ratchet for constitutional protection linked to the characteristics of the individual officer conducting the stop: If a driver is stopped by a particularly efficient officer, then he will be entitled to be released from the traffic stop after a shorter period of time than a driver stopped by a less efficient officer. Similarly, if a driver is stopped by an officer with access to technology that can shorten a records check, then he will be entitled to be released from the stop after a shorter period of time than an individual stopped by an officer without access to such technology.

I cannot accept that the search and seizure protections of the Fourth Amendment are so variable and can be made to turn upon such trivialities. We have repeatedly explained that the reasonableness inquiry must not hinge on the characteristics of the individual officer conducting the seizure. * * *

B

As if that were not enough, the majority also limits the duration of the stop to the time it takes the officer to complete a narrow category of "traffic-based inquiries." According to the majority, these inquiries include those that "serve the same objective as enforcement of the traffic code: ensuring that vehicles on the road are operated safely and responsibly." Inquiries directed to "detecting evidence of ordinary criminal wrongdoing" are not traffic-related inquiries and thus cannot count toward the overall duration of the stop.

* * *

The majority's approach draws an artificial line between dog sniffs and other common police practices. The lower courts have routinely confirmed that warrant checks are a constitutionally permissible part of a traffic stop, and the majority confirms that it finds no fault in these measures. Yet its reasoning suggests the opposite. Such warrant checks look more like they are directed to "detecting evidence of ordinary criminal wrongdoing" than to "ensuring that vehicles on the road are operated safely and responsibly." Perhaps one could argue that the existence of an outstanding warrant might make a driver less likely to operate his vehicle safely and responsibly on the road, but the same could be said about a driver in possession of contraband. A driver confronted by the police in either case might try to flee or become violent toward the officer. But under the majority's analysis, a dog sniff, which is directed at uncovering that problem, is not treated as a traffic-based inquiry. Warrant checks, arguably, should fare no better. * * *

Investigative questioning rests on the same basis as the dog sniff. "Asking questions is an essential part of police investigations." Hiibel v. Sixth Judicial Dist. Court of Nev., Humboldt Cty., 542 U.S. 177, 185 (2004). And the lower courts have routinely upheld such questioning during routine traffic stops. The majority's reasoning appears to allow officers to engage in *some* questioning aimed at detecting evidence of ordinary criminal wrongdoing. But it is hard to see how such inquiries fall within the seizure's "mission" of addressing the traffic violation that warranted the stop, or attending to related safety concerns. Its reasoning appears to come down to the principle that dogs are different.

C

On a more fundamental level, the majority's inquiry elides the distinction between traffic stops based on probable cause and those based on reasonable suspicion. * * *

Although all traffic stops must be executed reasonably, our precedents make clear that traffic stops justified by reasonable suspicion are subject to additional limitations that those justified by probable cause are not. A traffic stop based on reasonable suspicion, like all *Terry* stops, must be "justified at its inception" and "reasonably related in scope to the circumstances which justified the interference in the first place." It also "cannot continue for an excessive period of time or resemble a traditional arrest." By contrast, a stop based on probable cause affords an officer considerably more leeway. In such seizures, an officer may engage in a warrantless arrest of the driver, a warrantless search incident to arrest of the driver, and a warrantless search incident to arrest of the vehicle if it is reasonable to believe evidence relevant to the crime of arrest might be found there.

The majority casually tosses this distinction aside. It asserts that the traffic stop in this case, which was undisputedly initiated on the basis of probable cause, can last no longer than is in fact necessary to effectuate the mission of the stop. And, it assumes that the mission of the stop was merely to write a traffic ticket, rather than to consider making a custodial arrest. In support of that durational requirement, it relies primarily on cases involving *Terry* stops. * * *

The *only* case involving a traffic stop based on probable cause that the majority cites for its rule is *Caballes*. But, that decision provides no support for today's restructuring of our Fourth Amendment jurisprudence. In *Caballes*, the Court made clear that, in the context of a traffic stop supported by probable cause, "a dog sniff would not change the character of a traffic stop that is lawful at its inception and otherwise executed in a reasonable manner." To be sure, *the dissent* in *Caballes* would have "appl[ied] *Terry*'s reasonable-relation test . . . to determine whether the canine sniff impermissibly expanded the scope of the initially valid seizure of Caballes." But even it conceded that the *Caballes* majority had "implicitly [rejected] the application of *Terry* to a traffic stop converted, by calling in a dog, to a drug search."

By strictly limiting the tasks that define the durational scope of the traffic stop, the majority accomplishes today what the *Caballes* dissent could not: strictly limiting the scope of an officer's activities during a traffic stop justified by probable cause. In doing so, it renders the difference between probable cause and reasonable suspicion virtually meaningless in this context. That shift is supported neither by the Fourth Amendment nor by our precedents interpreting it. And, it results in a constitutional framework that lacks predictability. Had Officer Struble arrested, handcuffed, and taken Rodriguez to the police station for his traffic violation, he would have complied with the Fourth Amendment. But because he made Rodriguez wait for seven or eight extra minutes until a dog arrived, he evidently committed a constitutional violation. Such a view of the Fourth Amendment makes little sense.

III

Today's revision of our Fourth Amendment jurisprudence was also entirely unnecessary. Rodriguez suffered no Fourth Amendment violation here for an entirely independent reason: Officer Struble had reasonable suspicion to continue to hold him for investigative purposes. Our precedents make clear that the Fourth Amendment permits an officer to conduct an investigative traffic stop when that officer has "a particularized and objective basis for suspecting the particular person stopped of criminal activity." * * *

Officer Struble testified that he first became suspicious that Rodriguez was engaged in criminal activity for a number of reasons. When he approached the vehicle, he smelled an "overwhelming odor of air freshener coming from the vehicle," which is, in his experience, "a common attempt to conceal an odor that [people] don't want . . . to be smelled by the police." He also observed, upon approaching the front window on the passenger side of the vehicle, that Rodriguez's passenger, Scott Pollman, appeared nervous. Pollman pulled his hat down low, puffed nervously on a cigarette, and refused to make eye contact with him. The officer thought he was "more nervous than your typical passenger" who "do[esn't] have anything to worry about because [t]hey didn't commit a [traffic] violation."

Officer Struble's interactions with the vehicle's occupants only increased his suspicions. When he asked Rodriguez why he had driven onto the shoulder, Rodriguez claimed that he swerved to avoid a pothole. But that story could not be squared with Officer Struble's observation of the vehicle slowly driving off the road before being jerked back onto it. And when Officer Struble asked Pollman where they were coming from and where they were going, Pollman told him they were traveling from Omaha, Nebraska, back to Norfolk, Nebraska, after looking at a vehicle they were considering purchasing. Pollman told the officer that he had neither seen pictures of the vehicle nor confirmed title before the trip. As Officer Struble explained, it "seemed suspicious" to him "to drive . . . approximately two hours . . . late at night to see a vehicle sight unseen to possibly buy it," and to go from Norfolk to Omaha to look at it because "[u]sually people leave Omaha to go get vehicles, not the other way around" due to higher Omaha taxes.

* * * Taking into account all the relevant facts, Officer Struble possessed reasonable suspicion of criminal activity to conduct the dog sniff.

Rodriguez contends that reasonable suspicion cannot exist because each of the actions giving rise to the officer's suspicions could be entirely innocent, but our cases easily dispose of that argument. Acts that, by themselves, might be innocent can, when taken together, give rise to reasonable suspicion. * * *

* * *

I would conclude that the police did not violate the Fourth Amendment here. Officer Struble possessed probable cause to stop Rodriguez for driving on the shoulder, and he executed the subsequent stop in a reasonable manner. Our decision in *Caballes* requires no more. The majority's holding to the contrary is irreconcilable with *Caballes* and a number of other routine police practices, distorts the distinction between traffic stops justified by probable cause and those justified by reasonable suspicion, and abandons reasonableness as the touchstone of the Fourth Amendment. I respectfully dissent.

JUSTICE ALITO, dissenting.

* * *

The Court refuses to address the real Fourth Amendment question: whether the stop was unreasonably prolonged. Instead, the Court latches onto the fact that Officer Struble delivered the warning prior to the dog sniff and proclaims that the authority to detain based on a traffic stop ends when a citation or warning is handed over to the driver. The Court thus holds that the Fourth Amendment was violated, not because of the length of the stop, but simply because of the sequence in which Officer Struble chose to perform his tasks.

This holding is not only arbitrary; it is perverse since Officer Struble chose that sequence for the purpose of protecting his own safety and possibly the safety of others. * * *

In this case, Officer Struble was concerned that he was outnumbered at the scene, and he therefore called for backup and waited for the arrival of another officer before conducting the sniff. As a result, the sniff was not completed until seven or eight minutes after he delivered the warning. But Officer Struble could have proceeded with the dog sniff while he was waiting for the results of the records check on Pollman and before the arrival of the second officer. The drug-sniffing dog was present in Officer Struble's car. If he had chosen that riskier sequence of events, the dog sniff would have been completed before the point in time when, according to the Court's analysis, the authority to detain for the traffic stop ended. Thus, an action that would have been lawful had the officer made the *unreasonable* decision to risk his life became unlawful when the officer made the *reasonable* decision to wait a few minutes for backup. Officer Struble's error—apparently—was following prudent procedures motivated by legitimate safety concerns. The Court's holding therefore makes no practical sense. And nothing in the Fourth Amendment, which speaks of *reasonableness*, compels this arbitrary line.

The rule that the Court adopts will do little good going forward. It is unlikely to have any appreciable effect on the length of future traffic stops. Most officers will learn the prescribed sequence of events even if they cannot fathom the reason for that requirement. (I would love to be the proverbial fly on the wall when police instructors teach this rule to officers who make traffic stops.)

For these reasons and those set out in Justice Thomas's opinion, I respectfully dissent.

NOTES ON RODRIGUEZ

We place this case in the section on *Terry,* but as Justice Thomas notes in dissent, it is technically not a *Terry* case—Rodriguez was stopped for a traffic violation, but the officer had probable cause, not reasonable suspicion. Still, the majority clearly uses the *Terry* principles and looks at the case as involving a *Terry* stop.

In determining who has the better of the argument in *Rodriguez,* suppose an officer has no dog, stops a car for failing to make a complete stop at a stop sign, checks the driver's various documents, and issues a ticket. If the officer has no reasonable suspicion of any criminal behavior, it makes no sense to permit the officer to detain someone for almost ten more minutes to await a dog sniff. There is nothing "reasonable" about such an arbitrary detention, even though it is for a short time. It might be a short seizure, but a short seizure without reasonable suspicion is by definition unreasonable.

If one is not persuaded, consider an officer who stops a car that has not committed a traffic violation simply because the officer has a dog in the car and would like to do a dog sniff that will take less than two minutes unless drugs are detected, making the stop much shorter than that in Rodriguez. This type of arbitrary, suspicion-less stop was condemned in Delaware v. Prouse, 440 U.S. 648 (1979), where the Court held that an ad hoc inspection of a car for registration purposes, without any suspicion, violated the Fourth Amendment. *Prouse* is a reminder that one thing the Fourth Amendment protects against is arbitrary police actions.

Suppose a police department engages in a "slowdown" approach to traffic stops so that many stops take long enough for officers to call for drug-sniffing dogs based on hunches not supported by reasonable suspicion, or that drug-sniffing dogs are placed in every patrol car in a jurisdiction and officers are instructed to use the dogs before completing a stop. The question that would be raised is whether such actions would render these traffic stops "unreasonable" and/or whether the Court is really committed to the proposition that drug-sniffing dogs are not doing searches when deployed in these ways. In other words, might a drug-sniffing dog be considered a reasonable component of every routine traffic stop?

C. SEARCH INCIDENT TO ARREST: THE ARREST POWER RULE

3. Searches of the Person—and Containers on the Person— Incident to Arrest

Page 324. Delete the material under the headnote *"Searches of Smartphones and Other Electronics Found on an Arrestee"*; replace that material with the following:

In the following case, the Court refuses to extend the automatic search rule of *Robinson* to searches of cellphones found on an arrestee. It also discusses the influence of a case involving searches of automobiles incident to arrest. That case, Arizona v. Gant, is set forth in the Casebook at page 338 and it would be useful to read that case before reading the following case.

RILEY V. CALIFORNIA

Supreme Court of the United States, 2014.
134 S.Ct. 2473.

CHIEF JUSTICE ROBERTS delivered the opinion of the Court.

These two cases raise a common question: whether the police may, without a warrant, search digital information on a cell phone seized from an individual who has been arrested.

* * *

In the first case, petitioner David Riley was stopped by a police officer for driving with expired registration tags. In the course of the stop, the officer also learned that Riley's license had been suspended. The officer impounded Riley's car, pursuant to department policy, and another officer conducted an inventory search of the car. Riley was arrested for possession of concealed and loaded firearms when that search turned up two handguns under the car's hood.

An officer searched Riley incident to the arrest and found items associated with the "Bloods" street gang. He also seized a cell phone from Riley's pants pocket. * * * [T]he phone was a "smart phone," a cell phone with a broad range of other functions based on advanced computing capability, large storage capacity, and Internet connectivity. The officer accessed information on the phone and noticed that some words (presumably in text messages or a contacts list) were preceded by the letters "CK"—a label that, he believed, stood for "Crip Killers," a slang term for members of the Bloods gang.

At the police station about two hours after the arrest, a detective specializing in gangs further examined the contents of the phone. The detective testified that he "went through" Riley's phone "looking for evidence, because . . . gang members will often video themselves with guns or take pictures of themselves with the guns." Although there was "a lot of stuff" on the phone, particular files that "caught [the detective's] eye" included videos of young men sparring while someone yelled encouragement using the moniker "Blood." The police also found photographs of Riley standing in front of a car they suspected had been involved in a shooting a few weeks earlier. [Riley's motion to suppress the evidence found on his cellphone was denied and he was convicted of weapons-related and gang-related crimes. The lower courts affirmed the trial court's ruling that the search of the cellphone incident to arrest did not violate the Fourth Amendment.]

* * *

In the second case, a police officer performing routine surveillance observed respondent Brima Wurie make an apparent drug sale from a car. Officers subsequently arrested Wurie and took him to the police station. At the station, the officers seized two cell phones from Wurie's person. The one at issue here was a "flip phone," a kind of phone that is flipped open for use and that generally has a smaller range of features than a smart phone. Five to ten minutes after arriving at the station, the officers noticed that the phone was repeatedly receiving calls from a source identified as "my house" on the phone's external screen. A few minutes later, they opened the phone and saw a photograph of a woman and a baby set as the phone's wallpaper. They pressed one button on the phone to access its call log, then another button to determine the phone number associated with the "my house" label. They next used an online phone directory to trace that phone number to an apartment building.

When the officers went to the building, they saw Wurie's name on a mailbox and observed through a window a woman who resembled the woman in the photograph on Wurie's phone. They secured the apartment while obtaining a search warrant and, upon later executing the warrant, found and seized 215 grams of crack cocaine, marijuana, drug paraphernalia, a firearm and ammunition, and cash.

Wurie was charged with distributing crack cocaine, possessing crack cocaine with intent to distribute, and being a felon in possession of a firearm and ammunition. He moved to suppress the evidence obtained from the search of the apartment, arguing that it was the fruit of an unconstitutional search of his cell phone. The District Court denied the motion. Wurie was convicted on all three counts and sentenced to 262 months in prison.

A divided panel of the First Circuit reversed the denial of Wurie's motion to suppress and vacated Wurie's convictions for possession with intent to distribute and possession of a firearm as a felon. The court held that cell phones are distinct from other physical possessions that may be searched incident to arrest without a warrant, because of the amount of personal data cell phones contain and the negligible threat they pose to law enforcement interests. We granted certiorari.

* * *

Our cases have determined that where a search is undertaken by law enforcement officials to discover evidence of criminal wrongdoing, reasonableness generally requires the obtaining of a judicial warrant Such a warrant ensures that the inferences to support a search are "drawn by a neutral and detached magistrate instead of being judged by the officer engaged in the often competitive enterprise of ferreting out crime." Johnson v. United States, 333 U.S. 10, 14 (1948). In the absence of a warrant, a search is reasonable only if it falls within a specific exception to the warrant requirement.

The two cases before us concern the reasonableness of a warrantless search incident to a lawful arrest. In 1914, this Court first acknowledged in dictum "the right on the part of the Government, always recognized under English and American law, to search the person of the accused when legally arrested to discover and seize the fruits or evidences of crime." Weeks v. United States, 232 U.S. 383, 392. Since that time, it has been well accepted that such a search constitutes an exception to the warrant requirement. Indeed, the label "exception" is something of a misnomer in this context, as warrantless searches incident to arrest occur with far greater frequency than searches conducted pursuant to a warrant.

Although the existence of the exception for such searches has been recognized for a century, its scope has been debated for nearly as long. See

Arizona v. Gant, 556 U.S. 332, 350 (2009) (noting the exception's "checkered history"). That debate has focused on the extent to which officers may search property found on or near the arrestee. Three related precedents set forth the rules governing such searches:

The first, Chimel v. California, 395 U.S. 752 (1969), laid the groundwork for most of the existing search incident to arrest doctrine. Police officers in that case arrested Chimel inside his home and proceeded to search his entire three-bedroom house, including the attic and garage. In particular rooms, they also looked through the contents of drawers. The Court crafted the following rule for assessing the reasonableness of a search incident to arrest:

> "When an arrest is made, it is reasonable for the arresting officer to search the person arrested in order to remove any weapons that the latter might seek to use in order to resist arrest or effect his escape. Otherwise, the officer's safety might well be endangered, and the arrest itself frustrated. In addition, it is entirely reasonable for the arresting officer to search for and seize any evidence on the arrestee's person in order to prevent its concealment or destruction. . . . There is ample justification, therefore, for a search of the arrestee's person and the area 'within his immediate control'—construing that phrase to mean the area from within which he might gain possession of a weapon or destructible evidence."

The extensive warrantless search of Chimel's home did not fit within this exception, because it was not needed to protect officer safety or to preserve evidence.

Four years later, in United States v. Robinson, 414 U.S. 218 (1973), the Court applied the *Chimel* analysis in the context of a search of the arrestee's person. A police officer had arrested Robinson for driving with a revoked license. The officer conducted a patdown search and felt an object that he could not identify in Robinson's coat pocket. He removed the object, which turned out to be a crumpled cigarette package, and opened it. Inside were 14 capsules of heroin.

The Court of Appeals concluded that the search was unreasonable because Robinson was unlikely to have evidence of the crime of arrest on his person, and because it believed that extracting the cigarette package and opening it could not be justified as part of a protective search for weapons. This Court reversed, rejecting the notion that "case-by-case adjudication" was required to determine "whether or not there was present one of the reasons supporting the authority for a search of the person incident to a lawful arrest." As the Court explained, "[t]he authority to search the person incident to a lawful custodial arrest, while based upon the need to disarm and to discover evidence, does not depend on what a court may later decide was the probability in a particular arrest situation that weapons or evidence would in fact be found upon the person of the suspect." Instead, a "custodial arrest of a suspect based on probable cause is a reasonable intrusion under the Fourth Amendment; that intrusion being lawful, a search incident to the arrest requires no additional justification."

The Court thus concluded that the search of Robinson was reasonable even though there was no concern about the loss of evidence, and the arresting officer had no specific concern that Robinson might be armed. In doing so, the Court did not draw a line between a search of Robinson's person and a further examination of the cigarette pack found during that search. It merely noted that, "[h]aving in the course of a lawful search come upon the crumpled package of cigarettes, [the officer] was entitled to inspect it." A few years later, the Court clarified that this exception was limited to "personal property . . . immediately associated with the person of the arrestee." United States v. Chadwick, 433 U.S. 1, 15 (1977) (200-pound, locked footlocker could not be searched incident to arrest).

The search incident to arrest trilogy concludes with *Gant*, which analyzed searches of an arrestee's vehicle. *Gant*, like *Robinson*, recognized that the *Chimel* concerns for officer safety and evidence preservation underlie the search incident to arrest exception. As a result, the Court concluded that *Chimel* could authorize police to search a vehicle "only when the arrestee is unsecured and within reaching distance of the passenger compartment at the time of the search." *Gant* added, however, an independent exception for a warrantless search of a vehicle's passenger compartment "when it is reasonable to believe evidence relevant to the crime of arrest might be found in the vehicle." That exception stems not from *Chimel*, the Court explained, but from "circumstances unique to the vehicle context."

* * *

These cases require us to decide how the search incident to arrest doctrine applies to modern cell phones, which are now such a pervasive and insistent part of daily life that the proverbial visitor from Mars might conclude they were an important feature of human anatomy. A smart phone of the sort taken from Riley was unheard of ten years ago; a significant majority of American adults now own such phones. Even less sophisticated phones like Wurie's, which have already faded in popularity since Wurie was arrested in 2007, have been around for less than 15 years. Both phones are based on technology nearly inconceivable just a few decades ago, when *Chimel* and *Robinson* were decided.

Absent more precise guidance from the founding era, we generally determine whether to exempt a given type of search from the warrant requirement by assessing, on the one hand, the degree to which it intrudes upon an individual's privacy and, on the other, the degree to which it is needed for the promotion of legitimate governmental interests. Such a balancing of interests supported the search incident to arrest exception in *Robinson*, and a mechanical application of *Robinson* might well support the warrantless searches at issue here.

But while *Robinson*'s categorical rule strikes the appropriate balance in the context of physical objects, neither of its rationales has much force with respect to digital content on cell phones. On the government interest side, *Robinson* concluded that the two risks identified in *Chimel*—harm to officers and destruction of evidence—are present in all custodial arrests. There are no comparable risks when the search is of digital data. In addition, *Robinson* regarded any privacy interests retained by an individual after arrest as significantly diminished by the fact of the arrest itself. Cell phones, however, place vast quantities of personal information literally in the hands of individuals. A search of the information on a cell phone bears little resemblance to the type of brief physical search considered in *Robinson*.

We therefore decline to extend *Robinson* to searches of data on cell phones, and hold instead that officers must generally secure a warrant before conducting such a search.

* * *

We first consider each *Chimel* concern in turn. In doing so, we do not overlook *Robinson*'s admonition that searches of a person incident to arrest, "while based upon the need to disarm and to discover evidence," are reasonable regardless of "the probability in a particular arrest situation that weapons or evidence would in fact be found." Rather than requiring the "case-by-case adjudication" that *Robinson* rejected, we ask instead whether application of the search incident to arrest doctrine to this particular category of effects would "untether the rule from the justifications underlying the *Chimel* exception," *Gant, supra*, at 343. See also Knowles v. Iowa, 525 U.S. 113, 119 (1998) (declining to extend *Robinson* to the issuance of citations, "a situation where the concern for officer safety is not present to the same extent and the concern for destruction or loss of evidence is not present at all").

* * *

Digital data stored on a cell phone cannot itself be used as a weapon to harm an arresting officer or to effectuate the arrestee's escape. Law enforcement officers remain free to examine the physical aspects of a phone to ensure that it will not be used as a weapon—say, to determine whether there is a razor blade hidden between the phone and its case. Once an officer has secured a phone and eliminated any potential physical threats, however, data on the phone can endanger no one.

Perhaps the same might have been said of the cigarette pack seized from Robinson's pocket. Once an officer gained control of the pack, it was unlikely that Robinson could have accessed the pack's contents. But unknown physical objects may always pose risks, no matter how slight, during the tense atmosphere of a custodial arrest. The officer in *Robinson* testified that he could not identify the objects in the cigarette pack but knew they were not cigarettes. Given that, a further search was a reasonable protective measure. No such unknowns exist with respect to digital data. As the First Circuit explained, the officers who searched Wurie's cell phone "knew exactly what they would find therein: data. They also knew that the data could not harm them."

The United States and California both suggest that a search of cell phone data might help ensure officer safety in more indirect ways, for example by alerting officers that confederates of the arrestee are headed to the scene. There is undoubtedly a strong government interest in warning officers about such possibilities, but neither the United States nor California offers evidence to suggest that their concerns are based on actual experience. The proposed consideration would also represent a broadening of *Chimel's* concern that an *arrestee himself* might grab a weapon and use it against an officer "to resist arrest or effect his escape." And any such threats from outside the arrest scene do not lurk in all custodial arrests. Accordingly, the interest in protecting officer safety does not justify dispensing with the warrant requirement across the board. To the extent dangers to arresting officers may be implicated in a particular way in a particular case, they are better addressed through consideration of case-specific exceptions to the warrant requirement, such as the one for exigent circumstances.

* * *

The United States and California focus primarily on the second *Chimel* rationale: preventing the destruction of evidence.

Both Riley and Wurie concede that officers could have seized and secured their cell phones to prevent destruction of evidence while seeking a warrant. That is a sensible concession. See Illinois v. McArthur, 531 U.S. 326, 331–333 (2001). And once law enforcement officers have secured a cell phone, there is no longer any risk that the arrestee himself will be able to delete incriminating data from the phone.

The United States and California argue that information on a cell phone may nevertheless be vulnerable to two types of evidence destruction unique to digital data—remote wiping and data encryption. Remote wiping occurs when a phone, connected to a wireless network, receives a signal that erases stored data. This can happen when a third party sends a remote signal or when a phone is preprogrammed to delete data upon entering or leaving certain geographic areas (so-called "geofencing"). Encryption is a security feature that some modern cell phones use in addition to password protection. When such phones lock, data becomes protected by sophisticated encryption that renders a phone all but "unbreakable" unless police know the password.

As an initial matter, these broader concerns about the loss of evidence are distinct from *Chimel*'s focus on a defendant who responds to arrest by trying to conceal or destroy evidence within his reach. With respect to remote wiping, the Government's primary concern turns on the actions of third parties who are not present at the scene of arrest. And data encryption is even further afield. There, the Government focuses on the ordinary operation of a phone's security features, apart from *any* active attempt by a defendant or his associates to conceal or destroy evidence upon arrest.

We have also been given little reason to believe that either problem is prevalent. The briefing reveals only a couple of anecdotal examples of remote wiping triggered by an arrest. Similarly, the opportunities for officers to search a password-protected phone before data becomes encrypted are quite limited. Law enforcement officers are very unlikely to come upon such a phone in an unlocked state because most phones lock at the touch of a button or, as a default, after some very short period of inactivity. * * *

Moreover, in situations in which an arrest might trigger a remote-wipe attempt or an officer discovers an unlocked phone, it is not clear that the ability to conduct a warrantless search would make much of a difference. The need to effect the arrest, secure the scene, and tend to other pressing matters means that law enforcement officers may well not be able to turn their attention to a cell phone right away. Cell phone data would be vulnerable to remote wiping from the time an individual anticipates arrest to the time any eventual search of the phone is completed, which might be at the station house hours later. Likewise, an officer who seizes a phone in an unlocked state might not be able to begin his search in the short time remaining before the phone locks and data becomes encrypted.

In any event, as to remote wiping, law enforcement is not without specific means to address the threat. Remote wiping can be fully prevented by disconnecting a phone from the network. There are at least two simple ways to do this: First, law enforcement officers can turn the phone off or remove its battery. Second, if they are concerned about encryption or other potential problems, they can leave a phone powered on and place it in an enclosure that isolates the phone from radio waves. Such devices are commonly called "Faraday bags," after the English scientist Michael Faraday. They are essentially sandwich bags made of aluminum foil: cheap, lightweight, and easy to use. They may not be a complete answer to the problem, but at least for now they provide a reasonable response. In fact, a number of law enforcement agencies around the country already encourage the use of Faraday bags.

To the extent that law enforcement still has specific concerns about the potential loss of evidence in a particular case, there remain more targeted ways to address those concerns. If the police are truly confronted with a "now or never situation,"—for example, circumstances suggesting that a defendant's phone will be the target of an imminent remote-wipe attempt—they may be able to rely on exigent circumstances to search the phone immediately. Or, if officers happen to seize a phone in an unlocked state, they may be able to disable a phone's automatic-lock feature in order to prevent the phone from locking and encrypting data. Such a preventive measure could be analyzed under the principles set forth in our decision in *McArthur*, 531 U.S. 326, which approved officers' reasonable steps to secure a scene to preserve evidence while they awaited a warrant.

* * *

The search incident to arrest exception rests not only on the heightened government interests at stake in a volatile arrest situation, but also on an arrestee's reduced privacy interests upon being taken into police custody. *Robinson* focused primarily on the first of those rationales. But it also quoted with approval then-Judge Cardozo's account of the historical basis for the search incident to arrest exception: "Search of the person becomes lawful when grounds for arrest and accusation have been discovered, and the law is in the act of subjecting the body of the accused to its physical dominion." 414 U.S., at 232 (quoting People v. Chiagles, 237 N.Y. 193, 197, 142 N.E. 583, 584 (1923)); see also 414 U.S., at 237 (Powell, J., concurring) ("an individual lawfully subjected to a custodial arrest retains no significant Fourth Amendment interest in the privacy of his person"). Put simply, a patdown of Robinson's clothing and an inspection of the cigarette pack found in his pocket constituted only minor additional intrusions compared to the substantial government authority exercised in taking Robinson into custody.

The fact that an arrestee has diminished privacy interests does not mean that the Fourth Amendment falls out of the picture entirely. * * * To the contrary, when privacy-related concerns are weighty enough a search may require a warrant, notwithstanding the diminished expectations of privacy of the arrestee. One such example, of course, is *Chimel*. *Chimel* refused to "characteriz[e] the invasion of privacy that results from a top-to-bottom search of a man's house as 'minor.'" Because a search of the arrestee's entire house was a substantial invasion beyond the arrest itself, the Court concluded that a warrant was required.

Robinson is the only decision from this Court applying *Chimel* to a search of the contents of an item found on an arrestee's person. * * * Lower courts applying *Robinson* and *Chimel*, however, have approved searches of a variety of personal items carried by an arrestee. See, *e.g.,* United States v. Carrion, 809 F.2d 1120, 1123, 1128 (CA5 1987) (billfold and address book); United States v. Watson, 669 F.2d 1374, 1383–1384 (CA11 1982) (wallet); United States v. Lee, 501 F.2d 890, 892 (CADC 1974) (purse).

The United States asserts that a search of all data stored on a cell phone is "materially indistinguishable" from searches of these sorts of physical items. That is like saying a ride on horseback is materially indistinguishable from a flight to the moon. Both are ways of getting from point A to point B, but little else justifies lumping them together. Modern cell phones, as a category, implicate privacy concerns far beyond those implicated by the search of a cigarette pack, a wallet, or a purse. A conclusion that inspecting the contents of an arrestee's pockets works no substantial additional intrusion on privacy beyond the arrest itself may make sense as applied to physical items, but any extension of that reasoning to digital data has to rest on its own bottom.

* * *

Cell phones differ in both a quantitative and a qualitative sense from other objects that might be kept on an arrestee's person. The term "cell phone" is itself misleading shorthand; many of these devices are in fact minicomputers that also happen to have the capacity to be used as a telephone. They could just as easily be called cameras, video players, rolodexes, calendars, tape recorders, libraries, diaries, albums, televisions, maps, or newspapers.

One of the most notable distinguishing features of modern cell phones is their immense storage capacity. Before cell phones, a search of a person was limited by physical realities and tended as a general matter to constitute only a narrow intrusion on privacy. Most people cannot lug around every piece of mail they have received for the past several months, every picture they have taken, or every book or article they have read—nor would they have any reason to attempt to do so. And if they did, they would have to drag behind them a trunk of the sort held to require a search warrant in *Chadwick, supra,* rather than a container the size of the cigarette package in *Robinson.*

But the possible intrusion on privacy is not physically limited in the same way when it comes to cell phones. The current top-selling smart phone has a standard capacity of 16 gigabytes (and is available with up to 64 gigabytes). Sixteen gigabytes translates to millions of pages of text, thousands of pictures, or hundreds of videos. Cell phones couple that capacity with the ability to store many different types of information: Even the most basic phones that sell for less than $20 might hold photographs, picture messages, text messages, Internet browsing history, a calendar, a thousand-entry phone book, and so on. We expect that the gulf between physical practicability and digital capacity will only continue to widen in the future.

The storage capacity of cell phones has several interrelated consequences for privacy. First, a cell phone collects in one place many distinct types of information—an address, a note, a prescription, a bank statement, a video—that reveal much more in combination than any isolated record. Second, a cell phone's capacity allows even just one type of information to convey far more than previously possible. The sum of an individual's private life can be reconstructed through a thousand photographs labeled with dates, locations, and descriptions; the same cannot be said of a photograph or two of loved ones tucked into a wallet. Third, the data on a phone can date back to the purchase of the phone, or even earlier. A person might carry in his pocket a slip of paper reminding him to call Mr. Jones; he would not carry a record of all his communications with Mr. Jones for the past several months, as would routinely be kept on a phone.

Finally, there is an element of pervasiveness that characterizes cell phones but not physical records. Prior to the digital age, people did not typically carry a cache of sensitive personal information with them as they went about their day. Now it is the person who is not carrying a cell phone, with all that it contains, who is the exception. According to one poll, nearly three-quarters of smart phone users report being within five feet of their phones most of the time, with 12% admitting that they even use their phones in the shower. See Harris Interactive, 2013 Mobile Consumer Habits Study (June 2013). A decade ago police officers searching an arrestee might have occasionally stumbled across a highly personal item such as a diary. But those discoveries were likely to be few and far between. Today, by contrast, it is no exaggeration to say that many of the more than 90% of American adults who own a cell phone keep on their person a digital record of nearly every aspect of their lives—from the mundane to the intimate. Allowing the police to scrutinize such records on a routine basis is quite different from allowing them to search a personal item or two in the occasional case.

Although the data stored on a cell phone is distinguished from physical records by quantity alone, certain types of data are also qualitatively different. An Internet search and browsing history, for example, can be found on an Internet-enabled phone and could reveal an individual's private interests or concerns—perhaps a search for certain symptoms of disease, coupled with frequent visits to WebMD. Data on a cell phone can also reveal where a person has been. Historic location information is a standard feature on many smart phones and can reconstruct someone's specific movements down to the minute, not only around town but also within a particular building.

Mobile application software on a cell phone, or "apps," offer a range of tools for managing detailed information about all aspects of a person's life. There are apps for Democratic Party news and Republican Party news; apps for alcohol, drug, and gambling addictions; apps for sharing prayer requests; apps for tracking pregnancy symptoms; apps for planning your budget; apps for every conceivable hobby or pastime; apps for improving your romantic life. There are popular apps for buying or selling just about anything, and the records of such transactions may be accessible on the phone indefinitely. There are over a million apps available in each of the two major app stores; the phrase "there's an app for that" is now part of the popular lexicon. The average smart phone user has installed 33 apps, which together can form a revealing montage of the user's life.

In 1926, Learned Hand observed (in an opinion later quoted in *Chimel*) that it is "a totally different thing to search a man's pockets and use against him what they contain, from ransacking his house for everything which may incriminate him." United States v. Kirschenblatt, 16 F.2d 202, 203 (CA2). If his pockets contain a cell phone, however, that is no longer true. Indeed, a cell phone search would typically expose to the government far *more* than the most exhaustive search of a house: A phone not only contains in digital form many sensitive records previously found in the home; it also contains a broad array of private information never found in a home in any form—unless the phone is.

* * *

To further complicate the scope of the privacy interests at stake, the data a user views on many modern cell phones may not in fact be stored on the device itself. Treating a cell phone as a container whose contents may be searched incident to an arrest is a bit strained as an initial matter. See New York v. Belton, 453 U.S. 454, 460, n. 4 (1981) (describing a "container" as "any object capable of holding another object"). But the analogy crumbles entirely when a cell phone is used to access data located elsewhere, at the tap of a screen. That is what cell phones, with increasing frequency, are designed to do by taking advantage of "cloud computing." Cloud computing is the capacity of Internet-connected devices to display data stored on remote servers rather than on the device itself. Cell phone users often may not know whether particular information is stored on the device or in the cloud, and it generally makes little difference. Moreover, the same type of data may be stored locally on the device for one user and in the cloud for another.

The United States concedes that the search incident to arrest exception may not be stretched to cover a search of files accessed remotely—that is, a search of files stored in the cloud. Such a search would be like finding a key in a suspect's pocket and arguing that it allowed law enforcement to unlock and search a house. But officers searching a phone's data would not typically know whether the information they are viewing was stored locally at the time of the arrest or has been pulled from the cloud.

Although the Government recognizes the problem, its proposed solutions are unclear. It suggests that officers could disconnect a phone from the network before searching the device—the very solution whose feasibility it contested with respect to the threat of remote wiping. Alternatively, the Government proposes that law enforcement agencies "develop protocols to address" concerns raised by cloud computing. Probably a good idea, but the Founders did not fight a revolution to gain the right to government agency protocols. The possibility that a search might extend well beyond papers and effects in the physical proximity of an arrestee is yet another reason that the privacy interests here dwarf those in *Robinson*.

* * *

Apart from their arguments for a direct extension of *Robinson*, the United States and California offer various fallback options for permitting warrantless cell phone searches under certain circumstances. Each of the proposals is flawed and contravenes our general preference to provide clear guidance to law enforcement through categorical rules. "[I]f police are to have workable rules, the balancing of the competing interests . . . must in large part be done on a categorical basis—not in an ad hoc, case-by-case fashion by individual police officers." Michigan v. Summers, 452 U.S. 692, 705, n. 19 (1981).

The United States first proposes that the *Gant* standard be imported from the vehicle context, allowing a warrantless search of an arrestee's cell phone whenever it is reasonable to believe that the phone contains evidence of the crime of arrest. But *Gant* relied on "circumstances unique to the vehicle context" to endorse a search solely for the purpose of gathering evidence. JUSTICE SCALIA's *Thornton* opinion, on which *Gant* was based, explained that those unique circumstances are "a reduced expectation of privacy" and "heightened law enforcement needs" when it comes to motor vehicles. For reasons that we have explained, cell phone searches bear neither of those characteristics.

At any rate, a *Gant* standard would prove no practical limit at all when it comes to cell phone searches. In the vehicle context, *Gant* generally protects against searches for evidence of past crimes. In the cell phone context, however, it is reasonable to expect that incriminating information will be found on a phone regardless of when the crime occurred. Similarly, in the vehicle context *Gant* restricts broad searches resulting from minor crimes such as traffic violations. That would not necessarily be true for cell phones. It would be a particularly inexperienced or unimaginative law enforcement officer who could not come up with several reasons to suppose evidence of just about any crime could be found on a cell phone. Even an individual pulled over for something as basic as speeding might well have locational data dispositive of guilt on his phone. An individual pulled over for reckless driving might have evidence on the phone that shows whether he was texting while driving. The sources of potential pertinent information are virtually unlimited, so applying the *Gant* standard to cell phones would in effect give police officers unbridled discretion to rummage at will among a person's private effects.

The United States also proposes a rule that would restrict the scope of a cell phone search to those areas of the phone where an officer reasonably believes that information relevant to the crime, the arrestee's identity, or officer safety will be discovered. This approach would again impose few meaningful constraints on officers. The proposed categories would sweep in a great deal of information, and officers would not always be able to discern in advance what information would be found where.

We also reject the United States' final suggestion that officers should always be able to search a phone's call log, as they did in Wurie's case. The Government relies on Smith v. Maryland, 442 U.S. 735 (1979), which held that no warrant was required to use a pen register at telephone company premises to identify numbers dialed by a particular caller. The Court in that case, however, concluded that the use of a pen register was not a "search" at all under the Fourth Amendment. There is no dispute here that the officers engaged in a search of Wurie's cell phone. Moreover, call logs typically contain more than just phone numbers; they include any identifying information that an individual might add, such as the label "my house" in Wurie's case.

Finally, at oral argument California suggested a different limiting principle, under which officers could search cell phone data if they could have obtained the same information from a pre-digital counterpart. But the fact that a search in the pre-digital era could have turned up a photograph or two in a wallet does not justify a search of thousands of photos in a digital gallery. The fact that someone could have tucked a paper bank statement in a pocket does not justify a search of every bank statement from the last five years. And to make matters worse, such an analogue test would allow law enforcement to search a range of items contained on a phone, even though people would be unlikely to carry such a variety of information in physical form. In Riley's case, for example, it is implausible that he would have strolled around with video tapes, photo albums, and an address book all crammed into his pockets. But because each of those items has a pre-digital analogue, police under California's proposal would be able to search a phone for all of those items—a significant diminution of privacy.

In addition, an analogue test would launch courts on a difficult line-drawing expedition to determine which digital files are comparable to physical records. Is an e-mail equivalent to a letter? Is a voicemail equivalent to a phone message slip? It is not clear how officers could make these kinds of decisions before conducting a search, or how courts would apply the proposed rule after the fact. An analogue test would keep defendants and judges guessing for years to come.

* * *

We cannot deny that our decision today will have an impact on the ability of law enforcement to combat crime. Cell phones have become important tools in facilitating coordination and communication among members of criminal enterprises, and can provide valuable incriminating information about dangerous criminals. Privacy comes at a cost.

Our holding, of course, is not that the information on a cell phone is immune from search; it is instead that a warrant is generally required before such a search, even when a cell phone is seized incident to arrest. Our cases have historically recognized that the warrant requirement is "an important working part of our machinery of government," not merely "an inconvenience to be somehow 'weighed' against the claims of police efficiency." Coolidge v. New Hampshire, 403 U.S. 443, 481 (1971). Recent technological advances similar to those discussed here have, in addition, made the process of obtaining a warrant itself more efficient. See Missouri v. McNeely, 133 S.Ct. 1552 (2013) (ROBERTS, C.J., concurring in part and dissenting in part) (describing jurisdiction where "police officers can e-mail warrant requests to judges' iPads [and] judges have signed such warrants and e-mailed them back to officers in less than 15 minutes").

Moreover, even though the search incident to arrest exception does not apply to cell phones, other case-specific exceptions may still justify a warrantless search of a particular phone. One well-recognized exception applies when the exigencies of the situation make the needs of law enforcement so compelling that a warrantless search is objectively reasonable under the Fourth Amendment. Such exigencies could include the need to prevent the imminent destruction of evidence in individual cases, to pursue a fleeing suspect, and to assist persons who are seriously injured or are threatened with imminent injury. In *Chadwick*, for example, the Court held that the exception for searches incident to arrest did not justify a search of the trunk at issue, but noted that "if officers have reason to believe that luggage contains some immediately dangerous instrumentality, such as explosives, it would be foolhardy to transport it to the station house without opening the luggage."

In light of the availability of the exigent circumstances exception, there is no reason to believe that law enforcement officers will not be able to address some of the more extreme hypotheticals that have been suggested: a suspect texting an accomplice who, it is feared, is preparing to detonate a bomb, or a child abductor who may have information about the child's location on his cell phone. The defendants here recognize—indeed, they stress—that such fact-specific threats may justify a warrantless search of cell phone data. The critical point is that, unlike the search incident to arrest exception, the exigent circumstances exception requires a court to examine whether an emergency justified a warrantless search in each particular case.

———————

Our cases have recognized that the Fourth Amendment was the founding generation's response to the reviled "general warrants" and "writs of assistance" of the colonial era, which allowed British officers to rummage through homes in an unrestrained search for evidence of criminal activity. Opposition to such searches was in fact one of the driving forces behind the Revolution itself. In 1761, the patriot James Otis delivered a speech in Boston denouncing the use of writs of assistance. A young John Adams was there, and he would later write that "[e]very man of a crowded audience appeared to me to go away, as I did, ready to take arms against writs of assistance." 10 Works of John Adams 247–248 (C. Adams ed. 1856). According to Adams, Otis's speech was "the first scene of the first act of opposition to the arbitrary claims of Great Britain. Then and there the child Independence was born." *Id.,* at 248 (quoted in Boyd v. United States, 116 U.S. 616, 625 (1886)).

Modern cell phones are not just another technological convenience. With all they contain and all they may reveal, they hold for many Americans "the privacies of life," *Boyd, supra,* at 630. The fact that technology now allows an individual to carry such information in his hand does not make the information any less worthy of the protection for which the Founders fought. Our answer to the question of what police must do before searching a cell phone seized incident to an arrest is accordingly simple—get a warrant.

We reverse the judgment of the California Court of Appeal * * * and remand the case for further proceedings not inconsistent with this opinion. We affirm the judgment of the First Circuit * * * .

JUSTICE ALITO, concurring in part and concurring in the judgment.

I agree with the Court that law enforcement officers, in conducting a lawful search incident to arrest, must generally obtain a warrant before searching information stored or accessible on a cell phone. I write separately to address two points.

* * *

First, I am not convinced at this time that the ancient rule on searches incident to arrest is based exclusively (or even primarily) on the need to protect the safety of arresting officers and the need to prevent the destruction of evidence. This rule antedates the adoption of the Fourth Amendment by at least a century. In Weeks v. United States, 232 U.S. 383, 392 (1914), we held that the Fourth Amendment did not disturb this rule. And neither in *Weeks* nor in any of the authorities discussing the old common-law rule have I found any suggestion that it was based exclusively or primarily on the need to protect arresting officers or to prevent the destruction of evidence.

On the contrary, when pre-*Weeks* authorities discussed the basis for the rule, what was mentioned was the need to obtain probative evidence. [Justice Alito cites and discusses state cases and treatises from the 1800's.]

What ultimately convinces me that the rule is not closely linked to the need for officer safety and evidence preservation is that these rationales fail to explain the rule's well-recognized scope. It has long been accepted that written items found on the person of an arrestee may be examined and used at trial. But once these items are taken away from an arrestee (something that obviously must be done before the items are read), there is no risk that the arrestee will destroy them. Nor is there any risk that leaving these items unread will endanger the arresting officers.

The idea that officer safety and the preservation of evidence are the sole reasons for allowing a warrantless search incident to arrest appears to derive from the Court's reasoning in Chimel v. California, 395 U.S. 752 (1969), a case that involved the lawfulness of a search of the scene of an arrest, not the person of an arrestee. As I have explained, *Chimel*'s reasoning is questionable, see Arizona v. Gant, 556 U.S. 332, 361–363 (2009) (ALITO, J., dissenting), and I think it is a mistake to allow that reasoning to affect cases like these that concern the search of the person of arrestees.

* * *

Despite my view on the point discussed above, I agree that we should not mechanically apply the rule used in the predigital era to the search of a cell phone. Many cell phones now in use are capable of storing and accessing a quantity of information, some highly personal, that no person would ever have had on his person in hard-copy form. This calls for a new balancing of law enforcement and privacy interests.

The Court strikes this balance in favor of privacy interests with respect to all cell phones and all information found in them, and this approach leads to anomalies. For example, the Court's broad holding favors information in digital form over information in hard-copy form. Suppose that two suspects are arrested. Suspect number one has in his pocket a monthly bill for his land-line phone, and the bill lists an incriminating call to a long-distance number. He also has in his a wallet a few snapshots, and one of these is incriminating. Suspect number two has in his pocket a cell phone, the call log of which shows a call to the same incriminating number. In addition, a number of photos are stored in the memory of the cell phone, and one of these is incriminating. Under established law, the police may seize and examine the phone bill and the snapshots in the wallet without obtaining a warrant, but under the Court's holding today, the information stored in the cell phone is out.

While the Court's approach leads to anomalies, I do not see a workable alternative. Law enforcement officers need clear rules regarding searches incident to arrest, and it would take many cases and many years for the courts to develop more nuanced rules. And during that time, the nature of the electronic devices that ordinary Americans carry on their persons would continue to change.

* * *

This brings me to my second point. While I agree with the holding of the Court, I would reconsider the question presented here if either Congress or state legislatures, after assessing the legitimate needs of law enforcement and the privacy interests of cell phone owners, enact legislation that draws reasonable distinctions based on categories of information or perhaps other variables.

The regulation of electronic surveillance provides an instructive example. After this Court held that electronic surveillance constitutes a search even when no property interest is invaded, see Katz v. United States, 389 U.S. 347, 353–359 (1967), Congress responded by enacting Title III of the Omnibus Crime Control and Safe Streets Act of 1968, 82 Stat. 211. Since that time, electronic surveillance has been governed primarily, not by decisions of this Court, but by the statute, which authorizes but imposes detailed restrictions on electronic surveillance.

Modern cell phones are of great value for both lawful and unlawful purposes. They can be used in committing many serious crimes, and they present new and difficult law enforcement problems. At the same time, because of the role that these devices have come to play in contemporary life, searching their contents implicates very sensitive privacy interests that this Court is poorly positioned to understand and evaluate. Many forms of modern technology are making it easier and easier for both government and private entities to amass a wealth of information about the lives of ordinary Americans, and at the same time, many ordinary Americans are choosing to make public much information that was seldom revealed to outsiders just a few decades ago.

In light of these developments, it would be very unfortunate if privacy protection in the 21st century were left primarily to the federal courts using the blunt instrument of the Fourth Amendment. Legislatures, elected by the people, are in a better position than we are to assess and respond to the changes that have already occurred and those that almost certainly will take place in the future.

Page 328. Add the following headnote and case:

Breathalyzers and Blood Tests Incident to Arrest: Birchfield v. North Dakota

BIRCHFIELD V. NORTH DAKOTA
United States Supreme Court 2016.
136 S.Ct. 2160.

JUSTICE ALITO delivered the opinion of the Court.

Drunk drivers take a grisly toll on the Nation's roads, claiming thousands of lives, injuring many more victims, and inflicting billions of dollars in property damage every year. To fight this problem, all States have laws that prohibit motorists from driving with a blood alcohol concentration (BAC) that exceeds a specified level. But determining whether a driver's BAC is over the legal limit requires a test, and many drivers stopped on suspicion of drunk driving would not submit to testing if given the option. So every State also has long had what are termed "implied consent laws." These laws impose penalties on motorists who refuse to undergo testing when there is sufficient reason to believe they are violating the State's drunk-driving laws.

In the past, the typical penalty for noncompliance was suspension or revocation of the motorist's license. The cases now before us involve laws that go beyond that and make it a crime for a motorist to refuse to be tested after being lawfully arrested for driving while impaired. The question presented is whether such laws violate the Fourth Amendment's prohibition against unreasonable searches.

I

[Justice Alito discusses the history of state regulation of drunk driving, and the development of breath testing machines and blood tests.]

Measurement of BAC [blood alcohol content] based on a breath test requires the cooperation of the person being tested. The subject must take a deep breath and exhale through a mouthpiece that connects to the machine. * * * When a standard infrared device is used, the whole process takes only a few minutes from start to finish. Most evidentiary breath tests do not occur next to the vehicle, at the side of the road, but in a police station, where the controlled environment is especially conducive to reliable testing, or in some cases in the officer's patrol vehicle or in special mobile testing facilities.

Because the cooperation of the test subject is necessary when a breath test is administered and highly preferable when a blood sample is taken, the enactment of laws defining intoxication based on BAC made it necessary for States to find a way of securing such cooperation. So-called "implied consent" laws were enacted to achieve this result. They provided that cooperation with BAC testing was a condition of the privilege of driving on state roads and that the privilege would be rescinded if a suspected drunk driver refused to honor that condition. * * * Suspension or revocation of the motorist's driver's license remains the standard legal consequence of refusal. In addition, evidence of the motorist's refusal is admitted as evidence of likely intoxication in a drunk-driving prosecution.

In recent decades, the States and the Federal Government have toughened drunk-driving laws, and those efforts have corresponded to a dramatic decrease in alcohol-related fatalities * * * [B]ut this new structure threatened to undermine the effectiveness of implied consent laws. If the penalty for driving with a greatly elevated BAC or for repeat violations exceeds the penalty for refusing to submit to testing, motorists who fear conviction for the more severely punished offenses have an incentive to reject testing. And in some States, the refusal rate is high. On average, over one-fifth of all drivers asked to submit to BAC testing in 2011 refused to do so. * * *

To combat the problem of test refusal, some States have begun to enact laws making it a crime to refuse to undergo testing. Minnesota has taken this approach for decades. And that may partly explain why its refusal rate now is below the national average. * * * North Dakota adopted a similar law, in 2013. * * *

II

[Justice Alito describes the facts. Birchfield accidentally drove his car off a road, and showed signs of drunkenness, but refused the officers' demand to let his blood be drawn. He pleaded guilty for failing to cooperate, a misdemeanor, but his plea was conditional; while he admitted refusing the blood test, he argued that the Fourth Amendment prohibited criminalizing that refusal. The North Dakota Supreme Court reject that argument.

Bernard showed signs of intoxication but denied driving a truck that was stuck in a river. He was arrested for driving while impaired, and refused to take a breath test. Because he had four prior drunk driving convictions, he was charged with the most serious crime possible for refusing to cooperate—test refusal in the first degree—with a mandatory minimum sentence of three years' imprisonment. The Minnesota Supreme Court found that the conviction did not violate the Fourth Amendment.

Finally, Beylund was driving recklessly and when stopped the officer observed signs of intoxication. The officer arrested Beylund for driving while impaired and took him to a nearby hospital. After being informed that refusal is a crime in North Dakota, Beylund agreed to have his blood drawn and analyzed. A nurse took a blood sample, which revealed a blood alcohol concentration of 0.250%, more than three times the legal limit. Beylund's driver's license was suspended for two years and he appealed that decision, arguing that his consent to the blood test was coerced by the officer's warning that refusing to consent would itself be a crime. The North Dakota Supreme Court rejected that argument.]

We granted certiorari in all three cases and consolidated them for argument, in order to decide whether motorists lawfully arrested for drunk driving may be convicted of a crime or otherwise penalized for refusing to take a warrantless test measuring the alcohol in their bloodstream.

III

* * * [S]uccess for all three petitioners depends on the proposition that the criminal law ordinarily may not compel a motorist to submit to the taking of a blood sample or to a breath test unless a warrant authorizing such testing is issued by a magistrate. If, on the other hand, such warrantless searches comport with the Fourth Amendment, it follows that a State may criminalize the refusal to comply with a demand to submit to the required testing, just as a State may make it a crime for a person to obstruct the execution of a valid search warrant. And by the same token, if such warrantless searches are constitutional, there is no obstacle under federal law to the admission of the results that they yield in either a criminal prosecution or a civil or administrative proceeding. We therefore begin by considering whether the searches demanded in these cases were consistent with the Fourth Amendment.

IV

The Fourth Amendment * * * prohibits "unreasonable searches," and our cases establish that the taking of a blood sample or the administration of a breath test is a search. See Skinner v. Railway Labor Executives' Assn., 489 U.S. 602 (1989); Schmerber v. California, 384 U.S. 757 (1966). The question, then, is whether the warrantless searches at issue here were reasonable.

"[T]he text of the Fourth Amendment does not specify when a search warrant must be obtained." Kentucky v. King, 563 U.S. 452, 459 (2011). But "this Court has inferred that a warrant must [usually] be secured." King, 563 U.S., at 459. This usual requirement, however, is subject to a number of exceptions.

We have previously had occasion to examine whether one such exception—for "exigent circumstances"—applies in drunk-driving investigations. The exigent circumstances exception allows a warrantless search when an emergency leaves police insufficient time to seek a warrant. * * * In *Schmerber* we held that drunk driving *may* present such an exigency. There, an officer directed hospital personnel to take a blood sample from a driver who was receiving treatment for car crash injuries. The Court concluded that the officer "might reasonably have believed that he was confronted with an emergency" that left no time to seek a warrant because "the percentage of alcohol in the blood begins to diminish shortly after drinking stops." On the specific facts of that case, where time had already been lost taking the driver to the hospital and investigating the accident, the Court found no Fourth Amendment violation even though the warrantless blood draw took place over the driver's objection.

More recently, though, we have held that the natural dissipation of alcohol from the bloodstream does not *always* constitute an exigency justifying the warrantless taking of a blood sample. That was the holding of Missouri v. McNeely, 133 S.Ct. 1552 (2013), where the State of Missouri was seeking a *per se* rule that "whenever an officer has probable cause to believe an individual has been driving under the influence of alcohol, exigent circumstances will necessarily exist because BAC evidence is inherently evanescent." We disagreed, emphasizing that *Schmerber* had adopted a case-specific analysis depending on "all of the facts and circumstances of the particular case." * * *

While emphasizing that the exigent-circumstances exception must be applied on a case-by-case basis, the *McNeely* Court noted that other exceptions to the warrant requirement "apply categorically" rather than in a "case-specific" fashion. One of these, as the *McNeely* opinion recognized, is the long-established rule that a warrantless search may be conducted incident to a lawful arrest. But the Court pointedly did not address any potential justification for warrantless testing of drunk-driving suspects except for the exception "at issue in th[e] case," namely, the exception for exigent circumstances. * * *

In the three cases now before us, the drivers were searched or told that they were required to submit to a search after being placed under arrest for drunk driving. We therefore consider how the search-incident-to-arrest doctrine applies to breath and blood tests incident to such arrests.

V

A

The search-incident-to-arrest doctrine has an ancient pedigree. Well before the Nation's founding, it was recognized that officers carrying out a lawful arrest had the authority to make a warrantless search of the arrestee's person. * * * One Fourth Amendment historian has observed that, prior to American independence, "[a]nyone arrested could expect that not only his surface clothing but his body, luggage, and saddlebags would be searched and, perhaps, his shoes, socks, and mouth as well." W.

Cuddihy, The Fourth Amendment: Origins and Original Meaning: 602–1791, p. 420 (2009).

No historical evidence suggests that the Fourth Amendment altered the permissible bounds of arrestee searches. On the contrary, legal scholars agree that "the legitimacy of body searches as an adjunct to the arrest process had been thoroughly established in colonial times, so much so that their constitutionality in 1789 can not be doubted." *Id.,* at 752.

* * *

When this Court first addressed the question, we too confirmed (albeit in dicta) "the right on the part of the Government, always recognized under English and American law, to search the person of the accused when legally arrested to discover and seize the fruits or evidence of crime." Weeks v. United States, 232 U.S. 383, 392 (1914). The exception quickly became a fixture in our Fourth Amendment case law. But in the decades that followed, we grappled repeatedly with the question of the authority of arresting officers to search the area surrounding the arrestee, and our decisions reached results that were not easy to reconcile.

We attempted to clarify the law regarding searches incident to arrest in Chimel v. California, 395 U.S. 752, 754 (1969), a case in which officers had searched the arrestee's entire three-bedroom house. *Chimel* endorsed a general rule that arresting officers, in order to prevent the arrestee from obtaining a weapon or destroying evidence, could search both "the person arrested" and "the area within his immediate control." "[N]o comparable justification," we said, supported "routinely searching any room other than that in which an arrest occurs—or, for that matter, for searching through all the desk drawers or other closed or concealed areas in that room itself."

Four years later, in United States v. Robinson, 414 U.S. 218 (1973), we elaborated on *Chimel*'s meaning. We noted that the search-incident-to-arrest rule actually comprises "two distinct propositions": "The first is that a search may be made of the *person* of the arrestee by virtue of the lawful arrest. The second is that a search may be made of the area within the control of the arrestee." After a thorough review of the relevant common law history, we repudiated "case-by-case adjudication" of the question whether an arresting officer had the authority to carry out a search of the arrestee's person. The permissibility of such searches, we held, does not depend on whether a search of a *particular* arrestee is likely to protect officer safety or evidence * * * . Instead, the mere "fact of the lawful arrest" justifies "a full search of the person." In *Robinson* itself, that meant that police had acted permissibly in searching inside a package of cigarettes found on the man they arrested.

Our decision two Terms ago in Riley v. California, 134 S.Ct. 2473 (2014), reaffirmed "*Robinson*'s categorical rule" and explained how the rule should be applied in situations that could not have been envisioned when the Fourth Amendment was adopted. *Riley* concerned a search of data contained in the memory of a modern cell phone. "Absent more precise guidance from the founding era," the Court wrote, "we generally determine whether to exempt a given type of search from the warrant requirement by assessing, on the one hand, the degree to which it intrudes upon an individual's privacy and, on the other, the degree to which it is needed for the promotion of legitimate governmental interests."

Blood and breath tests to measure blood alcohol concentration are not as new as searches of cell phones, but here, as in *Riley,* the founding era does not provide any definitive guidance as to whether they should be allowed incident to arrest. Lacking such guidance, we engage in the same mode of analysis as in *Riley*: we examine "the degree to which [they] intrud[e] upon an individual's privacy and . . . the degree to which [they are] needed for the promotion of legitimate governmental interests."

B

We begin by considering the impact of breath and blood tests on individual privacy interests, and we will discuss each type of test in turn.

1

Years ago we said that breath tests do not "implicat[e] significant privacy concerns." *Skinner,* 489 U.S., at 626. That remains so today.

First, the physical intrusion is almost negligible. Breath tests do not require piercing the skin and entail a minimum of inconvenience. As Minnesota describes its version of the breath test, the process requires the arrestee to blow continuously for 4 to 15 seconds into a straw-like mouthpiece that is connected by a tube to the test machine. Independent sources describe other breath test devices in essentially the same terms. The effort is no more demanding than blowing up a party balloon.

Petitioner Bernard argues, however, that the process is nevertheless a significant intrusion because the arrestee must insert the mouthpiece of the machine into his or her mouth. But there is nothing painful or strange about this requirement. The use of a straw to drink beverages is a common practice and one to which few object.

Nor, contrary to Bernard, is the test a significant intrusion because it "does not capture an ordinary exhalation of the kind that routinely is exposed to the public" but instead requires a sample of "alveolar" (deep lung) air. Humans have never been known to assert a possessory interest in or any emotional attachment to *any* of the air in their lungs. The air that humans exhale is not part of their bodies. Exhalation is a natural process—indeed, one that is necessary for life. Humans cannot hold their breath for more than a few minutes, and all the air that is breathed into a breath analyzing machine, including deep lung air, sooner or later would be exhaled even without the test.

* * *

Second, breath tests are capable of revealing only one bit of information, the amount of alcohol in the subject's breath. In this respect, they contrast sharply with the sample of cells collected by the swab in Maryland v. King [Text, page 472]. Although the DNA obtained under the law at issue in that case could lawfully be used only for identification purposes, the process put into the possession of law enforcement authorities a sample from which a wealth of additional, highly personal information could potentially be obtained. A breath test, by contrast, results in a BAC reading on a machine, nothing more. No sample of anything is left in the possession of the police.

Finally, participation in a breath test is not an experience that is likely to cause any great enhancement in the embarrassment that is inherent in any arrest. The act of blowing into a straw is not inherently embarrassing, nor are evidentiary breath tests administered in a manner that causes embarrassment. Again, such tests are normally administered in private at a police station, in a patrol car, or in a mobile testing facility, out of public view. Moreover, once placed under arrest, the individual's expectation of privacy is necessarily diminished.

* * *

2

Blood tests are a different matter. They require piercing the skin and extract a part of the subject's body. And while humans exhale air from their lungs many times per minute, humans do not continually shed blood. It is true, of course, that people voluntarily submit to the taking of blood samples as part of a physical examination, and the process involves little pain or risk. Nevertheless, for many, the process is not one they relish. It is significantly more intrusive than blowing into a tube. Perhaps that is why many States' implied consent laws, including Minnesota's, specifically prescribe that breath tests be administered in the usual drunk-driving case instead of blood tests or give motorists a measure of choice over which test to take.

In addition, a blood test, unlike a breath test, places in the hands of law enforcement authorities a sample that can be preserved and from which it is possible to extract information beyond a simple BAC reading. Even if the law enforcement agency is precluded from testing the blood for any purpose other than to measure BAC, the potential remains and may result in anxiety for the person tested.

C

Having assessed the impact of breath and blood testing on privacy interests, we now look to the States' asserted need to obtain BAC readings for persons arrested for drunk driving.

1

The States and the Federal Government have a paramount interest in preserving the safety of **p**ublic highways. Although the number of deaths and injuries caused by motor vehicle accidents has declined over the years, the statistics are still staggering. Alcohol consumption is a leading cause of traffic fatalities and injuries. * * *

Justice SOTOMAYOR's partial dissent suggests that States' interests in fighting drunk driving are satisfied once suspected drunk drivers are arrested, since such arrests take intoxicated drivers off the roads where they might do harm. But of course States are not solely concerned with neutralizing the threat posed by a drunk driver who has already gotten behind the wheel. They also have a compelling interest in creating effective deterrents to drunken driving so such individuals make responsible decisions and do not become a threat to others in the first place.

To deter potential drunk drivers and thereby reduce alcohol-related injuries, the States and the Federal Government have taken the series of steps that we recounted earlier. We briefly recapitulate. After pegging inebriation to a specific level of blood alcohol, States passed implied consent laws to induce motorists to submit to BAC testing. While these laws originally provided that refusal to submit could result in the loss of the privilege of driving and the use of evidence of refusal in a drunk-driving prosecution, more recently States and the Federal Government have concluded that these consequences are insufficient. In particular, license suspension alone is unlikely to persuade the most dangerous offenders, such as those who drive with a BAC significantly above the current limit of 0.08% and recidivists, to agree to a test that would lead to severe criminal sanctions. The laws at issue in the present cases—which make it a crime to refuse to submit to a BAC test—are designed to provide an incentive to cooperate in such cases, and we conclude that they serve a very important function.

2

Petitioners and Justice SOTOMAYOR contend that the States and the Federal Government could combat drunk driving in other ways that do not have the same impact on personal privacy. Their arguments are unconvincing.

The chief argument on this score is that an officer making an arrest for drunk driving should not be allowed to administer a BAC test unless the officer procures a search warrant or could not do so in time to obtain usable test results. * * * This argument contravenes our decisions holding that the legality of a search incident to arrest must be judged on the basis of categorical rules. In *Robinson,* for example, no one claimed that the object of the search, a package of cigarettes, presented any danger to the arresting officer or was at risk of being destroyed in the time that it would have taken to secure a search warrant. The Court nevertheless upheld the constitutionality of a warrantless search of the package, concluding that a categorical rule was needed to give police adequate guidance: "A police officer's determination as to how and where to search the person of a suspect whom he has arrested is necessarily a quick *ad hoc* judgment which the Fourth Amendment does not require to be broken down in each instance into an analysis of each step in the search."

* * *

In advocating the case-by-case approach, petitioners and Justice SOTOMAYOR cite language in our *McNeely* opinion. But *McNeely* concerned an exception to the warrant requirement—for exigent circumstances—that always requires case-by-case determinations. That was the basis for our decision in that case. Although Justice SOTOMAYOR contends that the categorical search-incident-to-arrest doctrine and case-by-case exigent circumstances doctrine are actually parts of a single framework, in *McNeely* the Court was careful to note that the decision did not address any other exceptions to the warrant requirement.

Petitioners and Justice SOTOMAYOR next suggest that requiring a warrant for BAC testing in every case in which a motorist is arrested for drunk driving would not impose any great burden on the police or the courts. But of course the same argument could be made about searching through objects found on the arrestee's possession, which our cases permit even in the absence of a warrant. What about the cigarette package in *Robinson*? What if a motorist arrested for drunk driving has a flask in his pocket? What if a motorist arrested for driving while under the influence of marijuana has what appears to be a marijuana cigarette on his person? What about an unmarked bottle of pills?

If a search warrant were required for every search incident to arrest that does not involve exigent circumstances, the courts would be swamped. And even if we arbitrarily singled out BAC tests incident to arrest for this special treatment, as it appears the dissent would do, the impact on the courts would be considerable. The number of arrests every year for driving under the influence is enormous—more than 1.1 million in 2014. Particularly in sparsely populated areas, it would be no small task for courts to field a large new influx of warrant applications that could come on any day of the year and at any hour. In many jurisdictions, judicial officers have the authority to issue warrants only within their own districts, and in rural areas, some districts may have only a small number of judicial officers.

North Dakota, for instance, has only 51 state district judges spread across eight judicial districts. Those judges are assisted by 31 magistrates, and there are no magistrates in 20 of the State's 53 counties. At any given location in the State, then, relatively few state officials have authority to issue search warrants. Yet the State, with a population of roughly 740,000, sees nearly 7,000 drunk-driving arrests each year. With a small number of judicial officers authorized to issue warrants in some parts of the State, the burden of fielding BAC warrant applications 24 hours per day, 365 days of the year would not be the light burden that petitioners and Justice SOTOMAYOR suggest.

In light of this burden and our prior search-incident-to-arrest precedents, petitioners would at a minimum have to show some special need for warrants for BAC testing. It is therefore appropriate to consider the benefits that such applications would provide. Search warrants protect privacy in two main ways. First, they ensure that a search is not carried out unless a neutral magistrate makes an independent determination that there is probable cause to believe that evidence will be found. Second, if the magistrate finds probable cause, the warrant limits the intrusion on privacy by specifying the scope of the search—that is, the area that can be searched and the items that can be sought.

How well would these functions be performed by the warrant applications that petitioners propose? In order to persuade a magistrate that there is probable cause for a search warrant, the officer would typically recite the same facts that led the officer to find that there was probable cause for arrest, namely, that there is probable cause to believe that a BAC test will reveal that the motorist's blood alcohol level is over the limit. As these three cases suggest, * * * the facts that establish probable cause are largely the same from one drunk-driving stop to the next and consist largely of the officer's own characterization of his or her observations—for example, that there was a strong odor of alcohol, that the motorist wobbled when attempting to stand, that the motorist paused when reciting the alphabet or counting backwards, and so on. A magistrate would be in a poor position to challenge such characterizations.

As for the second function served by search warrants—delineating the scope of a search—the warrants in question here would not serve that function at all. In every case the scope of the warrant would simply be a BAC test of the arrestee. For these reasons, requiring the police to obtain a warrant in every case would impose a substantial burden but no commensurate benefit.

Petitioners advance other alternatives to warrantless BAC tests incident to arrest, but these are poor substitutes. * * * Birchfield identifies 19 strategies that he claims would be at least as effective as implied consent laws, including high-visibility sobriety checkpoints, installing ignition interlocks on repeat offenders' cars that would disable their operation when the driver's breath reveals a sufficiently high alcohol concentration, and alcohol treatment programs. But Birchfield ignores the fact that many of these measures, such as checkpoints, [are] significantly more costly than test refusal penalties. Others, such as ignition interlocks, target only a segment of the drunk-driver population. And still others, such as treatment programs, are already in widespread use, including in North Dakota and Minnesota. * * *

3

Petitioner Bernard objects to the whole idea of analyzing breath and blood tests as searches incident to arrest. That doctrine, he argues, does not protect the sort of governmental interests that warrantless breath and blood tests serve. On his reading, this Court's precedents permit a search of an arrestee solely to prevent the arrestee from obtaining a weapon or taking steps to destroy evidence. In *Chimel,* for example, the Court derived its limitation for the scope of the permitted search—"the area into which an arrestee might reach"—from the principle that officers may reasonably search "the area from within which he might gain possession of a weapon or destructible evidence." Stopping an arrestee from destroying evidence, Bernard argues, is critically different from preventing the loss of blood alcohol evidence as the result of the body's metabolism of alcohol, a natural process over which the arrestee has little control.

The distinction that Bernard draws between an arrestee's active destruction of evidence and the loss of evidence due to a natural process makes little sense. In both situations the State is justifiably concerned that evidence may be lost, and Bernard does not explain why the cause of the loss should be dispositive. * * *

Nor is there any reason to suspect that *Chimel*'s use of the word "destruction," was a deliberate decision to rule out evidence loss that is mostly beyond the arrestee's control. The case did not involve any evidence that was subject to dissipation through natural processes, and there is no sign in the opinion that such a situation was on the Court's mind.

* * *

Having assessed the effect of BAC tests on privacy interests and the need for such tests, we conclude that the Fourth Amendment permits warrantless breath tests incident to arrests for drunk driving. The impact of breath tests on privacy is slight, and the need for BAC testing is great.

We reach a different conclusion with respect to blood tests. Blood tests are significantly more intrusive, and their reasonableness must be judged in light of the availability of the less invasive alternative of a breath test. Respondents have offered no satisfactory justification for demanding the more intrusive alternative without a warrant.

Neither respondents nor their *amici* dispute the effectiveness of breath tests in measuring BAC. Breath tests have been in common use for many years. Their results are admissible in court and are widely credited by juries, and respondents do not dispute their accuracy or utility. What, then, is the justification for warrantless blood tests?

One advantage of blood tests is their ability to detect not just alcohol but also other substances that can impair a driver's ability to operate a car safely. A breath test cannot do this, but police have other measures at their disposal when they have reason to believe that a motorist may be under the influence of some other substance (for example, if a breath test indicates that a clearly impaired motorist has little if any alcohol in his blood). Nothing prevents the police from seeking a warrant for a blood test when there is sufficient time to do so in the particular circumstances or from relying on the exigent circumstances exception to the warrant requirement when there is not.

A blood test also requires less driver participation than a breath test. In order for a technician to take a blood sample, all that is needed is for the subject to remain still, either voluntarily or by being immobilized. Thus, it is possible to extract a blood sample from a subject who forcibly resists, but many States reasonably prefer not to take this step. North Dakota, for example, tells us that it generally opposes this practice because of the risk of dangerous altercations between police officers and arrestees in rural areas where the arresting officer may not have backup. Under current North Dakota law, only in cases involving an accident that results in death or serious injury may blood be taken from arrestees who resist.

It is true that a blood test, unlike a breath test, may be administered to a person who is unconscious (perhaps as a result of a crash) or who is unable to do what is needed to take a breath test due to profound intoxication or injuries. But we have no reason to believe that such situations are common in drunk-driving arrests, and when they arise, the police may apply for a warrant if need be.

A breath test may also be ineffective if an arrestee deliberately attempts to prevent an accurate reading by failing to blow into the tube for the requisite length of time or with the necessary force. But courts have held that such conduct qualifies as a refusal to undergo testing, and it may be prosecuted as such. And again, a warrant for a blood test may be sought.

Because breath tests are significantly less intrusive than blood tests and in most cases amply serve law enforcement interests, we conclude that a breath test, but not a blood test, may be administered as a search incident to a lawful arrest for drunk driving. As in all cases involving reasonable searches incident to arrest, a warrant is not needed in this situation.

VI

Having concluded that the search incident to arrest doctrine does not justify the warrantless taking of a blood sample, we must address respondents' alternative argument that such tests are justified based on the driver's legally implied consent to submit to them. It is well established that a search is reasonable when the subject consents, and that sometimes consent to a search need not be express but may be fairly inferred from context. Our prior opinions have referred approvingly to the general concept of implied-consent laws that impose civil penalties and evidentiary consequences on motorists who refuse to comply. Petitioners do not question the constitutionality of those laws, and nothing we say here should be read to cast doubt on them.

It is another matter, however, for a State not only to insist upon an intrusive blood test, but also to impose criminal penalties on the refusal to submit to such a test. There must be a limit to the consequences to which motorists may be deemed to have consented by virtue of a decision to drive on public roads.

* * * [W]e conclude that motorists cannot be deemed to have consented to submit to a blood test on pain of committing a criminal offense.

VII

Our remaining task is to apply our legal conclusions to the three cases before us.

Petitioner Birchfield was criminally prosecuted for refusing a warrantless blood draw, and therefore the search he refused cannot be justified as a search incident to his arrest or on the basis of implied consent. There is no indication in the record or briefing that a breath test would have failed to satisfy the State's interests in acquiring evidence to enforce its drunk-driving laws against Birchfield. And North Dakota has not presented any case-specific information to suggest that the exigent circumstances exception would have justified a warrantless search. Unable to see any other basis on which to justify a warrantless test of Birchfield's blood, we conclude that Birchfield was threatened with an unlawful search and that the judgment affirming his conviction must be reversed.

Bernard, on the other hand, was criminally prosecuted for refusing a warrantless breath test. That test *was* a permissible search incident to Bernard's arrest for drunk driving, an arrest whose legality Bernard has not contested. Accordingly, the Fourth Amendment did not require officers to obtain a warrant prior to demanding the test, and Bernard had no right to refuse it.

Unlike the other petitioners, Beylund was not prosecuted for refusing a test. He submitted to a blood test after police told him that the law required his submission, and his license was then suspended and he was fined in an administrative proceeding. The North Dakota Supreme Court held that Beylund's consent was voluntary on the erroneous assumption that the State could permissibly compel both blood and breath tests. Because voluntariness of consent to a search must be determined from the totality of all the circumstances, we leave it to the state court on remand to reevaluate Beylund's consent given the partial inaccuracy of the officer's advisory.

* * *

JUSTICE SOTOMAYOR, with whom JUSTICE GINSBURG joins, concurring in part and dissenting in part.

[Justice Sotomayor agreed with the majority that criminalizing refusal to undergo a blood test without a warrant was a violation of the Fourth Amendment. She disagreed, however, with the majority's holding that a warrantless breath test was permissible as a search incident to arrest—and therefore that the state could criminalize refusal. Excerpts from her opinion follow.]

[T]he Court cites the governmental interest in protecting the public from drunk drivers. See *ante,* at 2178–2179. But it is critical to note that once a person is stopped for drunk driving and arrested, he no longer poses an immediate threat to the public. Because the person is already in custody prior to the administration of the breath test, there can be no serious claim that the time it takes to obtain a warrant would increase the danger that drunk driver poses to fellow citizens.

* * *

[T]he Court and the States cite a governmental interest in minimizing the costs of gathering evidence of drunk driving. But neither has demonstrated that requiring police to obtain warrants for breath tests would impose a sufficiently significant burden on state resources to justify the elimination of the Fourth Amendment's warrant requirement. * * * States only need to obtain warrants for drivers who refuse testing and a significant majority of drivers voluntarily consent to breath tests, even in States without criminal penalties for refusal. In North Dakota, only 21% of people refuse breath tests and in Minnesota, only 12% refuse. Including States that impose only *civil* penalties for refusal, the average refusal rate is slightly higher at 24%. Say that North Dakota's and Minnesota's refusal rates rise to double the mean, or 48%. Each of their judges and magistrate judges would need to issue fewer than one extra warrant a week. That bears repeating: The Court finds a categorical exception to the warrant requirement because each of a State's judges and magistrate judges would need to issue less than one extra warrant a week.

* * *

This Court has already taken the weighty step of characterizing breath tests as "searches" for Fourth Amendment purposes. See *Skinner,* 489 U.S., at 616–617. That is because the typical breath test requires the subject to actively blow alveolar (or "deep lung") air into the machine. Although the process of physically blowing into the machine can be completed in as little as a few minutes, the end-to-end process can be significantly longer. The person administering the test must calibrate the machine, collect at least two separate samples from the arrestee, change the mouthpiece and reset the machine between each, and conduct any additional testing indicated by disparities between the two tests. Although some searches are certainly more invasive than breath tests, this Court cannot do justice to their status as Fourth Amendment "searches" if exaggerated time pressures, mere convenience in collecting evidence, and the "burden" of asking judges to issue an extra couple of warrants per month are costs so high as to render reasonable a search without a warrant. The Fourth Amendment becomes an empty promise of protecting citizens from unreasonable searches.

* * *

Without even considering the comparative effectiveness of case-by-case and categorical exceptions, the Court reaches for the categorical search-incident-to-arrest exception and enshrines it for all breath tests. The majority apparently assumes that any postarrest search should be analyzed under the search-incident-to-arrest doctrine. But * * * police officers may want to conduct a range of different searches after placing a person under arrest. Each of those searches must be separately analyzed for Fourth Amendment compliance. Two narrow types of postarrest searches are analyzed together under the rubric of our search-incident-to-arrest doctrine: Searches to disarm arrestees who could pose a danger before a warrant is obtained and searches to find evidence arrestees have an incentive to destroy before a warrant is obtained. Other forms of postarrest searches are analyzed differently because they present needs that require more tailored exceptions to the warrant requirement.

The fact that a person is under arrest does not tell us which of these warrant exceptions should apply to a particular kind of postarrest search. The way to analyze which exception, if any, is appropriate is to ask whether the exception best addresses the nature of the postarrest search and the needs it fulfills. Yet the majority never explains why the search-incident-to-arrest framework—its justifications, applications, and categorical scope—is best suited to breath tests.

To the contrary, the search-incident-to-arrest exception is particularly ill suited to breath tests. To the extent the Court discusses any fit between breath tests and the rationales underlying the search-incident-to-arrest exception, it says that evidence preservation is one of the core values served by the exception and worries that "evidence may be lost" if breath tests are not conducted. But, of course, the search-incident-to-arrest exception is concerned with evidence destruction only insofar as that destruction would occur before a warrant could be sought. And breath tests are not, except in rare circumstances, conducted at the time of arrest, before a warrant can be obtained, but at a separate location 40 to 120 minutes after an arrest is effectuated. That alone should be reason to reject an exception forged to address the immediate needs of arrests.

The exception's categorical reach makes it even less suitable here. The search-incident-to-arrest exception is applied categorically precisely because the needs it addresses could arise in every arrest. But the government's need to conduct a breath test is present only in arrests for drunk driving. And the asserted need to conduct a breath test without a warrant arises only when a warrant cannot be obtained during the significant built-in delay between arrest and testing. The conditions that require warrantless breath searches, in short, are highly situational and defy the logical underpinnings of the search-incident-to-arrest exception and its categorical application.

* * *

JUSTICE THOMAS, concurring in the judgment in part and dissenting in part.

The compromise the Court reaches today is not a good one. By deciding that some (but not all) warrantless tests revealing the blood alcohol concentration (BAC) of an arrested driver are constitutional, the Court contorts the search-incident-to-arrest exception to the Fourth Amendment's warrant requirement. The far simpler answer to the question presented is the one rejected in Missouri v. McNeely, 133 S.Ct. 1552 (2013). Here, the tests revealing the BAC of a driver suspected of driving drunk are constitutional under the exigent-circumstances exception to the warrant requirement.

I

Today's decision chips away at a well-established exception to the warrant requirement. Until recently, we have admonished that "[a] police officer's determination as to how and where to search the person of a suspect whom he has arrested is necessarily a quick ad hoc judgment which the Fourth Amendment does not require to be broken down in each instance into an analysis of each step in the search." United States v. Robinson, 414 U.S. 218, 235 (1973). Under our precedents, a search incident to lawful arrest "require[d] no additional justification." Ibid. Not until the recent decision in Riley v. California, 134 S.Ct. 2473 (2014), did the Court begin to retreat from this categorical approach because it feared that the search at issue, the "search of the information on a cell phone," bore "little resemblance to the type of brief physical search" contemplated by this Court's past search-incident-to-arrest decisions. I joined *Riley*, however, because the Court resisted the temptation to permit searches of some kinds of cellphone data and not others, and instead asked more generally whether that entire "category of effects" was searchable without a warrant.

Today's decision begins where *Riley* left off. The Court purports to apply *Robinson* but further departs from its categorical approach by holding that warrantless breath tests to prevent the destruction of BAC evidence are constitutional searches incident to arrest, but warrantless blood tests are not. That hairsplitting makes little sense. Either the search-incident-to-arrest exception permits bodily searches to prevent the destruction of BAC evidence, or it does not.

* * *

The Court was wrong in *McNeely*, and today's compromise is perhaps an inevitable consequence of that error. Both searches contemplated by the state laws at issue in these cases would be constitutional under the exigent-circumstances exception to the warrant requirement. I respectfully concur in the judgment in part and dissent in part.

D. PRETEXTUAL STOPS AND ARRESTS

Page 361. Add to the discussion in the headnote on *"Reasonable Mistake of Fact, Mistake of Law"*:

The discussion in text indicates that a stop will not be reasonable if the officer is mistaken about the law, i.e., that the officer thought that the actions of a suspect constituted a crime or offense when in fact the law did not prohibit the conduct. That mistakes of law provided no excuse was a principle embraced by all but one of the federal circuits and by most state courts. But the Supreme Court, in Heien v. North Carolina, 135 S.Ct. 530 (2014), held that a stop can be valid even though there is no violation under the law, so long as the law is ambiguous and could be reasonably read as having been violated.

In *Heien,* the defendant was pulled over for having one brake light out, in what appears from the record to be a pretextual stop: drugs were found in the course of the stop. The North Carolina statute was ambiguous on whether there was a violation if one brake light was still working. The state court on Heien's appeal reviewed the statute and ruled that a single brake light out was not a violation, and so the stop on the basis of a violation of the law was invalid. But, the Supreme Court, in an opinion by Chief Justice Roberts, upheld the stop, finding that the officer's interpretation of the ambiguous statute, while wrong, was reasonable. The court found no analytical distinction between reasonable mistakes of fact and reasonable mistakes of law. The Court emphasized that it wasn't sanctioning ignorance of the law, and that an officer who simply didn't know what the law was would not be making a reasonable mistake in stopping someone on the basis of the officer's unknowing misconception. In *Heien*, the officer was not ignorant of the law—the law was ambiguous and was susceptible to two reasonable interpretations.

Justice Sotomayor, in a lone dissent, decried the fact that the Court's decision would expand the possibilities of pretextual searches and arrests under *Whren.*

Heien is set forth in full in the section on reasonable suspicion earlier in this Supplement.

E. PLAIN VIEW AND PLAIN TOUCH SEIZURES

Page 366. Add after the headnote on *"Probable Cause to Seize an Item in Plain View: Arizona v. Hicks":*

Plain View, Probable Cause, and Legalized Marijuana

When an officer in the course of legal activity sees evidence that constitutes probable cause of crime in plain view, she can seize that evidence and the evidence might well support a further search under other doctrines, such as search incident to arrest or search of an automobile without a warrant. What if the officer in the course of legal activity sees a user-amount of marijuana? When a jurisdiction decriminalizes possession of small amounts of marijuana, the fact that an officer sees a person in possession of marijuana in plain view does not necessarily amount to probable cause. For example, in Commonwealth v. Sheridan, 470 Mass. 752, 25 N.E.3d 875 (Mass. 2015), the Massachusetts Supreme Judicial Court held that state officers who observe what appears to be a legally possessed amount of marijuana in a car during a traffic stop do not have probable cause to search the vehicle or any other justification to enter the vehicle to seize the drug. If federal law criminalizes possession of marijuana, however, federal officers with probable cause to believe that an individual possesses marijuana have authority to arrest the individual and to search a car if they see marijuana—even user amounts—in plain view.

H. ADMINISTRATIVE SEARCHES AND OTHER SEARCHES AND SEIZURES BASED ON "SPECIAL NEEDS"

2. Administrative Searches of Businesses

Page 427. Add after New York v. Burger:

In the following case, the Court took a more limited view than it had in *Burger* of the "heavily regulated industries" exception to the warrant requirement for businesses. In finding that hotels were not heavily regulated, the Court seems to reject the relevance of the indicia of regulation it had found in *Burger*—as Justice Scalia points out in his dissent.

CITY OF LOS ANGELES V. PATEL

Supreme Court of the United States, 2015.
135 S.Ct. 2443.

JUSTICE SOTOMAYOR delivered the opinion of the Court.

Respondents brought a Fourth Amendment challenge to a provision of the Los Angeles Municipal Code that compels every operator of a hotel to keep a record containing specified information concerning guests and to make this record available to any officer of the Los Angeles Police Department for inspection on demand. The questions presented are whether facial challenges to statutes can be brought under the Fourth Amendment and, if so, whether this provision of the Los Angeles Municipal Code is facially invalid. We hold facial challenges can be brought under the Fourth Amendment. We further hold that the provision of the Los Angeles Municipal Code that requires hotel operators to make their registries available to the police on demand is facially unconstitutional because it penalizes them for declining to turn over their records without affording them any opportunity for precompliance review.

I

A

Los Angeles Municipal Code (LAMC) § 41.49 requires hotel operators to record information about their guests, including: the guest's name and address; the number of people in each guest's party; the make, model, and license plate number of any guest's vehicle parked on hotel property; the guest's date and time of arrival and scheduled departure date; the room number assigned to the guest; the rate charged and amount collected for the room; and the method of payment. § 41.49(2). * * * This information can be maintained in either electronic or paper form, but it must be kept on the hotel premises in the guest reception or guest check-in area or in an office adjacent thereto for a period of 90 days. § 41.49(3)(a).

Section 41.49(3)(a)—the only provision at issue here—states, in pertinent part, that hotel guest records "shall be made available to any officer of the Los Angeles Police Department for inspection," provided that "[w]henever possible, the inspection shall be conducted at a time and in a manner that minimizes any interference with the operation of the business." A hotel operator's failure to make his or her guest records available for police inspection is a misdemeanor punishable by up to six months in jail and a $1,000 fine.

B

In 2003, respondents, a group of motel operators along with a lodging association, sued the city of Los Angeles in three consolidated cases challenging the constitutionality of § 41.49(3)(a). They sought declaratory and injunctive relief. The parties agreed that the sole issue in the action would be a facial constitutional challenge to § 41.49(3)(a) under the Fourth Amendment. They further stipulated that respondents have been subjected to mandatory record inspections under the ordinance without consent or a warrant.

Following a bench trial, the District Court entered judgment in favor of the City, holding that respondents' facial challenge failed because they lacked a reasonable expectation of privacy in the records subject to inspection. A divided panel of the Ninth Circuit affirmed on the same grounds. On rehearing en banc, however, the Court of Appeals reversed.

The en banc court first determined that a police officer's nonconsensual inspection of hotel records under § 41.49 is a Fourth Amendment "search" because "[t]he business records covered by § 41.49 are the hotel's private property" and the hotel therefore "has the right to exclude others from prying into the[ir] contents." Next, the court assessed "whether the searches authorized by § 41.49 are reasonable." Relying on Donovan v. Lone Steer, Inc., 464 U.S. 408 (1984), and See v. Seattle, 387 U.S. 541 (1967), the court held that § 41.49 is facially unconstitutional "as it authorizes inspections" of hotel records "without affording an opportunity to obtain judicial review of the reasonableness of the demand prior to suffering penalties for refusing to comply."

* * *

We granted certiorari, and now affirm.

II

We first clarify that facial challenges under the Fourth Amendment are not categorically barred or especially disfavored.

A

A facial challenge is an attack on a statute itself as opposed to a particular application. While such challenges are "the most difficult . . . to mount successfully," United States v. Salerno, 481 U.S. 739, 745 (1987), the Court has never held that these claims cannot be brought under any otherwise enforceable provision of the Constitution.

Fourth Amendment challenges to statutes authorizing warrantless searches are no exception. * * *

[C]laims for facial relief under the Fourth Amendment are unlikely to succeed when there is substantial ambiguity as to what conduct a statute authorizes: Where a statute consists of extraordinarily elastic categories, it may be impossible to tell whether and to what extent it deviates from the requirements of the Fourth Amendment.

[T]he Court has entertained facial challenges under the Fourth Amendment to statutes authorizing warrantless searches. See, e.g., Vernonia School District 47J v. Acton, 515 U.S. 646, 648 (1995) ("We granted certiorari to decide whether" petitioner's student athlete drug testing policy "violates the Fourth and Fourteenth Amendments to the United States Constitution"); Skinner v. Railway Labor Executives' Assn., 489 U.S. 602, 633, n. 10 (1989) ("[R]espondents have challenged the administrative scheme on its face. We deal therefore with whether the [drug] tests contemplated by the regulation can ever be conducted"). Perhaps more importantly, the Court has on numerous occasions declared statutes facially invalid under the Fourth Amendment. For instance, in Chandler v. Miller, 520 U.S. 305, 308–309 (1997), the Court struck down a Georgia statute requiring candidates for certain state offices to take and pass a drug test, concluding that this "requirement . . . [did] not fit within the closely guarded category of constitutionally permissible suspicionless searches." Similar examples abound. See, e.g., Ferguson v. Charleston, 532 U.S. 67, 86 (2001) (holding that a hospital policy authorizing "nonconsensual, warrantless, and suspicionless searches" contravened the Fourth Amendment); Payton v. New York, 445 U.S. 573, 574, 576 (1980) (holding that a New York statute "authoriz[ing] police officers to enter a private residence without a warrant and with force, if necessary, to make a routine felony arrest" was "not consistent with the Fourth Amendment").

B

Petitioner principally contends that facial challenges to statutes authorizing warrantless searches must fail because such searches will never be unconstitutional in all applications. In particular, the City points to situations where police are responding to an emergency, where the subject of the search consents to the intrusion, and where police are acting under a court-ordered warrant. While petitioner frames this argument as an objection to respondents' challenge in this case, its logic would preclude facial relief in every Fourth Amendment challenge to a statute authorizing warrantless searches. For this reason alone, the City's argument must fail: The Court's precedents demonstrate not only that facial challenges to statutes authorizing warrantless searches can be brought, but also that they can succeed.

Moreover, the City's argument misunderstands how courts analyze facial challenges. Under the most exacting standard the Court has prescribed for facial challenges, a plaintiff must establish that a law is unconstitutional in all of its applications. But when assessing whether a statute meets this standard, the Court has considered only applications of the statute in which it actually authorizes or prohibits conduct. * * *

[W]hen addressing a facial challenge to a statute authorizing warrantless searches, the proper focus of the constitutional inquiry is searches that the law actually authorizes, not those for which it is irrelevant. If exigency or a warrant justifies an officer's search, the subject of the search must permit it to proceed irrespective of whether it is authorized by statute. Statutes authorizing warrantless searches also do no work where the subject of a search has consented. Accordingly, the constitutional "applications" that petitioner claims prevent facial relief here are irrelevant to our analysis because they do not involve actual applications of the statute.

III

Turning to the merits of the particular claim before us, we hold that § 41.49(3)(a) is facially unconstitutional because it fails to provide hotel operators with an opportunity for precompliance review.

A

* * * [T]he Court has repeatedly held that searches conducted outside the judicial process, without prior approval by a judge or a magistrate judge, are *per se* unreasonable, subject only to a few specifically established and well-delineated exceptions. This rule "applies to commercial premises as well as to homes." Marshall v. Barlow's, Inc., 436 U.S. 307, 312 (1978).

Search regimes where no warrant is ever required may be reasonable where special needs make the warrant and probable-cause requirement impracticable, and where the "primary purpose" of the searches is "[d]istinguishable from the general interest in crime control," Indianapolis v. Edmond, 531 U.S. 32, 44 (2000). Here, we assume that the searches authorized by § 41.49 serve a "special need" other than conducting criminal investigations: They ensure compliance with the recordkeeping requirement, which in turn deters criminals from operating on the hotels' premises. The Court has referred to this kind of search as an "administrative search." Camara v. Municipal Court of City and County of San Francisco, 387 U.S. 523, 534 (1967). Thus, we consider whether § 41.49 falls within the administrative search exception to the warrant requirement.

The Court has held that absent consent, exigent circumstances, or the like, in order for an administrative search to be constitutional, the subject of the search must be afforded an opportunity to obtain precompliance review before a neutral decisionmaker. See *Lone Steer,* 464 U.S., at 415 (noting that an administrative search may proceed with only a subpoena where the subpoenaed party is sufficiently protected by the opportunity to "question the reasonableness of the subpoena, before suffering any penalties for refusing to comply with it, by raising objections in an action in district court"). And, we see no reason why this minimal requirement is inapplicable here. While the Court has never attempted to prescribe the exact form an opportunity for precompliance review must take, the City does not even attempt to argue that § 41.49(3)(a) affords hotel operators any opportunity whatsoever. Section 41.49(3)(a) is, therefore, facially invalid.

A hotel owner who refuses to give an officer access to his or her registry can be arrested on the spot. The Court has held that business owners cannot reasonably be put to this kind of choice. *Camara,* 387 U.S., at 533 (holding that "broad statutory safeguards are no substitute for individualized review, particularly when those safeguards may only be invoked at the risk of a criminal penalty"). Absent an opportunity for precompliance review, the ordinance creates an intolerable risk that searches authorized by it will exceed statutory limits, or be used as a pretext to harass hotel operators and their guests. Even if a hotel has been searched 10 times a day, every day, for three months, without any violation being found, the operator can only refuse to comply with an officer's demand to turn over the registry at his or her own peril.

To be clear, we hold only that a hotel owner must be afforded an *opportunity* to have a neutral decisionmaker review an officer's demand to search the registry before he or she faces penalties for failing to comply. Actual review need only occur in those rare instances where a hotel operator objects to turning over the registry. Moreover, this opportunity can be provided without imposing onerous burdens on those charged with an administrative scheme's enforcement. For instance, respondents accept that the searches authorized by § 41.49(3)(a) would be constitutional if they were performed pursuant to an administrative subpoena. These subpoenas, which are typically a simple form, can be issued by the individual seeking the record—here, officers in the field—without probable cause that a regulation is being infringed. Issuing a subpoena will usually be the full extent of an officer's burden because "the great majority of businessmen can be expected in normal course to consent to inspection without warrant." *Barlow's, Inc.,* 436 U.S., at 316. Indeed, the City has cited no evidence suggesting that without an ordinance authorizing on-demand searches, hotel operators would regularly refuse to cooperate with the police.

In those instances, however, where a subpoenaed hotel operator believes that an attempted search is motivated by illicit purposes, respondents suggest it would be sufficient if he or she could move to quash the subpoena before any search takes place. A neutral decisionmaker, including an administrative law judge, would then review the subpoenaed party's objections before deciding whether the subpoena is enforceable. Given the limited grounds on which a motion to quash can be granted, such challenges will likely be rare. And, in the even rarer event that an officer reasonably suspects that a hotel operator may tamper with the registry while the motion to quash is pending, he or she can guard the registry until the required hearing can occur, which ought not take long. Riley v. California, 573 U.S. ___, 134 S.Ct. 2473, 2476 (2014) (police may seize and hold a cell phone "to prevent destruction of evidence while seeking a warrant"); Illinois v. McArthur, 531 U.S. 326, 334 (2001) (citing cases upholding the constitutionality of "temporary restraints where [they are] needed to preserve evidence until police could obtain a warrant").

* * * In most contexts, business owners can be afforded at least an opportunity to contest an administrative search's propriety without unduly compromising the government's ability to achieve its regulatory aims.

Of course administrative subpoenas are only one way in which an opportunity for precompliance review can be made available. But whatever the precise form, the availability of precompliance review alters the dynamic between the officer and the hotel to be searched, and reduces the risk that officers will use these administrative searches as a pretext to harass business owners.

Finally, we underscore the narrow nature of our holding. Respondents have not challenged and nothing in our opinion calls into question those parts of § 41.49 that require hotel operators to maintain guest registries containing certain information. And, even absent legislative action to create a procedure along the lines discussed above, police will not be prevented from obtaining access to these documents. As they often do, hotel operators remain free to consent to searches of their registries and police can compel them to turn them over if they have a proper administrative warrant—including one that was issued *ex parte*—or if some other exception to the warrant requirement applies, including exigent circumstances.

B

Rather than arguing that § 41.49(3)(a) is constitutional under the general administrative search doctrine, the City and Justice SCALIA contend that hotels are "closely regulated," and that the ordinance is facially valid under the more relaxed standard that applies to searches of this category of businesses. They are wrong on both counts.

Over the past 45 years, the Court has identified only four industries that "have such a history of government oversight that no reasonable expectation of privacy . . . could exist for a proprietor over the stock of such an enterprise," *Barlow's, Inc.,* 436 U.S., at 313. Simply listing these industries refutes petitioner's argument that hotels should be counted among them. Unlike liquor sales, Colonnade Catering Corp. v. United States, 397 U.S. 72 (1970), firearms dealing, United States v. Biswell, 406 U.S. 311, 311–312 (1972), mining, Donovan v. Dewey, 452 U.S. 594 (1981), or running an automobile junkyard, New York v. Burger, 482 U.S. 691(1987), nothing inherent in the operation of hotels poses a clear and significant risk to the public welfare.

Moreover, "[t]he clear import of our cases is that the closely regulated industry . . . is the exception." *Barlow's, Inc.,* 436 U.S., at 313. To classify hotels as pervasively regulated would permit what has always been a narrow exception to swallow the rule. The City wisely refrains from arguing that § 41.49 itself renders hotels closely regulated. Nor do any of the other regulations on which petitioner and Justice SCALIA rely— regulations requiring hotels to, *inter alia,* maintain a license, collect taxes, conspicuously post their rates, and meet certain sanitary standards— establish a comprehensive scheme of regulation that distinguishes hotels from numerous other businesses. * * * If such general regulations were sufficient to invoke the closely regulated industry exception, it would be hard to imagine a type of business that would not qualify.

* * * History is relevant when determining whether an industry is closely regulated. See, *e.g., Burger,* 482 U.S., at 707. * * * The City and Justice SCALIA principally point to evidence that hotels were treated as public accommodations. For instance, the Commonwealth of Massachusetts required innkeepers to "furnish[ ] . . . suitable provisions and lodging, for the refreshment and entertainment of strangers and travellers, pasturing and stable room, hay and provender . . . for their horses and cattle." Brief for Petitioner 35 (quoting An Act For The Due Regulation Of Licensed Houses (1786)). But laws obligating inns to provide suitable lodging to all paying guests are not the same as laws subjecting inns to warrantless searches. Petitioner also asserts that for a long time, hotel owners left their registers open to widespread inspection. Setting aside that modern hotel registries contain sensitive information, such as driver's licenses and credit card numbers for which there is no historic analog, the fact that some hotels chose to make registries accessible to the public has little bearing on whether government authorities could have viewed these documents on demand without a hotel's consent.

Even if we were to find that hotels are pervasively regulated, § 41.49 would need to satisfy three additional criteria to be reasonable under the Fourth Amendment: (1) "[T]here must be a 'substantial' government interest that informs the regulatory scheme pursuant to which the inspection is made"; (2) "the warrantless inspections must be 'necessary' to further [the] regulatory scheme"; and (3) "the statute's inspection program, in terms of the certainty and regularity of its application, [must] provid[e] a constitutionally adequate substitute for a warrant." *Burger,* 482 U.S., at 702–703. We assume petitioner's interest in ensuring that hotels maintain accurate and complete registries might fulfill the first of these requirements, but conclude that § 41.49 fails the second and third prongs of this test.

The City claims that affording hotel operators any opportunity for precompliance review would fatally undermine the scheme's efficacy by giving operators a chance to falsify their records. The Court has previously rejected this exact argument, which could be made regarding any recordkeeping requirement. See *Barlow's, Inc.,* 436 U.S., at 320 ("[It is not] apparent why the advantages of surprise would be lost if, after being refused entry, procedures were available for the [Labor] Secretary to seek an *ex parte* warrant to reappear at the premises without further notice to the establishment being inspected"). We see no reason to accept it here.

* * *

Section 41.49 is also constitutionally deficient under the "certainty and regularity" prong of the closely regulated industries test because it fails sufficiently to constrain police officers' discretion as to which hotels to search and under what circumstances. While the Court has upheld inspection schemes of closely regulated industries that called for searches at least four times a year, *Dewey,* 452 U.S., at 604 or on a "regular basis," *Burger,* 482 U.S., at 711 § 41.49 imposes no comparable standard.

3

For the foregoing reasons, we agree with the Ninth Circuit that § 41.49(3)(a) is facially invalid insofar as it fails to provide any opportunity for precompliance review before a hotel must give its guest registry to the police for inspection. Accordingly, the judgment of the Ninth Circuit is affirmed.

It is so ordered.

JUSTICE SCALIA, with whom THE CHIEF JUSTICE and JUSTICE THOMAS join, dissenting.

* * * The purpose of this recordkeeping requirement is to deter criminal conduct, on the theory that criminals will be unwilling to carry on illicit activities in motel rooms if they must provide identifying information at check-in. Because this deterrent effect will only be accomplished if motels actually do require guests to provide the required information, the ordinance also authorizes police to conduct random spot checks of motels' guest registers to ensure that they are properly maintained. The ordinance limits these spot checks to the four corners of the register, and does not authorize police to enter any nonpublic area of the motel. To the extent possible, police must conduct these spot checks at times that will minimize any disruption to a motel's business.

The parties do not dispute the governmental interests at stake. Motels not only provide housing to vulnerable transient populations, they are also a particularly attractive site for criminal activity ranging from drug dealing and prostitution to human trafficking. Offering privacy and anonymity on the cheap, they have been employed as prisons for migrants smuggled across the border and held for ransom, and rendezvous sites where child sex workers meet their clients on threat of violence from their procurers.

Nevertheless, the Court today concludes that Los Angeles's ordinance is "unreasonable" inasmuch as it permits police to flip through a guest register to ensure it is being filled out without first providing an opportunity for the motel operator to seek judicial review. Because I believe that such a limited inspection of a guest register is eminently reasonable under the circumstances presented, I dissent.

I

I assume that respondents may bring a facial challenge to the City's ordinance under the Fourth Amendment. Even so, their claim must fail because * * * the law is constitutional in most, if not all, of its applications. * * *

II

The Fourth Amendment provides, in relevant part, that "[t]he right of the people to be secure in their persons, houses, papers, and effects, against unreasonable searches and seizures, shall not be violated, and no Warrants shall issue, but upon probable cause." Grammatically, the two clauses of the Amendment seem to be independent—and directed at entirely different actors. The former tells the executive what it must do when it conducts a search, and the latter tells the judiciary what it must do when it issues a search warrant. But in an effort to guide courts in applying the Search-and-Seizure Clause's indeterminate reasonableness standard, and to maintain coherence in our case law, we have used the Warrant Clause as a guidepost for assessing the reasonableness of a search, and have erected a framework of presumptions applicable to broad categories of searches conducted by executive officials. Our case law has repeatedly recognized, however, that these are mere presumptions, and the only constitutional *requirement* is that a search be reasonable.

When, for example, a search is conducted to enforce an administrative regime rather than to investigate criminal wrongdoing, we have been willing to modify the probable-cause standard so that a warrant may issue absent individualized suspicion of wrongdoing. Thus, our cases say a warrant may issue to inspect a structure for fire-code violations on the basis of such factors as the passage of time, the nature of the building, and the condition of the neighborhood. Camara v. Municipal Court of City and County of San Francisco, 387 U.S. 523, 538–539 (1967). As we recognized in that case, "reasonableness is still the ultimate standard. If a valid public interest justifies the intrusion contemplated, then there is probable cause to issue a suitably restricted search warrant." *Id.,* at 539. And precisely "because the ultimate touchstone of the Fourth Amendment is 'reasonableness,' " even the presumption that the search of a home without a warrant is unreasonable "is subject to certain exceptions." Brigham City v. Stuart, 547 U.S. 398, 403 (2006).

One exception to normal warrant requirements applies to searches of closely regulated businesses. "[W]hen an entrepreneur embarks upon such a business, he has voluntarily chosen to subject himself to a full arsenal of governmental regulation," and so a warrantless search to enforce those regulations is not unreasonable. Marshall v. Barlow's, Inc., 436 U.S. 307, 313 (1978). Recognizing that warrantless searches of closely regulated businesses may nevertheless *become* unreasonable if arbitrarily conducted, we have required laws authorizing such searches to satisfy three criteria: (1) There must be a " 'substantial' government interest that informs the regulatory scheme pursuant to which the inspection is made"; (2) "the warrantless inspections must be 'necessary to further [the] regulatory scheme' "; and (3) " 'the statute's inspection program, in terms of the certainty and regularity of its application, [must] provid[e] a constitutionally adequate substitute for a warrant.' " New York v. Burger, 482 U.S. 691, 702–703 (1987).

Los Angeles's ordinance easily meets these standards.

A

In determining whether a business is closely regulated, this Court has looked to factors including the duration of the regulatory tradition; the comprehensiveness of the regulatory regime; and the imposition of similar regulations by other jurisdictions. These factors are not talismans, but shed light on the expectation of privacy the owner of a business may reasonably have, which in turn affects the reasonableness of a warrantless search.

Reflecting the unique public role of motels and their commercial forebears, governments have long subjected these businesses to unique public duties, and have established inspection regimes to ensure compliance. As Blackstone observed, "Inns, in particular, being intended for the lodging and receipt of travellers, may be indicted, suppressed, and the inn-keepers fined, if they refuse to entertain a traveller without a very sufficient cause: for thus to frustrate the end of their institution is held to be disorderly behavior." 4 W. Blackstone, Commentaries on the Laws of England 168 (1765). Justice Story similarly recognized "[t]he soundness of the public policy of subjecting particular classes of persons to extraordinary responsibility, in cases where an extraordinary confidence is necessarily reposed in them, and there is an extraordinary temptation to fraud, or danger of plunder." J. Story, Commentaries on the Law of Bailments § 464, pp. 487–488 (5th ed. 1851). Accordingly, in addition to the obligation to receive any paying guest, "innkeepers are bound to take, not merely ordinary care, but uncommon care, of the goods, money, and baggage of their guests," *id.,* § 470, at 495, as travellers "are obliged to rely almost implicitly on the good faith of innholders, whose education and morals are none of the best, and who might have frequent opportunities of associating with ruffians and pilferers," *id.,* § 471, at 498.

These obligations were not merely aspirational. At the time of the founding, searches—indeed, warrantless searches—of inns and similar places of public accommodation were commonplace. For example, although Massachusetts was perhaps the State most protective against government searches, "the state code of 1788 still allowed tithingmen to search public houses of entertainment on every Sabbath without any sort of warrant." W. Cuddihy, Fourth Amendment: Origins and Original Meaning 602–1791, 743 (2009).

As this evidence demonstrates, the regulatory tradition governing motels is not only longstanding, but comprehensive. And the tradition continues in Los Angeles. The City imposes an occupancy tax upon transients who stay in motels, and makes the motel owner responsible for collecting it. It authorizes city officials to enter a motel, free of charge, during business hours in order to inspect and examine them to determine whether these tax provisions have been complied with. It requires all motels to obtain a "Transient Occupancy Registration Certificate," which must be displayed on the premises. State law requires motels to post in a conspicuous place a statement of rate or range of rates by the day for lodging, and forbids any charges in excess of those posted rates. Hotels must change bed linens between guests, Cal.Code Regs., tit. 25, § 40 (2015), and they must offer guests the option not to have towels and linens laundered daily. "Multiuse drinking utensils" may be placed in guest rooms only if they are "thoroughly washed and sanitized after each use" and "placed in protective bags." Cal.Code Regs., tit. 17, § 30852. And state authorities, like their municipal counterparts, "may at reasonable times enter and inspect any hotels, motels, or other public places" to ensure compliance. § 30858.

The regulatory regime at issue here is thus substantially *more* comprehensive than the regulations governing junkyards in *Burger,* where licensing, inventory-recording, and permit-posting requirements were found sufficient to qualify the industry as closely regulated. * * * The regulations we have described above reach into the "minutest detail[s]" of motel operations, *Barlow's, supra,* at 314 and those who enter that business today (like those who have entered it over the centuries) do so with an expectation that they will be subjected to especially vigilant governmental oversight.

Finally, this ordinance is not an outlier. The City has pointed us to more than 100 similar register-inspection laws in cities and counties across the country, and that is far from exhaustive. * * *

This copious evidence is surely enough to establish that "[w]hen a [motel operator] chooses to engage in this pervasively regulated business . . . he does so with the knowledge that his business records . . . will be subject to effective inspection." United States v. Biswell, 406 U.S. 311, 316 (1972). And *that* is the relevant constitutional test—not whether this regulatory superstructure is "the same as laws subjecting inns to warrantless searches," or whether, as an historical matter, government authorities not only required these documents to be kept but permitted them to be viewed on demand without a motel's consent.

The Court's observation that "[o]ver the past 45 years, the Court has identified only four industries" as closely regulated, is neither here nor there. Since we first concluded in Colonnade Catering that warrantless searches of closely regulated businesses are reasonable, we have only identified one industry as not closely regulated, see *Barlow's*, 436 U.S., at 313–314. The Court's statistic thus tells us more about how this Court exercises its discretionary review than it does about the number of industries that qualify as closely regulated. At the same time, lower courts, which do not have the luxury of picking the cases they hear, have identified many more businesses as closely regulated under the test we have announced: pharmacies, United States v. Gonsalves, 435 F.3d 64, 67 (C.A.1 2006); massage parlors, Pollard v. Cockrell, 578 F.2d 1002, 1014 (C.A.5 1978); commercial-fishing operations, United States v. Raub, 637 F.2d 1205, 1208–1209 (C.A.9 1980); day-care facilities, Rush v. Obledo, 756 F.2d 713, 720–721 (C.A.9 1985); nursing homes, People v. Firstenberg, 92 Cal.App.3d 570, 578–580, 155 Cal.Rptr. 80, 84–86 (1979); jewelers, People v. Pashigian, 150 Mich.App. 97, 100–101, 388 N.W.2d 259, 261–262 (1986) (per curiam); barbershops, Stogner v. Kentucky, 638 F.Supp. 1, 3 (W.D.Ky.1985); and yes, even rabbit dealers, Lesser v. Espy, 34 F.3d 1301, 1306–1307 (C.A.7 1994). Like automobile junkyards and catering companies that serve alcohol, many of these businesses are far from "intrinsically dangerous." This should come as no surprise. The reason closely regulated industries may be searched without a warrant has nothing to do with the risk of harm they pose; rather, it has to do with the expectations of those who enter such a line of work.

B

The City's ordinance easily satisfies the remaining *Burger* requirements: It furthers a substantial governmental interest, it is necessary to achieving that interest, and it provides an adequate substitute for a search warrant.

Neither respondents nor the Court question the substantial interest of the City in deterring criminal activity. The private pain and public costs imposed by drug dealing, prostitution, and human trafficking are beyond contention, and motels provide an obvious haven for those who trade in human misery.

Warrantless inspections are also necessary to advance this interest. Although the Court acknowledges that law enforcement can enter a motel room without a warrant when exigent circumstances exist, the whole reason criminals use motel rooms in the first place is that they offer privacy and secrecy, so that police will never come to discover these exigencies. The recordkeeping requirement, which all parties admit is permissible, therefore operates by *deterring* crime. Criminals, who depend on the anonymity that motels offer, will balk when confronted with a motel's demand that they produce identification. And a motel's evasion of the recordkeeping requirement fosters crime. In San Diego, for example, motel owners were indicted for collaborating with members of the Crips street gang in the prostitution of underage girls; the motel owners "set aside rooms apart from the rest of their legitimate customers where girls and women were housed, charged the gang members/pimps a higher rate for the rooms where 'dates' or 'tricks' took place, and warned the gang members of inquiries by law enforcement." Office of the Attorney General, Cal. Dept. of Justice, The State of Human Trafficking in California 25 (2012). The warrantless inspection requirement provides a necessary incentive for motels to maintain their registers thoroughly and accurately: They never know when law enforcement might drop by to inspect.

Respondents and the Court acknowledge that *inspections* are necessary to achieve the purposes of the recordkeeping regime, but insist that *warrantless* inspections are not. They have to acknowledge, however, that the motel operators who conspire with drug dealers and procurers may demand precompliance judicial review simply as a pretext to buy time for making fraudulent entries in their guest registers. The Court therefore must resort to arguing that warrantless inspections are not "necessary" because other alternatives exist.

The Court suggests that police could obtain an administrative subpoena to search a guest register and, if a motel moves to quash, the police could guard the registry pending a hearing on the motion. This proposal is equal parts 1984 and Alice in Wonderland. It protects motels from government inspection of their registers by authorizing government agents to seize the registers (if "guarding" entails forbidding the register to be moved) or to upset guests by a prolonged police presence at the motel. The Court also notes that police can obtain an *ex parte* warrant before conducting a register inspection. Presumably such warrants could issue without probable cause of wrongdoing by a particular motel, see *Camara,* 387 U.S., at 535–536; otherwise, this would be no alternative at all. Even so, under this regime police would have to obtain an *ex parte* warrant before *every* inspection. That is because law enforcement would have no way of knowing ahead of time which motels would refuse consent to a search upon request; and if they wait to obtain a warrant until consent is refused, motels will have the opportunity to falsify their guest registers while the police jump through the procedural hoops required to obtain a warrant. It is quite plausible that the costs of this always-get-a-warrant "alternative" would be prohibitive for a police force in one of America's largest cities, juggling numerous law-enforcement priorities, and confronting more than 2,000 motels within its jurisdiction. To be sure, the fact that obtaining a warrant might be costly will not by itself render a warrantless search reasonable under the Fourth Amendment; but it can render a warrantless search *necessary* in the context of an administrative-search regime governing closely regulated businesses.

But all that discussion is in any case irrelevant. The administrative search need only be reasonable. It is not the burden of Los Angeles to show that there are no less restrictive means of achieving the City's purposes. Sequestration or *ex parte* warrants were *possible* alternatives to the warrantless search regimes approved by this Court in *Colonnade Catering, Biswell, Dewey,* and *Burger.* By importing a least-restrictive-means test into *Burger*'s Fourth Amendment framework, today's opinion implicitly overrules that entire line of cases.

Finally, the City's ordinance provides an adequate substitute for a warrant. Warrants "advise the owner of the scope and objects of the search, beyond which limits the inspector is not expected to proceed." *Barlow's,* 436 U.S., at 323, 98 S.Ct. 1816. Ultimately, they aim to protect against "devolv[ing] almost unbridled discretion upon executive and administrative officers, particularly those in the field, as to when to search and whom to search." *Ibid.*

Los Angeles's ordinance provides that the guest register must be kept in the guest reception or guest check-in area, or in an adjacent office, and that it "be made available to any officer of the Los Angeles Police Department for inspection. Whenever possible, the inspection shall be conducted at a time and in a manner that minimizes any interference with the operation of the business." LAMC § 41.49(3). Nothing in the ordinance authorizes law enforcement to enter a nonpublic part of the motel. Compare this to the statute upheld in *Colonnade Catering,* which provided that " '[t]he Secretary or his delegate may enter, in the daytime, any building or place where any articles or objects subject to tax are made, produced, or kept, so far as it may be necessary for the purpose of examining said articles or objects,' " 397 U.S., at 73, n. 2; * * * or the one in *Burger,* which compelled junkyard operators to " 'produce such records and permit said agent or police officer to examine them and any vehicles or parts of vehicles which are subject to the record keeping requirements of this section and which are on the premises,' " 482 U.S., at 694, n. 1. The Los Angeles ordinance—which limits warrantless police searches to the pages of a guest register in a public part of a motel—circumscribes police discretion in much more exacting terms than the laws we have approved in our earlier cases.

The Court claims that Los Angeles's ordinance confers too much discretion because it does not adequately limit the *frequency* of searches. Without a trace of irony, the Court tries to distinguish Los Angeles's law from the laws upheld in *Dewey* and *Burger* by pointing out that the latter regimes required inspections at least four times a year and on a "regular basis," respectively. But the warrantless police searches of a business "10 times a day, every day, for three months" that the Court envisions under Los Angeles's regime, are entirely consistent with the regimes in *Dewey* and *Burger*; 10 times a day, every day, is "at least four times a year," and on a (much too) "regular basis."

That is not to say that the Court's hypothetical searches are necessarily constitutional. It is only to say that Los Angeles's ordinance presents no greater risk that such a hypothetical will materialize than the laws we have already upheld. As in our earlier cases, we should leave it to lower courts to consider on a case-by-case basis whether warrantless searches have been conducted in an unreasonably intrusive or harassing manner.

III

The Court reaches its wrongheaded conclusion not simply by misapplying our precedent, but by mistaking our precedent for the Fourth Amendment itself. Rather than bother with the text of that Amendment, the Court relies exclusively on our administrative-search cases. But the Constitution predates 1967, and it remains the supreme law of the land today. Although the categorical framework our jurisprudence has erected in this area may provide us guidance, it is guidance to answer the constitutional question at issue: whether the challenged search is *reasonable*.

An administrative, warrantless-search ordinance that narrowly limits the scope of searches to a single business record, that does not authorize entry upon premises not open to the public, and that is supported by the need to prevent fabrication of guest registers, is, to say the least, far afield from the laws at issue in the cases the Court relies upon. The Court concludes that such minor intrusions, permissible when the police are trying to tamp down the market in stolen auto parts, are "unreasonable" when police are instead attempting to stamp out the market in child sex slaves.

Because I believe that the limited warrantless searches authorized by Los Angeles's ordinance are reasonable under the circumstances, I respectfully dissent.

Editor's Note: Justice Alito wrote a separate dissent joined by Justice Thomas. He argued that the facial attack on the ordinance should fail because there were many situations in which the ordinance could be constitutionally applied.

VI. ELECTRONIC SURVEILLANCE, UNDERCOVER ACTIVITY, AND THE OUTER REACHES OF THE FOURTH AMENDMENT

D. THE FOREIGN INTELLIGENCE SURVEILLANCE ACT

Page 545. At the end of the section, add the following:

On June 2, 2015, President Obama signed the USA Freedom Act, which put certain limits on the NSA bulk data collection program that is discussed in the Text. As stated by Congressman Sensenbrenner, who introduced the legislation, the purpose of the USA Freedom Act is "[t]o rein in the dragnet collection of data by the National Security Agency (NSA) and other government agencies, increase transparency of the Foreign Intelligence Surveillance Court (FISC), provide businesses the ability to release information regarding FISA requests, and create an independent constitutional advocate to argue cases before the FISC."

The Act eliminates NSA bulk data collection. Instead, phone companies will retain the data and the NSA can obtain information about targeted individuals only with permission from the FISA court. The government does not need probable cause to obtain such an order. Rather, the government can get an order to do the following:

- production on an ongoing basis of call detail records created before, on, or after the date of the application relating to an authorized investigation to protect against international terrorism, in which case the specific selection term must specifically identify an individual, account, or personal device; or

- production of call detail records or other tangible things in any other manner, in which case the selection term must specifically identify an individual, a federal officer or employee, a group, an entity, an association, a corporation, a foreign power, an account, a physical or an electronic address, a personal device, or any other specific identifier but is prohibited from including, when not used as part of a specific identifier, a broad geographic region (including the United States, a city, county, state, zip code, or area code) or an electronic communication or remote computing service provider, unless the provider is itself a subject of an authorized investigation.

To obtain such an order, the government must show: (1) reasonable grounds to believe that the call detail records are relevant to such investigation; and (2) a reasonable, articulable suspicion that the specific selection term is associated with a foreign power or an agent of a foreign power engaged in international terrorism or activities in preparation for such terrorism.

The Freedom Act also purports to bring some sunlight into FISA court decisionmaking, and establishes a panel of civil libertarians that will have input into the policy-based decisions of FISA courts.

According to former Deputy Attorney General James Cole, even after the passage of the Freedom Act, the NSA could find a way to continue its bulk collection of American's phone records. He explained that "it's going to depend on how the [FISA] court interprets any number of the provisions" contained within the legislation.

The above description of the legislation only scratches the surface. For a full description of the USA Freedom Act, go to https://www.congress.gov/bill/114th-congress/house-bill/2048. It should be noted, for the purposes of a course on Constitutional Criminal Procedure, that it has never been definitively held that the NSA's bulk data program was *unconstitutional*. The Freedom Act is a legislative response to what Congress saw as offensive practices undertaken as a result of the NSA's reading of the PATRIOT Act to allow bulk data collection of phone calls.

VII. REMEDIES FOR FOURTH AMENDMENT VIOLATIONS

E. LIMITATIONS ON EXCLUSION

4. The Requirement of Causation and the Exception for Attenuation

Page 620. Add the following headnote before "5. Independent Source":

Discovery of an Outstanding Arrest Warrant After an Illegal Stop: Utah v. Strieff

UTAH V. STRIEFF
United States Supreme Court, 2016.
136 S.Ct. 2056.

JUSTICE THOMAS delivered the opinion of the Court.

To enforce the Fourth Amendment's prohibition against "unreasonable searches and seizures," this Court has at times required courts to exclude evidence obtained by unconstitutional police conduct. But the Court has also held that, even when there is a Fourth Amendment violation, this exclusionary rule does not apply when the costs of exclusion outweigh its deterrent benefits. In some cases, for example, the link between the unconstitutional conduct and the discovery of the evidence is too attenuated to justify suppression. The question in this case is whether this attenuation doctrine applies when an officer makes an unconstitutional investigatory stop; learns during that stop that the suspect is subject to a valid arrest warrant; and proceeds to arrest the suspect and seize incriminating evidence during a search incident to that arrest. We hold that the evidence the officer seized as part of the search incident to arrest is admissible because the officer's discovery of the arrest warrant attenuated the connection between the unlawful stop and the evidence seized incident to arrest.

I

This case began with an anonymous tip. In December 2006, someone called the South Salt Lake City police's drug-tip line to report "narcotics activity" at a particular residence. Narcotics detective Douglas Fackrell investigated the tip. Over the course of about a week, Officer Fackrell conducted intermittent surveillance of the home. He observed visitors who left a few minutes after arriving at the house. These visits were sufficiently frequent to raise his suspicion that the occupants were dealing drugs.

One of those visitors was respondent Edward Strieff. Officer Fackrell observed Strieff exit the house and walk toward a nearby convenience store. In the store's parking lot, Officer Fackrell detained Strieff, identified himself, and asked Strieff what he was doing at the residence.

As part of the stop, Officer Fackrell requested Strieff's identification, and Strieff produced his Utah identification card. Officer Fackrell relayed Strieff's information to a police dispatcher, who reported that Strieff had an outstanding arrest warrant for a traffic violation. Officer Fackrell then arrested Strieff pursuant to that warrant. When Officer Fackrell searched Strieff incident to the arrest, he discovered a baggie of methamphetamine and drug paraphernalia.

The State charged Strieff with unlawful possession of methamphetamine and drug paraphernalia. Strieff moved to suppress the evidence, arguing that the evidence was inadmissible because it was derived from an unlawful investigatory stop. At the suppression hearing, the prosecutor conceded that Officer Fackrell lacked reasonable suspicion for the stop but argued that the evidence should not be suppressed because the existence of a valid arrest warrant attenuated the connection between the unlawful stop and the discovery of the contraband.

The trial court agreed with the State and admitted the evidence. The court found that the short time between the illegal stop and the search weighed in favor of suppressing the evidence, but that two countervailing considerations made it admissible. First, the court considered the presence of a valid arrest warrant to be an "extraordinary intervening circumstance." Second, the court stressed the absence of flagrant misconduct by Officer Fackrell, who was conducting a legitimate investigation of a suspected drug house.

Strieff conditionally pleaded guilty to reduced charges of attempted possession of a controlled substance and possession of drug paraphernalia, but reserved his right to appeal the trial court's denial of the suppression motion. The Utah Court of Appeals affirmed.

The Utah Supreme Court reversed. It held that the evidence was inadmissible because only "a voluntary act of a defendant's free will (as in a confession or consent to search)" sufficiently breaks the connection between an illegal search and the discovery of evidence. Because Officer Fackrell's discovery of a valid arrest warrant did not fit this description, the court ordered the evidence suppressed.

We granted certiorari to resolve disagreement about how the attenuation doctrine applies where an unconstitutional detention leads to the discovery of a valid arrest warrant. We now reverse.

II

A

* * * Because officers who violated the Fourth Amendment were traditionally considered trespassers, individuals subject to unconstitutional searches or seizures historically enforced their rights through tort suits or self-help. Davies, Recovering the Original Fourth Amendment, 98 Mich. L. Rev. 547, 625 (1999). In the 20th century, however, the exclusionary rule—the rule that often requires trial courts to exclude unlawfully seized evidence in a criminal trial—became the principal judicial remedy to deter Fourth Amendment violations.

Under the Court's precedents, the exclusionary rule encompasses both the "primary evidence obtained as a direct result of an illegal search or seizure" and, relevant here, "evidence later discovered and found to be derivative of an illegality," the so-called "fruit of the poisonous tree." Segura v. United States, 468 U.S. 796, 804 (1984). But the significant costs of this rule have led us to deem it "applicable only . . . where its deterrence benefits outweigh its substantial social costs." Hudson v. Michigan, 547 U.S. 586, 591 (2006). "Suppression of evidence . . . has always been our last resort, not our first impulse." *Ibid*.

We have accordingly recognized several exceptions to the rule. Three of these exceptions involve the causal relationship between the unconstitutional act and the discovery of evidence. First, the independent source doctrine allows trial courts to admit evidence obtained in an unlawful search if officers independently acquired it from a separate, independent source. See Murray v. United States, 487 U.S. 533, 537 (1988). Second, the inevitable discovery doctrine allows for the admission of evidence that would have been discovered even without the unconstitutional source. See Nix v. Williams, 467 U.S. 431, 443–444 (1984). Third, and at issue here, is the attenuation doctrine: Evidence is admissible when the connection between unconstitutional police conduct and the evidence is remote or has been interrupted by some intervening circumstance, so that "the interest protected by the constitutional guarantee that has been violated would not be served by suppression of the evidence obtained." *Hudson, supra*, at 593.

B

Turning to the application of the attenuation doctrine to this case, we first address a threshold question: whether this doctrine applies at all to a case like this, where the intervening circumstance that the State relies on is the discovery of a valid, pre-existing, and untainted arrest warrant. The Utah Supreme Court declined to apply the attenuation doctrine because it read our precedents as applying the doctrine only "to circumstances involving an independent act of a defendant's 'free will' in confessing to a crime or consenting to a search." In this Court, Strieff has not defended this argument, and we disagree with it, as well. The attenuation doctrine evaluates the causal link between the government's unlawful act and the discovery of evidence, which often has nothing to do with a defendant's actions. And the logic of our prior attenuation cases is not limited to independent acts by the defendant.

It remains for us to address whether the discovery of a valid arrest warrant was a sufficient intervening event to break the causal chain between the unlawful stop and the discovery of drug-related evidence on Strieff's person. The three factors articulated in Brown v. Illinois, 422 U.S. 590 (1975), guide our analysis. First, we look to the "temporal proximity" between the unconstitutional conduct and the discovery of evidence to determine how closely the discovery of evidence followed the unconstitutional search. Second, we consider "the presence of intervening circumstances." Third, and "particularly" significant, we examine "the purpose and flagrancy of the official misconduct." In evaluating these factors, we assume without deciding (because the State conceded the point) that Officer Fackrell lacked reasonable suspicion to initially stop Strieff. And, because we ultimately conclude that the warrant breaks the causal chain, we also have no need to decide whether the warrant's existence alone would make the initial stop constitutional even if Officer Fackrell was unaware of its existence.

1

The first factor, temporal proximity between the initially unlawful stop and the search, favors suppressing the evidence. Our precedents have declined to find that this factor favors attenuation unless "substantial time" elapses between an unlawful act and when the evidence is obtained. Kaupp v. Texas, 538 U.S. 626, 63 (2003) (*per curiam*). Here, however,

Officer Fackrell discovered drug contraband on Strieff's person only minutes after the illegal stop. As the Court explained in *Brown*, such a short time interval counsels in favor of suppression; there, we found that the confession should be suppressed, relying in part on the "less than two hours" that separated the unconstitutional arrest and the confession.

In contrast, the second factor, the presence of intervening circumstances, strongly favors the State. In *Segura*, 468 U.S. 796, the Court addressed similar facts to those here and found sufficient intervening circumstances to allow the admission of evidence. There, agents had probable cause to believe that apartment occupants were dealing cocaine. They sought a warrant. In the meantime, they entered the apartment, arrested an occupant, and discovered evidence of drug activity during a limited search for security reasons. The next evening, the Magistrate Judge issued the search warrant. This Court deemed the evidence admissible notwithstanding the illegal search because the information supporting the warrant was "wholly unconnected with the [arguably illegal] entry and was known to the agents well before the initial entry."

Segura, of course, applied the independent source doctrine because the unlawful entry "did not contribute in any way to discovery of the evidence seized under the warrant." But the *Segura* Court suggested that the existence of a valid warrant favors finding that the connection between unlawful conduct and the discovery of evidence is "sufficiently attenuated to dissipate the taint." That principle applies here.

In this case, the warrant was valid, it predated Officer Fackrell's investigation, and it was entirely unconnected with the stop. And once Officer Fackrell discovered the warrant, he had an obligation to arrest Strieff. A warrant is a judicial mandate to an officer to conduct a search or make an arrest, and the officer has a sworn duty to carry out its provisions. Fackrell's arrest of Strieff thus was a ministerial act that was independently compelled by the pre-existing warrant. And once Officer Fackrell was authorized to arrest Strieff, it was undisputedly lawful to search Strieff as an incident of his arrest to protect Officer Fackrell's safety.

Finally, the third factor, "the purpose and flagrancy of the official misconduct," also strongly favors the State. The exclusionary rule exists to deter police misconduct. The third factor of the attenuation doctrine reflects that rationale by favoring exclusion only when the police misconduct is most in need of deterrence—that is, when it is purposeful or flagrant.

Officer Fackrell was at most negligent. In stopping Strieff, Officer Fackrell made two good-faith mistakes. First, he had not observed what time Strieff entered the suspected drug house, so he did not know how long Strieff had been there. Officer Fackrell thus lacked a sufficient basis to conclude that Strieff was a short-term visitor who may have been consummating a drug transaction. Second, because he lacked confirmation that Strieff was a short-term visitor, Officer Fackrell should have asked Strieff whether he would speak with him, instead of demanding that Strieff do so. Officer Fackrell's stated purpose was to "find out what was going on [in] the house." Nothing prevented him from approaching Strieff simply to ask. See Florida v. Bostick, 501 U.S. 429, 434 (1991)("[A] seizure does not occur simply because a police officer approaches an individual and asks a few questions"). But these errors in judgment hardly rise to a purposeful or flagrant violation of Strieff's Fourth Amendment rights.

* * *

Moreover, there is no indication that this unlawful stop was part of any systemic or recurrent police misconduct. To the contrary, all the evidence suggests that the stop was an isolated instance of negligence that occurred in connection with a bona fide investigation of a suspected drug house. Officer Fackrell saw Strieff leave a suspected drug house. And his suspicion about the house was based on an anonymous tip and his personal observations.

Applying these factors, we hold that the evidence discovered on Strieff's person was admissible because the unlawful stop was sufficiently attenuated by the pre-existing arrest warrant. Although the illegal stop was close in time to Strieff's arrest, that consideration is outweighed by two factors supporting the State. The outstanding arrest warrant for Strieff's arrest is a critical intervening circumstance that is wholly independent of the illegal stop. The discovery of that warrant broke the causal chain between the unconstitutional stop and the discovery of evidence by compelling Officer Fackrell to arrest Strieff. And, it is especially significant that there is no evidence that Officer Fackrell's illegal stop reflected flagrantly unlawful police misconduct.

2

We find Strieff's counterarguments unpersuasive.

First, he argues that the attenuation doctrine should not apply because the officer's stop was purposeful and flagrant. He asserts that Officer Fackrell stopped him solely to fish for evidence of suspected wrongdoing. But Officer Fackrell sought information from Strieff to find out what was happening inside a house whose occupants were legitimately suspected of dealing drugs. This was not a suspicionless fishing expedition in the hope that something would turn up.

Strieff argues, moreover, that Officer Fackrell's conduct was flagrant because he detained Strieff without the necessary level of cause (here, reasonable suspicion). But that conflates the standard for an illegal stop with the standard for flagrancy. For the violation to be flagrant, more severe police misconduct is required than the mere absence of proper cause for the seizure. See, *e.g., Kaupp*, 538 U.S., at 628 (finding flagrant violation where a warrantless arrest was made in the arrestee's home after police were denied a warrant and at least some officers knew they lacked probable cause). Neither the officer's alleged purpose nor the flagrancy of the violation rise to a level of misconduct to warrant suppression.

Second, Strieff argues that, because of the prevalence of outstanding arrest warrants in many jurisdictions, police will engage in dragnet searches if the exclusionary rule is not applied. We think that this outcome is unlikely. Such wanton conduct would expose police to civil liability. And in any event, the *Brown* factors take account of the purpose and flagrancy of police misconduct. Were evidence of a dragnet search presented here, the application of the *Brown* factors could be different. But there is no evidence that the concerns that Strieff raises with the criminal justice system are present in South Salt Lake City, Utah.

JUSTICE SOTOMAYOR, with whom JUSTICE GINSBURG joins as to parts I, II, and III, dissenting.

* * *

The Court today holds that the discovery of a warrant for an unpaid parking ticket will forgive a police officer's violation of your Fourth Amendment rights. Do not be soothed by the opinion's technical language: This case allows the police to stop you on the street, demand your identification, and check it for outstanding traffic warrants—even if you are doing nothing wrong. If the officer discovers a warrant for a fine you forgot to pay, courts will now excuse his illegal stop and will admit into evidence anything he happens to find by searching you after arresting you on the warrant. Because the Fourth Amendment should prohibit, not permit, such misconduct, I dissent.

* * *

II

It is tempting in a case like this, where illegal conduct by an officer uncovers illegal conduct by a civilian, to forgive the officer. After all, his instincts, although unconstitutional, were correct. But a basic principle lies at the heart of the Fourth Amendment: Two wrongs don't make a right.
* * *

* * *

Applying the exclusionary rule, the Utah Supreme Court correctly decided that Strieff's drugs must be excluded because the officer exploited his illegal stop to discover them. The officer found the drugs only after learning of Strieff's traffic violation; and he learned of Strieff's traffic violation only because he unlawfully stopped Strieff to check his driver's license.

The court also correctly rejected the State's argument that the officer's discovery of a traffic warrant unspoiled the poisonous fruit. The State analogizes finding the warrant to one of our earlier decisions, *Wong Sun v. United States*. There, an officer illegally arrested a person who, days later, voluntarily returned to the station to confess to committing a crime. 371 U.S., at 491. Even though the person would not have confessed "but for the illegal actions of the police," we noted that the police did not exploit their illegal arrest to obtain the confession. Because the confession was obtained by "means sufficiently distinguishable" from the constitutional violation, we held that it could be admitted into evidence. The State contends that the search incident to the warrant-arrest here is similarly distinguishable from the illegal stop.

But *Wong Sun* explains why Strieff's drugs must be excluded. We reasoned that a Fourth Amendment violation may not color every investigation that follows but it certainly stains the actions of officers who exploit the infraction. We distinguished evidence obtained by innocuous means from evidence obtained by exploiting misconduct after considering a variety of factors: whether a long time passed, whether there were "intervening circumstances," and whether the purpose or flagrancy of the misconduct was "calculated" to procure the evidence. Brown v. Illinois, 422 U.S. 590, 603–604 (1975).

These factors confirm that the officer in this case discovered Strieff's drugs by exploiting his own illegal conduct. The officer did not ask Strieff to volunteer his name only to find out, days later, that Strieff had a warrant against him. The officer illegally stopped Strieff and immediately ran a warrant check. The officer's discovery of a warrant was not some intervening surprise that he could not have anticipated. Utah lists over 180,000 misdemeanor warrants in its database, and at the time of the arrest, Salt Lake County had a "backlog of outstanding warrants" so large that it faced the "potential for civil liability." The officer's violation was also calculated to procure evidence. His sole reason for stopping Strieff, he acknowledged, was investigative—he wanted to discover whether drug activity was going on in the house Strieff had just exited.

The warrant check, in other words, was not an "intervening circumstance" separating the stop from the search for drugs. It was part and parcel of the officer's illegal "expedition for evidence in the hope that something might turn up." *Brown*, 422 U.S., at 605. Under our precedents, because the officer found Strieff's drugs by exploiting his own constitutional violation, the drugs should be excluded.

III

A

The Court sees things differently. To the Court, the fact that a warrant gives an officer cause to arrest a person severs the connection between illegal policing and the resulting discovery of evidence. This is a remarkable proposition: The mere existence of a warrant not only gives an officer legal cause to arrest and search a person, it also forgives an officer who, with no knowledge of the warrant at all, unlawfully stops that person on a whim or hunch.

* * *

According to the majority, *Segura* involves facts "similar" to this case and "suggest[s]" that a valid warrant will clean up whatever illegal conduct uncovered it. It is difficult to understand this interpretation. In *Segura*, the agents' illegal conduct in entering the apartment had nothing to do with their procurement of a search warrant. Here, the officer's illegal conduct in stopping Strieff was essential to his discovery of an arrest warrant. *Segura* would be similar only if the agents used information they illegally obtained from the apartment to procure a search warrant or discover an arrest warrant. Precisely because that was not the case, the Court admitted the untainted evidence.

* * *

The majority also posits that the officer could not have exploited his illegal conduct because he did not violate the Fourth Amendment on purpose. Rather, he made "good-faith mistakes." Never mind that the officer's sole purpose was to fish for evidence. The majority casts his unconstitutional actions as "negligent" and therefore incapable of being deterred by the exclusionary rule.

But the Fourth Amendment does not tolerate an officer's unreasonable searches and seizures just because he did not know any better. Even officers prone to negligence can learn from courts that exclude illegally obtained evidence. Indeed, they are perhaps the most in need of the education, whether by the judge's opinion, the prosecutor's future guidance, or an updated manual on criminal procedure. If the officers are in doubt about what the law requires, exclusion gives them an incentive to err on the side of constitutional behavior.

B

Most striking about the Court's opinion is its insistence that the event here was "isolated," with "no indication that this unlawful stop was part of any systemic or recurrent police misconduct." Respectfully, nothing about this case is isolated.

Outstanding warrants are surprisingly common. When a person with a traffic ticket misses a fine payment or court appearance, a court will issue a warrant. When a person on probation drinks alcohol or breaks curfew, a court will issue a warrant. The States and Federal Government maintain databases with over 7.8 million outstanding warrants, the vast majority of which appear to be for minor offenses. * * * The county in this case has had a "backlog" of such warrants. The Department of Justice recently reported that in the town of Ferguson, Missouri, with a population of 21,000, 16,000 people had outstanding warrants against them.

Justice Department investigations across the country have illustrated how these astounding numbers of warrants can be used by police to stop people without cause. In a single year in New Orleans, officers "made nearly 60,000 arrests, of which about 20,000 were of people with outstanding traffic or misdemeanor warrants from neighboring parishes for such infractions as unpaid tickets." In the St. Louis metropolitan area, officers "routinely" stop people—on the street, at bus stops, or even in court—for no reason other than "an officer's desire to check whether the subject had a municipal arrest warrant pending." In Newark, New Jersey, officers stopped 52,235 pedestrians within a 4-year period and ran warrant checks on 39,308 of them. The Justice Department analyzed these warrant-checked stops and reported that "approximately 93% of the stops would have been considered unsupported by articulated reasonable suspicion."

I do not doubt that most officers act in "good faith" and do not set out to break the law. That does not mean these stops are "isolated instance[s] of negligence," however. Many are the product of institutionalized training procedures. The New York City Police Department long trained officers to, in the words of a District Judge, "stop and question first, develop reasonable suspicion later." Ligon v. New York, 925 F.Supp.2d 478, 537–538 (SDNY), stay granted on other grounds, 736 F.3d 118 (CA2 2013). The Utah Supreme Court described as " 'routine procedure' or 'common practice' " the decision of Salt Lake City police officers to run warrant checks on pedestrians they detained without reasonable suspicion. State v. Topanotes, 2003 UT 30, ¶ 2, 76 P.3d 1159, 1160. In the related context of traffic stops, one widely followed police manual instructs officers looking for drugs to "run at least a warrants check on all drivers you stop. Statistically, narcotics offenders are . . . more likely to fail to appear on simple citations, such as traffic or trespass violations, leading to the issuance of bench warrants. Discovery of an outstanding warrant gives you cause for an immediate custodial arrest and search of the suspect." C. Remsberg, Tactics for Criminal Patrol 205–206 (1995); C. Epp et al., Pulled Over 23, 33–36 (2014).

The majority does not suggest what makes this case "isolated" from these and countless other examples. Nor does it offer guidance for how a defendant can prove that his arrest was the result of "widespread" misconduct. Surely it should not take a federal investigation of Salt Lake County before the Court would protect someone in Strieff's position.

IV

Writing only for myself, and drawing on my professional experiences, I would add that unlawful "stops" have severe consequences much greater than the inconvenience suggested by the name. This Court has given officers an array of instruments to probe and examine you. When we condone officers' use of these devices without adequate cause, we give them reason to target pedestrians in an arbitrary manner. We also risk treating members of our communities as second-class citizens.

Although many Americans have been stopped for speeding or jaywalking, few may realize how degrading a stop can be when the officer is looking for more. This Court has allowed an officer to stop you for whatever reason he wants—so long as he can point to a pretextual justification after the fact. That justification must provide specific reasons why the officer suspected you were breaking the law, but it may factor in your ethnicity, where you live, what you were wearing, and how you behaved. The officer does not even need to know which law you might have broken so long as he can later point to any possible infraction—even one that is minor, unrelated, or ambiguous.

The indignity of the stop is not limited to an officer telling you that you look like a criminal. The officer may next ask for your "consent" to inspect your bag or purse without telling you that you can decline. Regardless of your answer, he may order you to stand helpless, perhaps facing a wall with your hands raised. If the officer thinks you might be dangerous, he may then "frisk" you for weapons. This involves more than just a pat down. As onlookers pass by, the officer may "feel with sensitive fingers every portion of [your] body. A thorough search [may] be made of [your] arms and armpits, waistline and back, the groin and area about the testicles, and entire surface of the legs down to the feet."

The officer's control over you does not end with the stop. If the officer chooses, he may handcuff you and take you to jail for doing nothing more than speeding, jaywalking, or driving your pickup truck with your 3-year-old son and 5-year-old daughter without your seatbelt fastened. At the jail, he can fingerprint you, swab DNA from the inside of your mouth, and force you to shower with a delousing agent while you lift your tongue, hold out your arms, turn around, and lift your genitals. Even if you are innocent, you will now join the 65 million Americans with an arrest record and experience the "civil death" of discrimination by employers, landlords, and whoever else conducts a background check. And, of course, if you fail to pay bail or appear for court, a judge will issue a warrant to render you "arrestable on sight" in the future.

This case involves a *suspicionless* stop, one in which the officer initiated this chain of events without justification. As the Justice Department notes, many innocent people are subjected to the humiliations of these unconstitutional searches. The white defendant in this case shows that anyone's dignity can be violated in this manner. See M. Gottschalk, Caught 119–138 (2015). But it is no secret that people of color are disproportionate victims of this type of scrutiny. See M. Alexander, The New Jim Crow 95–136 (2010). For generations, black and brown parents have given their children "the talk"—instructing them never to run down the street; always keep your hands where they can be seen; do not even think of talking back to a stranger—all out of fear of how an officer with a gun will react to them. See, *e.g.*, W. E. B. Du Bois, The Souls of Black Folk (1903); J. Baldwin, The Fire Next Time (1963); T. Coates, Between the World and Me (2015).

By legitimizing the conduct that produces this double consciousness, this case tells everyone, white and black, guilty and innocent, that an officer can verify your legal status at any time. It says that your body is subject to invasion while courts excuse the violation of your rights. It implies that you are not a citizen of a democracy but the subject of a carceral state, just waiting to be cataloged.

We must not pretend that the countless people who are routinely targeted by police are "isolated." They are the canaries in the coal mine whose deaths, civil and literal, warn us that no one can breathe in this atmosphere. They are the ones who recognize that unlawful police stops corrode all our civil liberties and threaten all our lives. Until their voices matter too, our justice system will continue to be anything but.

* * *

I dissent.

JUSTICE KAGAN, with whom JUSTICE GINSBURG joins, dissenting.

If a police officer stops a person on the street without reasonable suspicion, that seizure violates the Fourth Amendment. And if the officer pats down the unlawfully detained individual and finds drugs in his pocket, the State may not use the contraband as evidence in a criminal prosecution. That much is beyond dispute. The question here is whether the prohibition on admitting evidence dissolves if the officer discovers, after making the stop but before finding the drugs, that the person has an outstanding arrest warrant. Because that added wrinkle makes no difference under the Constitution, I respectfully dissent.

* * *

This case * * * requires the Court to determine whether excluding the fruits of Officer Douglas Fackrell's unjustified stop of Edward Strieff would significantly deter police from committing similar constitutional violations in the future. And as the Court states, that inquiry turns on application of the "attenuation doctrine" * * * . Since Brown v. Illinois, 422 U.S. 590, 604–605 (1975), three factors have guided that analysis. First, the closer the "temporal proximity" between the unlawful act and the discovery of evidence, the greater the deterrent value of suppression. Second, the more "purpose[ful]" or "flagran[t]" the police illegality, the clearer the necessity, and better the chance, of preventing similar misbehavior. And third, the presence (or absence) of "intervening circumstances" makes a difference: The stronger the causal chain between the misconduct and the evidence, the more exclusion will curb future constitutional violations. Here, as shown below, each of those considerations points toward suppression: Nothing in Fackrell's discovery of an outstanding warrant so attenuated the connection between his wrongful behavior and his detection of drugs as to diminish the exclusionary rule's deterrent benefits.

Start where the majority does: The temporal proximity factor, it forthrightly admits, "favors suppressing the evidence." * * *

Move on to the purposefulness of Fackrell's conduct, where the majority is less willing to see a problem for what it is. The majority chalks up Fackrell's Fourth Amendment violation to a couple of innocent "mistakes." But far from a Barney Fife-type mishap, Fackrell's seizure of Strieff was a calculated decision, taken with so little justification that the State has never tried to defend its legality. * * * Fackrell frankly admitted that he had no basis for his action except that Strieff "was coming out of the house." * * * In Brown, the Court held [similar] facts to support suppression—and they do here as well. Swing and a miss for strike two.

Finally, consider whether any intervening circumstance broke the causal chain between the stop and the evidence. The notion of such a disrupting event comes from the tort law doctrine of proximate causation. And as in the tort context, a circumstance counts as intervening only when it is unforeseeable—not when it can be seen coming from miles away. For rather than breaking the causal chain, predictable effects (e.g., X leads naturally to Y leads naturally to Z) are its very links.

And Fackrell's discovery of an arrest warrant—the only event the majority thinks intervened—was an eminently foreseeable consequence of stopping Strieff. As Fackrell testified, checking for outstanding warrants during a stop is the "normal" practice of South Salt Lake City police. In other words, the department's standard detention procedures—stop, ask for identification, run a check—are partly designed to find outstanding warrants. And find them they will, given the staggering number of such warrants on the books. To take just a few examples: The State of California has 2.5 million outstanding arrest warrants (a number corresponding to about 9% of its adult population); Pennsylvania (with a population of about 12.8 million) contributes 1.4 million more; and New York City (population

8.4 million) adds another 1.2 million.[1] So outstanding warrants do not appear as bolts from the blue. They are the run-of-the-mill results of police stops—what officers look for when they run a routine check of a person's identification and what they know will turn up with fair regularity. In short, they are nothing like what intervening circumstances are supposed to be. Strike three.

The majority's misapplication of *Brown*'s three-part inquiry creates unfortunate incentives for the police—indeed, practically invites them to do what Fackrell did here. Consider an officer who, like Fackrell, wishes to stop someone for investigative reasons, but does not have what a court would view as reasonable suspicion. If the officer believes that any evidence he discovers will be inadmissible, he is likely to think the unlawful stop not worth making—precisely the deterrence the exclusionary rule is meant to achieve. But when he is told of today's decision? Now the officer knows that the stop may well yield admissible evidence: So long as the target is one of the many millions of people in this country with an outstanding arrest warrant, anything the officer finds in a search is fair game for use in a criminal prosecution. The officer's incentive to violate the Constitution thus increases: From here on, he sees potential advantage in stopping individuals without reasonable suspicion—exactly the temptation the exclusionary rule is supposed to remove. Because the majority thus places Fourth Amendment protections at risk, I respectfully dissent.

---

[1] What is more, outstanding arrest warrants are not distributed evenly across the population. To the contrary, they are concentrated in cities, towns, and neighborhoods where stops are most likely to occur—and so the odds of any given stop revealing a warrant are even higher than the above numbers indicate. One study found, for example, that Cincinnati, Ohio had over 100,000 outstanding warrants with only 300,000 residents. See Helland & Tabarrok, The Fugitive: Evidence on Public Versus Private Law Enforcement from Bail Jumping, 47 J. Law & Econ. 93, 98 (2004). And as JUSTICE SOTOMAYOR notes, 16,000 of the 21,000 people residing in the town of Ferguson, Missouri have outstanding warrants.

CHAPTER 3

SELF-INCRIMINATION AND CONFESSIONS

■ ■ ■

I. THE PRIVILEGE AGAINST COMPELLED SELF-INCRIMINATION

C. WHAT IS COMPULSION?

3. Comment on the Invocation of the Privilege

Page 671. Add after the end of the section on *"Adverse Inferences at Sentencing: Mitchell v. United States"*:

*No Clearly Established Right to an Adverse
Inference Instruction at the Penalty Phase
of a Capital Trial: White v. Woodall*

In White v. Woodall, 134 S.Ct. 1697 (2014), the Court reviewed a habeas petition from a capital proceeding, in which the defendant requested, but was not granted, an instruction that no adverse inference could be drawn from his failure to testify at the penalty phase of his capital trial. Under applicable standards of review in habeas, the petitioner was not entitled to relief unless his right to an instruction was "clearly established" by the Supreme Court's case law. The Court, in an opinion by Justice Scalia, held that there was no clearly established right to a "no-adverse-inference" instruction in a capital sentencing proceeding. Justice Scalia noted that the Court in *Mitchell* reserved the question of whether the sentencing judge could take into account the defendant's silence on questions of remorse, as opposed to questions about the crime itself; thus *Mitchell* could not be read to clearly establish a rule that an adverse inference instruction is always required at a sentencing proceeding. Moreover, Justice Scalia noted that *Mitchell* was a case in which the sentencing judge actively drew a negative inference from silence—it did not clearly follow that an instruction to the jury not to draw an inference would be required. Justice Breyer, joined by Justices Ginsburg and Sotomayor, dissented. The full opinion in White v. Woodall is set forth in Chapter 13 of this Supplement.

III. FIFTH AMENDMENT LIMITATIONS ON CONFESSIONS

A. MIRANDA v. ARIZONA

Page 754. In the discussion of *"Alternatives to Miranda",* at the end of the block paragraph, add the following:

According to The Innocence Project, "[t]o date, Connecticut, Illinois, Maine, Maryland, Michigan, Missouri, Montana, Nebraska, New Mexico, North Carolina, Ohio, Oregon, Wisconsin, and the District of Columbia have enacted legislation regarding the recording of custodial interrogations. State supreme courts have taken action in Alaska, Indiana, Iowa, Massachusetts, Minnesota, New Hampshire, and New Jersey. Approximately 850 jurisdictions have recording policies." http://www.innocenceproject.org/Content/False_Confessions__Recording_Of_Cust odial_Interrogations.php

In a Memorandum dated May 12, 2014, James M. Cole, Deputy Attorney General, announced a new Department of Justice policy, effective July 11, 2014, that establishes a presumption that federal prosecutors and law enforcement agents will record the entirety of custodial interrogations. There are exceptions. One is "where questioning is undertaken to gather national security-related intelligence or questioning concerning intelligence, sources, or methods, the public disclosure of which would cause damage to national security." There is a "residual exception" that applies "where the Special Agent in Charge and the United States Attorney, or their designees, agree that a significant and articulable law enforcement purpose requires setting [the presumption] aside."

The entire text of the Memorandum is set forth below:

> This policy establishes a presumption that the Federal Bureau of Investigation (FBI), the Drug Enforcement Administration (DEA), the Bureau of Alcohol, Tobacco, Firearms, and Explosives (ATF), and the United States Marshals Service (USMS) will electronically record statements made by individuals in their custody in the circumstances set forth below.

> This policy also encourages agents and prosecutors to consider electronic recording in investigative or other circumstances where the presumption does not apply. The policy encourages agents and prosecutors to consult with each other in such circumstances.

> This policy is solely for internal Department of Justice guidance. It is not intended to, does not, and may not be relied upon to create any rights or benefits, substantive or procedural, enforceable at law or in equity in any matter, civil or criminal, by any party against the

United States, its departments, agencies, or entities, its officers, employees, or agents, or any other person, nor does it place any limitation on otherwise lawful investigative and litigative prerogatives of the Department of Justice.

I.   Presumption of Recording. There is a presumption that the custodial statement of an individual in a place of detention with suitable recording equipment, following arrest but prior to initial appearance, will be electronically recorded, subject to the exceptions defined below. Such custodial interviews will be recorded without the need for supervisory approval.

a.   Electronic recording. This policy strongly encourages the use of video recording to satisfy the presumption. When video recording equipment considered suitable under agency policy is not available, audio recording may be utilized.

b.   Custodial interviews. The presumption applies only to interviews of persons in FBI, DEA, ATF or USMS custody. Interviews in non-custodial settings are excluded from the presumption.

c.   Place of detention. A place of detention is any structure where persons are held in connection with federal criminal charges where those persons can be interviewed. This includes not only federal facilities, but also any state, local, or tribal law enforcement facility, office, correctional or detention facility, jail, police or sheriff's station, holding cell, or other structure used for such purpose. Recording under this policy is not required while a person is waiting for transportation, or is en route, to a place of detention.

d.   Suitable recording equipment. The presumption is limited to a place of detention that has suitable recording equipment. With respect to a place of detention owned or controlled by FBI, DEA, ATF, or USMS, suitable recording equipment means:

(i)   an electronic recording device deemed suitable by the agency for the recording of interviews that,

(ii)   is reasonably designed to capture electronically the entirety of the interview. Each agency will draft its own policy governing placement, maintenance and upkeep of such equipment, as well as requirements for preservation and transfer of recorded content.

With respect to an interview by FBI, DEA, ATF, or USMS in a place of detention they do not own or control, but which has recording equipment, FBI, DEA, ATF, or USMS will each determine on a case by case basis whether that recording equipment meets or is equivalent to that agency's own requirements or is otherwise suitable for use in recording interviews for purposes of this policy.

e.   <u>Timing</u>. The presumption applies to persons in custody in a place of detention with suitable recording equipment following arrest but who have not yet made an initial appearance before a judicial officer under Federal Rule of Criminal Procedure 5.

f.   <u>Scope of offenses</u>. The presumption applies to interviews in connection with all federal crimes.

g.   <u>Scope of recording</u>. Electronic recording will begin as soon as the subject enters the interview area or room and will continue until the interview is completed.

h.   <u>Recording may be overt or covert</u>. Recording under this policy may be covert or overt. Covert recording constitutes consensual monitoring, which is allowed by federal law. *See* 18 U.S.C. § 2511(2)(c). Covert recording in fulfilling the requirement of this policy may be carried out without constraint by the procedures and approval requirements prescribed by other Department policies for consensual monitoring.

II.   Exceptions to the Presumption. A decision not to record any interview that would otherwise presumptively be recorded under this policy must be documented by the agent as soon as practicable. Such documentation shall be made available to the United States Attorney and should be reviewed in connection with a periodic assessment of this policy by the United States Attorney and the Special Agent in Charge or their designees.

a.   <u>Refusal by interviewee</u>. If the interviewee is informed that the interview will be recorded and indicates that he or she is willing to give a statement but only if it is not electronically recorded, then a recording need not take place.

b.   <u>Public Safety and National Security Exception</u>. Recording is not prohibited in any of the circumstances covered by this exception and the decision whether or not to record should wherever possible be the subject of consultation between the agent and the prosecutor. There is no presumption of electronic recording where questioning is done for the purpose of gathering public safety information under *New York v. Quarles*. The presumption of recording likewise does not apply to those limited circumstances where questioning is undertaken to gather national security-related intelligence or questioning concerning intelligence, sources, or methods, the public disclosure of which would cause damage to national security.

c.   <u>Recording is not reasonably practicable</u>. Circumstances may prevent, or render not reasonably practicable, the electronic recording of an interview that would otherwise be presumptively recorded. Such circumstances may include equipment malfunction, an unexpected need to move the interview, or a need for multiple interviews in a limited timeframe exceeding the available number of recording devices.

d.   Residual exception. The presumption in favor of recording may be overcome where the Special Agent in Charge and the United States Attorney, or their designees, agree that a significant and articulable law enforcement purpose requires setting it aside. This exception is to be used sparingly.

III. Extraterritoriality. The presumption does not apply outside of the United States. However, recording may be appropriate outside the United States where it is not otherwise precluded or made infeasible by law, regulation, treaty, policy, or practical concerns such as the suitability of recording equipment. The decision whether to record an interview B whether the subject is in foreign custody, U.S. custody, or not in custody B outside the United States should be the subject of consultation between the agent and the prosecutor, in addition to other applicable requirements and authorities.

IV. Administrative Issues.

a.   Training. Field offices of each agency shall, in connection with the implementation of this policy, collaborate with the local U.S. Attorney's Office to provide district-wide joint training for agents and prosecutors on best practices associated with electronic recording of interviews.

b.   Assignment of responsibilities. The investigative agencies will bear the cost of acquiring and maintaining, in places of detention they control where custodial interviews occur, recording equipment in sufficient numbers to meet expected needs for the recording of such interviews. Agencies will pay for electronic copies of recordings for distribution pre-indictment. Post-indictment, the United States Attorneys' offices will pay for transcripts of recordings, as necessary.

V.   Effective Date. This policy shall take effect on July 11, 2014.

CHAPTER 4

IDENTIFYING SUSPECTS

■ ■ ■

II. THE JUDICIAL RESPONSE

C. NON-CONSTITUTIONAL PROTECTIONS AGAINST UNRELIABLE IDENTIFICATIONS

Page 923. Add to the headnote on *"Jury Instructions"*:

In Commonwealth v. Gomes, 470 Mass. 352 (2015), the Massachusetts Supreme Judicial Court relied on research done by a Study Group and recognized five principles regarding identification evidence that it found to have achieved a "near consensus in the relevant scientific community"—and so would be included in a revised model jury instruction regarding eyewitness identification. The five principles are:

1. "Human memory does not function like a video recording but is a complex process that consists of three stages: acquisition, retention, and retrieval."

2. "An eyewitness's expressed certainty in an identification, standing alone, may not indicate the accuracy of the identification, especially where the witness did not describe that level of certainty when the witness first made the identification."

3. "High levels of stress can reduce an eyewitness's ability to make an accurate identification."

4. "Information that is unrelated to the initial viewing of the event, which an eyewitness receives before or after making an identification, can influence the witness's later recollection of the memory or of the identification."

5. "A prior viewing of a suspect at an identification procedure may reduce the reliability of a subsequent identification procedure in which the same suspect is shown."

The court offered a model instruction. Here are some of the pertinent provisions:

* * *

In evaluating eyewitness identification testimony, it is not essential that a witness be free from doubt as to the correctness of his or her identification of the defendant. However, you, the jury, must be satisfied beyond a reasonable doubt, based on all of the credible evidence, that this defendant is the person who committed [or participated in the commission of] the crime[s] before you may convict him/her.

* * *

Human beings have the ability to recognize other people from past experiences and to identify them at a later time, but research has shown that people sometimes make mistakes in identification. That research has focused on the factors that may affect the accuracy of an identification, including the nature of human memory.

Research has shown that human memory is not like a video recording that a witness need only replay to remember what happened. Memory is far more complex. The process of remembering consists of three stages: first, a person sees or otherwise acquires information about the original event; second, the person stores in the brain the information about the event for a period of time until, third, the person attempts to recall that stored information. At each of these stages, memory can be affected by a variety of factors.

Relying on some of the research that has been done in this area, I am going to list some specific factors you should consider in determining whether the identification testimony is accurate. By instructing you on the factors to consider, I am not expressing any opinion about the accuracy of any specific memory of any particular witness. You, the jury, must decide whether the witness's identification is accurate.

(1) *The witness's opportunity to view the event.* You should consider the opportunity the witness had to observe the offender at the time of the offense, how good a look the witness had of the offender, the degree of attention the witness was paying to the offender at that time, the distance between the witness and the offender, how good the lighting conditions were, and the length of time the witness had to observe the offender;

Add if relevant to the case:

[IF DISGUISE WAS INVOLVED OR FACE WAS OBSCURED] whether the offender was disguised or had his/her features obscured in some way;

[IF PERPETRATOR HAD DISTINCTIVE FACE OR FEATURE] whether the perpetrator had a distinctive face or feature;

[IF A WEAPON WAS INVOLVED] and whether the witness saw a weapon during the event—the visible presence of a weapon may reduce the reliability of an identification if the crime is of short duration, but the longer the event, the more time the witness has to adapt to the presence of the weapon.

(2) *Characteristics of the witness.* You should also consider characteristics of the witness when the observation was made, such as the quality of the witness's eyesight, whether the witness knew the offender, and, if so, how well, and whether the witness was under a high degree of stress—high levels of stress, compared to low to medium levels, can reduce an eyewitness's ability to accurately perceive an event;

Add if relevant to the case:

[IF DRUGS OR ALCOHOL WERE INVOLVED] whether the witness at the time of the observation was under the influence of alcohol or drugs, and if so, to what degree;

[IF WITNESS AND OFFENDER ARE OF DIFFERENT RACES] and whether the witness and the offender are of different races— research has shown that people of all races may have greater difficulty in accurately identifying members of a different race than they do in identifying members of their own race.

(3) *The time elapsed.* You should consider how much time elapsed between the event observed and the identification. Generally, memory is most accurate right after the event and begins to fade thereafter.

(4) *Witness's expressed certainty.* Research shows that a witness's expressed certainty in an identification, standing alone, may not be a reliable indicator of the accuracy of the identification, especially where the witness did not describe that level of certainty when the witness first made the identification.

(5) *Exposure to identification information from others.* A person's memory may be affected by information the person received between the incident and the identification, as well as after the identification, and the person may not realize that his or her memory has been affected. You may consider whether the witness was exposed to identifications made by other witnesses, to opinions or descriptions given by others, including police officers, or to any other information or influence. Such exposure may affect the independence and reliability of a witness's identification, and may inflate the witness's confidence in the identification.

An identification that is the product of some suggestive conduct by the police or others should be scrutinized with special caution and care. The risk that suggestion will affect the identification is greater where the witness did not get so good a look at the offender, because a witness who got a good look is less likely to be influenced by suggestion.

Add if relevant to the case:

[IF THERE WAS A PHOTOGRAPHIC ARRAY OR LINEUP] An identification may occur as part of the police investigation through the showing of an array of photographs or through a lineup of individuals. You may take into account that any identification that was made by picking the defendant out of a group of similar individuals is generally more reliable than one which results from the presentation of the defendant alone to a witness.

You should consider whether the police in conducting the photographic array or lineup followed established or recommended procedures that are designed to diminish the risk of suggestiveness. If there was evidence that any of those procedures were not followed, you should evaluate the identification with particular care and consider whether the failure to follow the procedure affected the reliability of the identification.

Where a witness identified the defendant in a photographic array [or in a lineup], you should consider the number of photographs in the array [or individuals in the lineup], whether there was anything about the defendant's photograph [or the defendant's appearance in the lineup] that made him/her stand out from the others, whether the person administering the photographic array [or lineup] did not know who was the suspect and therefore could not influence the witness's identification, and whether anything was said to the witness that would suggest that the suspect was among the persons shown in the photographic array [or lineup], or that would suggest that the witness should identify the suspect.

[IF THERE WAS A SHOWUP] An identification may occur as part of the police investigation through what is known as a showup, where a suspect is shown alone to a witness. An identification procedure in which a witness selects a person from a group of similar individuals in a photographic array or a lineup is generally less suggestive than a showup, which is to some degree inherently suggestive. You should consider how long after the initial event the showup took place, as a fresh memory of an event that occurred only a few hours earlier may reduce the risks arising from the inherently suggestive nature of a showup.

You should consider whether the police, in conducting the showup, followed established or recommended procedures that are designed to diminish the risk of suggestiveness. If any of those procedures were not followed, you should evaluate the identification with particular care and consider whether the failure to follow the procedure affected the reliability of the identification.

Add if relevant to the case:

[IF THERE WERE MULTIPLE VIEWINGS BY THE SAME WITNESS] You should consider whether the witness viewed the defendant in multiple identification procedures or events. When a witness views the same person in more than one identification procedure or event, it may be difficult to know whether a later identification comes from the witness's memory of the actual, original event, or from the witness's observation of the person at an earlier identification procedure or event.

(6) *Failure to identify or inconsistent identification.* You may take into account whether a witness ever tried and failed to make an identification of the defendant, or made an identification that was inconsistent with the identification that such witness made at trial.

(7) *Totality of the evidence.* You should consider all the relevant factors that I have discussed, viewed in the context of the totality of the evidence in this case, in evaluating the accuracy of a witness's identification testimony. Specifically, you should consider whether there was other evidence in the case, direct or circumstantial, that tends to support or not to support the accuracy of an identification. If you are not convinced beyond a reasonable doubt that the defendant was the person who committed [or participated in the commission of] the crime[s], you must find the defendant not guilty.

CHAPTER 5

THE RIGHT TO COUNSEL

■ ■ ■

IV. THE SCOPE OF THE RIGHT

C. THE RIGHT EXTENDED TO EXPERTS

Page 950. Add at the end of the section:

Ake Violation: McWilliams v. Dunn

The Court found that a capital defendant had a constitutional right to an appointed expert under *Ake*, and that the right was violated, in McWilliams v. Dunn, 137 S.Ct. 1790 (2017). Alabama charged petitioner McWilliams with rape and murder. Finding him indigent, the trial court appointed counsel, who requested a psychiatric evaluation of McWilliams. The court granted the motion and the State convened a panel of doctors, which concluded that McWilliams was competent to stand trial and had not been suffering from mental illness at the time of the alleged offense. A jury convicted McWilliams of capital murder and recommended a death sentence. Later, while the parties awaited McWilliams' judicial sentencing hearing, McWilliams' counsel asked for neurological and neuropsychological testing of McWilliams. The court agreed and McWilliams was examined by Dr. Goff. Dr. Goff filed a report two days before the judicial sentencing hearing. He concluded that McWilliams was likely exaggerating his symptoms, but nonetheless appeared to have some genuine neuropsychological problems. Just before the hearing, counsel also received updated records from the commission's evaluation and previously subpoenaed mental health records from the Alabama Department of Corrections. At the hearing, defense counsel requested a continuance in order to evaluate all the new material, and asked for the assistance of someone with expertise in psychological matters to review the findings. The trial court denied defense counsel's requests. At the conclusion of the hearing, the court sentenced McWilliams to death.

Justice Breyer, writing for five members of the Court, noted that "no one denies that the conditions that trigger application of *Ake* are present. McWilliams is and was an indigent defendant. His mental condition was relevant to the punishment he might suffer. And, that mental condition, i.e., his sanity at the time of the offense, was seriously in question.

Consequently, the Constitution, as interpreted in *Ake*, required the State to provide McWilliams with 'access to a competent psychiatrist who will conduct an appropriate examination and assist in evaluation, preparation, and presentation of the defense.'"

Justice Breyer concluded that the examination provided by the state through Dr. Goff was no substitute. He elaborated as follows:

> The Alabama appeals court held that "the requirements of Ake v. Oklahoma are met when the State provides the defendant with a competent psychiatrist." The State [purportedly] met this requirement in allowing Dr. Goff to examine McWilliams. This [is] plainly incorrect. *Ake* does not require just an examination. Rather, it requires the State to provide the defense with access to "a competent psychiatrist who will conduct an appropriate [1] examination and assist in [2] evaluation, [3] preparation, and [4] presentation of the defense."

> We are willing to assume that Alabama met the examination portion of this requirement by providing for Dr. Goff's examination of McWilliams. But what about the other three parts? Neither Dr. Goff nor any other expert helped the defense evaluate Goff's report or McWilliams' extensive medical records and translate these data into a legal strategy. Neither Dr. Goff nor any other expert helped the defense prepare and present arguments that might, for example, have explained that McWilliams' purported malingering was not necessarily inconsistent with mental illness * * * . Neither Dr. Goff nor any other expert helped the defense prepare direct or cross-examination of any witnesses, or testified at the judicial sentencing hearing himself.

> Since Alabama's provision of mental health assistance fell so dramatically short of what *Ake* requires, we must conclude that the Alabama court decision affirming McWilliams's conviction and sentence was "contrary to, or involved an unreasonable application of, clearly established Federal law." 28 U.S.C. § 2254(d)(1).

Justice Alito, joined by Chief Justice Roberts and Justice Thomas, dissented in *McWilliams*. He argued that there is no clearly established right under *Ake* to have a psychiatric expert who is a member of the defense team, as opposed to a neutral expert who is available to assist both the prosecution and the defense—and therefore the Alabama courts' determination that Dr. Goff's examination was sufficient under *Ake* could not be overturned on habeas review. Justice Gorsuch took no part in the case.

CHAPTER 8

DISCOVERY

■ ■ ■

IV. THE PROSECUTOR'S CONSTITUTIONAL DUTY TO DISCLOSE

B. APPLYING THE *BRADY* RULE

Page 1101. After the headnote discussing *Kyles v. Whitley*, add the following headnotes and material:

Another Fact-Intensive Application of Brady: Wearry v. Cain

WEARRY V. CAIN

Supreme Court of the United States, 2016.
136 S.Ct. 1002.

PER CURIAM.

Michael Wearry is on Louisiana's death row. Urging that the prosecution failed to disclose evidence supporting his innocence and that his counsel provided ineffective assistance at trial, Wearry unsuccessfully sought postconviction relief in state court. Contrary to the state postconviction court, we conclude that the prosecution's failure to disclose material evidence violated Wearry's due process rights. We reverse the state postconviction court's judgment on that account, and therefore do not reach Wearry's ineffective-assistance-of-counsel claim.

* * *

Sometime between 8:20 and 9:30 on the evening of April 4, 1998, Eric Walber was brutally murdered. Nearly two years after the murder, Sam Scott, at the time incarcerated, contacted authorities and implicated Michael Wearry. Scott initially reported that he had been friends with the victim; that he was at work the night of the murder; that the victim had come looking for him but had instead run into Wearry and four others; and that Wearry and the others had later confessed to shooting and driving over the victim before leaving his body on Blahut Road. In fact, the victim had not been shot, and his body had been found on Crisp Road.

Scott changed his account of the crime over the course of four later statements, each of which differed from the others in material ways. By the time Scott testified as the State's star witness at Wearry's trial, his story bore little resemblance to his original account. According to the version Scott told the jury, he had been playing dice with Wearry and others when the victim drove past. Wearry, who had been losing, decided to rob the victim. After Wearry and an acquaintance, Randy Hutchinson, stopped the victim's car, Hutchinson shoved the victim into the cargo area. Five men, including Scott, Hutchinson, and Wearry, proceeded to drive around, at one point encountering Eric Brown—the State's other main witness—and pausing intermittently to assault the victim. Finally, Scott related, Wearry and two others killed the victim by running him over. On cross-examination, Scott admitted that he had changed his account several times.

Consistent with Scott's testimony, Brown testified that on the night of the murder he had seen Wearry and others with a man who looked like the victim. Incarcerated on unrelated charges at the time of Wearry's trial, Brown acknowledged that he had made a prior inconsistent statement to the police, but had recanted and agreed to testify against Wearry, not for any prosecutorial favor, but solely because his sister knew the victim's sister. The State commented during its opening argument that Brown "is doing 15 years on a drug charge right now, [but] hasn't asked for a thing." During closing argument, the State reiterated that Brown "has no deal on the table" and was testifying because the victim's "family deserves to know."

Although the State presented no physical evidence at trial, it did offer additional circumstantial evidence linking Wearry to the victim. One witness testified that he saw Wearry in the victim's car on the night of the murder and, later, holding the victim's class ring. Another witness said he saw Wearry throwing away the victim's cologne. In some respects, however, these witnesses contradicted Scott's account. For example, the witness who reported seeing Wearry in the victim's car did not place Scott in the car.

Wearry's defense at trial rested on an alibi. He claimed that, at the time of the murder, he had been at a wedding reception in Baton Rouge, 40 miles away. Wearry's girlfriend, her sister, and her aunt corroborated Wearry's account. In closing argument, the State stressed that all three witnesses had personal relationships with Wearry. The State also presented two rebuttal witnesses: the bride at the wedding, who reported that the reception had ended by 8:30 or 9:00 (potentially leaving sufficient time for Wearry to have committed the crime); and three jail employees, who testified that they had overheard Wearry say that he was a bystander when the crime occurred.

The jury convicted Wearry of capital murder and sentenced him to death. His conviction and sentence were affirmed on direct appeal.

* * *

After Wearry's conviction became final, it emerged that the prosecution had withheld relevant information that could have advanced Wearry's plea. Wearry argued during state postconviction proceedings that three categories of belatedly revealed information would have undermined the prosecution and materially aided Wearry's defense at trial.

First, previously undisclosed police records showed that two of Scott's fellow inmates had made statements that cast doubt on Scott's credibility. One inmate had reported hearing Scott say that he wanted to "make sure [Wearry] gets the needle cause he jacked over me." The other inmate had told investigators—at a meeting Scott orchestrated—that he had witnessed the murder, but this inmate recanted the next day. "Scott had told him what to say," he explained, and had suggested that lying about having witnessed the murder "would help him get out of jail."

Second, the State had failed to disclose that, contrary to the prosecution's assertions at trial, Brown had twice sought a deal to reduce his existing sentence in exchange for testifying against Wearry. The police had told Brown that they would "talk to the D.A. if he told the truth."

Third, the prosecution had failed to turn over medical records on Randy Hutchinson. According to Scott, on the night of the murder, Hutchinson had run into the street to flag down the victim, pulled the victim out of his car, shoved him into the cargo space, and crawled into the cargo space himself. But Hutchinson's medical records revealed that, nine days before the murder, Hutchinson had undergone knee surgery to repair a ruptured patellar tendon. An expert witness * * * testified at the state collateral-review hearing that Hutchinson's surgically repaired knee could not have withstood running, bending, or lifting substantial weight. The State presented an expert witness who disagreed with Dr. Dworak's appraisal of Hutchinson's physical fitness.

During state postconviction proceedings, Wearry also maintained that his trial attorney had failed to uncover exonerating evidence. Wearry's trial attorney admitted at the state collateral-review hearing that he had conducted no independent investigation into Wearry's innocence and had relied solely on evidence the State and Wearry had provided. For example, despite Wearry's alibi, his attorney undertook no effort to locate independent witnesses from among the dozens of guests who had attended the wedding reception.

Counsel representing Wearry on collateral review conducted an independent investigation. This investigation revealed many witnesses lacking any personal relationship with Wearry who would have been willing to corroborate his alibi had they been called at trial. Collateral-review counsel's investigation also revealed that Scott's brother and sister-in-law would have been willing to testify at trial, as they did at the collateral-review hearing, that Scott was with them, mostly at a strawberry festival, until around 11:00 on the night of the murder.

* * *

"[T]he suppression by the prosecution of evidence favorable to an accused upon request violates due process where the evidence is material either to guilt or to punishment, irrespective of the good faith or bad faith of the prosecution." *Brady*. Evidence qualifies as material when there is any reasonable likelihood it could have affected the judgment of the jury. To prevail on his *Brady* claim, Wearry need not show that he "more likely than not" would have been acquitted had the new evidence been admitted. He must show only that the new evidence is sufficient to "undermine confidence" in the verdict.

Beyond doubt, the newly revealed evidence suffices to undermine confidence in Wearry's conviction. The State's trial evidence resembles a house of cards, built on the jury crediting Scott's account rather than Wearry's alibi. See United States v. Agurs, 427 U.S. 97, 113 (1976) ("[I]f the verdict is already of questionable validity, additional evidence of relatively minor importance might be sufficient to create a reasonable doubt."). The dissent asserts that, apart from the testimony of Scott and Brown, there was independent evidence pointing to Wearry as the murderer. But all of the evidence the dissent cites suggests, at most, that someone in Wearry's group of friends may have committed the crime, and that Wearry may have been involved in events related to the murder *after* it occurred. Perhaps, on the basis of this evidence, Louisiana might have charged Wearry as an accessory after the fact. But Louisiana instead charged Wearry with capital murder, and the only evidence directly tying him to that crime was Scott's dubious testimony, corroborated by the similarly suspect testimony of Brown.

As the dissent recognizes, "Scott did not have an exemplary record of veracity." Scott's credibility, already impugned by his many inconsistent stories, would have been further diminished had the jury learned that Hutchinson may have been physically incapable of performing the role Scott ascribed to him, that Scott had coached another inmate to lie about the murder and thereby enhance his chances to get out of jail, or that Scott may have implicated Wearry to settle a personal score. Moreover, any juror who found Scott more credible in light of Brown's testimony might have thought differently had she learned that Brown may have been motivated to come forward not by his sister's relationship with the victim's sister—as the prosecution had insisted in its closing argument—but by the possibility of a reduced sentence on an existing conviction. Even if the jury—armed with all of this new evidence—*could* have voted to convict Wearry, we have no confidence that it *would* have done so.

Reaching the opposite conclusion, the state postconviction court improperly evaluated the materiality of each piece of evidence in isolation rather than cumulatively, see *Kyles v. Whitley*, 514 U.S. 419, 441 (1995) (requiring a "cumulative evaluation" of the materiality of wrongfully withheld evidence), emphasized reasons a juror might disregard new evidence while ignoring reasons she might not, and failed even to mention the statements of the two inmates impeaching Scott.

* * *

Because Wearry's due process rights were violated, we grant his petition for a writ of certiorari and motion for leave to proceed *in forma pauperis,* reverse the judgment of the Louisiana postconviction court, and remand for further proceedings not inconsistent with this opinion.

It is so ordered.

JUSTICE ALITO, with whom JUSTICE THOMAS joins, dissenting.

Without briefing or argument, the Court reverses a 14-year-old murder conviction on the ground that the prosecution violated *Brady v. Maryland*, by failing to turn over certain information that tended to exculpate petitioner. There is no question in my mind that the prosecution should have disclosed this information, but whether the information was sufficient to warrant reversing petitioner's conviction is another matter. * * *

The Court argues that the information in question here could have affected the jury's verdict and that petitioner's conviction must therefore be reversed. The Court ably makes the case for reversal, but there is a reasonable contrary argument that petitioner's conviction should stand because the undisclosed information would *not* have affected the jury's verdict. I will briefly discuss the main points made in the *per curiam,* not for the purpose of showing that they are necessarily wrong, but to show that the *Brady* issue is not open and shut. * * *

The first item of information discussed by the Court is a police report that recounts statements made about Sam Scott, a key witness for the prosecution, by a fellow inmate. According to this report, Scott told the inmate: "I'm gonna make sure Mike [*i.e.,* petitioner] gets the needle cause he jacked over me." Scott, who had been serving a sentence on unrelated drug charges, reportedly told the inmate that he had been expecting to be released but that he "still [had not] gone home because of this," *i.e.,* petitioner's prosecution. As stated in the report, Scott said that he was now facing the possibility of a 10-year sentence, apparently for his admitted role in the events surrounding the murder. The report did not provide any further explanation for Scott's alleged statement that petitioner had "jacked [him] over."

The Court reads the report to suggest that Scott implicated petitioner in the murder "to settle a personal score." But if petitioner's counsel had actually attempted to use this evidence at trial, the net effect might well have been harmful, not helpful, to the defense. The undisclosed police report on which the Court relies may be read to mean that Scott blamed petitioner for putting him in the position of having to admit his own role in the events surrounding the murder and thereby expose himself to the 10-year sentence and lose an opportunity to secure early release from prison on the drug charges. If defense counsel had attempted to impeach Scott with this police report, the effort could have backfired by allowing the prosecution to return the jury's focus to a point the State emphasized often during trial, namely, that Scott's accusations were credible precisely because Scott had no motive to tell a story that was contrary to his own interests.

The Court next turns to an allegation that Scott had coached another prisoner to make up lies against petitioner. This prisoner never testified at trial, and there is a basis for arguing that this information would not have made a difference to the jury, which was well aware that Scott did not have an exemplary record of veracity. Scott himself admitted to fabricating information that he told the police during their investigations. In addition, a witness who *did* testify against petitioner at trial also accused Scott of asking him to lie, although admittedly this witness later denied making this accusation. Given that the jury convicted even with these quite serious strikes against Scott's credibility, there is reason to question whether the jury would have seriously considered a different verdict because of an accusation from someone who never took the stand.

Third, the Court observes that the prosecution failed to turn over evidence that another witness, Eric Brown, had asked for favorable treatment from the district attorney in exchange for testifying against petitioner. It is true—and troubling—that the prosecutor claimed in her opening statement that Brown had not sought favorable treatment. But even so, it is far from clear that disclosing the contradictory information had real potential to affect the trial's outcome. For one thing, there is no evidence that Brown (unlike Scott) actually received any deal, despite defense counsel's efforts in cross-examination to establish that Brown's testimony might have earned him leniency from the State. Moreover, Brown admitted during the exchange that he had manipulated his initial story to the police to avoid implicating himself in criminal activity. We know, then, that the jury harbored no illusions about the purity of Brown's motives, notwithstanding the prosecutor's opening misstatement.

Finally, the Court says that the medical records of Randy Hutchinson would have cast doubt on Scott's trial testimony that Hutchinson repeatedly dragged the victim into and out of a car and bludgeoned him with a stick. The records reveal that Hutchinson had knee surgery to repair his patellar tendon just nine days before the murder. But one of the State's witnesses testified at trial that he had seen records showing that Hutchinson had had surgery on his knee "about nine days before the homicide happened." The jury thus knew the most salient fact revealed by these records—that Scott had attributed significant strength and mobility to a man nine days removed from knee surgery. Given that these particular details about Hutchinson's actions were a relatively minor part of Scott's account of the crime and the State's case against petitioner, the significance of the undisclosed medical records is subject to reasonable dispute.

While the Court highlights the exculpatory quality of the withheld information, the Court downplays the considerable evidence of petitioner's guilt. Aside from Scott's and Brown's testimony, three witnesses told the jury that they saw petitioner and others driving around shortly after the murder in the victim's red car, which according to one of these witnesses had blood on its exterior. Petitioner offered to sell an Albany High School class ring to one of these witnesses and a set of new speakers to another. The third witness said he saw petitioner throw away a bottle of Tommy Hilfiger cologne. Meanwhile, the victim's mother testified that her son wore an Albany High class ring that was not recovered with his body, had received speakers as a gift shortly before his murder, and had a bottle of Tommy Hilfiger cologne with him on the night when he was killed. In addition, three jailers testified that petitioner called his father after his eventual arrest and stated that "he didn't know what he was doing in jail because he didn't do anything [and] was just an innocent bystander."

In short, this is far from a case in which the withheld information would have allowed the defense to undermine "the *only* evidence linking [petitioner] to the crime." Smith v. Cain, 132 S.Ct. 627, 630 (2012).

* * *

Whether disclosing the information at issue realistically could have changed the trial's outcome is indisputably an intensely factual question. Under *Brady,* we must evaluate the significance of the withheld information in light of *all* the proof at petitioner's trial. It is unusual and, in my judgment, unreasonable for us to decide such a question without full briefing and argument.

At this stage, all that we have from the State is its brief in opposition to the petition for certiorari. And the State had ample reason to believe when it submitted that brief that the question on the table was whether the Court should hear the case, not whether petitioner's conviction should be reversed. The State undoubtedly knew that we generally deny certiorari on factbound questions that do not implicate any disputed legal issue. Nothing warned the State that this petition was likely to produce an exception to that general rule. * * *

Why, then, has the Court decided to depart from our usual procedures and decide petitioner's fact-intensive *Brady* claim at this stage? Why not allow petitioner to raise that claim in a federal habeas proceeding? If the case took that course, it would not reach us until a district court and a court of appeals had studied the record and evaluated the likely impact of the information in question.

One consequence of waiting until the claim was raised in a federal habeas proceeding is that our review would then be governed by the Antiterrorism and Effective Death Penalty Act of 1996 (AEDPA). Under AEDPA, relief could be granted only if it could be said that the state court's rejection of the claim represented an "unreasonable application" of *Brady*. By intervening now before AEDPA comes into play, the Court avoids the application of that standard and is able to exercise plenary review. But if the *Brady* claim is as open-and-shut as the Court maintains, AEDPA would not present an obstacle to the granting of habeas relief. On the other hand, if reasonable jurists could disagree about the application of *Brady* to the facts of this case, there is no good reason to dispose of this case summarily. The State should be given the opportunity to make its full case.

In my view, therefore, summary reversal is highly inappropriate. The Court is anxious to vacate petitioner's conviction before the State has the opportunity to make its case. But if we are going to intervene at this stage, we should grant the petition and hear the case on the merits. There is room on our docket to give this case the careful consideration it deserves.

And Another Fact-Intensive Analysis of Brady Materiality: Turner v. United States

TURNER V. UNITED STATES
Supreme Court of the United States, 2017.
2017 WL 2674152.

JUSTICE BREYER delivered the opinion of the Court.

In *Brady* v. *Maryland*, 373 U.S. 83 (1963), this Court held that the government violates the Constitution's Due Process Clause "if it withholds evidence that is favorable to the defense and *material* to the defendant's guilt or punishment." Smith v. Cain, 565 U.S. 73, 75 (2012) (emphasis added) (summarizing *Brady* holding). In 1985 the seven petitioners in these cases were tried together in the Superior Court for the District of Columbia for the kidnaping, armed robbery, and murder of Catherine Fuller. Long after petitioners' convictions became final, it emerged that the Government possessed certain evidence that it failed to disclose to the defense. The only question before us here is whether that withheld evidence was "material" under *Brady*. The D. C. Superior Court, after a 16-day evidentiary hearing, determined that the withheld evidence was not material. The D. C. Court of Appeals reviewed the record, reached the same conclusion, and affirmed the Superior Court. After reviewing the record, we reach the same conclusion as did the lower courts.

I

In these fact-intensive cases, we set out here only a basic description of the record facts along with our reasons for reaching our conclusion. * * *

A

The Trial

On March 22, 1985, a grand jury indicted the seven petitioners—Timothy Catlett, Russell Overton, Levy Rouse, Kelvin Smith, Charles Turner, Christopher Turner, and Clifton Yarborough—and several others for the kidnaping, robbery, and murder of Catherine Fuller. The evidence produced at their joint trial showed that on October 1, 1984, at around 4:30 p.m., Catherine Fuller left her home to go shopping. At around 6 p.m., William Freeman, a street vendor, found Fuller's body inside an alley garage between Eighth and Ninth Street N. E., just a few blocks from Fuller's home. Fuller had been robbed, severely beaten, and sodomized with an object that caused extensive internal injuries.

The Government advanced the theory at trial that Fuller had been attacked in the alley by a large group of individuals, including petitioners; codefendants Steve Webb, Alfonso Harris, and Felicia Ruffin; as well as by Calvin Alston and Harry Bennett. The Government's evidentiary centerpiece consisted of testimony by Alston and Bennett, who confessed to participating in the offense and who cooperated with the Government in return for leniency. Although the testimony of Alston and Bennett diverged on minor details, it was consistent in stating that, and describing how, Fuller was attacked by a sizeable group of individuals, including petitioners and they themselves.

Alston testified that at about 4:10 p.m. on the day of the murder, he arrived in a park located on H Street between Eighth and Ninth Streets. He said he found a group of people gathered there. It included petitioners Levy Rouse, Russell Overton, Christopher Turner, Charles Turner, Kelvin Smith, Clifton Yarborough, and Timothy Catlett, as well as several codefendants and others. Those in the group were talking and singing while Catlett was banging out a beat. Alston suggested "getting paid" by robbing someone. Catlett, Overton, Rouse, Smith, Charles Turner, Christopher Turner, Yarborough, and several others agreed. Alston pointed at Catherine Fuller, who was walking on the other side of H Street near the corner of H and Eighth Streets. Those in the group said they were "game for getting paid." Alston, Rouse, Yarborough, and Charles Turner crossed H Street moving toward Eighth Street and followed Fuller down Eighth Street. The rest of the group crossed H Street and moved toward

Ninth Street. When Alston's group approached Fuller, Charles Turner shoved her into an alley that runs between Eighth and Ninth Streets. Charles Turner, Rouse, and Alston began punching Fuller. They were soon joined by Christopher Turner, Smith, and others. All of them continued to hit and kick Fuller until she fell to the ground. Rouse and Charles Turner then carried Fuller to the center of the alley and dropped her in front of a garage located at the point where the alley joins another, perpendicular alley that runs toward I Street. Someone dragged Fuller into the garage. Alston, Rouse, Charles Turner, Overton, Yarborough, and Catlett followed. Others stood outside. Members of the group tore Fuller's clothes off and struggled over her change purse. Overton and Charles Turner then held Fuller's legs, and Alston, Catlett, Harris, and Yarborough stood around her while Rouse sodomized her with a foot-long pipe. Shortly after, the group dispersed and left the alley.

Harry Bennett's testimony was similar. Bennett also described a group attack. He said that he had gone to the H Street park, where he saw Rouse, Overton, Christopher Turner, Smith, Catlett, and others gathered. Alston was talking to the group about "[g]etting paid" and said "let's go get that lady." At that point Alston, Rouse, Overton, and Webb crossed H Street and approached Fuller, while Catlett, Christopher Turner, Charles Turner, and Harris followed in a separate group. Bennett added that he himself went to the corner of Eighth and H Streets to watch for police. He then went into the alley and joined the group in kicking and beating Fuller. He testified that at least 12 people were there, with some beating Fuller and others watching or picking up her jewelry. Overton then dragged Fuller into the garage, and Bennett, Rouse, Christopher Turner, Charles Turner, Catlett, Smith, Harris, and Webb followed, as did some "girls." Alston and Steve Webb held Fuller's legs, and Rouse sodomized her with a pole. The group then dispersed from the garage and alley.

The Government presented several other witnesses who corroborated aspects of Alston's and Bennett's testimony, including the fact that Fuller was attacked by a group. Melvin Montgomery testified that he was in the H Street park on the afternoon of the murder. He saw Overton, Catlett, Rouse, Charles Turner, and others gathered there. The group was being noisy and singing a song about needing money. Somebody then said they were "going to get that one," and Montgomery saw that Overton was pointing to a woman standing on the corner of Eighth Street. Overton, Catlett, Rouse, Charles Turner, and others crossed H Street. Some headed toward Eighth Street while others went toward Ninth Street. Montgomery did not follow them.

Maurice Thomas, then 14 years old, testified that he witnessed the attack itself. Thomas lived in the neighborhood and knew many of the defendants. As he was walking home, he glanced down the Eighth Street alley and saw a group surrounding Fuller. Thomas saw Catlett pat Fuller down and then hit her. He then saw everyone in the group join in hitting her. Thomas said he knew Catlett, Yarborough, Rouse, Charles Turner, Christopher Turner, and Smith and recognized them in the group. Thomas heard Fuller calling for help. He ran home where he found his aunt, who told him not to tell anyone what he saw. Later that day, Thomas saw Catlett at a corner store, and heard Catlett say to someone that they "had to kill her" because "she spotted someone he was with."

On the afternoon of the murder, Carrie Eleby and Linda Jacobs were looking for petitioner Smith, who was Eleby's boyfriend, near the corner of H and Eighth Streets. They heard screams coming from where a "gang of boys" was beating somebody near the garage in the alley. Eleby and Jacobs approached the group. Eleby recognized Christopher Turner, Smith, Catlett, Rouse, Overton, Alston, and Webb kicking Fuller while Yarborough stood nearby. Both Eleby and Jacobs testified that they saw Rouse sodomize Fuller with a pole. Eleby added that Overton held Fuller's legs.

Finally, the Government played a videotape of a recorded statement that Yarborough, one of the petitioners, had given to detectives on December 9, 1984, approximately two months after the murder. Names were redacted. The video shows Yarborough describing in detail how he was part of a large group that forced Fuller into the alley, jointly robbed and assaulted her, and dragged her into the garage.

None of the defendants testified, nor did any of them try, through witnesses or other evidence, to rebut the prosecution witnesses' claim that Fuller was killed in a group attack. Rather, each petitioner pursued what was essentially a "not me, maybe them" defense, namely, that he was not part of the group that attacked Fuller. Each tried to establish this defense by impeaching witnesses who had placed that particular petitioner at the scene. Some, for example, provided evidence that Eleby and Jacobs had used PCP the day of Fuller's murder. Some also tried to establish alibis for the time of Fuller's death.

The jury convicted all seven petitioners, along with codefendant Steve Webb (who subsequently died). The jury acquitted codefendants Alfonso Harris and Felicia Ruffin. * * *

B

The Brady *Claims*

* * * After petitioners' convictions became final, it emerged that the Government possessed certain evidence that it had withheld from the defense at the time of trial. Petitioners discovered other withheld evidence in their review of the trial prosecutor's case file, which the Government turned over to petitioners in the course of the postconviction proceedings. Among other postconviction claims, petitioners contended that the

withheld evidence was both favorable and material, entitling them to relief under *Brady*.

The D. C. Superior Court considered petitioners' *Brady* claims as part of a 16-day evidentiary hearing. It rejected those claims, finding that "none of the undisclosed information was material." * * * At issue in those proceedings were the following seven specific pieces of evidence:

1. *The identity of James McMillan.* Freeman, the vendor who discovered Fuller's body in the alley garage, testified at trial that, while he was waiting for police to arrive, he saw two men run into the alley and stop near the garage for about five minutes before running away when an officer approached. One of the men had a bulge under his coat. Early in the trial, codefendant Harris' counsel had requested the identity of the two men to confirm that her client was not one of them. But the Government refused to disclose the men's identity.

In their postconviction review of the prosecutor's files, petitioners learned that Freeman had identified the two men he saw in the alley as James McMillan and Gerald Merkerson. McMillan lived in a house which opens in the back onto a connecting alley. In the weeks following Fuller's murder, but before petitioners' trial, McMillan was arrested for beating and robbing two women in the neighborhood. Neither attack included a sexual assault. Separately, petitioners learned that seven years after petitioners' trial, McMillan had robbed, sodomized, and murdered a young woman in an alley.

2. *The interview with Willie Luchie.* The prosecutor's notes also recorded an undisclosed interview with Willie Luchie, who told the prosecutor that he and three others walked through the alley on their way to an H Street liquor store between 5:30 and 5:45 p.m. on the evening of the murder. As the group walked by the garage, Luchie "heard several groans" and "remembers the doors to the garage being closed." Another person in the group recalled "hear[ing] some moans," while the other two persons did not recall hearing anything unusual. The group continued walking without looking into the garage or otherwise investigating the source of the sounds. They did not see McMillan or any other person in the alley when they passed through.

3. *The interviews with Ammie Davis.* Undisclosed notes written by a police officer and the prosecutor refer to two interviews with Ammie Davis, who had been arrested for disorderly conduct a few weeks after Fuller's murder. Davis initially told a police investigator that she had seen another individual, James Blue, beat Fuller to death in the alley. Shortly thereafter, she said she only saw Blue grab Fuller and push her into the alley. Davis also said that a girlfriend, whom she did not name, accompanied her. She promised to call the investigator with more details, but she did not do so.

About 9 months later (after petitioners were indicted but approximately 11 weeks before their trial), a prosecutor learned of the investigator's notes and interviewed Davis. The prosecutor's notes state that Davis did not provide any more details * * * . *Id.,* at 267–268. About two months later, which was shortly before petitioners' trial, Blue murdered Davis in an unrelated drug dispute.

During the postconviction evidentiary hearing, the prosecutor who interviewed Davis testified that he did not disclose Davis' statement because she acted "playful" and "not serious" during the interview and he found her to be "totally incredible." Additionally, the prosecutor stated that he knew Davis had previously falsely accused Blue of a different murder, and on another occasion had falsely accused a different individual of a different murder.

4. *Impeachment of Kaye Porter and Carrie Eleby.* Kaye Porter accompanied Eleby during an initial interview with homicide detectives. Porter agreed with Eleby that she had also heard Alston state that he was involved in robbing Fuller. An undisclosed prosecutorial note states that in a later interview with detectives, Porter stated that she did not actually recall hearing Alston's statement and just went along with what Eleby said. The note also states that Eleby likewise admitted that she had lied about Porter being present during Alston's statement and had asked Porter to support her.

5. *Impeachment of Carrie Eleby.* A prosecutor's un-disclosed note revealed that Eleby said she had been high on PCP during a January 9, 1985, meeting with investigators.

6. *Impeachment of Linda Jacobs.* An undisclosed note of an interview with Linda Jacobs said that the detective had "question[ed] her hard," and that she had "vacillated" about what she saw. The prosecutor recalled that the detective "kept raising his voice" and was "smacking his hand on the desk" during the interview.

7. *Impeachment of Maurice Thomas.* An undisclosed note of an interview with Maurice Thomas' aunt stated that she "does not recall Maurice ever telling her anything such as this."

II

A

The Government does not contest petitioners' claim that the withheld evidence was "favorable to the accused, either because it is exculpatory, or because it is impeaching." Strickler v. Greene, 527 U. S. 263, 281–282 (1999). Neither does the Government contest petitioners' claim that it suppressed the evidence * * * . [T]he Government assured the Court at oral argument that subsequent to petitioners' trial, it has adopted a "generous policy of discovery" in criminal cases under which it discloses any "information that a defendant might wish to use." As we have recognized, and as the Government agrees this is as it should be. Kyles v. Whitely, [Text, page 1098] (explaining that a "prudent prosecutor's" better course is to take care to disclose any evidence favorable to the defendant).

Petitioners and the Government, however, do contest the materiality of the undisclosed *Brady* information. * * *

Consequently, the issue before us here is legally simple but factually complex. We must examine the trial record, evaluate the withheld evidence in the context of the entire record, and determine in light of that examination whether there is a reasonable probability that, had the evidence been disclosed, the result of the proceeding would have been different. Having done so, we agree with the lower courts that there was no such reasonable probability.

B

Petitioners' main argument is that, had they known about McMillan's identity and Luchie's statement, they could have challenged the Government's basic theory that Fuller was killed in a group attack. Petitioners contend that they could have raised an alternative theory, namely, that a single perpetrator (or two at most) had attacked Fuller. According to petitioners, the groans that Luchie and his companion heard when they walked through the alley between 5:30 and 5:45 p.m. suggest that the attack was taking place inside the garage at that moment. The added facts that the garage was small and that Luchie's group saw no one in the alley could bolster a "single attacker" theory. Freeman's recollection that one garage door was open when he found Fuller's body at around 6 p.m., combined with Luchie's recollection that both doors were shut around 5:30 or 5:45 p.m., could suggest that one or two perpetrators were in the garage when Luchie walked by but left before Freeman arrived. McMillan's identity as one of the men Freeman saw enter the alley after Freeman discovered Fuller's body would have revealed McMillan's criminal convictions in the months before petitioners' trial. Petitioners argue that together, this evidence would have permitted the defense to knit together a theory that the group attack did not occur at all—and that it was actually McMillan, alone or with an accomplice, who murdered Fuller. They add that they could have used the investigators' failure to follow up on Ammie Davis' claim about James Blue, and the various pieces of withheld impeachment evidence, to suggest that an incomplete investigation had ended up accusing the wrong persons.

Considering the withheld evidence in the context of the entire record, however, we conclude that it is too little, too weak, or too distant from the main evidentiary points to meet *Brady*'s standards. As petitioners recognize, McMillan's guilt (or that of any other single, or near single, perpetrator) is inconsistent with petitioners' guilt only if there was no group attack. But a group attack was the very cornerstone of the Government's case. The witnesses may have differed on minor details, but virtually every witness to the crime itself agreed as to a main theme: that Fuller was killed by a large group of perpetrators. The evidence at trial was such that, even though petitioners knew that Freeman saw two men enter the alley after he discovered Fuller's body, that one appeared to have a bulky object hidden under his coat, and that both ran when the police arrived, none of the petitioners attempted to mount a defense that implicated those men as alternative perpetrators acting alone.

Is it reasonably probable that adding McMillan's identity, and Luchie's ambiguous statement that he heard groans but saw no one, could have led to a different result at trial? We conclude that it is not. The problem for petitioners is that their current alternative theory would have had to persuade the jury that both Alston and Bennett falsely confessed to being active participants in a group attack that never occurred; that Yarborough falsely implicated himself in that group attack and, through coordinated effort or coincidence, gave a highly similar account of how it occurred; that Thomas, a disinterested witness who recognized petitioners when he happened upon the attack and heard Catlett refer to it later that night, wholly fabricated his story; that both Eleby and Jacobs likewise testified to witnessing a group attack that did not occur; and that Montgomery in fact did not see petitioners and others, as a group, identify Fuller as a target and leave the park to rob her.

With respect to the undisclosed impeachment evidence, the record shows that it was largely cumulative of impeachment evidence petitioners already had and used at trial. For example, the jury heard multiple times about Eleby's frequent PCP use, including Eleby's own testimony that she and Jacobs had smoked PCP shortly before they witnessed Fuller's attack. In this context, it would not have surprised the jury to learn that Eleby used PCP on yet another occasion. Porter was a minor witness who was also impeached at trial with evidence about changes in her testimony over time, leaving little added significance to the note that she changed her mind about having agreed with Eleby's claims. The jury was also well aware of Jacobs' vacillation, as she was impeached on the stand with her shifting stories about what she witnessed. Knowledge that a detective raised his voice during an interview with her would have added little more. Nor do we see how the note about the statement by Thomas' aunt could have mattered much, given the facts that neither side chose to call the aunt as a witness and that the jury already knew, from Thomas' testimony, that his aunt had told him not to tell anyone what he saw. As for James Blue, petitioners argue that the investigators' delay in following up on Ammie Davis' statement could have led the jury to doubt the thoroughness of the investigation. But this likelihood is seriously undercut by notes about Davis' demeanor and lack of detail, and by her prior false accusations that

Blue committed a different murder and that yet another person committed yet a different murder.

We of course do not suggest that impeachment evidence is immaterial with respect to a witness who has already been impeached with other evidence. We conclude only that in the context of this trial, with respect to these witnesses, the cumulative effect of the withheld evidence is insufficient to undermine confidence in the jury's verdict.

III

On the basis of our review of the record, we agree with the lower courts that there is not a "reasonable probability" that the withheld evidence would have changed the outcome of petitioners' trial. The judgment of the D. C. Court of Appeals, accordingly, is affirmed.

It is so ordered.

Justice Gorsuch took no part in the consideration or decision of these cases.

JUSTICE KAGAN, with whom JUSTICE GINSBURG joins, dissenting.

Consider two criminal cases. In the first, the government accuses ten defendants of acting together to commit a vicious murder and robbery. At trial, each defendant accepts that the attack occurred almost exactly as the government describes—contending only that *he* wasn't part of the rampaging group. The defendants thus undermine each other's arguments at every turn. In the second case, the government makes the same arguments as before. But this time, all of the accused adopt a common defense, built around an alternative account of the crime. Armed with new evidence that someone else perpetrated the murder, the defendants vigorously dispute the government's gang-attack narrative and challenge the credibility of its investigation. The question this case presents is whether such a unified defense, relying on evidence unavailable in the first scenario, had a "reasonable probability" (less than a preponderance) of shifting even one juror's vote.

* * * With the undisclosed evidence, the whole tenor of the trial would have changed. Rather than relying on a "not me, maybe them" defense, all the defendants would have relentlessly impeached the Government's (thoroughly impeachable) witnesses and offered the jurors a way to view the crime in a different light. In my view, that could well have flipped one or more jurors—which is all *Brady* requires.

* * *

[T]he majority argues that "none of the [accused] attempted to mount [an alternative-perpetrator] defense" and that such a defense would have challenged "the very cornerstone of the Government's case." But that just proves my point. The defendants didn't offer an alternative-perpetrator defense because the Government prevented them from learning what made it credible: that one of the men seen near the garage had a record of assaulting and robbing middle-aged women, and that witnesses would back up the theory that only one or two individuals had committed the murder. Moreover, that defense had game-changing potential exactly *because* it challenged the cornerstone of the Government's case. Without the withheld evidence, each of the defendants had little choice but to accept the Government's framing of the crime as a group attack—and argue only that *he* wasn't there. That meant the defendants often worked at cross-purposes. In particular, each defendant not identified by a Government witness sought to bolster that witness's credibility, no matter the harm to his co-defendants. * * * Credible alternative-perpetrator evidence would have allowed the defendants to escape this cycle of mutually assured destruction. By enabling the defendants to jointly attack the Government's "cornerstone" theory, the withheld evidence would have reframed the case presented to the jury.

Still, the majority claims, an alternative-perpetrator defense would have had no realistic chance of changing the outcome because the Government had ample evidence of a group attack, including five witnesses who testified that they had participated in it or seen it happen. But the Government's case wasn't nearly the slam-dunk the majority suggests. No physical evidence tied any of the defendants to the crime—a highly surprising fact if, as the Government claimed, more than ten people carried out a spur-of-the-moment, rampage-like attack in a confined space. And as even the majority recognizes, the Government's five eyewitnesses had some serious credibility deficits. Two had been charged as defendants, and agreed to testify only in exchange for favorable plea deals. Two admitted they were high on PCP at the time. * * * One was an eighth-grader whose own aunt contradicted parts of his trial testimony. Even in the absence of an alternative account of the crime, the jury took more than a week—and many dozens of votes—to reach its final verdict. Had the defendants offered a unified counter-narrative, based on the withheld evidence, one or more jurors could well have concluded that the Government had not proved its case beyond a reasonable doubt.

Again, the issue here concerns the difference between two criminal cases. The Government got the case it most wanted—the one in which the defendants, each in an effort to save himself, formed something of a circular firing squad. And the Government avoided the case it most feared—the one in which the defendants acted jointly to show that a man known to assault women like Fuller committed her murder. The difference between the two cases lay in the Government's files—evidence of obvious relevance that prosecutors nonetheless chose to suppress. I think it could have mattered to the trial's outcome. For that reason, I respectfully dissent.

CHAPTER 10

TRIAL AND TRIAL-RELATED RIGHTS

■ ■ ■

I. THE RIGHT TO A SPEEDY TRIAL

Page 1203. Add a new section F (with the section on The Right to a Speedy Appeal changing to section G.):

F. THE RIGHT TO SPEEDY SENTENCING

In the following case, the Court discusses whether the constitutional guarantee of speedy trial extends to sentencing.

BETTERMAN V. MONTANA
Supreme Court of the United States, 2016.
136 S.Ct. 1609.

JUSTICE GINSBURG delivered the opinion of the Court.

* * * Does the Sixth Amendment's speedy trial guarantee apply to the sentencing phase of a criminal prosecution? That is the sole question this case presents. We hold that the guarantee protects the accused from arrest or indictment through trial, but does not apply once a defendant has been found guilty at trial or has pleaded guilty to criminal charges. For inordinate delay in sentencing, although the Speedy Trial Clause does not govern, a defendant may have other recourse, including, in appropriate circumstances, tailored relief under the Due Process Clauses of the Fifth and Fourteenth Amendments. Petitioner Brandon Betterman, however, advanced in this Court only a Sixth Amendment speedy trial claim. He did not preserve a due process challenge. We, therefore, confine this opinion to his Sixth Amendment challenge.

I

Ordered to appear in court on domestic assault charges, Brandon Betterman failed to show up and was therefore charged with bail jumping. After pleading guilty to the bail-jumping charge, he was jailed for over 14 months awaiting sentence on that conviction. The holdup, in large part, was due to institutional delay: the presentence report took nearly five months to complete; the trial court took several months to deny two presentence motions (one seeking dismissal of the charge on the ground of delay); and the court was slow in setting a sentencing hearing. Betterman was eventually sentenced to seven years' imprisonment, with four of those years suspended.

Arguing that the 14-month gap between conviction and sentencing violated his speedy trial right, Betterman appealed. The Montana Supreme Court affirmed his conviction and sentence, ruling that the Sixth Amendment's Speedy Trial Clause does not apply to postconviction, presentencing delay.

We granted certiorari to resolve a split among courts over whether the Speedy Trial Clause applies to such delay. Holding that the Clause does not apply to delayed sentencing, we affirm the Montana Supreme Court's judgment.

II

Criminal proceedings generally unfold in three discrete phases. First, the State investigates to determine whether to arrest and charge a suspect. Once charged, the suspect stands accused but is presumed innocent until conviction upon trial or guilty plea. After conviction, the court imposes sentence. There are checks against delay throughout this progression, each geared to its particular phase.

In the first stage—before arrest or indictment, when the suspect remains at liberty—statutes of limitations provide the primary protection against delay, with the Due Process Clause as a safeguard against fundamentally unfair prosecutorial conduct.

The Sixth Amendment's Speedy Trial Clause homes in on the second period: from arrest or indictment through conviction. The constitutional right, our precedent holds, does not attach until this phase begins, that is, when a defendant is arrested or formally accused. Today we hold that the right detaches upon conviction, when this second stage ends.

Prior to conviction, the accused is shielded by the presumption of innocence, the bedrock, axiomatic and elementary principle whose enforcement lies at the foundation of the administration of our criminal law. The Speedy Trial Clause implements that presumption by preventing undue and oppressive incarceration prior to trial, minimizing anxiety and concern accompanying public accusation, and limiting the possibilities that long delay will impair the ability of an accused to defend himself. As a measure protecting the presumptively innocent, the speedy trial right— like other similarly aimed measures—loses force upon conviction. Compare In re Winship, 397 U.S. 358, 364 (1970) (requiring "proof beyond a reasonable doubt of every fact necessary to constitute the crime"), with United States v. O'Brien, 560 U.S. 218, 224 (2010) ("Sentencing factors . . . can be proved . . . by a preponderance of the evidence."). Compare also 18 U.S.C. § 3142(b) (bail presumptively available for accused awaiting trial) with § 3143(a) (bail presumptively unavailable for those convicted awaiting sentence).

Our reading comports with the historical understanding. The speedy trial right, we have observed, "has its roots at the very foundation of our English law heritage. Its first articulation in modern jurisprudence appears to have been made in Magna Carta (1215). . . ." Klopfer v. North Carolina, 386 U.S. 213, 223 (1967). Regarding the Framers' comprehension of the right as it existed at the founding, we have cited Sir Edward Coke's Institutes of the Laws of England. Coke wrote that "the *innocent* shall not be worn and wasted by long imprisonment, but . . . speedily come to his *tria*[*l*]." 1 E. Coke, Second Part of the Institutes of the Laws of England 315 (1797) (emphasis added).

Reflecting the concern that a presumptively innocent person should not languish under an unresolved charge, the Speedy Trial Clause guarantees "the *accused*" "the right to a speedy . . . *trial*." U.S. Const., Amdt. 6 (emphasis added). At the founding, "accused" described a status preceding "convicted."

This understanding of the Sixth Amendment language—"accused" as distinct from "convicted," and "trial" as separate from "sentencing"— endures today. See, *e.g.,* Black's Law Dictionary 26 (10th ed. 2014) (defining "accused" as "a person who has been *arrested* and brought before a magistrate or who has been formally *charged*" (emphasis added)); Fed. Rule Crim. Proc. 32 (governing "Sentencing and Judgment," the rule appears in the chapter on "Post-Conviction Procedures," which follows immediately after the separate chapter headed "Trial").

This Court's precedent aligns with the text and history of the Speedy Trial Clause. Detaining the accused pretrial, we have said, disadvantages him, and the imposition is "especially unfortunate" as to those "ultimately found to be innocent." *Barker* [*v. Wingo*], 407 U.S., at 532–533. And in [*United States v.*] *Marion,* 404 U.S., at 320, addressing "the major evils protected against by the speedy trial guarantee," we observed: "Arrest is a public act that may seriously interfere with the defendant's liberty, whether he is free on bail or not, and that may disrupt his employment, drain his financial resources, curtail his associations, subject him to public obloquy, and create anxiety in him, his family and his friends." We acknowledged in *Marion* that even pre-arrest—a stage at which the right to a speedy trial does not arise—the passage of time "may impair memories, cause evidence to be lost, deprive the defendant of witnesses, and otherwise interfere with his ability to defend himself." Nevertheless, we determined, "this possibility of prejudice at trial is not itself sufficient reason to wrench the Sixth Amendment from its proper [arrest or charge triggered] context." Adverse consequences of postconviction delay, though subject to other checks, are similarly outside the purview of the Speedy Trial Clause.

The sole remedy for a violation of the speedy trial right—dismissal of the charges, see Strunk v. United States, 412 U.S. 434 (1973)—fits the preconviction focus of the Clause. It would be an unjustified windfall, in most cases, to remedy sentencing delay by vacating validly obtained convictions. Betterman concedes that a dismissal remedy ordinarily would not be in order once a defendant has been convicted.

The manner in which legislatures have implemented the speedy trial guarantee matches our reading of the Clause. Congress passed the Speedy Trial Act of 1974, 18 U.S.C. § 3161 *et seq.,* to give effect to the sixth amendment right. With certain exceptions, the Act directs—on pain of dismissal of the charges, § 3162(a)—that no more than 30 days pass between arrest and indictment, § 3161(b), and that no more than 70 days pass between indictment and trial, § 3161(c)(1). The Act says nothing, however, about the period between conviction and sentencing, suggesting that Congress did not regard that period as falling within the Sixth Amendment's compass. * * *

Betterman asks us to take account of the prevalence of guilty pleas and the resulting scarcity of trials in today's justice system. The sentencing hearing has largely replaced the trial as the forum for dispute resolution, Betterman urges. Therefore, he maintains, the concerns supporting the right to a speedy trial now recommend a speedy sentencing hearing. The modern reality, however, does not bear on the presumption-of-innocence protection at the heart of the Speedy Trial Clause. And factual disputes, if any there be, at sentencing, do not go to the question of guilt; they are geared, instead, to ascertaining the proper sentence within boundaries set by statutory minimums and maximums.

Moreover, a central feature of contemporary sentencing in both federal and state courts is preparation by the probation office, and review by the parties and the court, of a presentence investigation report. This aspect of the system requires some amount of wholly reasonable presentencing delay. Indeed, many—if not most—disputes are resolved, not at the hearing itself, but rather through the presentence-report process.

As we have explained, at the third phase of the criminal-justice process, *i.e.,* between conviction and sentencing, the Constitution's presumption-of-innocence-protective speedy trial right is not engaged. That does not mean, however, that defendants lack any protection against undue delay at this stage. The primary safeguard comes from statutes and rules. The federal rule on point directs the court to "impose sentence without unnecessary delay." Fed. Rule Crim. Proc. 32(b)(1). Many States have provisions to the same effect, and some States prescribe numerical time limits. Further, as at the prearrest stage, due process serves as a backstop against exorbitant delay. After conviction, a defendant's due process right to liberty, while diminished, is still present. He retains an interest in a sentencing proceeding that is fundamentally fair. But because Betterman advanced no due process claim here, we express no opinion on how he might fare under that more pliable standard.

The course of a criminal prosecution is composed of discrete segments. During the segment between accusation and conviction, the Sixth Amendment's Speedy Trial Clause protects the presumptively innocent from long enduring unresolved criminal charges. The Sixth Amendment speedy trial right, however, does not extend beyond conviction, which terminates the presumption of innocence. The judgment of the Supreme Court of Montana is therefore

Affirmed.

JUSTICE THOMAS, with whom JUSTICE ALITO joins, concurring.

I agree with the Court that the Sixth Amendment's Speedy Trial Clause does not apply to sentencing proceedings, except perhaps to bifurcated sentencing proceedings where sentencing enhancements operate as functional elements of a greater offense. I also agree with the Court's decision to reserve judgment on whether sentencing delays might violate the Due Process Clause. * * * We have never decided whether the Due Process Clause creates an entitlement to a reasonably prompt sentencing hearing. Today's opinion leaves us free to decide the proper analytical framework to analyze such claims if and when the issue is properly before us.

Justice SOTOMAYOR suggests that, for such claims, we should adopt the factors announced in Barker v. Wingo, 407 U.S. 514 (1972). I would not prejudge that matter. The factors listed in *Barker* may not necessarily translate to the delayed sentencing context. The Due Process Clause can be satisfied where a State has adequate procedures to redress an improper deprivation of liberty or property. In unusual cases where trial courts fail to sentence a defendant within a reasonable time, a State might fully satisfy due process by making traditional extraordinary legal remedies, such as mandamus, available. Or, much like the federal Speedy Trial Act regulates trials, see 18 U.S.C. § 3161, a State might remedy improper sentencing delay by statute. And a person who sleeps on these remedies, as Betterman did, may simply have no right to complain that his sentencing was delayed. We should await a proper presentation, full briefing, and argument before taking a position on this issue.

* * *

JUSTICE SOTOMAYOR, concurring.

I agree with the Court that petitioner cannot bring a claim under the Speedy Trial Clause for a delay between his guilty plea and his sentencing. As the majority notes, however, a defendant may have "other recourse" for such a delay, "including, in appropriate circumstances, tailored relief under the Due Process Clauses of the Fifth and Fourteenth Amendments." The Court has no reason to consider today the appropriate test for such a Due Process Clause challenge because petitioner has forfeited any such claim. I write separately to emphasize that the question is an open one.

The Due Process Clause is "flexible and calls for such procedural protections as the particular situation demands." Morrissey v. Brewer, 408 U.S. 471 (1972). This Court thus uses different tests to consider whether different kinds of delay run afoul of the Due Process Clause. In evaluating whether a delay in instituting judicial proceedings following a civil forfeiture violated the Due Process Clause, the Court applied the test from Barker v. Wingo, 407 U.S. 514 (1972)—the same test that the Court applies to violations of the Speedy Trial Clause. See United States v. $8,850, 461 U.S. 555, 564 (1983). Under the *Barker* test, courts consider four factors— the length of the delay, the reason for the delay, the defendant's assertion of his right, and prejudice to the defendant. None of the four factors is "either necessary or sufficient," and no one factor has a talismanic quality.

The Montana Supreme Court did not use the *Barker* test in evaluating petitioner's Due Process Clause claim. But it seems to me that the *Barker* factors capture many of the concerns posed in the sentencing delay context and that because the *Barker* test is flexible, it will allow courts to take account of any differences between trial and sentencing delays. The majority of the Circuits in fact use the *Barker* test for that purpose. See United States v. Sanders, 452 F.3d 572, 577 (C.A.6 2006) (collecting cases).

In the appropriate case, I would thus consider the correct test for a Due Process Clause delayed sentencing challenge.

III. CONSTITUTIONALLY BASED PROOF REQUIREMENTS

C. THE SCOPE OF THE REASONABLE DOUBT REQUIREMENT: WHAT IS AN ELEMENT OF THE CRIME?

2. Element of the Crime or Sentencing Factor?

Page 1236. After the headnote on *Ring v. Arizona*, add the following:

Application of Ring v. Arizona: Hurst v. Florida

In Hurst v. Florida, 136 S.Ct. 616 (2016), the Court reviewed a capital proceeding under Florida law, where state law provided that the death penalty was imposed by the judge, and the role of the jury was to provide an "advisory sentence" that the judge must accord great weight when imposing a sentence. To impose the death penalty, the judge was required to find facts that support the aggravating circumstances that warrant that punishment. The Court in *Hurst* found that this system ran afoul of the Sixth Amendment, according to the principles set forth in *Apprendi* and its progeny, including most importantly Ring v. Arizona. Justice Sotomayor, writing for the majority, declared as follows:

> In *Ring,* we concluded that Arizona's capital sentencing scheme violated *Apprendi's* rule because the State allowed a judge to find the facts necessary to sentence a defendant to death. An Arizona jury had convicted Timothy Ring of felony murder. Under state law, Ring could not be sentenced to death, the statutory maximum penalty for first-degree murder, unless further findings were made. Specifically, a judge could sentence Ring to death only after independently finding at least one aggravating circumstance. Ring's judge followed this procedure, found an aggravating circumstance, and sentenced Ring to death.

> The Court had little difficulty concluding that "the required finding of an aggravated circumstance exposed Ring to a greater punishment than that authorized by the jury's guilty verdict." Had Ring's judge not engaged in any factfinding, Ring would have received a life sentence. Ring's death sentence therefore violated his right to have a jury find the facts behind his punishment.

> The analysis the *Ring* Court applied to Arizona's sentencing scheme applies equally to Florida's. Like Arizona at the time of *Ring,* Florida does not require the jury to make the critical findings necessary to impose the death penalty. Rather, Florida requires a judge to find these facts. Although Florida incorporates an advisory jury verdict that Arizona lacked, we have previously made clear that this distinction is immaterial: "It is true that in Florida the jury recommends a sentence, but it does not make specific factual findings with regard to the existence of mitigating or aggravating circumstances and its recommendation is not binding on the trial judge. A Florida trial court no more has the assistance of a jury's findings of fact with respect to sentencing issues than does a trial judge in Arizona." Walton v. Arizona, 497 U.S. 639, 648 (1990).

> As with Timothy Ring, the maximum punishment Timothy Hurst could have received without any judge-made findings was life in prison without parole. As with Ring, a judge increased Hurst's authorized punishment based on her own factfinding. In light of *Ring,* we hold that Hurst's sentence violates the Sixth Amendment.

Justice Breyer concurred in the judgment.

Justice Alito dissented. He argued, as he had in previous cases, that *Apprendi* is inconsistent with the original understanding of the jury trial right. He also noted that the Florida law differed from that struck down in *Ring* in ways that called for a different result:

In *Ring*, the jury found the defendant guilty of felony murder and did no more. It did not make the findings required by the Eighth Amendment before the death penalty may be imposed in a felony-murder case. Nor did the jury find the presence of any aggravating factor, as required for death eligibility under Arizona law. Nor did it consider mitigating factors. And it did not determine whether a capital or noncapital sentence was appropriate. Under that system, the jury played no role in the capital sentencing process.

The Florida system is quite different. In Florida, the jury sits as the initial and primary adjudicator of the factors bearing on the death penalty. After unanimously determining guilt at trial, a Florida jury hears evidence of aggravating and mitigating circumstances. At the conclusion of this separate sentencing hearing, the jury may recommend a death sentence only if it finds that the State has proved one or more aggravating factors beyond a reasonable doubt and only after weighing the aggravating and mitigating factors.

Once the jury has made this decision, the trial court performs what amounts, in practical terms, to a reviewing function. The judge duplicates the steps previously performed by the jury and, while the court can impose a sentence different from that recommended by the jury, the judge must accord the jury's recommendation "great weight." * * * No Florida trial court has overruled a jury's recommendation of a life sentence for more than 15 years.

Under the Florida system, the jury plays a critically important role. Our decision in *Ring* did not decide whether this procedure violates the Sixth Amendment, and I would not extend *Ring* to cover the Florida system.

IV. TRIAL BY JURY

D. JURY SELECTION AND COMPOSITION

5. The Use of Peremptory Challenges

b. *Constitutional Limits on Peremptory Challenges*

Page 1322. After the headnote on *Snyder v. Louisiana*, add the following:

Another Fact-Intensive Review of Peremptory Challenges: Foster v. Chatman

FOSTER V. CHATMAN
Supreme Court of the United States, 2016.
136 S.Ct. 1737.

CHIEF JUSTICE ROBERTS delivered the opinion of the Court.

Petitioner Timothy Foster was convicted of capital murder and sentenced to death in a Georgia court. During jury selection at his trial, the State exercised peremptory strikes against all four black prospective jurors qualified to serve. Foster argued that the State's use of those strikes was racially motivated, in violation of our decision in Batson v. Kentucky, 476 U.S. 79 (1986). The trial court and the Georgia Supreme Court rejected Foster's *Batson* claim.

Foster then sought a writ of habeas corpus from the Superior Court of Butts County, Georgia, renewing his *Batson* objection. That court denied relief, and the Georgia Supreme Court declined to issue the Certificate of Probable Cause necessary under Georgia law for Foster to pursue an appeal. We granted certiorari and now reverse.

I

On the morning of August 28, 1986, police found Queen Madge White dead on the floor of her home in Rome, Georgia. White, a 79-year-old widow, had been beaten, sexually assaulted, and strangled to death. Her home had been burglarized. Timothy Foster subsequently confessed to killing White, and White's possessions were recovered from Foster's home and from Foster's two sisters. The State indicted Foster on charges of malice murder and burglary. He faced the death penalty.

District Attorney Stephen Lanier and Assistant District Attorney Douglas Pullen represented the State at trial. Jury selection proceeded in two phases: removals for cause and peremptory strikes. In the first phase, each prospective juror completed a detailed questionnaire, which the prosecution and defense reviewed. The trial court then conducted a juror-by-juror *voir dire* of approximately 90 prospective jurors. Throughout this process, both parties had the opportunity to question the prospective jurors and lodge challenges for cause. This first phase whittled the list down to 42 "qualified" prospective jurors. Five were black.

In the second phase, known as the "striking of the jury," both parties had the opportunity to exercise peremptory strikes against the array of qualified jurors. Pursuant to state law, the prosecution had ten such strikes; Foster twenty. The process worked as follows: The clerk of the court called the qualified prospective jurors one by one, and the State had the option to exercise one of its peremptory strikes. If the State declined to strike a particular prospective juror, Foster then had the opportunity to do so. If neither party exercised a peremptory strike, the prospective juror was selected for service. This second phase continued until 12 jurors had been accepted.

The morning the second phase began, Shirley Powell, one of the five qualified black prospective jurors, notified the court that she had just learned that one of her close friends was related to Foster. The court removed Powell for cause. That left four black prospective jurors: Eddie Hood, Evelyn Hardge, Mary Turner, and Marilyn Garrett.

The striking of the jury then commenced. The State exercised nine of its ten allotted peremptory strikes, removing all four of the remaining black prospective jurors. Foster immediately lodged a *Batson* challenge. The trial court rejected the objection and empaneled the jury. The jury convicted Foster and sentenced him to death.

[After his state appeals were rejected, Foster sought a writ of habeas corpus from the Superior Court of Butts County, Georgia, again pressing his *Batson* claim.] While the state habeas proceeding was pending, Foster filed a series of requests under the Georgia Open Records Act, seeking access to the State's file from his 1987 trial. In response, the State disclosed documents related to the jury selection at that trial. Over the State's objections, the state habeas court admitted those documents into evidence. They included the following:

(1) Four copies of the jury venire list. On each copy, the names of the black prospective jurors were highlighted in bright green. A legend in the upper right corner of the lists indicated that the green highlighting "represents Blacks." The letter "B" also appeared next to each black prospective juror's name. According to the testimony of Clayton Lundy, an investigator who assisted the prosecution during jury selection, these highlighted venire lists were circulated in the district attorney's office during jury selection. That allowed "everybody in the office"—approximately "10 to 12 people," including "[s]ecretaries, investigators, [and] district attorneys"—to look at them, share information, and

contribute thoughts on whether the prosecution should strike a particular juror. * * *

(2) A draft of an affidavit that had been prepared by Lundy "at Lanier's request" for submission to the state trial court in response to Foster's motion for a new trial. The typed draft detailed Lundy's views on ten black prospective jurors, stating "[m]y evaluation of the jurors are a[s] follows." Under the name of one of those jurors, Lundy had written:

> "If it comes down to having to pick one of the black jurors, [this one] might be okay. This is solely my opinion. . . . Upon picking of the jury after listening to all of the jurors we had to pick, if we had to pick a black juror I recommend that [this juror] be one of the jurors."

That text had been crossed out by hand; the version of the affidavit filed with the trial court did not contain the crossed-out language. Lundy testified that he "guess[ed]" the redactions had been done by Lanier.

(3) Three handwritten notes on black prospective jurors Eddie Hood, Louise Wilson, and Corrie Hinds. Annotations denoted those individuals as "B# 1," "B# 2," and "B# 3," respectively. Lundy testified that these were examples of the type of "notes that the team—the State would take down during voir dire to help select the jury in Mr. Foster's case."

(4) A typed list of the qualified jurors remaining after *voir dire*. It included "Ns" next to ten jurors' names, which Lundy told the state habeas court "signif[ied] the ten jurors that the State had strikes for during jury selection." Such an "N" appeared alongside the names of all five qualified black prospective jurors. The file also included a handwritten version of the same list, with the same markings. Lundy testified that he was unsure who had prepared or marked the two lists.

(5) A handwritten document titled "definite NO's," listing six names. The first five were those of the five qualified black prospective jurors. The State concedes that either Lanier or Pullen compiled the list, which Lundy testified was "used for preparation in jury selection."

(6) A handwritten document titled "Church of Christ." A notation on the document read: "NO. No Black Church."

(7) The questionnaires that had been completed by several of the black prospective jurors. On each one, the juror's response indicating his or her race had been circled.

In response to the admission of this evidence, the State introduced short affidavits from Lanier and Pullen. Lanier's affidavit stated:

> "I did not make any of the highlighted marks on the jury venire list. It was common practice in the office to highlight in yellow those jurors who had prior case experience. I did not instruct anyone to make the green highlighted marks. I reaffirm my testimony made during the

motion for new trial hearing as to how I used my peremptory jury strikes and the basis and reasons for those strikes."

Pullen's affidavit averred:

> "I did not make any of the highlighted marks on the jury venire list, and I did not instruct anyone else to make the highlighted marks. I did not rely on the highlighted jury venire list in making my decision on how to use my peremptory strikes."

Neither affidavit provided further explanation of the documents, and neither Lanier nor Pullen testified in the habeas proceeding.

After considering the evidence, the state habeas court denied relief. * * * The Georgia Supreme Court denied Foster the "Certificate of Probable Cause" necessary under state law for him to pursue an appeal, determining that his claim had no "arguable merit." We granted certiorari.

II

[The Chief Justice concluded that the state court determination was not based on an adequate and independent state ground, and so the Supreme Court had jurisdiction to decide the constitutional *Batson* claim.]

III

A

The Constitution forbids striking even a single prospective juror for a discriminatory purpose. Our decision in Batson v. Kentucky provides a three-step process for determining when a strike is discriminatory:

> First, a defendant must make a prima facie showing that a peremptory challenge has been exercised on the basis of race; second, if that showing has been made, the prosecution must offer a race-neutral basis for striking the juror in question; and third, in light of the parties' submissions, the trial court must determine whether the defendant has shown purposeful discrimination.

Both parties agree that Foster has demonstrated a prima facie case, and that the prosecutors have offered race-neutral reasons for their strikes. We therefore address only *Batson's* third step. That step turns on factual determinations, and, in the absence of exceptional circumstances, we defer to state court factual findings unless we conclude that they are clearly erroneous.

* * *

B

Foster centers his *Batson* claim on the strikes of two black prospective jurors, Marilyn Garrett and Eddie Hood. We turn first to Marilyn Garrett. According to Lanier, on the morning that the State was to use its strikes he had not yet made up his mind to remove Garrett. Rather, he decided to strike her only after learning that he would not need to use a strike on another black prospective juror, Shirley Powell, who was excused for cause that morning.

Ultimately, Lanier did strike Garrett. In justifying that strike to the trial court, he articulated a laundry list of reasons. Specifically, Lanier objected to Garrett because she: (1) worked with disadvantaged youth in her job as a teacher's aide; (2) kept looking at the ground during *voir dire*; (3) gave short and curt answers during *voir dire*; (4) appeared nervous; (5) was too young; (6) misrepresented her familiarity with the location of the crime; (7) failed to disclose that her cousin had been arrested on a drug charge; (8) was divorced; (9) had two children and two jobs; (10) was asked few questions by the defense; and (11) did not ask to be excused from jury service.

* * * On their face, Lanier's justifications for the strike seem reasonable enough. Our independent examination of the record, however, reveals that much of the reasoning provided by Lanier has no grounding in fact.

Lanier's misrepresentations to the trial court began with an elaborate explanation of how he ultimately came to strike Garrett:

> "[T]he prosecution considered this juror [to have] the most potential to choose from out of the four remaining blacks in the 42 [member] panel venire. However, a system of events took place on the morning of jury selection that caused the excusal of this juror. The [S]tate had, in his jury notes, *listed this juror as questionable*. The four negative challenges were allocated for Hardge, Hood, Turner and Powell. . . . But on the morning of jury selection, Juror Powell was excused for cause with no objections by [d]efense counsel. She was replaced by Juror Cadle [who] was acceptable to the State. This left the State with an additional strike it had not anticipated or allocated. Consequently, the State had to choose between [white] Juror Blackmon or Juror Garrett, the only two *questionable* jurors the State had left on the list."

Lanier then offered an extensive list of reasons for striking Garrett and explained that "[t]hese factors, with no reference to race, were considered by the prosecutor in this particular case to result in a juror less desirable from the prosecutor's viewpoint than Juror Blackmon." Lanier then compared Blackmon to Garrett. In contrast to Garrett, Juror Blackmon

> "was 46 years old, married 13 years to her husband who works at GE, buying her own home and [was recommended by a third party to] this prosecutor. She was no longer employed at Northwest Georgia Regional Hospital and she attended Catholic church on an irregular basis. She did not hesitate when answering the questions concerning

the death penalty, had good eye contact with the prosecutor and gave good answers on the insanity issue. She was perceived by the prosecutor as having a stable home environment, of the right age and no association with any disadvantaged youth organizations."

Lanier concluded that "the chances of [Blackmon] returning a death sentence were greater when all these factors were considered than Juror Garrett. Consequently, Juror Garrett was excused."

The trial court accepted this explanation in denying Foster's motion for a new trial. But the predicate for the State's account—that Garrett was "listed" by the prosecution as "questionable," making that strike a last-minute race-neutral decision—was false.

During jury selection, the State went first. As a consequence, the defense could accept any prospective juror not struck by the State without any further opportunity for the State to use a strike against that prospective juror. Accordingly, the State had to "pretty well select the ten specific people [it] intend[ed] to strike" in advance. The record evidence shows that Garrett was one of those "ten specific people."

That much is evident from the "definite NO's" list in the prosecution's file. Garrett's name appeared on that list, which the State concedes was written by one of the prosecutors. That list belies Lanier's assertion that the State considered allowing Garrett to serve. The title of the list meant what it said: Garrett was a "*definite* NO." The State from the outset was intent on ensuring that *none* of the jurors on that list would serve.

The first five names on the "definite NO's" list were Eddie Hood, Evelyn Hardge, Shirley Powell, Marilyn Garrett, and Mary Turner. All were black. The State struck each one except Powell (who, as discussed, was excused for cause at the last minute—though the prosecution informed the trial court that the "State was not, under any circumstances, going to take [Powell]." Only in the number six position did a white prospective juror appear, and she had informed the court during *voir dire* that she could not "say positively" that she could impose the death penalty even if the evidence warranted it. In short, contrary to the prosecution's submissions, the State's resolve to strike Garrett was never in doubt.

The State attempts to explain away the contradiction between the "definite NO's" list and Lanier's statements to the trial court as an example of a prosecutor merely "misspeak[ing]." But this was not some off-the-cuff remark; it was an intricate story expounded by the prosecution in writing, laid out over three single-spaced pages in a brief filed with the trial court.

Moreover, several of Lanier's reasons for *why* he chose Garrett over Blackmon are similarly contradicted by the record. Lanier told the court, for example, that he struck Garrett because "the defense did not ask her questions about" pertinent trial issues such as her thoughts on "insanity" or "alcohol," or "much questions on publicity." But the trial transcripts reveal that the defense asked her several questions on all three topics.

Still other explanations given by the prosecution, while not explicitly contradicted by the record, are difficult to credit because the State willingly accepted white jurors with the same traits that supposedly rendered Garrett an unattractive juror. Lanier told the trial court that he struck Garrett because she was divorced. But he declined to strike three out of the four prospective white jurors who were also divorced. Additionally, Lanier claimed that he struck Garrett because she was too young, and the "State was looking for older jurors that would not easily identify with the defendant." Yet Garrett was 34, and the State declined to strike eight white prospective jurors under the age of 36. Two of those white jurors served on the jury; one of those two was only 21 years old.

Lanier also explained to the trial court that he struck Garrett because he "felt that she was less than truthful" in her answers in *voir dire*. Specifically, the State pointed the trial court to the following exchange:

> "[Court]: Are you familiar with the neighborhood where [the victim] lived, North Rome?"
>
> "[Garrett]: No."

Lanier, in explaining the strike, told the trial court that in apparent contradiction to that exchange (which represented the only time that Garrett was asked about the topic during *voir dire*), he had "noted that [Garrett] attended Main High School, which is only two blocks from where [the victim] lived and certainly in the neighborhood. She denied any knowledge of the area."

We have no quarrel with the State's general assertion that it "could not trust someone who gave materially untruthful answers on voir dire." But even this otherwise legitimate reason is difficult to credit in light of the State's acceptance of (white) juror Duncan. Duncan gave practically the same answer as Garrett did during *voir dire*:

> "[Court]: Are you familiar with the neighborhood in which [the victim] live [d]?"
>
> "[Duncan]: No. I live in Atteiram Heights, but it's not—I'm not familiar with up there, you know."

But, as Lanier was aware, Duncan's "residence [was] less than a half a mile from the murder scene" and her workplace was located less than 250 yards away.

In sum, in evaluating the strike of Garrett, we are not faced with a single isolated misrepresentation.

C

We turn next to the strike of Hood. According to Lanier, Hood "was exactly what [the State] was looking for in terms of age, between forty and fifty, good employment and married." The prosecution nonetheless struck Hood, giving eight reasons for doing so. Hood: (1) had a son who was the same age as the defendant and who had previously been convicted of a crime; (2) had a wife who worked in food service at the local mental health institution; (3) had experienced food poisoning during *voir dire*; (4) was slow in responding to death penalty questions; (5) was a member of the Church of Christ; (6) had a brother who counseled drug offenders; (7) was not asked enough questions by the defense during *voir dire*; and (8) asked to be excused from jury service. An examination of the record, however, convinces us that many of these justifications cannot be credited.

As an initial matter, the prosecution's principal reasons for the strike shifted over time, suggesting that those reasons may be pretextual. In response to Foster's pre-trial *Batson* challenge, District Attorney Lanier noted all eight reasons, but explained:

> "*The only thing I was concerned about,* and I will state it for the record. He has an eighteen year old son which is about the same age as the defendant.

> "In my experience prosecuting over twenty-five murder cases . . . individuals having the same son as [a] defendant who is charged with murder [have] serious reservations and are more sympathetic and lean toward that particular person.

* * *

But by the time of Foster's subsequent motion for a new trial, Lanier's focus had shifted. He still noted the similarities between Hood's son and Foster, but that was no longer the key reason behind the strike. Lanier instead told the court that his paramount concern was Hood's membership in the Church of Christ: "The Church of Christ people, while they may not take a formal stand against the death penalty, they are very, very reluctant to vote for the death penalty." Hood's religion, Lanier now explained, was the most important factor behind the strike: "I evaluated the whole Eddie Hood. . . . And *the bottom line* on Eddie Hood is the Church of Christ affiliation."

Of course it is possible that Lanier simply misspoke in one of the two proceedings. But even if that were so, we would expect at least *one* of the two purportedly principal justifications for the strike to withstand closer scrutiny. Neither does.

Take Hood's son. If Darrell Hood's age was the issue, why did the State accept (white) juror Billy Graves, who had a 17-year-old son? And why did the State accept (white) juror Martha Duncan, even though she had a 20-year-old son?

The comparison between Hood and Graves is particularly salient. When the prosecution asked Hood if Foster's age would be a factor for him in sentencing, he answered "None whatsoever." Graves, on the other hand, answered the same question "probably so." Yet the State struck Hood and accepted Graves.

The State responds that Duncan and Graves were not similar to Hood because Hood's son had been convicted of theft, while Graves's and Duncan's sons had not. Lanier had described Darrell Hood's conviction to the trial court as being for "basically the same thing that this defendant is charged with." Nonsense. Hood's son had received a 12-month suspended sentence for stealing hubcaps from a car in a mall parking lot five years earlier. Foster was charged with capital murder of a 79-year-old widow after a brutal sexual assault. The "implausible" and "fantastic" assertion that the two had been charged with "basically the same thing" supports our conclusion that the focus on Hood's son can only be regarded as pretextual.

The prosecution's second principal justification for striking Hood—his affiliation with the Church of Christ, and that church's alleged teachings on the death penalty—fares no better. Hood asserted no fewer than four times during *voir dire* that he could impose the death penalty. A prosecutor is entitled to disbelieve a juror's *voir dire* answers, of course. But the record persuades us that Hood's race, and not his religious affiliation, was Lanier's true motivation.

The first indication to that effect is Lanier's mischaracterization of the record. On multiple occasions, Lanier asserted to the trial court that three white prospective jurors who were members of the Church of Christ had been struck for cause due to their opposition to the death penalty. That was not true. One of those prospective jurors was excused before even being questioned during *voir dire* because she was five-and-a-half months pregnant. Another was excused by the agreement of both parties because her answers on the death penalty made it difficult to ascertain her precise views on capital punishment. And the judge found cause to dismiss the third because she had already formed an opinion about Foster's guilt.

The prosecution's file fortifies our conclusion that any reliance on Hood's religion was pretextual. The file contains a handwritten document titled "Church of Christ." The document notes that the church "doesn't take a stand on [the] Death Penalty," and that the issue is "left for each individual member." The document then states: "NO. NO Black Church." The State tries to downplay the significance of this document by emphasizing that the document's author is unknown. That uncertainty is pertinent. But we think the document is nonetheless entitled to significant weight, especially given that it is consistent with our serious doubts about the prosecution's account of the strike.

Many of the State's secondary justifications similarly come undone when subjected to scrutiny. Lanier told the trial court that Hood "appeared to be confused and slow in responding to questions concerning his views on the death penalty." As previously noted, however, Hood unequivocally voiced his willingness to impose the death penalty, and a white juror who showed similar confusion served on the jury. According to the record, such confusion was not uncommon.

Lanier also stated that he struck Hood because Hood's wife worked at Northwest Regional Hospital as a food services supervisor. That hospital, Lanier explained, "deals a lot with mentally disturbed, mentally ill people," and so people associated with it tend "to be more sympathetic to the underdog." But Lanier expressed no such concerns about white juror Blackmon, who had worked at the same hospital. Blackmon, as noted, served on the jury.

Lanier additionally stated that he struck Hood because the defense "didn't ask [Hood] any question[s] about the age of the defendant," "his feelings about criminal responsibility involved in insanity," or "publicity." Yet again, the trial transcripts clearly indicate the contrary. See 2 Trial Transcript 280 ("Q: Is age a factor to you in trying to determine whether or not a defendant should receive a life sentence or a death sentence? A: None whatsoever."); *ibid.* ("Q: Do you have any feeling about the insanity defense? A: Do I have any opinion about that? I have not formed any opinion about that."); *id.,* at 281 ("Q: Okay. The publicity that you have heard, has that publicity affected your ability to sit as a juror in this case and be fair and impartial to the defendant? A: No, it has no effect on me.").

D

As we explained in Miller-El v. Dretke, [Text, page 1322] "[i]f a prosecutor's proffered reason for striking a black panelist applies just as well to an otherwise-similar nonblack [panelist] who is permitted to serve, that is evidence tending to prove purposeful discrimination." 545 U.S. 231, 241 (2005). With respect to both Garrett and Hood, such evidence is compelling. But that is not all. There are also the shifting explanations, the misrepresentations of the record, and the persistent focus on race in the prosecution's file. Considering all of the circumstantial evidence that "bear[s] upon the issue of racial animosity," we are left with the firm conviction that the strikes of Garrett and Hood were motivated in substantial part by discriminatory intent.

IV

Throughout all stages of this litigation, the State has strenuously objected that "race [was] not a factor" in its jury selection strategy. Indeed, at times the State has been downright indignant. See Trial Record 444 ("The Defenses's [*sic*] misapplication of the law and erroneous distortion of the facts are an attempt to discredit the prosecutor. . . . The State and this community demand an apology.")

The contents of the prosecution's file, however, plainly belie the State's claim that it exercised its strikes in a "color-blind" manner. The sheer number of references to race in that file is arresting. The State, however, claims that things are not quite as bad as they seem. The focus on black prospective jurors, it contends, does not indicate any attempt to exclude them from the jury. It instead reflects an effort to ensure that the State was "thoughtful and non-discriminatory in [its] consideration of black prospective jurors [and] to develop and maintain detailed information on those prospective jurors in order to properly defend against any suggestion that decisions regarding [its] selections were pretextual." *Batson*, after all, had come down only months before Foster's trial. The prosecutors, according to the State, were uncertain what sort of showing might be demanded of them and wanted to be prepared.

This argument falls flat. To begin, it reeks of afterthought, having never before been made in the nearly 30-year history of this litigation: not in the trial court, not in the state habeas court, and not even in the State's brief in opposition to Foster's petition for certiorari.

In addition, the focus on race in the prosecution's file plainly demonstrates a concerted effort to keep black prospective jurors off the jury. The State argues that it "was actively seeking a black juror." But this claim is not credible. An "N" appeared next to each of the black prospective jurors' names on the jury venire list. An "N" was also noted next to the name of each black prospective juror on the list of the 42 qualified prospective jurors; each of those names also appeared on the "definite NO's" list. And a draft affidavit from the prosecution's investigator stated his view that "[i]f it comes down to *having to pick* one of the black jurors, [Marilyn] Garrett, might be okay." Such references are inconsistent with attempts to actively seek a black juror.

The State's new argument today does not dissuade us from the conclusion that its prosecutors were motivated in substantial part by race when they struck Garrett and Hood from the jury 30 years ago. Two peremptory strikes on the basis of race are two more than the Constitution allows.

The order of the Georgia Supreme Court is reversed, and the case is remanded for further proceedings not inconsistent with this opinion.

It is so ordered.

[Justice Alito's opinion concurring in the judgment is omitted.]

* * *

JUSTICE THOMAS, dissenting.

* * *

Because the adjudication of his *Batson* claim is, at bottom, a credibility determination, we owe "great deference" to the state court's initial finding that the prosecution's race-neutral reasons for striking veniremen Eddie Hood and Marilyn Garrett were credible. On a record far less cold than today's, the Supreme Court of Georgia long ago (on direct appeal) rejected that claim by giving great deference to the trial court's credibility determinations. Evaluating the strike of venireman Hood, the court highlighted that his son had been convicted of a misdemeanor and that both his demeanor and religious affiliation indicated that he might be reluctant to impose the death penalty. And the prosecution reasonably struck venireman Garrett, according to the court, because it feared that she would sympathize with Foster given her work with "low-income, underprivileged children" and because she was "related to someone with a drug or alcohol problem." That should have been the last word on Foster's *Batson* claim.

But now, Foster has access to the prosecution's file. By allowing Foster to relitigate his *Batson* claim by bringing this newly discovered evidence to the fore, the Court upends *Batson*'s deferential framework. Foster's new evidence does not justify this Court's reassessment of who was telling the truth nearly three decades removed from *voir dire.*

* * *

The notion that this "newly discovered evidence" could warrant relitigation of a *Batson* claim is flabbergasting. * * * Time and again, we have said that the credibility of the attorney is best judged by the trial court and can be overturned only if it is clearly erroneous.

But the Court today invites state prisoners to go searching for new "evidence" by demanding the files of the prosecutors who long ago convicted them. If those prisoners succeed, then apparently this Court's doors are open to conduct the credibility determination anew. * * * I cannot go along with that sort of sandbagging of state courts. New evidence should not justify the relitigation of *Batson* claims. * * *

Today, without first seeking clarification from Georgia's highest court that it decided a federal question, the Court affords a death-row inmate another opportunity to relitigate his long-final conviction. In few other circumstances could I imagine the Court spilling so much ink over a factbound claim arising from a state postconviction proceeding. It was the trial court that observed the veniremen firsthand and heard them answer the prosecution's questions, and its evaluation of the prosecution's credibility on this point is certainly far better than this Court's nearly 30 years later. I respectfully dissent.

F. THE TRIAL JUDGE AND THE RIGHT TO JURY TRIAL

3. Challenges Against the Judge

Page 1337. At the end of the section, add the following cases:

Judge with a Conflict of Interest Due to Previous Role as Prosecutor: Williams v. Pennsylvania

In Williams v. Pennsylvania, 136 S.Ct. 1899 (2016), the Court held that the due process rights of a capital defendant were violated, when one of the Justices of the State Supreme Court who denied his *Brady* claim had previously served as the district attorney who made the decision on behalf of the state to seek the death penalty. The Court determined that the Due Process Clause required recusal of the State Supreme Court justice under these circumstances. Justice Kennedy, writing for five members of the Court, first discussed the protection afforded by the Due Process Clause against judicial bias:

> Due process guarantees "an absence of actual bias" on the part of a judge. Bias is easy to attribute to others and difficult to discern in oneself. To establish an enforceable and workable framework, the Court's precedents apply an objective standard that, in the usual case, avoids having to determine whether actual bias is present. The Court asks not whether a judge harbors an actual, subjective bias, but instead whether, as an objective matter, "the average judge in his position is likely to be neutral, or whether there is an unconstitutional potential for bias." Of particular relevance to the instant case, the Court has determined that an unconstitutional potential for bias exists when the same person serves as both accuser and adjudicator in a case. This objective risk of bias is reflected in the due process maxim that "no man can be a judge in his own case and no man is permitted to try cases where he has an interest in the outcome."

> The due process guarantee that "no man can be a judge in his own case" would have little substance if it did not disqualify a former prosecutor from sitting in judgment of a prosecution in which he or she had made a critical decision. * * * No attorney is more integral to the accusatory process than a prosecutor who participates in a major adversary decision. When a judge has served as an advocate for the State in the very case the court is now asked to adjudicate, a serious question arises as to whether the judge, even with the most diligent effort, could set aside any personal interest in the outcome. There is, furthermore, a risk that the judge would be so psychologically wedded to his or her previous position as a prosecutor that the judge would consciously or unconsciously avoid the appearance of having erred or

changed position. In addition, the judge's own personal knowledge and impression of the case, acquired through his or her role in the prosecution, may carry far more weight with the judge than the parties' arguments to the court.

Justice Kennedy found the conflict of interest to be particularly potent in this case because the *Brady* claim accused a prosecutor that the state justice had previously supervised, of suppressing materially exculpatory evidence. Justice Kennedy concluded that "Chief Justice Castille's significant, personal involvement in a critical decision in Williams's case gave rise to an unacceptable risk of actual bias. This risk so endangered the appearance of neutrality that his participation in the case must be forbidden if the guarantee of due process is to be adequately implemented."

Chief Justice Roberts, joined by Justice Alito, dissented. He argued the Due Process Clause was not violated because the state justice's decision—to seek the death penalty—was not related to the decision to reject the *Brady* claim. Justice Thomas wrote a separate dissent in which he concluded as follows:

> This is not a case about the "accused." It is a case about the due process rights of the already convicted. Whatever those rights might be, they do not include policing alleged violations of state codes of judicial ethics in postconviction proceedings. The Due Process Clause does not require any and all conceivable procedural protections that Members of this Court think Western liberal democratic government ought to guarantee to its citizens.

Showing of Actual Bias Not Required: Rippo v. Baker

In the per curiam decision in Rippo v. Baker, 137 S.Ct. 905 (2017) the Court considered the defendant's claim of a due process violation because his trial judge was the target of a criminal investigation in which the District Attorney was taking part. The state courts ruled against the defendant on the ground that his allegations "did not support the assertion that the trial judge was actually biased [against him] in this case."

The Supreme Court remanded because the Nevada courts' requirement of showing "actual bias" was too strict. The Court explained as follows:

> Under our precedents, the Due Process Clause may sometimes demand recusal even when a judge has no actual bias. Recusal is required when, objectively speaking, the probability of actual bias on the part of the judge or decisionmaker is too high to be constitutionally tolerable. See Williams v. Pennsylvania, 136 S.Ct. 1899, 1905 (2016) ("The Court asks not whether a judge harbors an actual, subjective bias, but instead whether, as an objective matter, the average judge in

his position is likely to be neutral, or whether there is an unconstitutional potential for bias"). Our decision in *Bracy* [Text page 1336] is not to the contrary: Although we explained that the petitioner there had pointed to facts suggesting actual, subjective bias, we did not hold that a litigant must show as a matter of course that a judge was actually biased in the litigant's case—much less that he must do so when, as here, he does not allege a theory of "camouflaging bias." The Nevada Supreme Court did not ask the question our precedents require: whether, considering all the circumstances alleged, the risk of bias was too high to be constitutionally tolerable. As a result, we * * * vacate the judgment below and remand the case for further proceedings not inconsistent with this opinion

VII. THE RIGHT TO EFFECTIVE ASSISTANCE OF COUNSEL

A. INEFFECTIVENESS AND PREJUDICE

3. Assessing Counsel's Effectiveness

Page 1412. Add the following two headnotes at the end of the section:

Failure to Challenge a Widely Accepted Analysis That Is Later Discredited: Maryland v. Kulbicki

In Maryland v. Kulbicki, 136 S.Ct. 2 (2015) (per curiam), the Court summarily reversed the Maryland Court of Appeals' grant of habeas corpus relief from a state murder conviction. Kulbicki argued that his lawyers were ineffective for failing to challenge expert testimony that the bullet fragment found in the victim's brain matched a bullet fragment found in Kulbicki's truck. The expert employed the "comparative bullet lead analysis" (CBLA) that was widely used at the time of trial. Eleven years later, that process had fallen out of favor and was found by the courts to be not generally accepted by the scientific community. The Court held that "[c]ounsel did not perform deficiently by dedicating their time and focus to elements of the defense that did not involve poking methodological holes in a then-uncontroversial mode of ballistics analysis." The Court added that it was highly unlikely that due diligence would have uncovered an obscure report—prepared four years before the defendant's trial by the same FBI agent who testified for the State—suggesting that CBLA was an invalid way to compare bullet fragments. It concluded that the lower court had "demanded something close to 'perfect advocacy'—far more than the 'reasonable competence' the right to counsel guarantees."

Insufficient Deference Given by Reviewing Court to Counsel's Decision Not to Object: Woods v. Etherton

In Woods v. Etherton, 136 S.Ct. 1149 (2016), the defendant was convicted of drug offenses. At his trial the court admitted evidence of an anonymous tip to law enforcement that led to his arrest. The defendant had been arrested while driving a car with a passenger, and a search of the car uncovered cocaine. The officers made the arrest after receiving an anonymous tip was that two men were driving in a car carrying cocaine. The defendant was convicted and argued that his trial counsel was ineffective for failing to object to admission of the tip on the ground that it violated his right to confrontation. The Court of Appeals, on habeas review, agreed with the defendant—but the Supreme Court reversed that ruling in a unanimous per curiam decision. The Court held that the Court of Appeals gave insufficient deference to the state court's determination that the anonymous tips were properly admitted for the non-hearsay purpose of explaining the context of the police investigation. The Court stated that a "fairminded jurist" could conclude "that repetition of the tip did not establish that the uncontested facts it conveyed were submitted for their truth. Such a jurist might reach that conclusion by placing weight on the fact that the truth of the facts was not disputed. No precedent of this Court clearly forecloses that view." Therefore trial counsel could not be found ineffective for failing to press the debatable constitutional question. Moreover, the Court concluded that "it would not be objectively unreasonable for a fair-minded judge to conclude" that the failure to raise the Confrontation claim "was not due to incompetence but because the facts of the tip were uncontested and in any event consistent with Etherton's defense"—that the drugs belonged to the passenger.

5.   Assessing Prejudice

Page 1427. Add after the headnote and discussion of Smith v. Spisak:

Defense's Calling of Expert in the Penalty Phase of a Capital Trial, Who Testified That the Defendant Was Dangerous Because He Was Black, Was Ineffective and Prejudicial: Buck v. Davis

In Buck v. Davis, 137 S.Ct. 759 (2017), the future dangerousness of the defendant was contested by the parties in the penalty phase of Buck's trial for capital murder. The defense counsel called a psychologist, who testified that Buck was unlikely to act violently in the future, because his violent acts were triggered by romantic relationships with women, which presumably he wouldn't have when imprisoned for life. But defense counsel also asked the expert about the assertion in his report regarding "statistical factors"—including an assertion that a black person (like Buck) is more likely to be dangerous than a white person. The expert then testified to this belief on both direct and cross-examination. Buck was sentenced to death.

The Supreme Court vacated the death sentence in an opinion by Chief Justice Roberts, on the ground that defense counsel's decision to invite the defense expert to testify about a supposed statistical connection between race and future dangerousness was ineffective and prejudicial.

The Court found little trouble in concluding that defense counsel acted ineffectively. The Chief Justice concluded as follows:

> Given that the jury had to make a finding of future dangerousness before it could impose a death sentence, Dr. Quijano's report said, in effect, that the color of Buck's skin made him more deserving of execution. It would be patently unconstitutional for a state to argue that a defendant is liable to be a future danger because of his race. No competent defense attorney would introduce such evidence about his own client.

The more difficult question was whether Buck was prejudiced by counsel's decision, or as the Court put it, "whether Buck had demonstrated a reasonable probability that, without Dr. Quijano's testimony on race, at least one juror would have harbored a reasonable doubt about whether Buck was likely to be violent in the future." The state argued that the jury would have sentenced Buck to death anyway, given the brutality of the crime and his lack of remorse. But Chief Judge Roberts observed that the state had to prove future dangerousness beyond a reasonable doubt, and the brutality of the crime and lack of remorse did not necessarily prove that Buck would be dangerous in the future. He asserted that the most important evidence about future dangerousness came improperly from the defendant's expert. The Chief Justice explained as follows:

> Deciding the key issue of Buck's dangerousness involved an unusual inquiry. The jurors were not asked to determine a historical fact concerning Buck's conduct, but to render a predictive judgment inevitably entailing a degree of speculation. Buck, all agreed, had committed acts of terrible violence. Would he do so again?

> Buck's prior violent acts had occurred outside of prison, and within the context of romantic relationships with women. If the jury did not impose a death sentence, Buck would be sentenced to life in prison, and no such romantic relationship would be likely to arise. A jury could conclude that those changes would minimize the prospect of future dangerousness.

> But one thing would never change: the color of Buck's skin. Buck would always be black. And according to Dr. Quijano, that immutable characteristic carried with it an "[i]ncreased probability" of future

violence. Here was hard statistical evidence—from an expert—to guide an otherwise speculative inquiry.

And it was potent evidence. Dr. Quijano's testimony appealed to a powerful racial stereotype—that of black men as "violence prone." In combination with the substance of the jury's inquiry, this created something of a perfect storm. Dr. Quijano's opinion coincided precisely with a particularly noxious strain of racial prejudice, which itself coincided precisely with the central question at sentencing. The effect of this unusual confluence of factors was to provide support for making a decision on life or death on the basis of race.

This effect was heightened due to the source of the testimony. Dr. Quijano took the stand as a medical expert bearing the court's imprimatur. The jury learned at the outset of his testimony that he held a doctorate in clinical psychology, had conducted evaluations in some 70 capital murder cases, and had been appointed by the trial judge (at public expense) to evaluate Buck. Reasonable jurors might well have valued his opinion concerning the central question before them.

The Chief Justice conceded that the expert's testimony about race and future dangerousness was brief, but concluded that "when a jury hears expert testimony that expressly makes a defendant's race directly pertinent on the question of life or death, the impact of that evidence cannot be measured simply by how much air time it received at trial or how many pages it occupies in the record. Some toxins can be deadly in small doses."

Finally, the Chief Justice rejected the argument that prejudice was minimized because the objectionable testimony came at the hands of the defense, rather than the prosecution:

In fact, the distinction could well cut the other way. A prosecutor is seeking a conviction. Jurors understand this and may reasonably be expected to evaluate the government's evidence and arguments in light of its motivations. When a defendant's own lawyer puts in the offending evidence, it is in the nature of an admission against interest, more likely to be taken at face value. The effect of Dr. Quijano's testimony on Buck's sentencing cannot be dismissed as "*de minimis.*" Buck has demonstrated prejudice.

Justice Thomas dissented, arguing that evidence of the heinousness of the crime and the defendant's clear lack of remorse were sufficient to support the jury's finding of future dangerousness.

6.   Per Se Ineffectiveness and Prejudice

Page 1434. Add the following headnote at the end of the section:

Absence of Counsel for Ten Minutes During Presentation of Evidence Unrelated to the Defendant Is Not Clearly Per Se Prejudicial Under Cronic: *Woods v. Donald*

In Woods v. Donald, 135 S.Ct. 1372 (2015) (per curiam), lower federal courts on habeas held that Donald was denied his right to effective assistance of counsel when his attorney was absent for approximately ten minutes during Donald's joint trial with two other defendants. Under the relevant statute governing habeas review, the federal court can grant relief only if the state court has violated clearly established federal law as determined by the Supreme Court. 28 U.S.C. § 2254(d)(1). The question for the Supreme Court was whether, under its case law, the absence of counsel for that ten minute period clearly constituted a deprivation of the right to effective assistance of counsel.

The lower courts had relied on United States v. Cronic, 466 U.S. 648 (1984) to find a violation, but the Supreme Court found that *Cronic* did not clearly control the fact situation presented. In this case, Donald's defense counsel absented himself from the government's presentation of a chart chronicling phone calls that did not include Donald. Donald's attorney indicated before a recess that he had no "dog in this race" when the defense counsel for the other defendants objected to the government's introduction of the chart. Donald's lawyer returned after the trial was underway for approximately 10 minutes and the trial judge informed him that the focus had been on the chart. Donald's lawyer reiterated that he had no interest in that subject.

The Supreme Court stated it had "never addressed whether the rule announced in *Cronic* applies to testimony regarding codefendants' actions." It also concluded that "[w]ithin the contours of *Cronic,* a fair-minded jurist could conclude that a presumption of prejudice is not warranted by counsel's short absence during testimony about other defendants where that testimony was irrelevant to the defendant's theory of the case." The Court emphasized that its ruling was "only in the narrow context of federal habeas review" and expressed no view on the underlying Sixth Amendment question.

7. The Right to Effective Assistance of Counsel at the Guilty Plea Stage

Page 1455. Add the following two cases after Lafler v. Cooper:

Reasonable Probability of Going to Trial Even Without a Strong Defense: Lee v. United States

LEE V. UNITED STATES
Supreme Court of the United States, 2017.
137 S.Ct. 1958.

CHIEF JUSTICE ROBERTS delivered the opinion of the Court.

Petitioner Jae Lee was indicted on one count of possessing ecstasy with intent to distribute. Although he has lived in this country for most of his life, Lee is not a United States citizen, and he feared that a criminal conviction might affect his status as a lawful permanent resident. His attorney assured him there was nothing to worry about—the Government would not deport him if he pleaded guilty. So Lee, who had no real defense to the charge, opted to accept a plea that carried a lesser prison sentence than he would have faced at trial.

Lee's attorney was wrong: The conviction meant that Lee was subject to mandatory deportation from this country. Lee seeks to vacate his conviction on the ground that, in accepting the plea, he received ineffective assistance of counsel in violation of the Sixth Amendment. Everyone agrees that Lee received objectively unreasonable representation. The question presented is whether he can show he was prejudiced as a result.

I

Jae Lee moved to the United States from South Korea in 1982. * * * In the 35 years he has spent in the country, Lee has never returned to South Korea. He did not become a United States citizen, living instead as a lawful permanent resident.

* * * In 2008, a confidential informant told federal officials that Lee had sold the informant approximately 200 ecstasy pills and two ounces of hydroponic marijuana over the course of eight years. The officials obtained a search warrant for Lee's house, where they found 88 ecstasy pills, three Valium tablets, $32,432 in cash, and a loaded rifle. Lee admitted that the drugs were his and that he had given ecstasy to his friends.

A grand jury indicted Lee on one count of possessing ecstasy with intent to distribute in violation of 21 U.S.C. § 841(a)(1). Lee retained an attorney and entered into plea discussions with the Government. The attorney advised Lee that going to trial was "very risky" and that, if he pleaded guilty, he would receive a lighter sentence than he would if convicted at trial. Lee informed his attorney of his noncitizen status and repeatedly asked him whether he would face deportation as a result of the criminal proceedings. The attorney told Lee that he would not be deported as a result of pleading guilty. Based on that assurance, Lee accepted the plea and the District Court sentenced him to a year and a day in prison, though it deferred commencement of Lee's sentence for two months so that Lee could manage his restaurants over the holiday season.

Lee quickly learned, however, that a prison term was not the only consequence of his plea. Lee had pleaded guilty to what qualifies as an "aggravated felony" under the Immigration and Nationality Act, and a noncitizen convicted of such an offense is subject to mandatory deportation, Lee filed a motion under 28 U.S.C. § 2255 to vacate his conviction and sentence, arguing that his attorney had provided constitutionally ineffective assistance.

At an evidentiary hearing on Lee's motion, both Lee and his plea-stage counsel testified that "deportation was the determinative issue in Lee's decision whether to accept the plea." * * * Lee's attorney testified that he thought Lee's case was a "bad case to try" because Lee's defense to the charge was weak. The attorney nonetheless acknowledged that if he had known Lee would be deported upon pleading guilty, he would have advised him to go to trial. Based on the hearing testimony, a Magistrate Judge recommended that Lee's plea be set aside and his conviction vacated because he had received ineffective assistance of counsel.

The District Court, however, denied relief. Applying our two-part test for ineffective assistance claims from Strickland v. Washington, 466 U.S. 668 (1984), the District Court concluded that * * * "[i]n light of the overwhelming evidence of Lee's guilt," Lee "would have almost certainly" been found guilty and received "a significantly longer prison sentence, and subsequent deportation," had he gone to trial. Lee therefore could not show he was prejudiced by his attorney's erroneous advice. * * *

The Court of Appeals for the Sixth Circuit affirmed the denial of relief. On appeal, the Government conceded that the performance of Lee's attorney had been deficient. To establish that he was prejudiced by that deficient performance, the court explained, Lee was required to show "a reasonable probability that, but for counsel's errors, he would not have pleaded guilty and would have insisted on going to trial." (quoting Hill v. Lockhart, 474 U.S. 52, 59 (1985)). Lee had "no *bona fide* defense, not even a weak one," so he "stood to gain nothing from going to trial but more prison time." * * * [T]he Court of Appeals concluded that Lee could not show prejudice. We granted certiorari.

II

The Sixth Amendment guarantees a defendant the effective assistance of counsel at "critical stages of a criminal proceeding," including when he enters a guilty plea. Lafler v. Cooper, 566 U.S. 156, 165 (2012). To demonstrate that counsel was constitutionally ineffective, a defendant must show that counsel's representation fell below an objective standard of reasonableness and that he was prejudiced as a result. The first requirement is not at issue in today's case: The Government concedes that Lee's plea-stage counsel provided inadequate representation when he assured Lee that he would not be deported if he pleaded guilty. The question is whether Lee can show he was prejudiced by that erroneous advice.

A

* * * When a defendant alleges his counsel's deficient performance led him to accept a guilty plea rather than go to trial, we do not ask whether, had he gone to trial, the result of that trial "would have been different" than the result of the plea bargain. That is because, while we ordinarily apply a strong presumption of reliability to judicial proceedings, we cannot accord any such presumption to judicial proceedings that never took place.

We instead consider whether the defendant was prejudiced by the denial of the entire judicial proceeding to which he had a right. As we held in Hill v. Lockhart, when a defendant claims that his counsel's deficient performance deprived him of a trial by causing him to accept a plea, the defendant can show prejudice by demonstrating a "reasonable probability that, but for counsel's errors, he would not have pleaded guilty and would have insisted on going to trial."

The dissent contends that a defendant must also show that he would have been better off going to trial. That is true when the defendant's decision about going to trial turns on his prospects of success and those are affected by the attorney's error—for instance, where a defendant alleges that his lawyer should have but did not seek to suppress an improperly obtained confession. Premo v. Moore, 562 U.S. 115, 118 (2011).

Not all errors, however, are of that sort. Here Lee knew, correctly, that his prospects of acquittal at trial were grim, and his attorney's error had nothing to do with that. The error was instead one that affected Lee's understanding of the consequences of pleading guilty. The Court confronted precisely this kind of error in *Hill*. Rather than asking how a hypothetical trial would have played out absent the error, the Court considered whether there was an adequate showing that the defendant, properly advised, would have opted to go to trial. The Court rejected the defendant's claim because he had "alleged no special circumstances that might support the conclusion that he placed particular emphasis on his parole eligibility in deciding whether or not to plead guilty." [Chief Justice Roberts distinguishes Missouri v. Frye and Lafler v. Cooper (Text pages 1445–55), as cases where the defendant *rejected* a plea on bad advice and went to trial.]

Lee, on the other hand, argues he can establish prejudice under *Hill* because he never would have accepted a guilty plea had he known that he would be deported as a result. Lee insists he would have gambled on trial, risking more jail time for whatever small chance there might be of an acquittal that would let him remain in the United States. The Government responds that, since Lee had no viable defense at trial, he would almost certainly have lost and found himself still subject to deportation, with a lengthier prison sentence to boot. Lee, the Government contends, cannot show prejudice from accepting a plea where his only hope at trial was that something unexpected and unpredictable might occur that would lead to an acquittal.

B

* * *

A defendant without any viable defense will be highly likely to lose at trial. And a defendant facing such long odds will rarely be able to show prejudice from accepting a guilty plea that offers him a better resolution than would be likely after trial. But that is not because the prejudice inquiry in this context looks to the probability of a conviction for its own sake. It is instead because defendants obviously weigh their prospects at trial in deciding whether to accept a plea. Where a defendant has no plausible chance of an acquittal at trial, it is highly likely that he will accept a plea if the Government offers one.

But common sense (not to mention our precedent) recognizes that there is more to consider than simply the likelihood of success at trial. The decision whether to plead guilty also involves assessing the respective consequences of a conviction after trial and by plea. When those consequences are, from the defendant's perspective, similarly dire, even the smallest chance of success at trial may look attractive. For example, a defendant with no realistic defense to a charge carrying a 20-year sentence may nevertheless choose trial, if the prosecution's plea offer is 18 years. Here Lee alleges that avoiding deportation was *the* determinative factor for him; deportation after some time in prison was not meaningfully different from deportation after somewhat less time. He says he accordingly would have rejected any plea leading to deportation—even if it shaved off prison time—in favor of throwing a "Hail Mary" at trial.

The Government urges that, in such circumstances, the possibility of an acquittal after trial is "irrelevant to the prejudice inquiry," pointing to our statement in *Strickland* that "[a] defendant has no entitlement to the luck of a lawless decisionmaker." That statement, however, was made in the context of discussing the presumption of reliability we apply to judicial proceedings. * * * [T]hat presumption has no place where, as here, a defendant was deprived of a proceeding altogether. In a presumptively reliable proceeding, "the possibility of arbitrariness, whimsy, caprice, 'nullification,' and the like" must by definition be ignored. *Strickland,* 466 U.S., at 695. But where we are instead asking what an individual defendant would have done, the possibility of even a highly improbable result may be pertinent to the extent it would have affected his decisionmaking.

C

"Surmounting *Strickland*'s high bar is never an easy task," Padilla v. Kentucky, 559 U.S. 356, 371 (2010), and the strong societal interest in finality has special force with respect to convictions based on guilty pleas. Courts should not upset a plea solely because of *post hoc* assertions from a defendant about how he would have pleaded but for his attorney's deficiencies. Judges should instead look to contemporaneous evidence to substantiate a defendant's expressed preferences.

In the unusual circumstances of this case, we conclude that Lee has adequately demonstrated a reasonable probability that he would have rejected the plea had he known that it would lead to mandatory deportation. There is no question that deportation was the determinative issue in Lee's decision whether to accept the plea deal. Lee asked his attorney repeatedly whether there was any risk of deportation from the proceedings, and both Lee and his attorney testified at the evidentiary hearing below that Lee would have gone to trial if he had known about the deportation consequences.

Lee demonstrated as much at his plea colloquy: When the judge warned him that a conviction "could result in your being deported," and asked "[d]oes that at all affect your decision about whether you want to plead guilty or not," Lee answered "Yes, Your Honor." When the judge inquired "[h]ow does it affect your decision," Lee responded "I don't understand," and turned to his attorney for advice. Only when Lee's counsel assured him that the judge's statement was a "standard warning" was Lee willing to proceed to plead guilty.

There is no reason to doubt the paramount importance Lee placed on avoiding deportation. Deportation is always a particularly severe penalty, *Padilla,* 559 U.S., at 365, and we have "recognized that preserving the client's right to remain in the United States may be more important to the client than any potential jail sentence." Id. At the time of his plea, Lee had lived in the United States for nearly three decades, had established two businesses in Tennessee, and was the only family member in the United States who could care for his elderly parents—both naturalized American citizens. In contrast to these strong connections to the United States, there is no indication that he had any ties to South Korea; he had never returned there since leaving as a child.

The Government argues, however, that under Padilla v. Kentucky, a defendant "must convince the court that a decision to reject the plea bargain would have been rational under the circumstances." The Government contends that Lee cannot make that showing because he was going to be deported either way; going to trial would only result in a longer sentence before that inevitable consequence.

We cannot agree that it would be irrational for a defendant in Lee's position to reject the plea offer in favor of trial. But for his attorney's incompetence, Lee would have known that accepting the plea agreement would *certainly* lead to deportation. Going to trial? *Almost* certainly. If deportation were the "determinative issue" for an individual in plea discussions, as it was for Lee; if that individual had strong connections to this country and no other, as did Lee; and if the consequences of taking a chance at trial were not markedly harsher than pleading, as in this case, that "almost" could make all the difference. Balanced against holding on to some chance of avoiding deportation was a year or two more of prison time. Not everyone in Lee's position would make the choice to reject the plea. But we cannot say it would be irrational to do so.

Lee's claim that he would not have accepted a plea had he known it would lead to deportation is backed by substantial and uncontroverted evidence. Accordingly we conclude Lee has demonstrated a "reasonable probability that, but for [his] counsel's errors, he would not have pleaded guilty and would have insisted on going to trial." *Hill,* 474 U.S., at 59.

The judgment of the United States Court of Appeals for the Sixth Circuit is reversed, and the case is remanded for further proceedings consistent with this opinion.

JUSTICE GORSUCH took no part in the consideration or decision of this case.

JUSTICE THOMAS, with whom JUSTICE ALITO joins except for Part I, dissenting.

The Court today holds that a defendant can undo a guilty plea, well after sentencing and in the face of overwhelming evidence of guilt, because he would have chosen to pursue a defense at trial with no reasonable chance of success if his attorney had properly advised him of the immigration consequences of his plea. Neither the Sixth Amendment nor this Court's precedents support that conclusion. I respectfully dissent.

I

As an initial matter, I remain of the view that the Sixth Amendment to the Constitution does not require counsel to provide accurate advice concerning the potential removal consequences of a guilty plea. Padilla v. Kentucky, 559 U.S. 356, 388 (2010) (Scalia, J., joined by THOMAS, J., dissenting). I would therefore affirm the Court of Appeals on the ground

that the Sixth Amendment does not apply to the allegedly ineffective
assistance in this case.

II

Because the Court today announces a novel standard for prejudice at
the plea stage, I further dissent on the separate ground that its standard
does not follow from our precedents.

A

* * *

To establish prejudice under *Strickland,* a defendant must show a
reasonable probability that, but for counsel's unprofessional errors, the
result of the proceeding would have been different. *Strickland* made clear
that the "result of the proceeding" refers to the outcome of the defendant's
criminal prosecution as a whole. It defined "reasonable probability" as "a
probability sufficient to undermine confidence *in the outcome.*" (emphasis
added). * * * *Strickland* * * * requires a defendant to establish that he
would have been better off in the end had his counsel not erred.

B

The majority misapplies this Court's precedents when it concludes
that a defendant may establish prejudice by showing only that "he would
not have pleaded guilty and would have insisted on going to trial," without
showing that "the result of that trial would have been different than the
result of the plea bargain." In reaching this conclusion, the Court relies
almost exclusively on the single line from *Hill* that "the defendant must
show that there is a reasonable probability that, but for counsel's errors,
he would not have pleaded guilty and would have insisted on going to trial."
* * * In *Hill,* the Court concluded that the defendant had not made that
showing, so it rejected his claim. The Court did not, however, further hold
that a defendant can establish prejudice by making that showing alone.

* * *

The majority today abandons any pretense of applying *Strickland* to
claims of ineffective assistance of counsel that arise at the plea stage. It
instead concludes that one standard applies when a defendant goes to trial
(*Strickland*); another standard applies when a defendant accepts a plea
(*Hill*); and yet another standard applies when counsel does not apprise the
defendant of an available plea or when the defendant rejects a plea (*Frye*
and *Lafler*). That approach leaves little doubt that the Court has opened a
whole new field of constitutionalized criminal procedure—"plea-bargaining
law"—despite its repeated assurances that it has been applying the same
Strickland standard all along. In my view, we should take the Court's
precedents at their word and conclude that "[a]n error by counsel . . . does

not warrant setting aside the judgment of a criminal proceeding if the error had no effect on the judgment." *Strickland,* 466, U.S., at 691.

III

Applying the ordinary *Strickland* standard in this case, I do not think a defendant in petitioner's circumstances could show a reasonable probability that the result of his criminal proceeding would have been different had he not pleaded guilty. Petitioner does not dispute that he possessed large quantities of illegal drugs or that the Government had secured a witness who had purchased the drugs directly from him. * * *

In the face of overwhelming evidence of guilt and in the absence of a bona fide defense, a reasonable court or jury applying the law to the facts of this case would find the defendant guilty. * * * A defendant in petitioner's shoes, therefore, would have suffered the same deportation consequences regardless of whether he accepted a plea or went to trial. He is thus plainly better off for having accepted his plea: had he gone to trial, he not only would have faced the same deportation consequences, he also likely would have received a higher prison sentence. Finding that petitioner has established prejudice in these circumstances turns *Strickland* on its head.

* * *

Counseling Client to Withdraw a Cooperation Agreement on the Basis of the Client's Protestation of Innocence: Burt v. Titlow

BURT V. TITLOW

Supreme Court of the United States, 2014.
134 S.Ct. 10.

JUSTICE ALITO delivered the opinion of the Court.

When a state prisoner asks a federal court to set aside a sentence due to ineffective assistance of counsel during plea bargaining, our cases require that the federal court use a "doubly deferential" standard of review that gives both the state court and the defense attorney the benefit of the doubt. Cullen v. Pinholster, 131 S.Ct. 1388 (2011). In this case, the Sixth Circuit failed to apply that doubly deferential standard by refusing to credit a state court's reasonable factual finding and by assuming that counsel was ineffective where the record was silent. Because [AEDPA and *Strickland*] do not permit federal judges to so casually second-guess the decisions of their state-court colleagues or defense attorneys, the Sixth Circuit's decision must be reversed.

* * *

Respondent Titlow and Billie Rogers, respondent's aunt, murdered Billie's husband Don by pouring vodka down his throat and smothering him with a pillow. With help from attorney Richard Lustig, respondent reached an agreement with state prosecutors to testify against Billie, plead guilty to manslaughter, and receive a 7- to 15-year sentence. As confirmed at a plea hearing, Lustig reviewed the State's evidence with respondent "over a long period of time," and respondent understood that that evidence could support a conviction for first-degree murder. The Michigan trial court approved the plea bargain.

Three days before Billie Rogers' trial was to commence, however, respondent retained a new lawyer, Frederick Toca. With Toca's help, respondent demanded a substantially lower minimum sentence (three years, instead of seven) in exchange for the agreement to plead guilty and testify. When the prosecutor refused to accede to the new demands, respondent withdrew the plea, acknowledging in open court the consequences of withdrawal (including reinstatement of the first-degree murder charge). Without respondent's critical testimony, Billie Rogers was acquitted, and later died.

Respondent subsequently stood trial. During the course of the trial, respondent denied any intent to harm Don Rogers or any knowledge, at the time respondent covered his mouth or poured vodka down his throat, that Billie intended to harm him. Indeed, respondent testified to attempting to *prevent* Billie from harming her husband. The jury, however, elected to believe respondent's previous out-of-court statements, which squarely demonstrated participation in the killing, and convicted respondent of second-degree murder. The trial court imposed a 20- to 40-year term of imprisonment.

On direct appeal, respondent argued that Toca advised withdrawal of the guilty plea without taking time to learn more about the case, thereby failing to realize the strength of the State's evidence and providing ineffective assistance of counsel. [The State appellate court found no ineffectiveness. On habeas review, the district court denied relief but the Sixth Circuit reversed and granted the writ.] The Sixth Circuit * * * found that the factual predicate for the state court's decision—that the withdrawal of the plea was based on respondent's assertion of innocence— was an unreasonable interpretation of the factual record, given Toca's explanation at the withdrawal hearing that "the decision to withdraw Titlow's plea was based on the fact that the State's plea offer was substantially higher than the Michigan guidelines for second-degree murder." Further observing that "[t]he record in this case contains no evidence" that Toca fully informed respondent of the possible consequences of withdrawing the guilty plea, the Sixth Circuit held that Toca rendered ineffective assistance of counsel that resulted in respondent's loss of the benefit of the plea bargain. Citing our decision in Lafler v. Cooper, 132 S.Ct.

1376, the Sixth Circuit remanded this case with instructions that the prosecution must reoffer the original plea agreement to respondent, and that the state court should "consul[t]" the plea agreement and "fashion" a remedy for the violation of respondent's Sixth Amendment right to effective assistance of counsel during plea bargaining.

On remand, the prosecution followed the Sixth Circuit's instructions and reoffered the plea agreement it had offered some 10 years before—even though, in light of Billie Rogers' acquittal and subsequent death, respondent was no longer able to deliver on the promises originally made to the prosecution. At the plea hearing, however, respondent balked, refusing to provide a factual basis for the plea which the court could accept. Respondent admitted to pouring vodka down Don Rogers' throat, but denied assisting in killing him or knowing that pouring vodka down his throat could lead to his death. As at trial, respondent testified to attempting to prevent Billie Rogers from harming her husband. Eventually, after conferring with current counsel (not Toca), respondent admitted to placing Don Rogers in danger by pouring vodka down his throat with the knowledge that his death could result. The trial court took the plea under advisement, where the matter stands at present. We granted certiorari.

* * *

[Justice Alito emphasizes the "doubly deferential" standard for review of effective assistance of counsel claims under AEDPA.] AEDPA recognizes a foundational principle of our federal system: State courts are adequate forums for the vindication of federal rights. * * * Indeed, state courts have the solemn responsibility equally with the federal courts to safeguard constitutional rights, and this Court has refused to sanction any decision that would reflect negatively upon a state court's ability to do so. Especially where a case involves such a common claim as ineffective assistance of counsel under *Strickland*—a claim state courts have now adjudicated in countless criminal cases for nearly 30 years—there is no intrinsic reason why the fact that a man is a federal judge should make him more competent, or conscientious, or learned than his neighbor in the state courthouse. * * *

The record readily supports the [State court's] factual finding that Toca advised withdrawal of the guilty plea only after respondent's proclamation of innocence. Respondent passed a polygraph denying planning to kill Don Rogers or being in the room when he died. Thereafter, according to an affidavit in the record, respondent discussed the case with a jailer, who advised against pleading guilty if respondent was not in fact guilty. That conversation set into motion respondent's decision to retain Toca. Those facts, together with the timing of Toca's hiring—on the eve of the trial at which respondent was to self-incriminate—strongly suggest that respondent had second thoughts about confessing in open court and proclaimed innocence to Toca. That conclusion is further bolstered by respondent's maintenance of innocence of Don Rogers' death at trial.

* * *

The only evidence the Sixth Circuit cited for its conclusion that the plea withdrawal was not based on respondent's proclamation of innocence was that, when Toca moved to withdraw the guilty plea, he "did not refer to Titlow's claims of innocence," but instead "explained that the decision to withdraw [the] plea was based on the fact that the State's plea offer was substantially higher than the Michigan guidelines" for manslaughter. * * *

But the [State court] * * * correctly recognized that there is nothing inconsistent about a defendant's asserting innocence on the one hand and refusing to plead guilty to manslaughter accompanied by higher-than-normal punishment on the other. Indeed, a defendant convinced of his or her own innocence may have a particularly optimistic view of the likelihood of acquittal, and therefore be more likely to drive a hard bargain with the prosecution before pleading guilty. Viewing the record as a whole, we conclude that the Sixth Circuit improperly set aside a reasonable state-court determination of fact in favor of its own debatable interpretation of the record.

Accepting as true the factual determination that respondent proclaimed innocence to Toca, the Sixth Circuit's *Strickland* analysis cannot be sustained. Although a defendant's proclamation of innocence does not relieve counsel of his normal responsibilities under *Strickland,* it may affect the advice counsel gives. The [State court's] conclusion that Toca's advice satisfied *Strickland* fell within the bounds of reasonableness under AEDPA, given that respondent was claiming innocence and only days away from offering self-incriminating testimony in open court pursuant to a plea agreement involving an above-guidelines sentence. The Sixth Circuit's conclusion to the contrary was error.

Even more troubling is the Sixth Circuit's conclusion that Toca was ineffective because the "record in this case contains no evidence that" he gave constitutionally adequate advice on whether to withdraw the guilty plea. We have said that counsel should be "strongly presumed to have rendered adequate assistance and made all significant decisions in the exercise of reasonable professional judgment," *Strickland,* and that the burden to show that counsel's performance was deficient rests squarely on the defendant. The Sixth Circuit turned that presumption of effectiveness on its head. It should go without saying that the absence of evidence cannot overcome the "strong presumption that counsel's conduct [fell] within the wide range of reasonable professional assistance." * * *

The Sixth Circuit pointed to a single fact in support of its conclusion that Toca failed to adequately advise respondent: his failure to retrieve respondent's file from Lustig before withdrawing the guilty plea. But here, too, the Sixth Circuit deviated from *Strickland's* strong presumption of effectiveness. The record does not reveal how much Toca was able to glean about respondent's case from other sources; he may well have obtained copies of the critical materials from prosecutors or the court. * * *

In any event, the same considerations were relevant to entering and withdrawing the guilty plea, and respondent admitted in open court when initially pleading guilty that Lustig had explained the State's evidence and that this evidence would support a conviction for first-degree murder. Toca was justified in relying on this admission to conclude that respondent understood the strength of the prosecution's case and nevertheless wished to withdraw the plea. With respondent having knowingly entered the guilty plea, we think any confusion about the strength of the State's evidence upon withdrawing the plea less than a month later highly unlikely.

Despite our conclusion that there was no factual or legal justification for overturning the state court's decision, we recognize that Toca's conduct in this litigation was far from exemplary. He may well have violated the rules of professional conduct by accepting respondent's publication rights as partial payment for his services, and he waited weeks before consulting respondent's first lawyer about the case. But the Sixth Amendment does not guarantee the right to perfect counsel; it promises only the right to effective assistance, and we have held that a lawyer's violation of ethical norms does not make the lawyer *per se* ineffective. See Mickens v. Taylor, 535 U.S. 162 (2002). Troubling as Toca's actions were, they were irrelevant to the narrow question that was before the Sixth Circuit: whether the state court reasonably determined that respondent was adequately advised before deciding to withdraw the guilty plea. Because the Michigan Court of Appeals' decision that respondent was so advised is reasonable and supported by the record, the Sixth Circuit's judgment is reversed.

JUSTICE SOTOMAYOR, concurring.

In my view, this case turns on Vonlee Titlow's failure to present enough evidence of what Frederick Toca did or did not do in the handful of days after she hired him and before she withdrew her plea. As our opinion notes, she bore the burden of overcoming two presumptions: that Toca performed effectively and that the state court ruled correctly. She failed to carry this burden. We need not say more, and indeed we do not say more. I therefore join the Court's opinion in full. I write separately, however, to express my understanding of our opinion's limited scope, particularly with respect to * * * statements that it makes about the adequacy of Toca's performance.

JUSTICE GINSBURG, concurring in the judgment.

While I join the Court's judgment, I find dubious the [State court's] conclusion that Toca acted reasonably in light of Titlow's protestations of innocence. Toca became Titlow's counsel on the recommendation of the deputy sheriff to whom Titlow professed innocence. As the Court rightly observes, Toca's conduct was "far from exemplary." With virtually no time to make an assessment of Titlow's chances of prevailing at trial, and without consulting the lawyer who had negotiated Titlow's plea, Toca told Titlow he could take the case to trial and win. With Toca's aid, Titlow's plea was withdrawn just three days after Toca's retention as defense counsel. At sentencing, the prosecutor volunteered that Titlow had been the "victim of some bad advice."

Nevertheless, one thing is crystal clear. The prosecutor's agreement to the plea bargain hinged entirely on Titlow's willingness to testify at her aunt's trial. Once Titlow reneged on that half of the deal, the bargain failed. Absent an extant bargain, there was nothing to renew. In short, the prosecutor could not be ordered to "renew" a plea proposal never offered in the first place. With the plea offer no longer alive, Titlow was convicted after a trial free from reversible error. For these reasons, I join the Court's judgment.

C. INEFFECTIVE ASSISTANCE WITHOUT FAULT ON THE PART OF DEFENSE COUNSEL

Page 1468. At the end of the headnote on *"Impairing Defense Strategy"*, add the following:

In Glebe v. Frost, 135 S.Ct. 1429 (2014) (per curiam), a habeas petitioner relied on *Herring* to argue that per se reversible error occurred when the state trial court restricted defense counsel from making a particular argument in closing. Trial counsel wanted to argue to the jury in the alternative: 1) that the prosecution failed to prove that the defendant was an accomplice to robberies; and 2) that in committing the crime, the defendant was acting under duress. The trial judge insisted that defense counsel choose one argument or the other for closing, as the arguments were inconsistent. Defense counsel limited his closing argument to duress, and the defendant was convicted. On habeas review, Frost argued that the trial judge's restriction violated his right to effective counsel and that this violation was a "structural" error that could not be assessed for harmlessness. (See Chapter 13 for a discussion of structural errors).

Because the case was on habeas review, Frost was required to show not just that an error occurred but that the state court violated clearly established law as determined by the Supreme Court. 22 U.S.C. § 2254(d). The Court found that *Herring* did *not* clearly establish that a trial court was prohibited from requiring defense counsel to choose between inconsistent arguments. The Court reasoned as follows:

> *Herring* held that complete denial of summation violates the Assistance of Counsel Clause. According to the Ninth Circuit, *Herring* further held that this denial amounts to structural error. We need not opine on the accuracy of that interpretation. For even assuming that *Herring* established that *complete denial* of summation amounts to structural error, it did not clearly establish that the *restriction* of summation also amounts to structural error. A court could reasonably conclude, after all, that prohibiting all argument differs from prohibiting argument in the alternative.

F. THE RIGHT TO COUNSEL OF CHOICE

2. Rendering the Defendant Unable to Pay for Counsel of Choice

Page 1496. Add the following at the end of the section:

Freezing Untainted Assets That Would Be Used to Pay for Counsel: Luis v. United States

LUIS V. UNITED STATES
Supreme Court of the United States, 2016.
136 S.Ct. 1083.

JUSTICE BREYER **announced the judgment of the Court and delivered an opinion in which** THE CHIEF JUSTICE, JUSTICE GINSBURG, **and** JUSTICE SOTOMAYOR **join.**

A federal statute provides that a court may freeze before trial certain assets belonging to a criminal defendant accused of violations of federal health care or banking laws. See 18 U.S.C. § 1345. Those assets include: (1) property "obtained as a result of" the crime, (2) property "traceable" to the crime, and (3) other "property of equivalent value." § 1345(a)(2). In this case, the Government has obtained a court order that freezes assets belonging to the third category of property, namely, property that is untainted by the crime, and that belongs fully to the defendant. That order, the defendant says, prevents her from paying her lawyer. She claims that insofar as it does so, it violates her Sixth Amendment "right . . . to have the Assistance of Counsel for [her] defence." We agree.

I

In October 2012, a federal grand jury charged the petitioner, Sila Luis, with paying kickbacks, conspiring to commit fraud, and engaging in other crimes all related to health care. The Government claimed that Luis had fraudulently obtained close to $45 million, almost all of which she had already spent. Believing it would convict Luis of the crimes charged, and hoping to preserve the $2 million remaining in Luis' possession for payment of restitution and other criminal penalties (often referred to as criminal forfeitures, which can include innocent—not just tainted—assets, a point of critical importance here), the Government sought a pretrial order prohibiting Luis from dissipating her assets. And the District Court ultimately issued an order prohibiting her from "dissipating, or otherwise disposing of . . . assets, real or personal . . . up to the equivalent value of the proceeds of the Federal health care fraud ($45 million)."

The Government and Luis agree that this court order will prevent Luis from using her own untainted funds, *i.e.*, funds not connected with the crime, to hire counsel to defend her in her criminal case. * * * Although the District Court recognized that the order might prevent Luis from obtaining counsel of her choice, it held "that there is no Sixth Amendment right to use untainted, substitute assets to hire counsel."

The Eleventh Circuit upheld the District Court. We granted Luis' petition for certiorari.

II

The question presented is "[w]hether the pretrial restraint of a criminal defendant's legitimate, untainted assets (those not traceable to a criminal offense) needed to retain counsel of choice violates the Fifth and Sixth Amendments." We see no reasonable way to interpret the relevant statutes to avoid answering this constitutional question. Hence, we answer it, and our answer is that the pretrial restraint of legitimate, untainted assets needed to retain counsel of choice violates the Sixth Amendment. The nature and importance of the constitutional right taken together with the nature of the assets lead us to this conclusion.

A

No one doubts the fundamental character of a criminal defendant's Sixth Amendment right to the "Assistance of Counsel." [Justice Breyer cites and quotes from *Gideon v. Wainright*.]

It is consequently not surprising: *first*, that this Court's opinions often refer to the right to counsel as "fundamental"; *second*, that commentators describe the right as a "great engin[e] by which an innocent man can make the truth of his innocence visible"; *third*, that we have understood the right to require that the Government provide counsel for an indigent defendant accused of all but the least serious crimes; and *fourth*, that we have considered the wrongful deprivation of the right to counsel a "structural" error that so "affec[ts] the framework within which the trial proceeds" that courts may not even ask whether the error harmed the defendant.

Given the necessarily close working relationship between lawyer and client, the need for confidence, and the critical importance of trust, neither is it surprising that the Court has held that the Sixth Amendment grants a defendant "a fair opportunity to secure counsel of his own choice." This "fair opportunity" for the defendant to secure counsel of choice has limits. A defendant has no right, for example, to an attorney who is not a member of the bar, or who has a conflict of interest due to a relationship with an opposing party. And an indigent defendant, while entitled to adequate representation, has no right to have the Government pay for his preferred representational choice.

We nonetheless emphasize that the constitutional right at issue here is fundamental: "[T]he Sixth Amendment guarantees a defendant the right to be represented by an otherwise qualified attorney whom that defendant can afford to hire."

B

The Government cannot, and does not, deny Luis' right to be represented by a qualified attorney whom she chooses and can afford. But the Government would undermine the value of that right by taking from Luis the ability to use the funds she needs to pay for her chosen attorney. The Government points out that, while freezing the funds may have this consequence, there are important interests on the other side of the legal equation: It wishes to guarantee that those funds will be available later to help pay for statutory penalties (including forfeiture of untainted assets) and restitution, should it secure convictions. And it points to two cases from this Court, *Caplin & Drysdale*, and [*United States v.*] *Monsanto* [both set forth in the Text at pages 1489–92], which, in the Government's view, hold that the Sixth Amendment does not pose an obstacle to its doing so here. In our view, however, the nature of the assets at issue here differs from the assets at issue in those earlier cases. And that distinction makes a difference.

1

The relevant difference consists of the fact that the property here is untainted; *i.e.*, it belongs to the defendant, pure and simple. In this respect it differs from a robber's loot, a drug seller's cocaine, a burglar's tools, or other property associated with the planning, implementing, or concealing of a crime. The Government may well be able to freeze, perhaps to seize, assets of the latter, "tainted" kind before trial. As a matter of property law the defendant's ownership interest is imperfect. The robber's loot belongs to the victim, not to the defendant. * * * The cocaine is contraband, long considered forfeitable to the Government wherever found. * * * And title to property used to commit a crime (or otherwise "traceable" to a crime) often passes to the Government at the instant the crime is planned or committed. * * *

The property at issue here, however, is not loot, contraband, or otherwise "tainted." It belongs to the defendant. That fact undermines the Government's reliance upon precedent, for both *Caplin & Drysdale* and *Monsanto* relied critically upon the fact that the property at issue was "tainted," and that title to the property therefore had passed from the defendant to the Government before the court issued its order freezing (or otherwise disposing of) the assets.

* * *

The Court in those cases * * * acknowledged that whether property is "forfeitable" or subject to pretrial restraint under Congress' scheme is a nuanced inquiry that very much depends on who has the superior interest in the property at issue. * * *

The distinction * * * is thus an important one, not a technicality. It is the difference between what is yours and what is mine. In *Caplin & Drysdale* and *Monsanto*, the Government wanted to impose restrictions upon (or seize) property that the Government had probable cause to believe was the proceeds of, or traceable to, a crime. The relevant statute said that the Government took title to those tainted assets as of the time of the crime. And the defendants in those cases consequently had to concede that the disputed property was in an important sense the Government's at the time the court imposed the restrictions.

This is not to say that the Government "owned" the tainted property outright (in the sense that it could take possession of the property even before obtaining a conviction). Rather, it is to say that the Government even before trial had a "substantial" interest in the tainted property sufficient to justify the property's pretrial restraint. * * *

If we analogize to bankruptcy law, the Government [in *Caplin & Drysdale* and *Monsanto*] became something like a secured creditor with a lien on the defendant's tainted assets superior to that of most any other party. * * *

Here, by contrast, the Government seeks to impose restrictions upon Luis' *un*tainted property without any showing of any equivalent governmental interest in that property. Again, if this were a bankruptcy case, the Government would be at most an unsecured creditor. Although such creditors someday might collect from a debtor's general assets, they cannot be said to have any present claim to, or interest in, the debtor's property. * * * At least regarding her untainted assets, Luis can at this point reasonably claim that the property is still "mine," free and clear.

2

This distinction between (1) what is primarily "mine" (the defendant's) and (2) what is primarily "yours" (the Government's) does not by itself answer the constitutional question posed, for the law of property sometimes allows a person without a present interest in a piece of property to impose restrictions upon a current owner, say, to prevent waste. A holder of a reversionary interest, for example, can prevent the owner of a life estate from wasting the property. * * * And holders of a contingent, future executory interest in property (an interest that might become possessory at some point down the road) can, in limited circumstances, enjoin the activities of the current owner. The Government here seeks a somewhat analogous order, *i.e.*, an order that will preserve Luis' untainted assets so that they will be available to cover the costs of forfeiture and restitution if she is convicted, and if the court later determines that her tainted assets are insufficient or otherwise unavailable.

The Government finds statutory authority for its request in language authorizing a court to enjoin a criminal defendant from, for example, disposing of innocent "property of equivalent value" to that of tainted property. 18 U.S.C. § 1345(a)(2)(B)(i). But Luis needs some portion of those same funds to pay for the lawyer of her choice. Thus, the legal conflict arises. And, in our view, insofar as innocent (*i.e.*, untainted) funds are needed to obtain counsel of choice, we believe that the Sixth Amendment prohibits the court order that the Government seeks.

Three basic considerations lead us to this conclusion. First, the nature of the competing interests argues against this kind of court order. On the one side we find, as we have previously explained, a Sixth Amendment right to assistance of counsel that is a fundamental constituent of due process of law. * * * The order at issue in this case would seriously undermine that constitutional right.

On the other side we find interests that include the Government's contingent interest in securing its punishment of choice (namely, criminal forfeiture) as well as the victims' interest in securing restitution (notably, from funds belonging to the defendant, not the victims). While these interests are important, to deny the Government the order it requests will not inevitably undermine them, for, at least sometimes, the defendant may possess other assets—say, "tainted" property—that might be used for forfeitures and restitution. Nor do the interests in obtaining payment of a criminal forfeiture or restitution order enjoy constitutional protection. Rather, despite their importance, compared to the right to counsel of choice, these interests would seem to lie somewhat further from the heart of a fair, effective criminal justice system.

Second, relevant legal tradition offers virtually no significant support for the Government's position. Rather, tradition argues to the contrary. Describing the 18th-century English legal world (which recognized only a limited right to counsel), Blackstone wrote that "only" those "goods and chattels" that "a man has *at the time of conviction* shall be forfeited." 4 W. Blackstone, Commentaries on the Laws of England 388 (1765) (emphasis added); see 1 J. Chitty, Practical Treatise on the Criminal Law 737 (1816) ("[T]he party indicted may sell any of [his property] . . . to assist him in preparing for his defense on the trial").

* * *

We have found no decision of this Court authorizing unfettered, pretrial forfeiture of the defendant's own "innocent" property—property with no connection to the charged crime. Nor do we see any grounds for distinguishing the historic preference against preconviction *forfeitures* from the preconviction *restraint* at issue here. As far as Luis' Sixth Amendment right to counsel of choice is concerned, a restraining order might as well be a forfeiture; that is, the restraint itself suffices to completely deny this constitutional right.

Third, as a practical matter, to accept the Government's position could well erode the right to counsel to a considerably greater extent than we have so far indicated. To permit the Government to freeze Luis' untainted assets would unleash a principle of constitutional law that would have no obvious stopping place. The statutory provision before us authorizing the present restraining order refers only to "banking law violation[s]" and "Federal health care offense[s]." 18 U.S.C. § 1345(a)(2). But, in the Government's view, Congress could write more statutes authorizing pretrial restraints in cases involving other illegal behavior—after all, a broad range of such behavior can lead to postconviction forfeiture of untainted assets.

Moreover, the financial consequences of a criminal conviction are steep. Even beyond the forfeiture itself, criminal fines can be high, and restitution orders expensive. See, *e.g.*, § 1344 ($1 million fine for bank fraud); § 3571 (mail and wire fraud fines of up to $250,000 for individuals and $500,000 for organizations). How are defendants whose innocent assets are frozen in cases like these supposed to pay for a lawyer— particularly if they lack "tainted assets" because they are innocent, a class of defendants whom the right to counsel certainly seeks to protect?

These defendants, rendered indigent, would fall back upon publicly paid counsel, including overworked and underpaid public defenders. As the Department of Justice explains, only 27 percent of county-based public defender offices have sufficient attorneys to meet nationally recommended caseload standards. And as one *amicus* points out, "[m]any federal public defender organizations and lawyers appointed under the Criminal Justice Act serve numerous clients and have only limited resources." The upshot is a substantial risk that accepting the Government's views would—by increasing the government-paid-defender workload—render less effective the basic right the Sixth Amendment seeks to protect.

3

We add that the constitutional line we have drawn should prove workable. That line distinguishes between a criminal defendant's (1) tainted funds and (2) innocent funds needed to pay for counsel. We concede, as JUSTICE KENNEDY points out, that money is fungible; and sometimes it will be difficult to say whether a particular bank account contains tainted or untainted funds. But the law has tracing rules that help courts implement the kind of distinction we require in this case. With the help of those rules, the victim of a robbery, for example, will likely obtain the car that the robber used stolen money to buy. See, *e.g.*, 1 G. Palmer, Law of Restitution § 2.14, p. 175 (1978) ("tracing" permits a claim against "an asset which is traceable to or the product of" tainted funds); 4 A. Scott, Law of Trusts § 518, pp. 3309–3314 (1956) (describing the tracing rules governing commingled accounts). And those rules will likely also prevent Luis from benefiting from many of the money transfers and purchases JUSTICE KENNEDY describes.

Courts use tracing rules in cases involving fraud, pension rights, bankruptcy, trusts, etc. They consequently have experience separating tainted assets from untainted assets, just as they have experience determining how much money is needed to cover the costs of a lawyer.

* * *

For the reasons stated, we conclude that the defendant in this case has a Sixth Amendment right to use her own "innocent" property to pay a reasonable fee for the assistance of counsel. On the assumptions made here, the District Court's order prevents Luis from exercising that right. We consequently vacate the judgment of the Court of Appeals and remand the case for further proceedings.

JUSTICE THOMAS, concurring in the judgment.

I agree with the plurality that a pretrial freeze of untainted assets violates a criminal defendant's Sixth Amendment right to counsel of choice. But I do not agree with the plurality's balancing approach. Rather, my reasoning rests strictly on the Sixth Amendment's text and common-law backdrop.

The Sixth Amendment provides important limits on the Government's power to freeze a criminal defendant's forfeitable assets before trial. And, constitutional rights necessarily protect the prerequisites for their exercise. The right "to have the Assistance of Counsel," U.S. Const., Amdt. 6, thus implies the right to use lawfully owned property to pay for an attorney. Otherwise the right to counsel—originally understood to protect only the right to hire counsel of choice—would be meaningless. History confirms this textual understanding. The common law limited pretrial asset restraints to tainted assets. Both this textual understanding and history establish that the Sixth Amendment prevents the Government from freezing untainted assets in order to secure a potential forfeiture. The freeze here accordingly violates the Constitution.

* * *

The Sixth Amendment denies the Government unchecked power to freeze a defendant's assets before trial simply to secure potential forfeiture upon conviction. If that bare expectancy of criminal punishment gave the Government such power, then a defendant's right to counsel of choice would be meaningless, because retaining an attorney requires resources.

* * *

An unlimited power to freeze a defendant's potentially forfeitable assets in advance of trial would eviscerate the Sixth Amendment's original meaning and purpose. * * * If the Government's mere expectancy of a total forfeiture upon conviction were sufficient to justify a complete pretrial asset freeze, then Congress could render the right to counsel a nullity in felony cases. That would have shocked the Framers. * * * [B]efore adoption of the Sixth Amendment, felony cases (not misdemeanors) were *precisely* when the common law denied defendants the right to counsel. With an unlimited power to freeze assets before trial, the Government could well revive the common-law felony rule that the Sixth Amendment was designed to abolish.

The modern, judicially created right to Government-appointed counsel does not obviate these concerns. As understood in 1791, the Sixth Amendment protected a defendant's right to retain an attorney he could afford. It is thus no answer, as the principal dissent replies, that defendants rendered indigent by a pretrial asset freeze can resort to public defenders. The dissent's approach nullifies the *original understanding* of the right to counsel. To ensure that the right to counsel has meaning, the Sixth Amendment limits the assets the Government may freeze before trial to secure eventual forfeiture.

* * *

The dissenters object that, before trial, a defendant has an identical property interest in tainted and untainted assets. Perhaps so. I need not take a position on the matter. Either way, that fact is irrelevant. Because the pretrial asset freeze here crosses into untainted assets, for which there is no historical tradition, it is unconstitutional. Any such incursion violates the Sixth Amendment.

* * *

JUSTICE KENNEDY, with whom JUSTICE ALITO joins, dissenting.

The plurality and JUSTICE THOMAS find in the Sixth Amendment a right of criminal defendants to pay for an attorney with funds that are forfeitable upon conviction so long as those funds are not derived from the crime alleged. That unprecedented holding rewards criminals who hurry to spend, conceal, or launder stolen property by assuring them that they may use their own funds to pay for an attorney after they have dissipated the proceeds of their crime. It matters not, under today's ruling, that the defendant's remaining assets must be preserved if the victim or the Government is to recover for the property wrongfully taken. By granting a defendant a constitutional right to hire an attorney with assets needed to make a property-crime victim whole, the plurality and JUSTICE THOMAS ignore this Court's precedents and distort the Sixth Amendment right to counsel.

The result reached today makes little sense in cases that involve fungible assets preceded by fraud, embezzlement, or other theft. An example illustrates the point. Assume a thief steals $1 million and then wins another $1 million in a lottery. After putting the sums in separate accounts, he or she spends $1 million. If the thief spends his or her lottery winnings, the Government can restrain the stolen funds in their entirety. The thief has no right to use those funds to pay for an attorney. Yet if the thief heeds today's decision, he or she will spend the stolen money first; for if the thief is apprehended, the $1 million won in the lottery can be used for an attorney. This result is not required by the Constitution.

[Justice Kennedy discusses *Caplin & Monsanto*.]

The principle the Court announced in *Caplin & Drysdale* and *Monsanto* controls the result here. Those cases establish that a pretrial restraint of assets forfeitable upon conviction does not contravene the Sixth Amendment even when the defendant possesses no other funds with which to pay for an attorney. The restraint itself does not prevent a defendant from seeking to convince his or her counsel of choice to take on the representation without advance payment. It does not disqualify any attorney the defendant might want. And it does not prevent a defendant from borrowing funds to pay for an attorney who is otherwise too expensive. To be sure, a pretrial restraint may make it difficult for a defendant to secure counsel who insists that high defense costs be paid in advance. That difficulty, however, does not result in a Sixth Amendment violation any more than high taxes or other government exactions that impose a similar burden.

* * *

[T]he Government has the same "strong . . . interest in obtaining full recovery of all forfeitable assets" here as it did in *Caplin & Drysdale* and *Monsanto*. If Luis is convicted, the Government has a right to recover Luis' substitute assets—the money she kept for herself while spending the taxpayer dollars she is accused of stealing. Just as the Government has an interest in ensuring Luis' presence at trial—an interest that can justify a defendant's pretrial detention—so too does the Government have an interest in ensuring the availability of her substitute assets after trial, an interest that can justify pretrial restraint.

One need look no further than the Court's concluding words in *Monsanto* to know the proper result here: "[N]o constitutional violation occurs when, after probable cause [to believe that a defendant's assets will be forfeitable] is adequately established, the Government obtains an order barring a defendant from . . . dissipating his assets prior to trial." The Government, having established probable cause to believe that Luis' substitute assets will be forfeitable upon conviction, should be permitted to obtain a restraining order barring her from spending those funds prior to trial. Luis should not be allowed to circumvent that restraint by using the funds to pay for a high, or even the highest, priced defense team she can find.

* * *

Caplin & Drysdale and *Monsanto* cannot be distinguished based on "the nature of the assets at issue." Title to the assets in those cases did not pass from the defendant to the Government until conviction. As a result, the assets restrained before conviction in *Monsanto* were on the same footing as the assets restrained here: There was probable cause to believe that the assets would belong to the Government upon conviction. But when the court issued its restraining order, they did not. The Government had no greater ownership interest in Monsanto's tainted assets than it has in Luis' substitute assets.

The plurality seeks to avoid this conclusion by relying on the relation-back doctrine. In its view the doctrine gives the Government title to tainted assets upon the commission of a crime rather than upon conviction or judgment of forfeiture. * * *

The plurality is correct to note that *Caplin & Drysdale* discussed the relation-back provision in the forfeiture statute at issue. The *Caplin & Drysdale* Court did not do so, however, to suggest that forfeitable assets can be restrained only when the assets are tainted. Rather, the Court referred to the provision to rebut the law firm's argument that the United States has less of an interest in forfeitable property than robbery victims have in their stolen property. * * * True, the assets in *Caplin & Drysdale* and *Monsanto* happened to be derived from the criminal activity alleged; but the Court's reasoning in those cases was based on the Government's entitlement to recoup money from criminals who have profited from their crimes, not on tracing or identifying the actual assets connected to the crime. For this reason, the principle the Court announced in those cases applies whenever the Government obtains (or will obtain) title to assets upon conviction. * * *

The principle the plurality and JUSTICE THOMAS announce today— that a defendant has a right to pay for an attorney with forfeitable assets so long as those assets are not related to or the direct proceeds of the crime alleged—has far-reaching implications. There is no clear explanation why this principle does not extend to the exercise of other constitutional rights. If defendants have a right to spend forfeitable assets on attorney's fees, why not on exercises of the right to speak, practice one's religion, or travel? * * *

The result today also creates arbitrary distinctions between defendants. Money, after all, is fungible. There is no difference between a defendant who has preserved his or her own assets by spending stolen money and a defendant who has spent his or her own assets and preserved stolen cash instead. Yet the plurality and concurrence—for different reasons—find in the Sixth Amendment the rule that greater protection is given to the defendant who, by spending, laundering, exporting, or concealing stolen money first, preserves his or her remaining funds for use on an attorney.

The true winners today are sophisticated criminals who know how to make criminal proceeds look untainted. They do so every day. * * * They structure their transactions to avoid triggering recordkeeping and reporting requirements. And they open bank accounts in other people's names and through shell companies, all to disguise the origins of their funds.

* * *

Notwithstanding that the Government established probable cause to believe that Luis committed numerous crimes and used the proceeds of those crimes to line her and her family's pockets, the plurality and JUSTICE THOMAS reward Luis' decision to spend the money she is accused of stealing rather than her own. They allow Luis to bankroll her private attorneys as well as the best and most industrious investigators, experts, paralegals, and law clerks money can buy—a legal defense team Luis claims she cannot otherwise afford. The Sixth Amendment does not provide such an unfettered right to counsel of choice.

* * * As a result of the District Court's order, Luis simply cannot afford the legal team she desires unless they are willing to represent her without advance payment. For Sixth Amendment purposes, the only question here is whether Luis' right to adequate representation is protected. That question is not before the Court. Neither Luis nor the plurality nor JUSTICE THOMAS suggests that Luis will receive inadequate representation if she is not able to use the restrained funds. And this is for

good reason. Given the large volume of defendants in the criminal justice system who rely on public representation, it would be troubling to suggest that a defendant who might be represented by a public defender will receive inadequate representation. Since Luis cannot afford the legal team she desires, and because there is no indication that she will receive inadequate representation as a result, she does not have a cognizable Sixth Amendment complaint.

The plurality does warn that accepting the Government's position "would—by increasing the government-paid-defender workload—render less effective the basic right the Sixth Amendment seeks to protect." Public-defender offices, the plurality suggests, already lack sufficient attorneys to meet nationally recommended caseload standards. But concerns about the caseloads of public-defender offices do not justify a constitutional command to treat a defendant accused of committing a lucrative crime differently than a defendant who is indigent from the outset. The Constitution does not require victims of property crimes to fund subsidies for members of the private defense bar.

* * *

Finally, the plurality posits that its decision "should prove workable" because courts "have experience separating tainted assets from untainted assets, just as they have experience determining how much money is needed to cover the costs of a lawyer." Neither of these assurances is adequate.

As to the first, the plurality cites a number of sources for the proposition that courts have rules that allow them to implement the distinction it adopts. Those rules, however, demonstrate the illogic of the conclusion that there is a meaningful difference between the actual dollars stolen and the dollars of equivalent value in a defendant's bank account. The plurality appears to agree that, if a defendant is indicted for stealing $1 million, the Government can obtain an order preventing the defendant from spending the $1 million he or she is believed to have stolen. The situation gets more complicated, however, when the defendant deposits the stolen $1 million into an account that already has $1 million. If the defendant then spends $1 million from the account, it cannot be determined with certainty whether the money spent was stolen money rather than money the defendant already had. The question arises, then, whether the Government can restrain the remaining million.

One of the treatises on which the plurality relies answers that question. The opinion cites A. Scott's Law of Trusts to support the claim that "the law has tracing rules that help courts implement the kind of distinction ... require[d] in this case." The treatise says that, if a "wrongdoer has mingled misappropriated money with his own money and later makes withdrawals from the mingled fund," assuming the withdrawals do not result in a zero balance, a person who has an interest in the misappropriated money can recover it from the amount remaining in the account. 4 A. Scott, Law of Trusts § 518, pp. 3309–3310 (1956). Based on this rule, one would expect the plurality to agree that, in the above hypothetical, the Government could restrain up to the full amount of the stolen funds—that is, the full $1 million—without having to establish whether the $1 million the defendant spent was stolen money or not. If that is so, it is hard to see why its opinion treats as different a situation where the defendant has two bank accounts—one with the $1 million from before the crime and one with the stolen $1 million. The Sixth Amendment provides no justification for the decision to mandate different treatment in these all-but-identical situations.

* * *

JUSTICE KAGAN, dissenting.

I find *United States* v. *Monsanto* a troubling decision. It is one thing to hold, as this Court did in *Caplin & Drysdale* that a convicted felon has no Sixth Amendment right to pay his lawyer with funds adjudged forfeitable. Following conviction, such assets belong to the Government, and "[t]here is no constitutional principle that gives one person the right to give another's property to a third party." But it is quite another thing to say that the Government may, prior to trial, freeze assets that a defendant needs to hire an attorney, based on nothing more than "probable cause to believe that the property will ultimately be proved forfeitable." At that time, the presumption of innocence still applies, and the Government's interest in the assets is wholly contingent on future judgments of conviction and forfeiture. I am not altogether convinced that, in this decidedly different circumstance, the Government's interest in recovering the proceeds of crime ought to trump the defendant's (often highly consequential) right to retain counsel of choice.

But the correctness of *Monsanto* is not at issue today. Petitioner Sila Luis has not asked this Court either to overrule or to modify that decision; she argues only that it does not answer the question presented here. And because Luis takes *Monsanto* as a given, the Court must do so as well.

On that basis, I agree with the principal dissent that *Monsanto* controls this case. Because the Government has established probable cause to believe that it will eventually recover Luis's assets, she has no right to use them to pay an attorney. * * *

The plurality reaches a contrary result only by differentiating between the direct fruits of criminal activity and substitute assets that become subject to forfeiture when the defendant has run through those proceeds. But * * * the Government's and the defendant's respective legal interests in those two kinds of property, prior to a judgment of guilt, are exactly the same: The defendant maintains ownership of either type, with the Government holding only a contingent interest. * * *

And given that money is fungible, the plurality's approach leads to utterly arbitrary distinctions as among criminal defendants who are in fact guilty. The thief who immediately dissipates his ill-gotten gains and thereby preserves his other assets is no more deserving of chosen counsel than the one who spends those two pots of money in reverse order. Yet the plurality would enable only the first defendant, and not the second, to hire the lawyer he wants. I cannot believe the Sixth Amendment draws that irrational line, much as I sympathize with the plurality's effort to cabin *Monsanto.* Accordingly, I would affirm the judgment below.

CHAPTER 11

SENTENCING

■ ■ ■

I. INTRODUCTION

D. CONSTITUTIONAL LIMITATIONS ON PUNISHMENT

2. Eighth Amendment Limitations on Sentencing

Page 1536. Add at the end of the *Note on the Death Penalty*:

Justice Kennedy wrote for a 5–4 majority in Hall v. Florida, 134 S.Ct. 1986 (2014), which examined Florida's reaction to the Court's decision in *Atkins* that the execution of persons with intellectual disabilities violated the Eighth and Fourteenth Amendments.

Hall moved to vacate the death sentence imposed upon him based on evidence of mental disability which included an IQ test score of 71. The trial court denied his motion, ruling that a Florida statute required Hall to show an IQ score of 70 or below before he would be permitted to present any additional intellectual disability evidence. The Florida Supreme Court held that the 70-point threshold was constitutional. The Supreme Court disagreed.

Justice Kennedy reiterated that *Atkins* established that no legitimate penological purpose is served by executing the intellectually disabled—and that the prohibition on executing such individuals protects the integrity of the trial process and limits the risk of wrongful conviction of individuals who are more likely to give false confessions, are often poor witnesses, and have difficulty providing meaningful assistance to their counsel.

The majority relied on the fact that an IQ test has a standard error of measurement (SEM), which recognizes that an IQ score is inherently imprecise and is better understood as a range, *e.g.*, five points on either side of the recorded score. The majority concluded that the Florida threshold was inconsistent with established medical practice. That practice demands consideration of other evidence in addition to a specific IQ score in assessing a defendant's intellectual capacity, and recognizes the imprecision of a specific IQ score. The majority also asserted that the vast majority of death penalty states reject a strict 70 point cutoff and recognize the SEM, providing strong evidence that they do not regard such a cutoff as humane.

In the end, the majority held that a defendant must be permitted to present additional evidence of intellectual disability when an IQ score falls within the SEM.

Justice Alito's dissent, joined by the Chief Justice and Justices Scalia and Thomas, disagreed with the majority that the vast majority of death penalty states rejected the Florida bright-line approach. The dissent argued that the majority "adopts a uniform national rule that is both conceptually unsound and likely to result in confusion," and that instead of striking down the Florida statute based on objective societal factors the majority was relying "on the evolving standards of professional societies, most notably the American Psychiatric Association (APA)." Justice Alito pointed to four problems with reliance on such professional groups: (1) they sometimes rescind or change their standards; (2) courts will be required either to follow every change in professional thinking or judge the validity of each new change for themselves; (3) courts must determine which professional organizations are entitled to special deference, and there may be cases in which they disagree; and (4) professional standards are adopted for reasons that are quite different from a decision on whether the imposition of a death sentence in a particular case would serve a valid penological end.

Thereafter, in Moore v. Texas, 137 S.Ct. 1039 (2017), Justice Ginsburg, writing for the Court, declared that the medical community's current (and developing) standards impose a constraint on a state's determination of whether the capital defendant is intellectually disabled. The Court vacated a death penalty because the state was relying on decades-old case law to determine intellectual disability, while ignoring the more recent diagnostic framework established in the medical community. Chief Justice Roberts, joined by Justices Thomas and Alito, dissented.

E. SENTENCING ALTERNATIVES OTHER THAN INCARCERATION

3. Restitution

Page 1548. Before the first full paragraph, add the following:

In Paroline v. United States, 134 S.Ct. 1710 (2014), the Court addressed the circuit split referred to in Text, i.e., whether restitution to victims of child pornography requires proof that the defendant proximately caused the victim's injury. Paroline pleaded guilty to possessing child pornography, including two images of "Amy" being sexually abused by her uncle when she was a child. Amy sought restitution for the psychological harm she suffered from knowing that the pictures of her were being seen by thousands of people over the Internet. The Court, in an opinion by Justice Kennedy for five Justices, read the restitution statute (18 U.S.C. § 2259) to require a showing by the government that the defendant proximately caused the victim's injuries. The Court rejected the victim's argument that every possessor should be responsible for the entirety of her damages as too extreme a position, especially in light of the purposes of imposing restitution as a part of a criminal punishment. Justice Kennedy elaborated as follows:

> The striking outcome of this reasoning—that each possessor of the victim's images would bear the consequences of the acts of the many thousands who possessed those images—illustrates why the Court has been reluctant to adopt aggregate causation logic in an incautious manner, especially in interpreting criminal statutes where there is no language expressly suggesting Congress intended that approach. Even if one were to refer just to the law of torts, it would be a major step to say there is a sufficient causal link between the injury and the wrong so that all the victim's general losses were "suffered . . . as a proximate result of [Paroline's] offense." § 2259(b)(3)(F).

> And there is special reason not to do so in the context of criminal restitution. Aside from the manifest procedural differences between criminal sentencing and civil tort lawsuits, restitution serves purposes that differ from (though they overlap with) the purposes of tort law. See, *e.g.,* Kelly v. Robinson, 479 U.S. 36, 49 (1986) (noting that restitution is, *inter alia,* "an effective rehabilitative penalty"). Legal fictions developed in the law of torts cannot be imported into criminal restitution and applied to their utmost limits without due consideration of these differences.

> Contrary to the victim's suggestion, this is not akin to a case in which a "gang of ruffians" collectively beats a person, or in which a woman is "gang raped by five men on one night or by five men on five sequential nights." First, this case does not involve a set of wrongdoers acting in concert; for Paroline had no contact with the overwhelming majority of the offenders for whose actions the victim would hold him accountable. Second, adopting the victim's approach would make an individual possessor liable for the combined consequences of the acts of not just 2, 5, or even 100 independently acting offenders; but instead, a number that may reach into the tens of thousands.

> It is unclear whether it could ever be sensible to embrace the fiction that this victim's entire losses were the "proximate result," of a single possessor's offense. Paroline's contribution to the causal process underlying the victim's losses was very minor, both compared to the combined acts of all other relevant offenders, and in comparison to the contributions of other individual offenders, particularly distributors (who may have caused hundreds or thousands of further viewings) and the initial producer of the child pornography. Congress gave no indication that it intended its statute to be applied in the expansive manner the victim suggests, a manner contrary to the bedrock

principle that restitution should reflect the consequences of the defendant's own conduct, not the conduct of thousands of geographically and temporally distant offenders acting independently, and with whom the defendant had no contact.

The reality is that the victim's suggested approach would amount to holding each possessor of her images liable for the conduct of thousands of other independently acting possessors and distributors, with no legal or practical avenue for seeking contribution. That approach is so severe it might raise questions under the Excessive Fines Clause of the Eighth Amendment.

The victim (and the government) in *Paroline* argued that under a strict requirement of proximate cause, the victim would never be able to recover *anything* from an individual wrongdoer, because the victim's damages stemmed from the fact that there was an entire market of individuals accessing the offensive pictures over the Internet. Justice Kennedy was sympathetic to this argument, and essentially crafted a compromise approach—between the victim's position that each user should be liable for all of her injuries and the defendant's position that the victim could not recover anything from a single user because the harm was coming from the market. Justice Kennedy set forth the Court's position in the following passage:

> The contention that the victim's entire losses from the ongoing trade in her images were "suffered . . . as a proximate result" of Paroline's offense * * * must be rejected. But that does not mean the broader principles underlying the aggregate causation theories the Government and the victim cite are irrelevant to determining the proper outcome in cases like this. The cause of the victim's general losses is the trade in her images. And Paroline is a part of that cause, for he is one of those who viewed her images. While it is not possible to identify a discrete, readily definable incremental loss he caused, it is indisputable that he was a part of the overall phenomenon that caused her general losses. Just as it undermines the purposes of tort law to turn away plaintiffs harmed by several wrongdoers, it would undermine the remedial and penological purposes of 18 U.S.C. § 2259 to turn away victims in cases like this.

> With respect to the statute's remedial purpose, there can be no question that it would produce anomalous results to say that no restitution is appropriate in these circumstances. It is common ground that the victim suffers continuing and grievous harm as a result of her knowledge that a large, indeterminate number of individuals have viewed and will in the future view images of the sexual abuse she endured. Harms of this sort are a major reason why child pornography is outlawed. The unlawful conduct of everyone who reproduces,

distributes, or possesses the images of the victim's abuse—including Paroline—plays a part in sustaining and aggravating this tragedy. And there can be no doubt Congress wanted victims to receive restitution for harms like this. The law makes restitution "mandatory," for child-pornography offenses * * * language that indicates Congress' clear intent that victims of child pornography be compensated by the perpetrators who contributed to their anguish. It would undermine this intent to apply the statute in a way that would render it a dead letter in child-pornography prosecutions of this type.

* * *

In this special context, where it can be shown both that a defendant possessed a victim's images and that a victim has outstanding losses caused by the continuing traffic in those images but where it is impossible to trace a particular amount of those losses to the individual defendant by recourse to a more traditional causal inquiry, a court applying 18 U.S.C. § 2259 should order restitution in an amount that comports with the defendant's relative role in the causal process that underlies the victim's general losses. The amount would not be severe in a case like this, given the nature of the causal connection between the conduct of a possessor like Paroline and the entirety of the victim's general losses from the trade in her images, which are the product of the acts of thousands of offenders. It would not, however, be a token or nominal amount. The required restitution would be a reasonable and circumscribed award imposed in recognition of the indisputable role of the offender in the causal process underlying the victim's losses and suited to the relative size of that causal role. This would serve the twin goals of helping the victim achieve eventual restitution for all her child-pornography losses and impressing upon offenders the fact that child-pornography crimes, even simple possession, affect real victims.

Justice Kennedy sought to provide guidance on how the proper amount of restitution could be determined:

There remains the question of how district courts should go about determining the proper amount of restitution. At a general level of abstraction, a court must assess as best it can from available evidence the significance of the individual defendant's conduct in light of the broader causal process that produced the victim's losses. This cannot be a precise mathematical inquiry and involves the use of discretion and sound judgment. But that is neither unusual nor novel, either in the wider context of criminal sentencing or in the more specific domain of restitution. * * *

There are a variety of factors district courts might consider in determining a proper amount of restitution, and it is neither necessary nor appropriate to prescribe a precise algorithm for determining the proper restitution amount at this point in the law's development. Doing so would unduly constrain the decisionmakers closest to the facts of any given case. But district courts might, as a starting point, determine the amount of the victim's losses caused by the continuing traffic in the victim's images * * * then set an award of restitution in consideration of factors that bear on the relative causal significance of the defendant's conduct in producing those losses. These could include the number of past criminal defendants found to have contributed to the victim's general losses; reasonable predictions of the number of future offenders likely to be caught and convicted for crimes contributing to the victim's general losses; any available and reasonably reliable estimate of the broader number of offenders involved (most of whom will, of course, never be caught or convicted); whether the defendant reproduced or distributed images of the victim; whether the defendant had any connection to the initial production of the images; how many images of the victim the defendant possessed; and other facts relevant to the defendant's relative causal role.

Chief Justice Roberts, joined by Justices Scalia and Thomas, "regretfully" dissented in *Paroline.* The Chief Justice contended that Congress had not authorized the majority's compromise approach to assessing restitution for victims of child pornography. In his view, "the restitution statute that Congress wrote for child pornography offenses makes it impossible to award relief" for damages caused by viewing the pictures of the victim over the Internet—because the statute requires proof of damage by a preponderance of the evidence. The Chief Justice concluded that it could not be possible to show that Paroline caused Amy any damage by a preponderance, because even without his viewing, Amy would have suffered the same damages from viewing by thousands of others. The Chief Justice concluded as follows:

> The Court's decision today means that Amy will not go home with nothing. But it would be a mistake for that salutary outcome to lead readers to conclude that Amy has prevailed or that Congress has done justice for victims of child pornography. The statute as written allows no recovery; we ought to say so, and give Congress a chance to fix it.

Justice Sotomayor wrote a separate dissent in *Paroline.* She argued that the statute should be read to allow apportionment of a victim's damages, and that each convicted defendant should have a payment schedule imposed in light of their financial circumstances.

II. GUIDELINES SENTENCING

D. SUPREME COURT CONSTRUCTION OF THE FEDERAL SENTENCING GUIDELINES

2. Application of Advisory Guidelines After *Booker*

Page 1588. Add the following after the headnote on *Peugh v. United States*:

Incorrect Sentencing That Ends Up to Be in the Correct Guidelines Range: Molina-Martinez v. United States

MOLINA-MARTINEZ v. UNITED STATES

Supreme Court of the United States, 2016.
136 S.Ct. 1338.

JUSTICE KENNEDY delivered the opinion of the Court.

This case involves the Federal Sentencing Guidelines. In sentencing petitioner, the District Court applied a Guidelines range higher than the applicable one. The error went unnoticed by the court and the parties, so no timely objection was entered. The error was first noted when, during briefing to the Court of Appeals for the Fifth Circuit, petitioner himself raised the mistake. The Court of Appeals refused to correct the error because, in its view, petitioner could not establish a reasonable probability that but for the error he would have received a different sentence. Under that court's decisions, if a defendant's ultimate sentence falls within what would have been the correct Guidelines range, the defendant, on appeal, must identify "additional evidence" to show that use of the incorrect Guidelines range did in fact affect his sentence. Absent that evidence, in the Court of Appeals' view, a defendant who is sentenced under an incorrect range but whose sentence is also within what would have been the correct range cannot demonstrate he has been prejudiced by the error.

Most Courts of Appeals have not adopted so rigid a standard. Instead, in recognition of the Guidelines' central role in sentencing, other Courts of Appeals have concluded that a district court's application of an incorrect Guidelines range can itself serve as evidence of an effect on substantial rights. See, *e.g.,* United States v. Sabillon-Umana, 772 F.3d 1328, 1333 (C.A.10 2014) (application of an erroneous Guidelines range "runs the risk of affecting the ultimate sentence *regardless of* whether the court ultimately imposes a sentence within or outside" that range). These courts recognize that, in most cases, when a district court adopts an incorrect Guidelines range, there is a reasonable probability that the defendant's sentence would be different absent the error. This Court granted certiorari to reconcile the difference in approaches.

I

A

The Sentencing Guidelines provide the framework for the tens of thousands of federal sentencing proceedings that occur each year. Congress directed the United States Sentencing Commission (USSC or Commission) to establish the Guidelines. 28 U.S.C. § 994(a)(1). The goal was to achieve "*uniformity* in sentencing . . . imposed by different federal courts for similar criminal conduct, as well as *proportionality* in sentencing through a system that imposes appropriately different sentences for criminal conduct of different severity." Rita v. United States, 551 U.S. 338, 349 (2007). To those ends, the Commission engaged in a deliberative and dynamic process to create Guidelines that account for a variety of offenses and circumstances. As part of that process, the Commission considered the objectives of federal sentencing identified in the Sentencing Reform Act of 1984—the same objectives that federal judges must consider when sentencing defendants. The result is a set of elaborate, detailed Guidelines that aim to embody federal sentencing objectives both in principle and in practice.

Uniformity and proportionality in sentencing are achieved, in part, by the Guidelines' significant role in sentencing. The Guidelines enter the sentencing process long before the district court imposes the sentence. The United States Probation Office first prepares a presentence report which includes a calculation of the advisory Guidelines range it considers to be applicable. The applicable Guidelines range is based on the seriousness of a defendant's offense (indicated by his "offense level") and his criminal history (indicated by his "criminal history category"). The presentence report explains the basis for the Probation Office's calculations and sets out the sentencing options under the applicable statutes and Guidelines. It also contains detailed information about the defendant's criminal history and personal characteristics, such as education and employment history.

At the outset of the sentencing proceedings, the district court must determine the applicable Guidelines range. To do so, the court considers the presentence report as well as any objections the parties might have. The court then entertains the parties' arguments regarding an appropriate sentence, including whether the sentence should be within the Guidelines range or not. Although the district court has discretion to depart from the Guidelines, the court "must consult those Guidelines and take them into account when sentencing." United States v. Booker, 543 U.S. 220, 264 (2005).

B

The Guidelines are complex, and so there will be instances when a district court's sentencing of a defendant within the framework of an incorrect Guidelines range goes unnoticed. In that circumstance, because the defendant failed to object to the miscalculation, appellate review of the error is governed by Federal Rule of Criminal Procedure 52(b).

Rule 52, in both its parts, is brief. It states:

"(a) Harmless Error. Any error, defect, irregularity, or variance that does not affect substantial rights must be disregarded.

"(b) Plain Error. A plain error that affects substantial rights may be considered even though it was not brought to the court's attention."

The starting point for interpreting and applying paragraph (b) of the Rule, upon which this case turns, is the Court's decision in United States v. Olano, 507 U.S. 725 (1993). *Olano* instructs that a court of appeals has discretion to remedy a forfeited error provided certain conditions are met. First, there must be an error that has not been intentionally relinquished or abandoned. Second, the error must be plain—that is to say, clear or obvious. Third, the error must have affected the defendant's substantial rights, which in the ordinary case means he or she must show a reasonable probability that, but for the error, the outcome of the proceeding would have been different. Once these three conditions have been met, the court of appeals should exercise its discretion to correct the forfeited error if the error "seriously affects the fairness, integrity or public reputation of judicial proceedings." *Olano, supra,* at 736.

II

The petitioner here, Saul Molina-Martinez, pleaded guilty to being unlawfully present in the United States after having been deported following an aggravated felony conviction * * * . As required, the Probation Office prepared a presentence report that related Molina-Martinez's offense of conviction, his criminal history, his personal characteristics, and the available sentencing options. The report also included the Probation Office's calculation of what it believed to be Molina-Martinez's Guidelines range. The Probation Office calculated Molina-Martinez's total offense level as 21. It concluded that Molina-Martinez's criminal history warranted 18 points, which included 11 points for five aggravated burglary convictions from 2011. Those 18 criminal history points resulted in a criminal history category of VI. That category, combined with an offense level of 21, resulted in a Guidelines range of 77 to 96 months.

At the sentencing hearing Molina-Martinez's counsel and the Government addressed the court. The Government acknowledged that the Probation Office had "recommended the low end on this case, 77 months." But, the prosecution told the court, it "disagree[d] with that recommendation," and was "asking for a high end sentence of 96 months"— the top of the Guidelines range. Like the Probation Office, counsel for Molina-Martinez urged the court to enter a sentence at the bottom of the Guidelines range. Counsel asserted that "77 months is a severe sentence" and that "after the 77 months, he'll be deported with probably a special release term." A sentence of 77 months, counsel continued, "is more than adequate to ensure he doesn't come back again."

After hearing from the parties, the court stated it was adopting the presentence report's factual findings and Guidelines calculations. It then ordered Molina-Martinez's sentence:

> "It's the judgment of the Court that the defendant, Saul Molina-Martinez, is hereby committed to the custody of the Bureau of Prisons to be imprisoned for a term of 77 months. Upon release from imprisonment, Defendant shall be placed on supervised release for a term of three years without supervision."

The court provided no further explanation for the sentence.

On appeal, Molina-Martinez * * * identified for the first time what he believed to be an error in the calculation of his criminal history points under the Guidelines. * * * The error, Molina-Martinez explained, occurred because the Probation Office failed to apply § 4A1.2(a)(2) of the Guidelines. That provision addresses how multiple sentences imposed on the same day are to be counted for purposes of determining a defendant's criminal history. It instructs that, when prior sentences were imposed on the same day, they should be counted as a single sentence unless the offenses "were separated by an intervening arrest (*i.e.,* the defendant is arrested for the first offense prior to committing the second offense)."

Molina-Martinez's presentence report included five aggravated burglary convictions for which he had been sentenced on the same day. The Probation Office counted each sentence separately, which resulted in the imposition of 11 criminal history points. Molina-Martinez contended this was error because none of the offenses were separated by an intervening arrest and because he had been sentenced for all five burglaries on the same day. Under a correct calculation, in his view, the burglaries should have resulted in 5 criminal history points instead of 11. That would have lowered his criminal history category from VI to V. The correct criminal history category, in turn, would have resulted in a Guidelines range of 70 to 87 months rather than 77 to 96 months. Had the correct range been used, Molina-Martinez's 77-month sentence would have been in the middle of the range, not at the bottom.

Molina-Martinez acknowledged that, because he did not object in the District Court, he was entitled to relief only if he could satisfy Rule 52(b)'s requirements. He nevertheless maintained relief was warranted because the error was plain, affected his substantial rights, and impugned the fairness, integrity, and public reputation of judicial proceedings.

The Court of Appeals disagreed. * * * It reasoned that, when a correct sentencing range overlaps with an incorrect range, the reviewing court "do[es] not assume, in the absence of additional evidence, that the sentence [imposed] affects a defendant's substantial rights." Molina-Martinez, the court ruled, had not put forth the additional evidence necessary to show that the error affected his substantial rights. * * *

III

The Court of Appeals for the Fifth Circuit stands generally apart from other Courts of Appeals with respect to its consideration of unpreserved Guidelines errors. This Court now holds that its approach is incorrect.

Nothing in the text of Rule 52(b), its rationale, or the Court's precedents supports a requirement that a defendant seeking appellate review of an unpreserved Guidelines error make some further showing of prejudice beyond the fact that the erroneous, and higher, Guidelines range set the wrong framework for the sentencing proceedings. This is so even if the ultimate sentence falls within both the correct and incorrect range. When a defendant is sentenced under an incorrect Guidelines range— whether or not the defendant's ultimate sentence falls within the correct range—the error itself can, and most often will, be sufficient to show a reasonable probability of a different outcome absent the error.

A

Today's holding follows from the essential framework the Guidelines establish for sentencing proceedings. The Court has made clear that the Guidelines are to be the sentencing court's "starting point and . . . initial benchmark." Gall v. United States, 552 U.S. 38, 49 (2007). Federal courts understand that they "*must* begin their analysis with the Guidelines and remain cognizant of them throughout the sentencing process." *Peugh* [*v. United States*], [Text, page 1587]. * * *

The Guidelines' central role in sentencing means that an error related to the Guidelines can be particularly serious. A district court that improperly calculates a defendant's Guidelines range, for example, has committed a significant procedural error. * * *

The Commission's statistics demonstrate the real and pervasive effect the Guidelines have on sentencing. In most cases district courts continue to impose either within-Guidelines sentences or sentences that depart downward from the Guidelines on the Government's motion. In less than 20% of cases since 2007 have district courts "imposed above- or below- Guidelines sentences absent a Government motion." *Peugh,* 133 S.Ct., at 2084. As the Court has recognized, "when a Guidelines range moves up or down, offenders' sentences [tend to] move with it." *Peugh, supra,* 133 S.Ct., at 2084. * * *

These sources confirm that the Guidelines are not only the starting point for most federal sentencing proceedings but also the lodestar. * * * In the usual case, then, the systemic function of the selected Guidelines range will affect the sentence. * * * From the centrality of the Guidelines in the sentencing process it must follow that, when a defendant shows that the district court used an incorrect range, he should not be barred from relief on appeal simply because there is no other evidence that the sentencing outcome would have been different had the correct range been used.

* * * There may be instances when, despite application of an erroneous Guidelines range, a reasonable probability of prejudice does not exist. The sentencing process is particular to each defendant, of course, and a reviewing court must consider the facts and circumstances of the case before it. The record in a case may show, for example, that the district court thought the sentence it chose was appropriate irrespective of the Guidelines range. Judges may find that some cases merit a detailed explanation of the reasons the selected sentence is appropriate. And that explanation could make it clear that the judge based the sentence he or she selected on factors independent of the Guidelines. The Government remains free to point to parts of the record—including relevant statements by the judge—to counter any ostensible showing of prejudice the defendant may make. Where, however, the record is silent as to what the district court might have done had it considered the correct Guidelines range, the court's reliance on an incorrect range in most instances will suffice to show an effect on the defendant's substantial rights. Indeed, in the ordinary case a defendant will satisfy his burden to show prejudice by pointing to the application of an incorrect, higher Guidelines range and the sentence he received thereunder. Absent unusual circumstances, he will not be required to show more.

The Court of Appeals' rule to the contrary fails to take account of the dynamics of federal sentencing. In a significant number of cases the sentenced defendant will lack the additional evidence the Court of Appeals' rule would require, for sentencing judges often say little about the degree to which the Guidelines influenced their determination. District courts, as a matter of course, use the Guidelines range to instruct them regarding the appropriate balance of the relevant federal sentencing factors. This Court has told judges that they need not provide extensive explanations for within-Guidelines sentences because circumstances may well make clear that the judge rests his decision upon the Commission's own reasoning. In these situations, reviewing courts may presume that a sentence imposed within a properly calculated Guidelines range is reasonable. As a result, the cases where the Guidelines are most likely to have influenced the district court's sentencing decision—those where the court chose a sentence within what it believed to be the applicable Guidelines range—are also the cases least likely to provide the defendant with evidence of the Guidelines' influence beyond the sentence itself. The defendants in these cases should not be prevented by a categorical rule from establishing on appeal that there is a reasonable probability the Guidelines range applied by the sentencing court had an effect on their within-Guidelines sentence.

B

This case illustrates the unworkable nature of the Court of Appeals' additional evidence rule. Here the court held that Molina-Martinez could not establish an effect on his substantial rights. Yet the record points to a different conclusion. The District Court said nothing specific about why it chose the sentence it imposed. It merely adopted the guideline applications in the presentence investigation report, which set the range at 77 to 96 months; rejected the Government's argument for a sentence at the top of the Guidelines range; and agreed with the defendant's request for, and the Probation Office's recommendation of, a sentence at the bottom of the range. As intended, the Guidelines served as the starting point for the sentencing and were the focal point for the proceedings that followed.

The 77-month sentence the District Court selected is conspicuous for its position as the lowest sentence within what the District Court believed to be the applicable range. * * * [T]he District Court's selection of a sentence at the bottom of the range, despite the Government's request for the maximum Guidelines sentence, evinced an intention to give the minimum recommended by the Guidelines. The District Court said nothing to suggest that it would have imposed a 77-month sentence regardless of the Guidelines range. Given these circumstances, there is at least a reasonable probability that the District Court would have imposed a different sentence had it known that 70 months was in fact the lowest sentence the Commission deemed appropriate.

IV

* * *

The Government expresses concern over the judicial resources needed for the resentencing proceedings that might result from the Court's holding. It is doubtful today's holding will result in much of an increased burden. As already noted, today's holding is consistent with the approach taken by most Courts of Appeals. Yet only a small fraction of cases are remanded for resentencing because of Guidelines related errors. See 2014 Sourcebook S-6, S-153 (Tables 2 and 62) (of the roughly 75,000 cases sentenced in 2014, only 620 resulted in a remand for resentencing because of a statutory or Guidelines related error). [A]ppellate courts retain broad discretion in determining whether a remand for resentencing is necessary. Courts have, for example, developed mechanisms short of a full remand to determine whether a district court in fact would have imposed a different sentence absent the error. See, *e.g.,* United States v. Currie, 739 F.3d 960, 967 (C.A.7 2014) (ordering "limited remand so that the district judge [could] consider, and state on the record, whether she would have imposed the same sentence . . . knowing that [the defendant] was subject to a five-year rather than a ten-year statutory minimum term of imprisonment"). And even when a Court of Appeals does decide that resentencing is appropriate, a remand for resentencing, while not costless, does not invoke the same difficulties as a remand for retrial does. * * *

———

In the ordinary case the Guidelines accomplish their purpose. They serve as the starting point for the district court's decision and anchor the court's discretion in selecting an appropriate sentence. It follows, then, that in most cases the Guidelines range will affect the sentence. When that is so, a defendant sentenced under an incorrect Guidelines range should be able to rely on that fact to show a reasonable probability that the district court would have imposed a different sentence under the correct range. That probability is all that is needed to establish an effect on substantial rights for purposes of obtaining relief under Rule 52(b).

The contrary judgment of the Court of Appeals for the Fifth Circuit is reversed, and the case is remanded for further proceedings consistent with this opinion.

It is so ordered.

JUSTICE ALITO, with whom JUSTICE THOMAS joins, concurring in part and concurring in the judgment.

I agree with the Court that the Fifth Circuit's rigid approach to unpreserved Guidelines errors is incorrect. And I agree that petitioner has shown a reasonable probability that the District Court would have imposed a different sentence in his case if his recommended Guidelines sentence had been accurately calculated. Unlike the Court, however, I would not speculate about how often the reasonable probability test will be satisfied in future cases. The Court's predictions in dicta about how plain-error review will play out are predicated on the view that sentencing judges will continue to rely very heavily on the Guidelines in the future, but that prediction may not turn out to be accurate. We should not make predictions about the future effects of Guidelines errors, particularly since some may misunderstand those predictions as veiled directives.

* * *

The Court's proclamations about what will occur in "most" cases are based on Sentencing Commission statistics indicating that the Guidelines tend to influence sentences. Perhaps these statistics are probative of the Guidelines' current impact on sentencing. But they provide an unstable and shifting basis for the Court's prophecies about the future. The Guidelines are now entirely advisory, and in time the lower courts may increasingly drift away from the Guidelines and back toward the sentencing regime that prevailed prior to their issuance. As circumstances change, and as judges who spent decades applying mandatory Guidelines ranges are replaced with new judges less wedded to the Guidelines, the statistics underlying the Court's forecasts may change dramatically. Because I cannot join the Court's questionable predictions, I concur only in part and in the judgment.

Page 1590. Add the following at the end of the section:

Sentencing Guidelines Cannot Be Subject to Void-for-Vagueness Challenges: Beckles v. United States

In Beckles v. United States, 137 S.Ct. 886 (2017), the defendant was found eligible for a sentencing enhancement under the Guidelines because he was a career offender and his offense qualified as a "crime of violence." The Guidelines definition of "crime of violence" tracked a federal penal statute that the Supreme Court had previously found to be void-for-vagueness under the Due Process Clause. The defendant relied on the Supreme Court's striking down the penal statute as a basis for attack on the Sentencing Guidelines. But the Supreme Court held that Sentencing Guidelines (unlike penal statutes) cannot be subject to void-for-vagueness challenges. Justice Thomas, writing for seven Justices, reasoned that allowing a void for vagueness challenge was inconsistent with Supreme Court precedent upholding essentially unlimited sentencing discretion. He explained as follows:

> The limited scope of the void-for-vagueness doctrine in this context is rooted in the history of federal sentencing. Instead of enacting specific sentences for particular federal crimes, Congress historically permitted district courts wide discretion to decide whether the offender should be incarcerated and for how long. For most crimes, Congress set forth a range of sentences, and sentencing courts had almost unfettered discretion to select the actual length of a defendant's sentence within the customarily wide range Congress had enacted. That discretion allowed district courts to craft individualized sentences, taking into account the facts of the crime and the history of the defendant. * * *

> Yet in the long history of discretionary sentencing, this Court has "never doubted the authority of a judge to exercise broad discretion in imposing a sentence within a statutory range." United States v. Booker, 543 U.S. 220, 233; see also, e.g., *Apprendi,* 120 S.Ct. 2348 ("[N]othing in this history suggests that it is impermissible for judges to exercise discretion . . . in imposing a judgment within the range prescribed by statute").

More specifically, our cases have never suggested that a defendant can successfully challenge as vague a sentencing statute conferring discretion to select an appropriate sentence from within a statutory range, even when that discretion is unfettered. * * * Indeed, no party to this case suggests that a system of purely discretionary sentencing could be subject to a vagueness challenge.

Turning specifically to the Guidelines, Justice Thomas concluded that a void-for-vagueness challenge was inapt because the Guidelines are, after *Booker,* discretionary and not binding.

Because they merely guide the district courts' discretion, the Guidelines are not amenable to a vagueness challenge. As discussed above, the system of purely discretionary sentencing that predated the Guidelines was constitutionally permissible. If a system of unfettered discretion is not unconstitutionally vague, then it is difficult to see how the present system of guided discretion could be.

The advisory Guidelines also do not implicate the twin concerns underlying vagueness doctrine—providing notice and preventing arbitrary enforcement. As to notice, even perfectly clear Guidelines could not provide notice to a person who seeks to regulate his conduct so as to avoid particular penalties within the statutory range. That is because even if a person behaves so as to avoid an enhanced sentence under the career-offender guideline, the sentencing court retains discretion to impose the enhanced sentence. * * * All of the notice required is provided by the applicable statutory range, which establishes the permissible bounds of the court's sentencing discretion.

The advisory Guidelines also do not implicate the vagueness doctrine's concern with arbitrary enforcement. Laws that regulate persons or entities, we have explained, must be sufficiently clear that those enforcing the law do not act in an arbitrary or discriminatory way. The Guidelines, however, do not regulate the public by prohibiting any conduct or by establishing minimum and maximum penalties for any crime. Rather, the Guidelines advise sentencing courts how to exercise their discretion within the bounds established by Congress. In this case, for example, the District Court did not "enforce" the career-offender Guideline against petitioner. It enforced 18 U.S.C. § 922(g)(1)'s prohibition on possession of a firearm by a felon—which prohibited petitioner's conduct—and § 924(e)(1)'s mandate of a sentence of 15 years to life imprisonment—which fixed the permissible range of petitioner's sentence. The court relied on the career-offender Guideline merely for advice in exercising its discretion to choose a sentence within those statutory limits.

Justice Thomas closed by emphasizing that the Guidelines are not free from all constitutional concerns. He noted some limitations:

> Our holding today does not render the advisory Guidelines immune from constitutional scrutiny. This Court held in *Peugh*, for example, that a "retrospective increase in the Guidelines range applicable to a defendant" violates the Ex Post Facto Clause." But the void-for-vagueness and ex post facto inquiries are analytically distinct. Our ex post facto cases have focused on whether a change in law creates a significant risk of a higher sentence. A retroactive change in the Guidelines creates such a risk because sentencing decisions are anchored by the Guidelines, which establish the framework for sentencing. In contrast, the void-for-vagueness doctrine requires a different inquiry. The question is whether a law regulating private conduct by fixing permissible sentences provides notice and avoids arbitrary enforcement by clearly specifying the range of penalties available.

* * *

> The Court has also recognized in the Eighth Amendment context that a district court's reliance on a vague sentencing factor in a capital case, even indirectly, can taint the sentence. But our approach to vagueness under the Due Process Clause is not interchangeable with the rationale of our cases construing and applying the Eighth Amendment.

> Finally, our holding today also does not render "sentencing procedure[s]" entirely "immune from scrutiny under the due process clause." Williams v. United States, 337 U.S., at 252; see, e.g., Townsend v. Burke, 334 U.S. 736, 741 (1948) (holding that due process is violated when a court relies on "extensively and materially false" evidence to impose a sentence on an uncounseled defendant). We hold only that the advisory Sentencing Guidelines * * * are not subject to a challenge under the void-for-vagueness doctrine.

Justices Ginsburg and Sotomayor concurred only in the judgment. They argued that the Guideline under which Beckles was sentenced was not in fact constitutionally vague, so it was unnecessary to reach the broad holding that the majority did. Justice Sotomayor wrote separately to argue that the Guidelines should be subject to scrutiny as void-for-vagueness. She concluded that "[i]t violates the Due Process Clause to condemn someone to prison on the basis of a sentencing rule so shapeless as to resist interpretation. But the Court's decision today permits exactly that result."

CHAPTER 12

DOUBLE JEOPARDY

■ ■ ■

II. THE EFFECT OF AN ACQUITTAL

Page 1621. Add after the headnote on *Evans v. Michigan*:

Dismissal When the Government Refuses to Participate in the Trial After the Jury Has Been Empanelled: Martinez v. Illinois

In the following per curiam opinion, the Court reiterates its bright-line rule that jeopardy attaches after the jury has been empanelled (see Text at p. 1624); and it holds that a dismissal due to the government's refusal to participate in the trial constitutes an acquittal for double jeopardy purposes.

MARTINEZ V. ILLINOIS
United States Supreme Court, 2014.
134 S.Ct. 2070.

PER CURIAM.

The trial of Esteban Martinez was set to begin on May 17, 2010. His counsel was ready; the State was not. When the court swore in the jury and invited the State to present its first witness, the State declined to present any evidence. So Martinez moved for a directed not-guilty verdict, and the court granted it. The State appealed, arguing that the trial court should have granted its motion for a continuance. The question is whether the Double Jeopardy Clause bars the State's attempt to appeal in the hope of subjecting Martinez to a new trial.

The Illinois Supreme Court manifestly erred in allowing the State's appeal, on the theory that jeopardy never attached because Martinez "was never at risk of conviction." Our cases have repeatedly stated the bright-line rule that "jeopardy attaches when the jury is empaneled and sworn." Crist v. Bretz, 437 U.S. 28, 35 (1978). There is simply no doubt that Martinez was subjected to jeopardy. And because the trial court found the State's evidence insufficient to sustain a conviction, there is equally no doubt that Martinez may not be retried.

We therefore grant Martinez's petition for certiorari and reverse the judgment of the Illinois Supreme Court.

* * *

The State of Illinois indicted Martinez in August 2006 on charges of aggravated battery and mob action against Avery Binion and Demarco Scott. * * * [The government had trouble getting Binion and Scott to appear as witnesses, and the court granted a number of continuances. Eventually a trial date was set for May 17, 2010.] On the morning of May 17, however, Binion and Scott were again nowhere to be found. At 8:30, when the trial was set to begin, the State asked for a brief continuance. The court offered to delay swearing the jurors until a complete jury had been empaneled and told the State that it could at that point either have the jury sworn or move to dismiss its case. When Binion and Scott still had not shown up after the jury was chosen, the court offered to call the other cases on its docket so as to delay swearing the jury a bit longer. But when all these delays had run out, Binion and Scott were still nowhere in sight. The State filed a written motion for a continuance, arguing that it was "unable to proceed" without Binion and Scott. The court denied that motion:

> "The case before the Court began on July 7, 2006. In two months we will then be embarking upon half a decade of pending a Class 3 felony. Avery Binion, Jr., and Demarco [Scott] are well known in Elgin, both are convicted felons. One would believe that the Elgin Police Department would know their whereabouts. They were ordered to be in court today. The Court will issue body writs for both of these gentlemen.
>
> "In addition, the State's list of witnesses indicates twelve witnesses. Excluding Mr. Scott and Mr. Binion, that's ten witnesses. The Court would anticipate it would take every bit of today and most of tomorrow to get through ten witnesses. By then the People may have had a chance to execute the arrest warrant body writs for these two gentlemen.
>
> "The Court will deny the motion for continuance. I will swear the jury in in 15, 20 minutes. Perhaps you might want to send the police out to find these two gentlemen."

After a brief recess, the court offered to delay the start of the trial for several more hours if the continuance would "be of any help" to the State. But when the State made clear that Binion and Scott's "whereabouts" remained "unknown," the court concluded that the delay "would be a further waste of time." [The prosecutor indicated to the judge that if the trial was held in the absence of the two witnesses, the prosecution would not participate.]

The jury was then sworn. After instructing the jury, the court directed the State to proceed with its opening statement. The prosecutor demurred: "Your Honor, respectfully, the State is not participating in this case." After the defense waived its opening statement, the court directed the State to call its first witness. Again, the prosecutor demurred: "Respectfully, your Honor, the State is not participating in this matter." The defense then moved for a judgment of acquittal. [The court granted the motion, referring to its order as a "dismissal" of the charges.]

* * *

The State appealed, arguing that the trial court should have granted a continuance. Martinez responded that the State's appeal was improper because he had been acquitted. The Illinois Appellate Court sided with the State, holding that jeopardy had never attached and that the trial court had erred in failing to grant a continuance.

The Illinois Supreme Court granted review on the jeopardy issue and affirmed. It [reasoned that] Martinez "was never at risk of conviction"— and jeopardy therefore did not attach—because "[t]he State indicated it would not participate prior to the jury being sworn." And because Martinez "was not placed in jeopardy," the court held, the trial "court's entry of directed verdicts of not guilty did not constitute true acquittals." * * *

This case presents two issues. First, did jeopardy attach to Martinez? Second, if so, did the proceeding end in such a manner that the Double Jeopardy Clause bars his retrial? Our precedents clearly dictate an affirmative answer to each question.

* * *

There are few if any rules of criminal procedure clearer than the rule that "jeopardy attaches when the jury is empaneled and sworn." * * *

Our clearest exposition of this rule came in *Crist*, which addressed the constitutionality of a Montana statute providing that jeopardy did not attach until the swearing of the first witness. As *Crist* explains, "the precise point at which jeopardy [attaches] in a jury trial might have been open to argument before this Court's decision in Downum v. United States, 372 U.S. 734 [(1963)]," in which "the Court held that the Double Jeopardy Clause prevented a second prosecution of a defendant whose first trial had ended just after the jury had been sworn and before any testimony had been taken." But *Downum* put any such argument to rest: Its holding "necessarily pinpointed the stage in a jury trial when jeopardy attaches, and [it] has since been understood as explicit authority for the proposition that jeopardy attaches when the jury is empaneled and sworn."

The Illinois Supreme Court misread our precedents in suggesting that the swearing of the jury is anything other than a bright line at which jeopardy attaches. * * *

The Illinois Supreme Court's error was consequential, for it introduced confusion into what we have consistently treated as a bright-line rule: A jury trial begins, and jeopardy attaches, when the jury is sworn. We have never suggested the exception perceived by the Illinois Supreme Court—that jeopardy may not have attached where, under the circumstances of a particular case, the defendant was not genuinely at risk of conviction. Martinez was subjected to jeopardy because the jury in his case was sworn.

* * *

The conclusion that jeopardy has attached, however, begins, rather than ends, the inquiry as to whether the Double Jeopardy Clause bars retrial. The remaining question is whether the jeopardy ended in such a manner that the defendant may not be retried. Here, there is no doubt that Martinez's jeopardy ended in a manner that bars his retrial: The trial court acquitted him of the charged offenses. Perhaps the most fundamental rule in the history of double jeopardy jurisprudence has been that a verdict of acquittal could not be reviewed without putting a defendant twice in jeopardy, and thereby violating the Constitution.

Our cases have defined an acquittal to encompass any ruling that the prosecution's proof is insufficient to establish criminal liability for an offense. And the trial court clearly made such a ruling here. After the State declined to present evidence against Martinez, his counsel moved for directed findings of not guilty to both counts, and the court granted the motion for a directed finding. That is a textbook acquittal: a finding that the State's evidence cannot support a conviction.

The Illinois Supreme Court thought otherwise. It first opined that "[b]ecause [Martinez] was not placed in jeopardy, the [trial] court's entry of directed verdicts of not guilty did not constitute true acquittals." But the premise of that argument is incorrect: Martinez was in jeopardy, for the reasons given above. The court went on to "note that, in directing findings of not guilty," the trial court "referred to its action as a 'dismissal' rather than an acquittal." Under our precedents, however, that is immaterial: We have emphasized that what constitutes an "acquittal" is not to be controlled by the form of the judge's action; it turns on whether the ruling of the judge, whatever its label, actually represents a resolution of some or all of the factual elements of the offense charged. United States v. Scott, 437 U.S. 82, 96 (1978) ("We have previously noted that the trial judge's characterization of his own action cannot control the classification of the action").

Here * * * the trial court's action was an acquittal because the court acted on its view that the prosecution had failed to prove its case. * * *

The functional rule adopted by the Illinois Supreme Court is not necessary to avoid unfairness to prosecutors or to the public. On the day of trial, the court was acutely aware of the significance of swearing a jury. It repeatedly delayed that act to give the State additional time to find its witnesses. It had previously granted the State a number of continuances for the same purpose. And, critically, the court told the State on the day of trial that it could "move to dismiss [its] case" before the jury was sworn. Had the State accepted that invitation, the Double Jeopardy Clause would not have barred it from recharging Martinez. Instead, the State participated in the selection of jurors and did not ask for dismissal before the jury was sworn. * * * Here, the State knew, or should have known, that an acquittal forever bars the retrial of the defendant when it occurs after jeopardy has attached. The Illinois Supreme Court's holding is understandable, given the significant consequence of the State's mistake, but it runs directly counter to our precedents and to the protection conferred by the Double Jeopardy Clause.

* * *

VIII.   COLLATERAL ESTOPPEL

Page 1679. Add after the headnote on *Yeager v. United States*:

In Bravo-Fernandez v. United States, 137 S.Ct. 352 (2016), the defendant and a public official (Martinez) were tried together on charges regarding an alleged bribe that Bravo-Fernandez paid to Martinez. Specifically they were charged with (1) bribery, (2) conspiracy to commit bribery, and (3) a violation of the Travel Act, because the bribe involved an all-expense paid trip from Puerto Rico to Las Vegas. The jury convicted the defendants of bribery but acquitted them of the conspiracy and Travel Act violations. These verdicts were inconsistent, because if there was a bribe then there had to be a conspiracy and travel involved—the only fact disputed at trial was whether there was a bribe. The defendants appealed the bribery conviction, and it was vacated by the Court of Appeals, on grounds of instructional error. On retrial on the bribery charge, the defendants moved for acquittal on grounds of issue preclusion, arguing that the acquittal on the other counts should preclude the government from retrying on the vacated count.

The Court, in a unanimous opinion by Justice Ginsburg, disagreed and held that trial on the bribery charge was not precluded by the prior acquittals. She stated the problem and explained the Court's reasoning in the following passage:

> This case concerns the issue-preclusion component of the Double Jeopardy Clause. In criminal prosecutions, as in civil litigation, the issue-preclusion principle means that "when an issue of ultimate fact has once been determined by a valid and final judgment, that issue cannot again be litigated between the same parties in any future lawsuit." Ashe v. Swenson, 397 U.S. 436, 443 (1970).

> Does issue preclusion apply when a jury returns inconsistent verdicts, convicting on one count and acquitting on another count,

where both counts turn on the very same issue of ultimate fact? In such a case, this Court has held, both verdicts stand. The Government is barred by the Double Jeopardy Clause from challenging the acquittal, but because the verdicts are rationally irreconcilable, the acquittal gains no preclusive effect, United States v. Powell, 469 U.S. 57, 68 (1984).

Does issue preclusion attend a jury's acquittal verdict if the same jury in the same proceeding fails to reach a verdict on a different count turning on the same critical issue? This Court has answered yes, in those circumstances, the acquittal has preclusive force. Yeager v. United States, 557 U.S. 110, 121–122 (2009). As "there is no way to decipher what a hung count represents," we reasoned, a jury's failure to decide "has no place in the issue-preclusion analysis." See *id.*, at 125 ("[T]he fact that a jury hangs is evidence of nothing—other than, of course, that it has failed to decide anything.").

In the case before us, the jury returned irreconcilably inconsistent verdicts of conviction and acquittal. Without more, *Powell* would control. There could be no retrial of charges that yielded acquittals but, in view of the inconsistent verdicts, the acquittals would have no issue-preclusive effect on charges that yielded convictions. In this case, however, unlike *Powell,* the guilty verdicts were vacated on appeal because of error in the judge's instructions unrelated to the verdicts' inconsistency. Petitioners urge that, just as a jury's failure to decide has no place in issue-preclusion analysis, so vacated guilty verdicts should not figure in that analysis.

We hold otherwise. One cannot know from the jury's report why it returned no verdict. "A host of reasons" could account for a jury's failure to decide—"sharp disagreement, confusion about the issues, exhaustion after a long trial, to name but a few." *Yeager,* 557 U.S., at 121. But actual inconsistency in a jury's verdicts is a reality; vacatur of a conviction for unrelated legal error does not reconcile the jury's inconsistent returns. We therefore bracket this case with *Powell,* not *Yeager,* and affirm the judgment of the Court of Appeals, which held that issue preclusion does not apply when verdict inconsistency renders unanswerable "what the jury necessarily decided."

Justice Thomas wrote a short concurring opinion, asserting that "[a]s originally understood, the Double Jeopardy Clause did not have an issue-preclusion prong" and that "[i]n an appropriate case, we should reconsider the holdings of *Ashe* and *Yeager*." But he joined the majority opinion because the Court declined to extend those cases.

IX.   DUAL SOVEREIGNS

Page 1685 After the headnote on *Heath v. Alabama*, add the following:

Puerto Rico and the Federal Government Are Not Separate Sovereigns for Purposes of the Double Jeopardy Clause: Commonwealth of Puerto Rico v. Sanchez Valle

In Commonwealth of Puerto Rico v. Sanchez Valle, 136 S.Ct. 1863 (2016), the Supreme Court considered whether a defendant could be prosecuted twice for the same offense when one prosecution was brought by the Commonwealth of Puerto Rico and the other by the Federal Government. The Court, in an opinion by Justice Kagan, held that Puerto Rico and the United States were not separate sovereigns for purposes of the Double Jeopardy Clause, and therefore the defendant could not be prosecuted for the same firearms offense in both a Puerto Rican and a Federal Court. Justice Kagan explained as follows:

> The Double Jeopardy Clause of the Fifth Amendment prohibits more than one prosecution for the "same offence." But under what is known as the dual-sovereignty doctrine, a single act gives rise to distinct offenses—and thus may subject a person to successive prosecutions—if it violates the laws of separate sovereigns. To determine whether two prosecuting authorities are different sovereigns for double jeopardy purposes, this Court asks a narrow, historically focused question. The inquiry does not turn, as the term "sovereignty" sometimes suggests, on the degree to which the second entity is autonomous from the first or sets its own political course. Rather, the issue is only whether the prosecutorial powers of the two jurisdictions have independent origins—or, said conversely, whether those powers derive from the same "ultimate source."

> * * *

> For whatever reason, the test we have devised to decide whether two governments are distinct for double jeopardy purposes overtly disregards common indicia of sovereignty. Under that standard, we do not examine the extent of control that one prosecuting authority wields over the other. The degree to which an entity exercises self-governance—whether autonomously managing its own affairs or continually submitting to outside direction—plays no role in the analysis. Nor do we care about a government's more particular ability to enact and enforce its own criminal laws. In short, the inquiry (despite its label) does not probe whether a government possesses the usual attributes, or acts in the common manner, of a sovereign entity.

Rather, as Puerto Rico itself acknowledges, our test hinges on a single criterion: the "ultimate source" of the power undergirding the respective prosecutions. Whether two prosecuting entities are dual sovereigns in the double jeopardy context, we have stated, depends on whether they draw their authority to punish the offender from distinct sources of power. The inquiry is thus historical, not functional— looking at the deepest wellsprings, not the current exercise, of prosecutorial authority. If two entities derive their power to punish from wholly independent sources (imagine here a pair of parallel lines), then they may bring successive prosecutions. Conversely, if those entities draw their power from the same ultimate source (imagine now two lines emerging from a common point, even if later diverging), then they may not.

Under that approach, the States are separate sovereigns from the Federal Government (and from one another). The States' powers to undertake criminal prosecutions * * * do not derive from the Federal Government. Instead, the States rely on authority originally belonging to them before admission to the Union and preserved to them by the Tenth Amendment. * * * State prosecutions therefore have their most ancient roots in an inherent sovereignty unconnected to, and indeed pre-existing, the U.S. Congress.

Justice Kagan undertook an extensive analysis of Puerto Rico's relationship with the United States, and ultimately concluded that it was not a separate sovereign for purposes of the Double Jeopardy Clause because its authority to establish and enforce criminal laws came from Congress. She concluded as follows:

Puerto Rico boasts a relationship to the United States that has no parallel in our history. And since the events of the early 1950's, an integral aspect of that association has been the Commonwealth's wide-ranging self-rule, exercised under its own Constitution. As a result of that charter, Puerto Rico today can avail itself of a wide variety of futures. But for purposes of the Double Jeopardy Clause, the future is not what matters—and there is no getting away from the past. Because the ultimate source of Puerto Rico's prosecutorial power is the Federal Government—because when we trace that authority all the way back, we arrive at the doorstep of the U.S. Capitol—the Commonwealth and the United States are not separate sovereigns. That means the two governments cannot "twice put" [the defendant] "in jeopardy" for the "same offence."

Justice Ginsburg, joined by Justice Thomas, concurred in the judgment, questioning whether there should be a double jeopardy carve-out for prosecutions by separate sovereigns at all. She expressed an interest in reconsidering the dual sovereignty doctrine in a subsequent case.

Justice Thomas wrote a separate opinion concurring in part and concurring in the judgment.

Justice Breyer, joined by Justice Sotomayor, dissented. He engaged in an extensive analysis of the history of the relationship between the United States and Puerto Rico. He concluded as follows:

> This history of statutes, language, organic acts, traditions, statements, and other actions, taken by all three branches of the Federal Government and by Puerto Rico, convinces me that the United States has entered into a compact one of the terms of which is that the "source" of Puerto Rico's criminal law ceased to be the U.S. Congress and became Puerto Rico itself, its people, and its constitution. The evidence of that grant of authority is far stronger than the evidence of congressional silence that led this Court to conclude that Indian tribes maintained a similar sovereign authority. Indeed, it is difficult to see how we can conclude that the tribes do possess this authority but Puerto Rico does not. Regardless, for the reasons given, I would hold for Double Jeopardy Clause purposes that the criminal law of Puerto Rico and the criminal law of the Federal Government do not find their legitimacy-conferring origin in the same "source."

CHAPTER 13

POST-CONVICTION CHALLENGES

■ ■ ■

II. GROUNDS FOR DIRECT ATTACKS ON A CONVICTION

A. INSUFFICIENT EVIDENCE

2. **The Standard of Appellate Review of Sufficiency of the Evidence**

Page 1704. Add the following at the bottom of the page:

Assessment of Sufficiency Where the Jury Instructions Add an Extra Element to the Crime: Musacchio v. United States

In Musacchio v. United States, 136 S.Ct. 709 (2016), the trial judge misinstructed the jury that it had to find two facts rather than one: the instruction was that the jury had to find that the defendant intentionally accessed a computer without authorization *and* exceeded authorized use, whereas the statute under which Musacchio was charged makes it a crime if a person "intentionally accesses a computer without authorization *or* exceeds authorized use." The Government failed to object to this jury instruction that, in essence, erroneously added an element that it had to prove. The defendant was nonetheless convicted, and appealed on grounds of insufficient evidence. One question for the Supreme Court was whether the sufficiency review would have to evaluate the evidence in light of the elements of the crime, or instead in light of the more stringent elements provided in the jury instruction.

The Court, in a unanimous opinion written by Justice Thomas, ruled that a sufficiency challenge must be assessed against the elements of the charged crime, not against the elements set forth in an erroneously heightened jury instruction. Justice Thomas elaborated as follows:

> On sufficiency review, a reviewing court makes a limited inquiry tailored to ensure that a defendant receives the minimum that due process requires: a "meaningful opportunity to defend" against the charge against him and a jury finding of guilt "beyond a reasonable doubt." Jackson v. Virginia, 443 U.S. 307, 314–315 (1979). The reviewing court considers only the "legal" question "whether, after

viewing the evidence in the light most favorable to the prosecution, *any* rational trier of fact could have found the essential elements of the crime beyond a reasonable doubt." *Id.,* at 319. That limited review does not intrude on the jury's role "to resolve conflicts in the testimony, to weigh the evidence, and to draw reasonable inferences from basic facts to ultimate facts." *Ibid.*

A reviewing court's limited determination on sufficiency review thus does not rest on how the jury was instructed. When a jury finds guilt after being instructed on all elements of the charged crime plus one more element, the jury has made all the findings that due process requires. If a jury instruction requires the jury to find guilt on the elements of the charged crime, a defendant will have had a meaningful opportunity to defend against the charge. And if the jury instruction requires the jury to find those elements "beyond a reasonable doubt," the defendant has been accorded the procedure that this Court has required to protect the presumption of innocence. The Government's failure to introduce evidence of an additional element does not implicate the principles that sufficiency review protects. All that a defendant is entitled to on a sufficiency challenge is for the court to make a "legal" determination whether the evidence was strong enough to reach a jury at all. The Government's failure to object to the heightened jury instruction thus does not affect the court's review for sufficiency of the evidence.

Justice Thomas noted that Musacchio did not contest that the indictment properly charged him with the statutory elements for conspiracy to obtain unauthorized access. Nor did he dispute that the evidence was sufficient to convict him of the crime charged in the indictment—of conspiring to make unauthorized access. Accordingly, the Court rejected his sufficiency challenge.

D. THE EFFECT OF AN ERROR ON THE VERDICT

1. Harmless Error

Page 1721. Add the following new headnotes after the headnote on *Rivera v. Illinois*:

Restricting Closing Argument Is Not Clearly Structural Error: Glebe v. Frost

In Glebe v. Frost, 135 S.Ct. 1429 (2014) (per curiam), a habeas petitioner argued that a structural error occurred when the state trial court restricted defense counsel from making a particular argument in closing. Trial counsel wanted to argue to the jury in closing 1) that the prosecution failed to prove that the defendant was an accomplice to robberies; and 2) that in committing the crime, the defendant was acting under duress. The trial judge insisted that defense counsel choose one argument or the other to close, as the arguments were inconsistent. Defense counsel limited his closing argument to duress, and the defendant was convicted. On direct review, the state court found the trial court's restriction to be a due process violation, but also found the error to be harmless. On habeas review, Frost argued that the state court erred in finding harmless error, because the restriction of counsel's argument was a "structural" error that could not be assessed for harmlessness.

Because the case was on habeas review, Frost was required to show not just that an error occurred but that the state court violated clearly established law as determined by the Supreme Court. 22 U.S.C. § 2254(d). The Court concluded that assuming an error occurred, it was not clearly established that the error was structural. It declared that "[o]nly the rare type of error—in general, one that infects the entire trial process and necessarily renders it fundamentally unfair—requires automatic reversal. None of our cases clearly requires placing improper restriction of closing argument in this narrow category."

Frost argued that the Court's decision in Herring v. New York, 442 U.S. 853 (1975), clearly established that structural error occurred in his case. In *Herring,* [Text, page 1468], the Court found a violation of due process when the trial court prevented defense counsel from making a closing argument. But the Court in *Frost* held that *Herring* did *not* clearly establish that a trial court was prohibited from requiring defense counsel to choose between inconsistent arguments. The Court reasoned as follows:

> *Herring* held that complete denial of summation violates the Assistance of Counsel Clause. According to the Ninth Circuit, *Herring* further held that this denial amounts to structural error. We need not opine on the accuracy of that interpretation. For even assuming that *Herring* established that *complete denial* of summation amounts to structural error, it did not clearly establish that the *restriction* of summation also amounts to structural error. A court could reasonably conclude, after all, that prohibiting all argument differs from prohibiting argument in the alternative.

Structural Error Not Raised Until Collateral Attack for Ineffective Assistance of Counsel: Weaver v. Massachusetts

The Court in Weaver v. Massachusetts, 137 S.Ct. 1899, 2017 WL 2674153, considered whether a structural error must result in automatic reversal when the error was not raised until the defendant complained about it on collateral attack in the form of an ineffective assistance of counsel claim. The ineffective assistance claim was that defense counsel failed to object to the exclusion of the public during two days of jury selection.

Justice Kennedy, writing for six members of the Court, held that when a structural error is raised collaterally as a ground for ineffective assistance, the defendant must show prejudice under *Strickland*. He first laid out an overview of the Court's case law on structural error; he noted that the Court had found three different types of errors that it has defined as structural:

> First, an error has been deemed structural in some instances if the right at issue is not designed to protect the defendant from erroneous conviction but instead protects some other interest. This is true of the defendant's right to conduct his own defense, which, when exercised, "usually increases the likelihood of a trial outcome unfavorable to the defendant." McKaskle v. Wiggins, 465 U.S. 168, 177, n. 8 (1984). That right is based on the fundamental legal principle that a defendant must be allowed to make his own choices about the proper way to protect his own liberty. Because harm is irrelevant to the basis underlying the right, the Court has deemed a violation of that right structural error. See United States v. Gonzalez-Lopez, 548 U.S. 140, 149, n. 4 (2006).

> Second, an error has been deemed structural if the effects of the error are simply too hard to measure. For example, when a defendant is denied the right to select his or her own attorney, the precise "effect of the violation cannot be ascertained." Ibid. Because the government will, as a result, find it almost impossible to show that the error was harmless beyond a reasonable doubt, the efficiency costs of letting the government try to make the showing are unjustified.

> Third, an error has been deemed structural if the error always results in fundamental unfairness. For example, if an indigent defendant is denied an attorney or if the judge fails to give a reasonable-doubt instruction, the resulting trial is always a fundamentally unfair one. See Gideon v. Wainwright, 372 U.S. 335, 343–345 (1963) (right to an attorney); Sullivan v. Louisiana, 508 U.S. 275, 279 (1993) (right to a reasonable-doubt instruction). It therefore would be futile for the government to try to show harmlessness.

> These categories are not rigid. In a particular case, more than one of these rationales may be part of the explanation for why an error is deemed to be structural. For these purposes, however, one point is critical: An error can count as structural even if the error does not lead to fundamental unfairness in every case.

Next, Justice Kennedy evaluated the right to a public trial [discussed in Chapter Ten of the Text] and why the deprivation of that right is a structural error—but also why it is not the type of structural error that always leads to fundamental unfairness:

> [A] violation of the right to a public trial is a structural error. It is relevant to determine why that is so. In particular, the question is whether a public-trial violation counts as structural because it always leads to fundamental unfairness or for some other reason.

> In Waller v. Georgia, 467 U.S. 39 (1984), the state court prohibited the public from viewing a weeklong suppression hearing out of concern for the privacy of persons other than those on trial. Although it recognized that there would be instances where closure was justified, this Court noted that "such circumstances will be rare" and that the closure in question was unjustified. Still, the Court did not order a new trial. Instead it ordered a new suppression hearing that was open to the public. If the same evidence was found admissible in that renewed pretrial proceeding, the Court held, no new trial as to guilt would be necessary. This was despite the structural aspect of the violation.

> Some 25 years after the *Waller* decision, the Court issued its per curiam ruling in Presley v. Georgia, 558 U.S. 209. In that case, as here, the courtroom was closed to the public during jury voir dire. Unlike here, however, there was a trial objection to the closure, and the issue was raised on direct appeal. * * * Although the Court expressly noted that courtroom closure may be ordered in some circumstances, the Court also stated that it was "still incumbent upon" the trial court "to consider all reasonable alternatives to closure."

> These opinions teach that courtroom closure is to be avoided, but that there are some circumstances when it is justified. The problems that may be encountered by trial courts in deciding whether some closures are necessary, or even in deciding which members of the public should be admitted when seats are scarce, are difficult ones. For example, there are often preliminary instructions that a judge may want to give to the venire as a whole, rather than repeating those instructions (perhaps with unintentional differences) to several groups of potential jurors. On the other hand, various constituencies of the public—the family of the accused, the family of the victim, members of the press, and other persons—all have their own interests in observing the selection of jurors. How best to manage these problems is not a topic discussed at length in any decision or commentary the Court has found.

> So although the public-trial right is structural, it is subject to exceptions. Though these cases should be rare, a judge may deprive a defendant of his right to an open courtroom by making proper factual findings in support of the decision to do so. The fact that the public-

trial right is subject to these exceptions suggests that not every public-trial violation results in fundamental unfairness.

* * *

Indeed, the Court has not said that a public-trial violation renders a trial fundamentally unfair in every case. In the two cases in which the Court has discussed the reasons for classifying a public-trial violation as structural error, the Court has said that a public-trial violation is structural for a different reason: because of the "difficulty of assessing the effect of the error." *Gonzalez-Lopez,* 548 U.S., at 149, n. 4; see also *Waller, supra,* at 49, n. 9.

The public-trial right also protects some interests that do not belong to the defendant. After all, the right to an open courtroom protects the rights of the public at large, and the press, as well as the rights of the accused. So one other factor leading to the classification of structural error is that the public-trial right furthers interests other than protecting the defendant against unjust conviction. These precepts confirm the conclusion the Court now reaches that, while the public-trial right is important for fundamental reasons, in some cases an unlawful closure might take place and yet the trial still will be fundamentally fair from the defendant's standpoint.

Justice Kennedy concluded that when the violation of the right to public trial is not raised until part of an ineffective assistance claim, the prejudice requirement of *Strickland* is applicable.

The prejudice showing is in most cases a necessary part of a *Strickland* claim. The reason is that a defendant has a right to effective representation, not a right to an attorney who performs his duties "mistake-free." As a rule, therefore, a violation of the Sixth Amendment right to effective representation is not complete until the defendant is prejudiced.

That said, the concept of prejudice is defined in different ways depending on the context in which it appears. In the ordinary *Strickland* case, prejudice means a reasonable probability that, but for counsel's unprofessional errors, the result of the proceeding would have been different. But the *Strickland* Court cautioned that the prejudice inquiry is not meant to be applied in a "mechanical" fashion. For when a court is evaluating an ineffective-assistance claim, the ultimate inquiry must concentrate on "the fundamental fairness of the proceeding." Petitioner therefore argues that under a proper interpretation of *Strickland,* even if there is no showing of a reasonable probability of a different outcome, relief still must be granted if the convicted person shows that attorney errors rendered the trial fundamentally unfair. For the analytical purposes of this case, the Court will assume that petitioner's interpretation of *Strickland* is the correct one. In light of the Court's ultimate holding, however, the Court need not decide that question here.

As explained above, not every public-trial violation will in fact lead to a fundamentally unfair trial. Nor can it be said that the failure to object to a public-trial violation always deprives the defendant of a reasonable probability of a different outcome. Thus, when a defendant raises a public-trial violation via an ineffective-assistance-of-counsel claim, *Strickland* prejudice is not shown automatically. Instead, the burden is on the defendant to show either a reasonable probability of a different outcome in his or her case or, as the Court has assumed for these purposes, to show that the particular public-trial violation was so serious as to render his or her trial fundamentally unfair.

Justice Kennedy found a critical difference between structural errors raised at the time of trial or direct review, and those raised in the course of an ineffective counsel claim:

> The reason for placing the burden on the petitioner in this case, however, derives both from the nature of the error, and the difference between a public-trial violation preserved and then raised on direct review and a public-trial violation raised as an ineffective-assistance-of-counsel claim. * * * [W]hen a defendant objects to a courtroom closure, the trial court can either order the courtroom opened or explain the reasons for keeping it closed. When a defendant first raises the closure in an ineffective-assistance claim, however, the trial court is deprived of the chance to cure the violation either by opening the courtroom or by explaining the reasons for closure.

> Furthermore, when state or federal courts adjudicate errors objected to during trial and then raised on direct review, the systemic costs of remedying the error are diminished to some extent. That is because, if a new trial is ordered on direct review, there may be a reasonable chance that not too much time will have elapsed for witness memories still to be accurate and physical evidence not to be lost. There are also advantages of direct judicial supervision. Reviewing courts, in the regular course of the appellate process, can give instruction to the trial courts in a familiar context that allows for elaboration of the relevant principles based on review of an adequate record. For instance, in this case, the factors and circumstances that might justify a temporary closure are best considered in the regular appellate process and not in the context of a later proceeding, with its added time delays.

> When an ineffective-assistance-of-counsel claim is raised in postconviction proceedings, the costs and uncertainties of a new trial are greater because more time will have elapsed in most cases. The finality interest is more at risk, * * * and direct review often has given

at least one opportunity for an appellate review of trial proceedings. These differences justify a different standard for evaluating a structural error depending on whether it is raised on direct review or raised instead in a claim alleging ineffective assistance of counsel.

> In sum, an ineffective-assistance claim can function as a way to escape rules of waiver and forfeiture and raise issues not presented at trial, thus undermining the finality of jury verdicts. For this reason, the rules governing ineffective-assistance claims must be applied with scrupulous care.

Justice Kennedy emphasized that "[n]either the reasoning nor the holding here calls into question the Court's precedents determining that certain errors are deemed structural and require reversal because they cause fundamental unfairness, either to the defendant in the specific case or by pervasive undermining of the systemic requirements of a fair and open judicial process." He explained that the structural errors evaluated in previous cases "necessitated automatic reversal after they were preserved and then raised on direct appeal."

Turning to the case at hand, Justice Kennedy found that the error in excluding the public from two days of jury selection was not prejudicial:

> It is of course possible that potential jurors might have behaved differently if petitioner's family had been present. And it is true that the presence of the public might have had some bearing on juror reaction. But here petitioner offered no evidence or legal argument establishing prejudice in the sense of a reasonable probability of a different outcome but for counsel's failure to object.

> In other circumstances a different result might obtain. If, for instance, defense counsel errs in failing to object when the government's main witness testifies in secret, then the defendant might be able to show prejudice with little more detail. Even in those circumstances, however, the burden would remain on the defendant to make the prejudice showing, because a public-trial violation does not always lead to a fundamentally unfair trial.

> In light of the above assumption that prejudice can be shown by a demonstration of fundamental unfairness, the remaining question is whether petitioner has shown that counsel's failure to object rendered the trial fundamentally unfair. The Court concludes that petitioner has not made the showing. Although petitioner's mother and her minister were indeed excluded from the courtroom for two days during jury selection, petitioner's trial was not conducted in secret or in a remote place. The closure was limited to the jury *voir dire*; the courtroom remained open during the evidentiary phase of the trial; the closure decision apparently was made by court officers rather than the judge; there were many members of the venire who did not become

jurors but who did observe the proceedings; and there was a record made of the proceedings that does not indicate any basis for concern, other than the closure itself.

Justice Kennedy concluded as follows:

> In the criminal justice system, the constant, indeed unending, duty of the judiciary is to seek and to find the proper balance between the necessity for fair and just trials and the importance of finality of judgments. When a structural error is preserved and raised on direct review, the balance is in the defendant's favor, and a new trial generally will be granted as a matter of right. When a structural error is raised in the context of an ineffective-assistance claim, however, finality concerns are far more pronounced. For this reason, and in light of the other circumstances present in this case, petitioner must show prejudice in order to obtain a new trial. As explained above, he has not made the required showing.

Justice Thomas, joined by Justice Gorsuch, wrote a short concurring opinion, stating that there were open questions as to two of the Court's assumptions: that the right to a public trial extends to jury selection, and that *Strickland* prejudice can be found by errors that lead to fundamental unfairness.

Justice Alito, joined by Justice Thomas, concurred in the judgment, seeing the case as presenting a straightforward application of *Strickland* prejudice requirements. He concluded that "in order to obtain relief under *Strickland,* Weaver must show that the result of his trial was unreliable. He could do so by demonstrating a reasonable likelihood that his counsel's error affected the verdict. Alternatively, he could establish that the error falls within the very short list of errors for which prejudice [under *Strickland*] is presumed. Weaver has not attempted to make either argument, so his claim must be rejected."

Justice Breyer, joined by Justice Kagan, dissented in *Weaver*. He argued that all structural errors require automatic reversal and therefore could not be evaluated under *Strickland* prejudice standards. He explained as follows:

> Even if some structural errors do not create fundamental unfairness, *all* structural errors nonetheless have features that make them defy analysis by harmless-error standards. This is why *all* structural errors—not just the "fundamental unfairness" ones—are exempt from harmlessness inquiry and warrant automatic reversal on direct review. Those same features mean that *all* structural errors defy an actual-prejudice analysis under *Strickland*.

> For instance, the majority concludes that some errors—such as the public-trial error at issue in this case—have been labeled

"structural" because they have effects that "are simply too hard to measure." But how could any error whose effects are inherently indeterminate prove susceptible to actual-prejudice analysis under *Strickland*? Just as the difficulty of assessing the effect of such an error would turn harmless-error analysis into "a speculative inquiry into what might have occurred in an alternate universe," *Gonzalez-Lopez, supra,* at 149, n. 4, 150, so too would it undermine a defendant's ability to make an actual-prejudice showing to establish an ineffective-assistance claim.

The problem is evident with regard to public-trial violations. This Court has recognized that "the benefits of a public trial are frequently intangible, difficult to prove, or a matter of chance." Waller v. Georgia, 467 U.S. 39, 49, n. 9 (1984). As a result, a requirement that prejudice be shown would in most cases deprive the defendant of the public-trial guarantee, for it would be difficult to envisage a case in which he would have evidence available of specific injury. In order to establish actual prejudice from an attorney's failure to object to a public-trial violation, a defendant would face the nearly impossible burden of establishing how his trial might have gone differently had it been open to the public.

* * *

In my view, we should not require defendants to take on a task that is normally impossible to perform. Nor would I give lower courts the unenviably complex job of deciphering which structural errors really undermine fundamental fairness and which do not—that game is not worth the candle. I would simply say that just as structural errors are categorically insusceptible to harmless-error analysis on direct review, so too are they categorically insusceptible to actual-prejudice analysis in *Strickland* claims. A showing that an attorney's constitutionally deficient performance produced a structural error should consequently be enough to entitle a defendant to relief. I respectfully dissent.

III. COLLATERAL ATTACK

B. FEDERAL HABEAS CORPUS: THE PROCEDURAL FRAMEWORK

3. Factual Findings and Mixed Questions of Law and Fact

Page 1753. Add after the section on *Williams v. Taylor*:

Application of Deferential AEDPA Standards of Review and Rejection of Relief for "Unreasonable Failure to Extend" Existing Precedent: White v. Woodall

In the following case, the Court once again chides a lower federal court for failing to give proper deference to state court applications of fact to law. It also discusses a question left open by Williams v. Taylor: whether habeas relief can be granted because the state court failed to properly *extend* existing law.

WHITE V. WOODALL
Supreme Court of the United States, 2014.
134 S.Ct. 1697.

JUSTICE SCALIA delivered the opinion of the Court.

Respondent brutally raped, slashed with a box cutter, and drowned a 16-year-old high-school student. After pleading guilty to murder, rape, and kidnaping, he was sentenced to death. The Kentucky Supreme Court affirmed the sentence, and we denied certiorari. Ten years later, the Court of Appeals for the Sixth Circuit granted respondent's petition for a writ of habeas corpus on his Fifth Amendment claim. In so doing, it disregarded the limitations of 28 U.S.C. § 2254(d)—a provision of law that some federal judges find too confining, but that all federal judges must obey. We reverse.

* * *

On the evening of January 25, 1997, Sarah Hansen drove to a convenience store to rent a movie. When she failed to return home several hours later, her family called the police. Officers eventually found the vehicle Hansen had been driving a short distance from the convenience store. They followed a 400- to 500-foot trail of blood from the van to a nearby lake, where Hansen's unclothed, dead body was found floating in the water. Hansen's throat had been slashed twice with each cut approximately 3.5 to 4 inches long, and her windpipe was totally severed.

Authorities questioned respondent when they learned that he had been in the convenience store on the night of the murder. Respondent gave conflicting statements regarding his whereabouts that evening. Further investigation revealed that respondent's fingerprints were on the van the victim was driving, blood was found on respondent's front door, blood on his clothing and sweatshirt was consistent with the blood of the victim, and DNA on vaginal swabs taken from the victim was consistent with respondent's.

Faced with overwhelming evidence of his guilt, respondent pleaded guilty to capital murder. He also pleaded guilty to capital kidnaping and first-degree rape, the statutory aggravating circumstance for the murder. At the ensuing penalty-phase trial, respondent called character witnesses but declined to testify himself. Defense counsel asked the trial judge to instruct the jury that "[a] defendant is not compelled to testify and the fact that the defendant did not testify should not prejudice him in any way." The trial judge denied the request, and the Kentucky Supreme Court affirmed that denial. While recognizing that the Fifth Amendment requires a no-adverse-inference instruction to protect a nontestifying defendant at the guilt phase, see Carter v. Kentucky, 450 U.S. 288 (1981), the court held that *Carter* and our subsequent cases did not require such an instruction [at the penalty phase]. We denied respondent's petition for a writ of certiorari from that direct appeal.

In 2006, respondent filed this petition for habeas corpus in Federal District Court. The District Court granted relief, holding, as relevant here, that the trial court's refusal to issue a no-adverse-inference instruction at the penalty phase violated respondent's Fifth Amendment privilege against self-incrimination. The Court of Appeals affirmed and ordered Kentucky to either resentence respondent within 180 days or release him. We granted certiorari.

* * *

Section 2254(d) of Title 28 provides that "[a]n application for a writ of habeas corpus on behalf of a person in custody pursuant to the judgment of a State court shall not be granted with respect to any claim that was adjudicated on the merits in State court proceedings unless the adjudication of the claim . . . resulted in a decision that was contrary to, or involved an unreasonable application of, clearly established Federal law, as determined by the Supreme Court of the United States." This standard * * * is difficult to meet. "Clearly established Federal law" for purposes of § 2254(d)(1) includes only "the holdings, as opposed to the dicta, of this Court's decisions." Williams v. Taylor, 529 U.S. 362, 412 (2000). And an "unreasonable application of" those holdings must be "objectively unreasonable," not merely wrong; even "clear error" will not suffice. Rather, "[a]s a condition for obtaining habeas corpus from a federal court, a state prisoner must show that the state court's ruling on the claim being presented in federal court was so lacking in justification that there was an error well understood and comprehended in existing law beyond any possibility for fairminded disagreement." Harrington v. Richter, 131 S.Ct. 770, 786–787 (2011).

Both the Kentucky Supreme Court and the Court of Appeals identified as the relevant precedents in this area our decisions in *Carter,* Estelle v. Smith, 451 U.S. 454 (1981), and Mitchell v. United States, 526 U.S. 314 (1999). *Carter* held that a no-adverse-inference instruction is required at the *guilt* phase. *Estelle* concerned the introduction at the penalty phase of the results of an involuntary, un-*Mirandized* pretrial psychiatric examination. And *Mitchell* disapproved a trial judge's drawing of an adverse inference from the defendant's silence at sentencing "with regard to factual determinations respecting the circumstances and details of the crime."

It is clear that the Kentucky Supreme Court's conclusion is not "contrary to" the actual holding of any of these cases. 28 U.S.C. § 2254(d)(1). The Court of Appeals held, however, that the "Kentucky Supreme Court's denial of this constitutional claim was an unreasonable application of" those cases. In its view, "reading *Carter, Estelle,* and *Mitchell* together, the only reasonable conclusion is that" a no-adverse-inference instruction was required at the penalty phase.[2]

We need not decide here, and express no view on, whether the conclusion that a no-adverse-inference instruction was required would be correct in a case not reviewed through the lens of § 2254(d)(1). For we are satisfied that the issue was, at a minimum, not "beyond any possibility for fairminded disagreement." *Harrington, supra,* 131 S.Ct., at 787.

We have, it is true, held that the privilege against self-incrimination applies to the penalty phase. But it is not uncommon for a constitutional rule to apply somewhat differently at the penalty phase than it does at the guilt phase. We have never directly held that *Carter* applies at a sentencing phase where the Fifth Amendment interests of the defendant are different.

Indeed, *Mitchell* itself leaves open the possibility that some inferences might permissibly be drawn from a defendant's penalty-phase silence. In that case, the District Judge had actually *drawn* from the defendant's silence an adverse inference about the drug quantity attributable to the defendant. We held that this ran afoul of the defendant's "right to remain silent at sentencing." (citing Griffin v. California, 380 U.S. 609, 614 (1965)). But we framed our holding narrowly, in terms implying that it was limited to inferences pertaining to the facts of the crime: "We decline to adopt an exception for the sentencing phase of a criminal case *with regard to factual determinations respecting the circumstances and details of the crime.*"

---

[2] The Court of Appeals also based its conclusion that respondent "was entitled to receive a no adverse inference instruction" on one of its own cases. That was improper. As we cautioned the Sixth Circuit two Terms ago, a lower court may not "consul[t] its own precedents, rather than those of this Court, in assessing" a habeas claim governed by § 2254. Parker v. Matthews, 132 S.Ct. 2148, 2155 (2012) (*per curiam*).

Mitchell, 526 U.S., at 328 (emphasis added). "The Government retains," we said, *"the burden of proving facts relevant to the crime . . .* and cannot enlist the defendant in this process at the expense of the self-incrimination privilege." *Id.,* at 330 (emphasis added). And *Mitchell* included an express reservation of direct relevance here: "Whether silence bears upon the determination of a lack of remorse, or upon acceptance of responsibility for purposes of the downward adjustment provided in § 3E1.1 of the United States Sentencing Guidelines (1998), is a separate question. It is not before us, and we express no view on it." *Ibid.*

Mitchell's reservation is relevant here for two reasons. First, if *Mitchell* suggests that *some* actual inferences might be permissible at the penalty phase, it certainly cannot be read to require a *blanket* no-adverse-inference instruction at every penalty-phase trial. And it was a blanket instruction that was requested and denied in this case; respondent's requested instruction would have informed the jury that "[a] defendant is not compelled to testify and the fact that the defendant did not testify should not prejudice him *in any way.*" Counsel for respondent conceded at oral argument that remorse was at issue during the penalty-phase trial, yet the proposed instruction would have precluded the jury from considering respondent's silence as indicative of his lack of remorse. * * * This alone suffices to establish that the Kentucky Supreme Court's conclusion was not "objectively unreasonable."

Second, regardless of the scope of respondent's proposed instruction, any inferences that could have been drawn from respondent's silence would arguably fall within the class of inferences as to which *Mitchell* leaves the door open. Respondent pleaded guilty to all of the charges he faced, including the applicable aggravating circumstances. Thus, Kentucky could not have shifted to respondent its "burden of proving facts relevant to the crime." Respondent's own admissions had already established every relevant fact on which Kentucky bore the burden of proof. There are reasonable arguments that the logic of *Mitchell* does not apply to such cases.

* * *

In arguing for a contrary result, respondent leans heavily on the notion that a state-court "determination may be set aside . . . if, under clearly established federal law, the state court was unreasonable in refusing to extend the governing legal principle to a context in which the principle should have controlled." The Court of Appeals and District Court relied on the same proposition in sustaining respondent's Fifth Amendment claim.

* * *

[T]his Court has never adopted the unreasonable-refusal-to-extend rule on which respondent relies. It has not been so much as endorsed in a majority opinion, let alone relied on as a basis for granting habeas relief. To the extent the unreasonable-refusal-to-extend rule differs from the one embraced in *Williams* and reiterated many times since, we reject it. Section 2254(d)(1) provides a remedy for instances in which a state court unreasonably *applies* this Court's precedent; it does not require state courts to *extend* that precedent or license federal courts to treat the failure to do so as error. Thus, "if a habeas court must extend a rationale before it can apply to the facts at hand," then by definition the rationale was not "clearly established at the time of the state-court decision." AEDPA's carefully constructed framework would be undermined if habeas courts introduced rules not clearly established under the guise of extensions to existing law.

This is not to say that § 2254(d)(1) requires an identical factual pattern before a legal rule must be applied. To the contrary, state courts must reasonably apply the rules squarely established by this Court's holdings to the facts of each case. The difference between applying a rule and extending it is not always clear, but certain principles are fundamental enough that when new factual permutations arise, the necessity to apply the earlier rule will be beyond doubt. The critical point is that relief is available under § 2254(d)(1)'s unreasonable-application clause if, and only if, it is so obvious that a clearly established rule applies to a given set of facts that there could be no fairminded disagreement on the question.

Perhaps the logical next step from *Carter, Estelle,* and *Mitchell* would be to hold that the Fifth Amendment requires a penalty-phase no-adverse-inference instruction in a case like this one; perhaps not. Either way, we have not yet taken that step, and there are reasonable arguments on both sides—which is all Kentucky needs to prevail in this AEDPA case. The appropriate time to consider the question as a matter of first impression would be on direct review, not in a habeas case governed by § 2254(d)(1).

* * *

Because the Kentucky Supreme Court's rejection of respondent's Fifth Amendment claim was not objectively unreasonable, the Sixth Circuit erred in granting the writ. We therefore need not reach its further holding that the trial court's putative error was not harmless. The judgment of the Court of Appeals is reversed, and the case is remanded for further proceedings consistent with this opinion.

JUSTICE BREYER, with whom JUSTICE GINSBURG and JUSTICE SOTOMAYOR join, dissenting.

* * *

This Court's decisions in Carter v. Kentucky, and Estelle v. Smith, clearly establish that a criminal defendant is entitled to a requested no-adverse-inference instruction in the penalty phase of a capital trial. First consider *Carter*. The Court held that a trial judge "has the constitutional obligation, upon proper request," to give a requested no-adverse-inference instruction in order "to minimize the danger that the jury will give evidentiary weight to a defendant's failure to testify." This is because when "the jury is left to roam at large with only its untutored instincts to guide it," it may "draw from the defendant's silence broad inferences of guilt." A trial court's refusal to give a requested no-adverse-inference instruction thus "exacts an impermissible toll on the full and free exercise of the [Fifth Amendment] privilege."

Now consider *Estelle*. The Court held that "so far as the protection of the Fifth Amendment privilege is concerned," it could "discern no basis to distinguish between the guilt and penalty phases" of a defendant's "capital murder trial." The State had introduced at the penalty phase the defendant's compelled statements to a psychiatrist, in order to show the defendant's future dangerousness. Defending the admission of those statements, the State argued that the defendant "was not entitled to the protection of the Fifth Amendment because [his statements were] used only to determine punishment after conviction, not to establish guilt." This Court rejected the State's argument on the ground that the Fifth Amendment applies equally to the penalty phase and the guilt phase of a capital trial.

What is unclear about the resulting law? If the Court holds in Case A that the First Amendment prohibits Congress from discriminating based on viewpoint, and then holds in Case B that the Fourteenth Amendment incorporates the First Amendment as to the States, then it is clear that the First Amendment prohibits the States from discriminating based on viewpoint. By the same logic, because the Court held in *Carter* that the Fifth Amendment requires a trial judge to give a requested no-adverse-inference instruction during the guilt phase of a trial, and held in *Estelle* that there is no basis for distinguishing between the guilt and punishment phases of a capital trial for purposes of the Fifth Amendment, it is clear that the Fifth Amendment requires a judge to provide a requested no-adverse-inference instruction during the penalty phase of a capital trial.

* * *

Failing to consider together the legal principles established by *Carter* and *Estelle*, the state court confined those cases to their facts. It held that *Carter* did not apply because Woodall had already pleaded guilty—that is, because Woodall requested a no-adverse-inference instruction at the penalty phase rather than the guilt phase of his trial. And it concluded that *Estelle* did not apply because *Estelle* was not a "jury instruction case." The Kentucky Supreme Court unreasonably failed to recognize that together *Carter* and *Estelle* compel a requested no-adverse-inference instruction at the penalty phase of a capital trial. And reading *Mitchell* to rein in the law in contemplation of never-before-recognized exceptions to this normal rule would be an unreasonable *retraction* of clearly established law, not a proper failure to "extend" it. Because the Sixth Circuit correctly applied clearly established law in granting Woodall's habeas petition, I would affirm.

D. LIMITATIONS ON OBTAINING HABEAS RELIEF

3. Procedural Default

c. The Meaning of "Cause and Prejudice"

Page 1790. Add the following at the bottom of the page:

In Davila v. Davis, 137 S.Ct. 2058, the Court held that *Coleman* and not *Martinez* applied to a default of a claim allegedly caused by ineffectiveness of appellate counsel in state post-conviction proceedings. Therefore the defendant's procedural default—failure to raise a claim on appeal—was not excused and habeas relief was not available to him. The Court held that the *Martinez* Court provided a limited exception to the *Coleman* rule that precludes a finding of cause when counsel was ineffective in failing to raise the claim. The Court in *Martinez* did not intend to replace *Coleman* in the context of appellate ineffectiveness. Justice Thomas wrote the opinion for five Members of the Court. Justice Breyer, joined by Justices Ginsburg, Sotomayor, and Kagan, dissented.

4. Adequate and Independent State Grounds

Page 1803. After the headnote on *Walker v. Martin*, add the following:

State Law Rule Finding Procedural Default for Failure to Raise a Claim on Direct Appeal Is an Adequate and Independent State Ground: Johnson v. Lee

The Supreme Court, in the per curiam opinion in Johnson v. Lee, 136 S.Ct. 1802 (2016), took the Ninth Circuit to task for failure to recognize that a California procedural rule was an adequate state ground that barred habeas review. The California "Dixon" rule provides that a defendant procedurally defaults a claim raised for the first time on state collateral review if he could have raised it earlier on direct appeal. Lee fell afoul of the rule, but the Ninth Circuit found that the Dixon rule was not an adequate ground to bar habeas relief, because it found the rule to be irregularly applied and not always cited by the California courts in dismissing a claim on collateral review. But the Supreme Court found that the rule had been consistently applied by the state courts, and that the failure of a few California courts to specifically cite *Dixon* was of no moment. The Court stated that "every State shares this procedural bar in some form" and that "[f]or such well-established and ubiquitous rules, it takes more than a few outliers to show inadequacy." The Court concluded as follows:

> By treating every missing citation as a sign of inconsistency, the Court of Appeals posed an unnecessary dilemma for California. The court forced the State to choose between the finality of its judgment and a burdensome opinion-writing requirement. Federal courts have no authority, however, to impose mandatory opinion-writing standards on state courts as the price of federal respect for their procedural rules. The Ninth Circuit's decision is thus fundamentally at odds with the federalism and comity concerns that motivate the adequate state ground doctrine in the habeas context.

The Federal Rules of Criminal Procedure

■ ■ ■

TITLE I.   APPLICABILITY

Rule 1. Scope; Definitions

(a) Scope.

(1) *In General.* These rules govern the procedure in all criminal proceedings in the United States district courts, the United States courts of appeals, and the Supreme Court of the United States.

(2) *State or Local Judicial Officer.* When a rule so states, it applies to a proceeding before a state or local judicial officer.

(3) *Territorial Courts.* These rules also govern the procedure in all criminal proceedings in the following courts:

(A)   the district court of Guam;

(B)   the district court for the Northern Mariana Islands, except as otherwise provided by law; and

(C)   the district court of the Virgin Islands, except that the prosecution of offenses in that court must be by indictment or information as otherwise provided by law.

(4) *Removed Proceedings.* Although these rules govern all proceedings after removal from a state court, state law governs a dismissal by the prosecution.

(5) *Excluded Proceedings.* Proceedings not governed by these rules include:

(A)   the extradition and rendition of a fugitive;

(B)   a civil property forfeiture for violating a federal statute;

(C)   the collection of a fine or penalty;

(D)   a proceeding under a statute governing juvenile delinquency to the extent the procedure is inconsistent with the statute, unless Rule 20(d) provides otherwise;

(E)   a dispute between seamen under 22 U.S.C. §§ 256–258; and

(F)   a proceeding against a witness in a foreign country under 28 U.S.C. § 1784.

(b) Definitions. The following definitions apply to these rules:

(1) "Attorney for the government" means:

(A) the Attorney General or an authorized assistant;

(B) a United States attorney or an authorized assistant;

(C) when applicable to cases arising under Guam law, the Guam Attorney General or other person whom Guam law authorizes to act in the matter; and

(D) any other attorney authorized by law to conduct proceedings under these rules as a prosecutor.

(2) "Court" means a federal judge performing functions authorized by law.

(3) "Federal judge" means:

(A) a justice or judge of the United States as these terms are defined in 28 U.S.C. § 451;

(B) a magistrate judge; and

(C) a judge confirmed by the United States Senate and empowered by statute in any commonwealth, territory, or possession to perform a function to which a particular rule relates.

(4) "Judge" means a federal judge or a state or local judicial officer.

(5) "Magistrate judge" means a United States magistrate judge as defined in 28 U.S.C. §§ 631–639.

(6) "Oath" includes an affirmation.

(7) "Organization" is defined in 18 U.S.C. § 18.

(8) "Petty offense" is defined in 18 U.S.C. § 19.

(9) "State" includes the District of Columbia, and any commonwealth, territory, or possession of the United States.

(10) "State or local judicial officer" means:

(A) a state or local officer authorized to act under 18 U.S.C. § 3041; and

(B) a judicial officer empowered by statute in the District of Columbia or in any commonwealth, territory, or possession to perform a function to which a particular rule relates.

(11) "Telephone" means any technology for transmitting live electronic voice communication.

(12) "Victim" means a "crime victim" as defined in 18 U.S.C. § 3771(e).

(c) Authority of a Justice or Judge of the United States. When these rules authorize a magistrate judge to act, any other federal judge may also act.

Rule 2. Interpretation

These rules are to be interpreted to provide for the just determination of every criminal proceeding, to secure simplicity in procedure and fairness in administration, and to eliminate unjustifiable expense and delay.

TITLE II.   PRELIMINARY PROCEEDINGS

Rule 3. The Complaint

The complaint is a written statement of the essential facts constituting the offense charged. Except as provided in Rule 4.1, it must be made under oath before a magistrate judge or, if none is reasonably available, before a state or local judicial officer.

Rule 4. Arrest Warrant or Summons on a Complaint

(a) Issuance. If the complaint or one or more affidavits filed with the complaint establish probable cause to believe that an offense has been committed and that the defendant committed it, the judge must issue an arrest warrant to an officer authorized to execute it. At the request of an attorney for the government, the judge must issue a summons, instead of a warrant, to a person authorized to serve it. A judge may issue more than one warrant or summons on the same complaint. If an individual fails to appear in response to a summons, a judge may, and upon request of an attorney for the government must, issue a warrant. If an organizational defendant fails to appear in response to a summons, a judge may take any action authorized by United States law.

(b) Form.

(1) *Warrant.* A warrant must:

(A) contain the defendant's name or, if it is unknown, a name or description by which the defendant can be identified with reasonable certainty;

(B) describe the offense charged in the complaint;

(C) command that the defendant be arrested and brought without unnecessary delay before a magistrate judge or, if none is reasonably available, before a state or local judicial officer; and

(D) be signed by a judge.

(2) *Summons.* A summons must be in the same form as a warrant except that it must require the defendant to appear before a magistrate judge at a stated time and place.

(c) Execution or Service, and Return.

(1) *By Whom.* Only a marshal or other authorized officer may execute a warrant. Any person authorized to serve a summons in a federal civil action may serve a summons.

(2) *Location.* A warrant may be executed, or a summons served, within the jurisdiction of the United States or anywhere else a federal statute authorizes an arrest. A summons to an organization under Rule 4(c)(3)(D) may also be served at a place not within a judicial district of the United States.

(3) *Manner.*

(A) A warrant is executed by arresting the defendant. Upon arrest, an officer possessing the original or a duplicate original warrant must show it to the defendant. If the officer does not possess the warrant, the officer must inform the defendant of the warrant's existence and of the offense charged and, at the defendant's request, must show the original or a duplicate original warrant to the defendant as soon as possible.

(B) A summons is served on an individual defendant:

(i) by delivering a copy to the defendant personally; or

(ii) by leaving a copy at the defendant's residence or usual place of abode with a person of suitable age and discretion residing at that location and by mailing a copy to the defendant's last known address.

(C) A summons is served on an organization in a judicial district of the United States by delivering a copy to an officer, to a managing or general agent, or to another agent appointed or legally authorized to receive service of process. If the agent is one authorized by statute and the statute so requires, a copy must also be mailed to the organization.

(D) A summons is served on an organization not within a judicial district of the United States:

(i) by delivering a copy, in a manner authorized by the foreign jurisdiction's law, to a managing or general agent, or to an agent appointed or legally authorized to receive service of process; or

(ii) by any other means that gives notice, including one that is:

(a) stipulated by the parties;

(b) undertaken by a foreign authority in response to a letter rogatory, a letter of request, or a request submitted under an applicable international agreement; or

(c) permitted by an international agreement.

(4) *Return.*

(A) After executing a warrant, the officer must return it to the judge before whom the defendant is brought in accordance with Rule 5. The officer may do so by reliable electronic means. At the request of an attorney for the government, an unexecuted warrant must be brought back to and canceled by a magistrate judge or, if none is reasonably available, by a state or local judicial officer.

(B) The person to whom a summons was delivered for service must return it on or before the return day.

(C) At the request of an attorney for the government, a judge may deliver an unexecuted warrant, an unserved summons, or a copy of the warrant or summons to the marshal or other authorized person for execution or service.

(d) Warrant by Telephone or Other Reliable Electronic Means. In accordance with Rule 4.1, a magistrate judge may issue a warrant or summons based on information communicated by telephone or other reliable electronic means.

Rule 4.1. Complaint, Warrant, or Summons by Telephone or Other Reliable Electronic Means

(a) In General. A magistrate judge may consider information communicated by telephone or other reliable electronic means when reviewing a complaint or deciding whether to issue a warrant or summons.

(b) Procedures. If a magistrate judge decides to proceed under this rule, the following procedures apply:

(1) *Taking Testimony Under Oath.* The judge must place under oath—and may examine—the applicant and any person on whose testimony the application is based.

(2) *Creating a Record of the Testimony and Exhibits.*

(A) *Testimony Limited to Attestation.* If the applicant does no more than attest to the contents of a written affidavit submitted by reliable electronic means, the judge must acknowledge the attestation in writing on the affidavit.

(B) *Additional Testimony or Exhibits.* If the judge considers additional testimony or exhibits, the judge must:

(i) have the testimony recorded verbatim by an electronic recording device, by a court reporter, or in writing;

(ii) have any recording or reporter's notes transcribed, have the transcription certified as accurate, and file it;

(iii) sign any other written record, certify its accuracy, and file it; and

(iv) make sure that the exhibits are filed.

(3) *Preparing a Proposed Duplicate Original of a Complaint, Warrant, or Summons.* The applicant must prepare a proposed duplicate original of a complaint, warrant, or summons, and must read or otherwise transmit its contents verbatim to the judge.

(4) *Preparing an Original Complaint, Warrant, or Summons.* If the applicant reads the contents of the proposed duplicate original, the judge must enter those contents into an original complaint, warrant, or summons. If the applicant transmits the contents by reliable electronic means, the transmission received by the judge may serve as the original.

(5) *Modification.* The judge may modify the complaint, warrant, or summons. The judge must then:

(A) transmit the modified version to the applicant by reliable electronic means; or

(B) file the modified original and direct the applicant to modify the proposed duplicate original accordingly.

(6) *Issuance.* To issue the warrant or summons, the judge must:

(A) sign the original documents;

(B) enter the date and time of issuance on the warrant or summons; and

(C) transmit the warrant or summons by reliable electronic means to the applicant or direct the applicant to sign the judge's name and enter the date and time on the duplicate original.

(c) Suppression Limited. Absent a finding of bad faith, evidence obtained from a warrant issued under this rule is not subject to suppression on the ground that issuing the warrant in this manner was unreasonable under the circumstances.

Rule 5. Initial Appearance

(a) In General.

(1) *Appearance Upon an Arrest.*

(A) A person making an arrest within the United States must take the defendant without unnecessary delay before a magistrate judge, or before a state or local judicial officer as Rule 5(c) provides, unless a statute provides otherwise.

(B) A person making an arrest outside the United States must take the defendant without unnecessary delay before a magistrate judge, unless a statute provides otherwise.

(2) *Exceptions.*

(A) An officer making an arrest under a warrant issued upon a complaint charging solely a violation of 18 U.S.C. § 1073 need not comply with this rule if:

(i) the person arrested is transferred without unnecessary delay to the custody of appropriate state or local authorities in the district of arrest; and

(ii) an attorney for the government moves promptly, in the district where the warrant was issued, to dismiss the complaint.

(B) If a defendant is arrested for violating probation or supervised release, Rule 32.1 applies.

(C) If a defendant is arrested for failing to appear in another district, Rule 40 applies.

(3) *Appearance Upon a Summons.* When a defendant appears in response to a summons under Rule 4, a magistrate judge must proceed under Rule 5(d) or (e), as applicable.

(b) Arrest Without a Warrant. If a defendant is arrested without a warrant, a complaint meeting Rule 4(a)'s requirement of probable cause must be promptly filed in the district where the offense was allegedly committed.

(c) Place of Initial Appearance; Transfer to Another District.

(1) *Arrest in the District Where the Offense Was Allegedly Committed.* If the defendant is arrested in the district where the offense was allegedly committed:

(A) the initial appearance must be in that district; and

(B) if a magistrate judge is not reasonably available, the initial appearance may be before a state or local judicial officer.

(2) *Arrest in a District Other Than Where the Offense Was Allegedly Committed.* If the defendant was arrested in a district other than where the offense was allegedly committed, the initial appearance must be:

(A) in the district of arrest; or

(B) in an adjacent district if:

(i) the appearance can occur more promptly there; or

(ii) the offense was allegedly committed there and the initial appearance will occur on the day of arrest.

(3) *Procedures in a District Other Than Where the Offense Was Allegedly Committed.* If the initial appearance occurs in a district other than where the offense was allegedly committed, the following procedures apply:

(A) the magistrate judge must inform the defendant about the provisions of Rule 20;

(B) if the defendant was arrested without a warrant, the district court where the offense was allegedly committed must first issue a warrant before the magistrate judge transfers the defendant to that district;

(C) the magistrate judge must conduct a preliminary hearing if required by Rule 5.1;

(D) the magistrate judge must transfer the defendant to the district where the offense was allegedly committed if:

(i) the government produces the warrant, a certified copy of the warrant, or a reliable electronic form of either; and

(ii) the judge finds that the defendant is the same person named in the indictment, information, or warrant; and

(E) when a defendant is transferred and discharged, the clerk must promptly transmit the papers and any bail to the clerk in the district where the offense was allegedly committed.

(4) *Procedure for Persons Extradited to the United States.* If the defendant is surrendered to the United States in accordance with a request for the defendant's extradition, the initial appearance must be in the district (or one of the districts) where the offense is charged.

(d) Procedure in a Felony Case.

(1) *Advice.* If the defendant is charged with a felony, the judge must inform the defendant of the following:

(A) the complaint against the defendant, and any affidavit filed with it;

(B) the defendant's right to retain counsel or to request that counsel be appointed if the defendant cannot obtain counsel;

(C) the circumstances, if any, under which the defendant may secure pretrial release;

(D) any right to a preliminary hearing;

(E) the defendant's right not to make a statement, and that any statement made may be used against the defendant; and

(F) that a defendant who is not a United States citizen may request that an attorney for the government or a federal law enforcement official notify a consular officer from the defendant's country of nationality that the defendant has been arrested—but that even without the defendant's request, a treaty or other international agreement may require consular notification.

(2) *Consulting with Counsel.* The judge must allow the defendant reasonable opportunity to consult with counsel.

(3) *Detention or Release.* The judge must detain or release the defendant as provided by statute or these rules.

(4) *Plea.* A defendant may be asked to plead only under Rule 10.

(e) Procedure in a Misdemeanor Case. If the defendant is charged with a misdemeanor only, the judge must inform the defendant in accordance with Rule 58(b)(2).

(f) Video Teleconferencing. Video teleconferencing may be used to conduct an appearance under this rule if the defendant consents.

Rule 5.1. Preliminary Hearing

(a) In General. If a defendant is charged with an offense other than a petty offense, a magistrate judge must conduct a preliminary hearing unless:

(1) the defendant waives the hearing;

(2) the defendant is indicted;

(3) the government files an information under Rule 7(b) charging the defendant with a felony;

(4) the government files an information charging the defendant with a misdemeanor; or

(5) the defendant is charged with a misdemeanor and consents to trial before a magistrate judge.

(b) Selecting a District. A defendant arrested in a district other than where the offense was allegedly committed may elect to have the preliminary hearing conducted in the district where the prosecution is pending.

(c) Scheduling. The magistrate judge must hold the preliminary hearing within a reasonable time, but no later than 14 days after the initial appearance if the defendant is in custody and no later than 21 days if not in custody.

(d) Extending the Time. With the defendant's consent and upon a showing of good cause—taking into account the public interest in the prompt disposition of criminal cases—a magistrate judge may extend the time limits in Rule 5.1(c) one or more times. If the defendant does not consent, the magistrate judge may extend the time limits only on a showing that extraordinary circumstances exist and justice requires the delay.

(e) Hearing and Finding. At the preliminary hearing, the defendant may cross-examine adverse witnesses and may introduce evidence but may not object to evidence on the ground that it was unlawfully acquired. If the magistrate judge finds probable cause to believe an offense has been committed and the defendant committed it, the magistrate judge must promptly require the defendant to appear for further proceedings.

(f) Discharging the Defendant. If the magistrate judge finds no probable cause to believe an offense has been committed or the defendant committed it, the magistrate judge must dismiss the complaint and discharge the defendant. A discharge does not preclude the government from later prosecuting the defendant for the same offense.

(g) Recording the Proceedings. The preliminary hearing must be recorded by a court reporter or by a suitable recording device. A recording of the proceeding may be made available to any party upon request. A copy of the recording and a transcript may be provided to any party upon request and upon any payment required by applicable Judicial Conference regulations.

(h) Producing a Statement.

(1) *In General.* Rule 26.2(a)–(d) and (f) applies at any hearing under this rule, unless the magistrate judge for good cause rules otherwise in a particular case.

(2) *Sanctions for Not Producing a Statement.* If a party disobeys a Rule 26.2 order to deliver a statement to the moving party, the magistrate judge must not consider the testimony of a witness whose statement is withheld.

TITLE III.   THE GRAND JURY, THE INDICTMENT, AND THE INFORMATION

Rule 6. The Grand Jury

(a) Summoning a Grand Jury.

(1) *In General.* When the public interest so requires, the court must order that one or more grand juries be summoned. A grand jury must have 16 to 23 members, and the court must order that enough legally qualified persons be summoned to meet this requirement.

(2) *Alternate Jurors.* When a grand jury is selected, the court may also select alternate jurors. Alternate jurors must have the same qualifications and be selected in the same manner as any other juror. Alternate jurors replace jurors in the same sequence in which the alternates were selected. An alternate juror who replaces a juror is subject to the same challenges, takes the same oath, and has the same authority as the other jurors.

(b) Objection to the Grand Jury or to a Grand Juror.

(1) *Challenges.* Either the government or a defendant may challenge the grand jury on the ground that it was not lawfully drawn, summoned, or selected, and may challenge an individual juror on the ground that the juror is not legally qualified.

(2) *Motion to Dismiss an Indictment.* A party may move to dismiss the indictment based on an objection to the grand jury or on an individual juror's lack of legal qualification, unless the court has previously ruled on the same objection under Rule 6(b)(1). The motion to dismiss is governed by 28 U.S.C. § 1867(e). The court must not dismiss the indictment on the ground that a grand juror was not legally qualified if the record shows that at least 12 qualified jurors concurred in the indictment.

(c) Foreperson and Deputy Foreperson. The court will appoint one juror as the foreperson and another as the deputy foreperson. In the foreperson's absence, the deputy foreperson will act as the foreperson. The foreperson may administer oaths and affirmations and will sign all indictments. The foreperson—or another juror designated by the foreperson—will record the number of jurors concurring in every indictment and will file the record with the clerk, but the record may not be made public unless the court so orders.

(d) Who May Be Present.

(1) *While the Grand Jury Is in Session.* The following persons may be present while the grand jury is in session: attorneys for the government, the witness being questioned, interpreters when needed, and a court reporter or an operator of a recording device.

(2) *During Deliberations and Voting.* No person other than the jurors, and any interpreter needed to assist a hearing-impaired or speech-impaired juror, may be present while the grand jury is deliberating or voting.

(e) Recording and Disclosing the Proceedings.

(1) *Recording the Proceedings.* Except while the grand jury is deliberating or voting, all proceedings must be recorded by a court reporter or by a suitable recording device. But the validity of a prosecution is not affected by the unintentional failure to make a recording. Unless the court orders otherwise, an attorney for the government will retain control of the recording, the reporter's notes, and any transcript prepared from those notes.

(2) *Secrecy.*

(A) No obligation of secrecy may be imposed on any person except in accordance with Rule 6(e)(2)(B).

(B) Unless these rules provide otherwise, the following persons must not disclose a matter occurring before the grand jury:

(i) a grand juror;

(ii) an interpreter;

(iii) a court reporter;

(iv) an operator of a recording device;

(v) a person who transcribes recorded testimony;

(vi) an attorney for the government; or

(vii) a person to whom disclosure is made under Rule 6(e)(3)(A)(ii) or (iii).

(3) *Exceptions.*

(A) Disclosure of a grand-jury matter—other than the grand jury's deliberations or any grand juror's vote—may be made to:

(i) an attorney for the government for use in performing that attorney's duty;

(ii) any government personnel—including those of a state, state subdivision, Indian tribe, or foreign government—that an attorney for the government considers necessary to assist in performing that attorney's duty to enforce federal criminal law; or

(iii) a person authorized by 18 U.S.C. § 3322.

(B) A person to whom information is disclosed under Rule 6(e)(3)(A)(ii) may use that information only to assist an attorney for the government in performing that attorney's duty to enforce federal criminal law. An attorney for the government must promptly provide the court that impaneled the grand jury with the names of all persons to whom a disclosure has been made, and must certify that the attorney has advised those persons of their obligation of secrecy under this rule.

(C) An attorney for the government may disclose any grand-jury matter to another federal grand jury.

(D) An attorney for the government may disclose any grand-jury matter involving foreign intelligence, counterintelligence (as defined in 50 U.S.C. § 3003), or foreign intelligence information (as defined in Rule 6(e)(3)(D)(iii)) to any federal law enforcement, intelligence, protective, immigration, national defense, or national security official to assist the official receiving the information in the performance of that official's duties. An attorney for the government may also disclose any grand-jury matter involving, within the United States or elsewhere, a threat of attack or other grave hostile acts of a foreign power or its agent, a threat of domestic or international sabotage or terrorism, or clandestine intelligence gathering activities by an intelligence service or network of a foreign power or by its agent, to any appropriate federal, state, state subdivision, Indian tribal, or foreign government official, for the purpose of preventing or responding to such threat or activities.

(i) Any official who receives information under Rule 6(e)(3)(D) may use the information only as necessary in the conduct of that person's official duties subject to any limitations on the unauthorized disclosure of such information. Any state, state subdivision, Indian tribal, or foreign government official who receives information under Rule 6(e)(3)(D) may use the information only in a manner consistent with any guidelines issued by the Attorney General and the Director of National Intelligence.

(ii) Within a reasonable time after disclosure is made under Rule 6(e)(3)(D), an attorney for the government must file, under seal, a notice with the court in the district where the grand jury convened stating that such information was disclosed and the departments, agencies, or entities to which the disclosure was made.

(iii) As used in Rule 6(e)(3)(D), the term "foreign intelligence information" means:

(a) information, whether or not it concerns a United States person, that relates to the ability of the United States to protect against—

• actual or potential attack or other grave hostile acts of a foreign power or its agent;

• sabotage or international terrorism by a foreign power or its agent; or

• clandestine intelligence activities by an intelligence service or network of a foreign power or by its agent; or

(b) information, whether or not it concerns a United States person, with respect to a foreign power or foreign territory that relates to—

• the national defense or the security of the United States; or

• the conduct of the foreign affairs of the United States.

(E) The court may authorize disclosure—at a time, in a manner, and subject to any other conditions that it directs—of a grand-jury matter:

(i) preliminarily to or in connection with a judicial proceeding;

(ii) at the request of a defendant who shows that a ground may exist to dismiss the indictment because of a matter that occurred before the grand jury;

(iii) at the request of the government, when sought by a foreign court or prosecutor for use in an official criminal investigation;

(iv) at the request of the government if it shows that the matter may disclose a violation of State, Indian tribal, or foreign criminal law, as long as the disclosure is to an appropriate state, state-subdivision, Indian tribal, or foreign government official for the purpose of enforcing that law; or

(v) at the request of the government if it shows that the matter may disclose a violation of military criminal law under the Uniform Code of Military Justice, as long as the disclosure is to an appropriate military official for the purpose of enforcing that law.

(F) A petition to disclose a grand-jury matter under Rule 6(e)(3)(E)(i) must be filed in the district where the grand jury convened. Unless the hearing is ex parte—as it may be when the government is the petitioner—the petitioner must serve the petition on, and the court must afford a reasonable opportunity to appear and be heard to:

> (i)   an attorney for the government;
>
> (ii) the parties to the judicial proceeding; and
>
> (iii) any other person whom the court may designate.

(G) If the petition to disclose arises out of a judicial proceeding in another district, the petitioned court must transfer the petition to the other court unless the petitioned court can reasonably determine whether disclosure is proper. If the petitioned court decides to transfer, it must send to the transferee court the material sought to be disclosed, if feasible, and a written evaluation of the need for continued grand-jury secrecy. The transferee court must afford those persons identified in Rule 6(e)(3)(F) a reasonable opportunity to appear and be heard.

(4) *Sealed Indictment.* The magistrate judge to whom an indictment is returned may direct that the indictment be kept secret until the defendant is in custody or has been released pending trial. The clerk must then seal the indictment, and no person may disclose the indictment's existence except as necessary to issue or execute a warrant or summons.

(5) *Closed Hearing.* Subject to any right to an open hearing in a contempt proceeding, the court must close any hearing to the extent necessary to prevent disclosure of a matter occurring before a grand jury.

(6) *Sealed Records.* Records, orders, and subpoenas relating to grand-jury proceedings must be kept under seal to the extent and as long as necessary to prevent the unauthorized disclosure of a matter occurring before a grand jury.

(7) *Contempt.* A knowing violation of Rule 6, or of any guidelines jointly issued by the Attorney General and the Director of National Intelligence under Rule 6, may be punished as a contempt of court.

(f) Indictment and Return. A grand jury may indict only if at least 12 jurors concur. The grand jury—or its foreperson or deputy foreperson—must return the indictment to a magistrate judge in open court. To avoid unnecessary cost or delay, the magistrate judge may take the return by video teleconference from the court where the grand jury sits. If a complaint or information is pending against the defendant and 12 jurors do not concur in the indictment, the foreperson must promptly and in writing report the lack of concurrence to the magistrate judge.

(g) Discharging the Grand Jury. A grand jury must serve until the court discharges it, but it may serve more than 18 months only if the court, having determined that an extension is in the public interest, extends the grand jury's service. An extension may be granted for no more than 6 months, except as otherwise provided by statute.

(h) Excusing a Juror. At any time, for good cause, the court may excuse a juror either temporarily or permanently, and if permanently, the court may impanel an alternate juror in place of the excused juror.

(i) "Indian Tribe" Defined. "Indian tribe" means an Indian tribe recognized by the Secretary of the Interior on a list published in the Federal Register under 25 U.S.C. § 479a–1.

Rule 7. The Indictment and the Information

(a) When Used.

(1) *Felony.* An offense (other than criminal contempt) must be prosecuted by an indictment if it is punishable:

(A) by death; or

(B) by imprisonment for more than one year.

(2) *Misdemeanor.* An offense punishable by imprisonment for one year or less may be prosecuted in accordance with Rule 58(b)(1).

(b) Waiving Indictment. An offense punishable by imprisonment for more than one year may be prosecuted by information if the defendant—in open court and after being advised of the nature of the charge and of the defendant's rights—waives prosecution by indictment.

(c) Nature and Contents.

(1) *In General.* The indictment or information must be a plain, concise, and definite written statement of the essential facts constituting the offense charged and must be signed by an attorney for the government. It need not contain a formal introduction or conclusion. A count may incorporate by reference an allegation made in another count. A count may allege that the means by which the defendant committed the offense are unknown or that the defendant committed it by one or more specified means. For each count, the indictment or information must give the official or customary citation of the statute, rule, regulation, or other provision of law that the defendant is alleged to have violated. For purposes of an indictment referred to in section 3282 of title 18, United States Code, for which the identity of the defendant is unknown, it shall be sufficient for the indictment to describe the defendant as an individual whose name is unknown, but who has a particular DNA profile, as that term is defined in section 3282.

(2) *Citation Error.* Unless the defendant was misled and thereby prejudiced, neither an error in a citation nor a citation's omission is a ground to dismiss the indictment or information or to reverse a conviction.

(d) **Surplusage.** Upon the defendant's motion, the court may strike surplusage from the indictment or information.

(e) **Amending an Information.** Unless an additional or different offense is charged or a substantial right of the defendant is prejudiced, the court may permit an information to be amended at any time before the verdict or finding.

(f) **Bill of Particulars.** The court may direct the government to file a bill of particulars. The defendant may move for a bill of particulars before or within 14 days after arraignment or at a later time if the court permits. The government may amend a bill of particulars subject to such conditions as justice requires.

Rule 8. Joinder of Offenses or Defendants

(a) **Joinder of Offenses.** The indictment or information may charge a defendant in separate counts with 2 or more offenses if the offenses charged—whether felonies or misdemeanors or both—are of the same or similar character, or are based on the same act or transaction, or are connected with or constitute parts of a common scheme or plan.

(b) **Joinder of Defendants.** The indictment or information may charge 2 or more defendants if they are alleged to have participated in the same act or transaction, or in the same series of acts or transactions, constituting an offense or offenses. The defendants may be charged in one or more counts together or separately. All defendants need not be charged in each count.

Rule 9. Arrest Warrant or Summons on an Indictment or Information

(a) **Issuance.** The court must issue a warrant—or at the government's request, a summons—for each defendant named in an indictment or named in an information if one or more affidavits accompanying the information establish probable cause to believe that an offense has been committed and that the defendant committed it. The court may issue more than one warrant or summons for the same defendant. If a defendant fails to appear in response to a summons, the court may, and upon request of an attorney for the government must, issue a warrant. The court must issue the arrest warrant to an officer authorized to execute it or the summons to a person authorized to serve it.

(b) Form.

(1) *Warrant.* The warrant must conform to Rule 4(b)(1) except that it must be signed by the clerk and must describe the offense charged in the indictment or information.

(2) *Summons.* The summons must be in the same form as a warrant except that it must require the defendant to appear before the court at a stated time and place.

(c) Execution or Service; Return; Initial Appearance.

(1) *Execution or Service.*

(A) The warrant must be executed or the summons served as provided in Rule 4(c)(1), (2), and (3).

(B) The officer executing the warrant must proceed in accordance with Rule 5(a)(1).

(2) *Return.* A warrant or summons must be returned in accordance with Rule 4(c)(4).

(3) *Initial Appearance.* When an arrested or summoned defendant first appears before the court, the judge must proceed under Rule 5.

(d) Warrant by Telephone or Other Means. In accordance with Rule 4.1, a magistrate judge may issue an arrest warrant or summons based on information communicated by telephone or other reliable electronic means.

TITLE IV. ARRAIGNMENT AND PREPARATION FOR TRIAL

Rule 10. Arraignment

(a) In General. An arraignment must be conducted in open court and must consist of:

(1) ensuring that the defendant has a copy of the indictment or information;

(2) reading the indictment or information to the defendant or stating to the defendant the substance of the charge; and then

(3) asking the defendant to plead to the indictment or information.

(b) Waiving Appearance. A defendant need not be present for the arraignment if:

(1) the defendant has been charged by indictment or misdemeanor information;

(2) the defendant, in a written waiver signed by both the defendant and defense counsel, has waived appearance and has affirmed that the defendant received a copy of the indictment or information and that the plea is not guilty; and

(3) the court accepts the waiver.

(c) Video Teleconferencing. Video teleconferencing may be used to arraign a defendant if the defendant consents.

Rule 11. Pleas

(a) Entering a Plea.

(1) *In General.* A defendant may plead not guilty, guilty, or (with the court's consent) nolo contendere.

(2) *Conditional Plea.* With the consent of the court and the government, a defendant may enter a conditional plea of guilty or nolo contendere, reserving in writing the right to have an appellate court review an adverse determination of a specified pretrial motion. A defendant who prevails on appeal may then withdraw the plea.

(3) *Nolo Contendere Plea.* Before accepting a plea of nolo contendere, the court must consider the parties' views and the public interest in the effective administration of justice.

(4) *Failure to Enter a Plea.* If a defendant refuses to enter a plea or if a defendant organization fails to appear, the court must enter a plea of not guilty.

(b) Considering and Accepting a Guilty or Nolo Contendere Plea.

(1) *Advising and Questioning the Defendant.* Before the court accepts a plea of guilty or nolo contendere, the defendant may be placed under oath, and the court must address the defendant personally in open court. During this address, the court must inform the defendant of, and determine that the defendant understands, the following:

(A) the government's right, in a prosecution for perjury or false statement, to use against the defendant any statement that the defendant gives under oath;

(B) the right to plead not guilty, or having already so pleaded, to persist in that plea;

(C) the right to a jury trial;

(D) the right to be represented by counsel—and if necessary have the court appoint counsel—at trial and at every other stage of the proceeding;

(E) the right at trial to confront and cross-examine adverse witnesses, to be protected from compelled self-incrimination, to testify and present evidence, and to compel the attendance of witnesses;

(F) the defendant's waiver of these trial rights if the court accepts a plea of guilty or nolo contendere;

(G) the nature of each charge to which the defendant is pleading;

(H) any maximum possible penalty, including imprisonment, fine, and term of supervised release;

(I)   any mandatory minimum penalty;

(J)   any applicable forfeiture;

(K) the court's authority to order restitution;

(L) the court's obligation to impose a special assessment;

(M) in determining a sentence, the court's obligation to calculate the applicable sentencing-guideline range and to consider that range, possible departures under the Sentencing Guidelines, and other sentencing factors under 18 U.S.C. § 3553(a);

(N) the terms of any plea-agreement provision waiving the right to appeal or to collaterally attack the sentence; and

(O) that, if convicted, a defendant who is not a United States citizen may be removed from the United States, denied citizenship, and denied admission to the United States in the future.

(2) *Ensuring That a Plea Is Voluntary.* Before accepting a plea of guilty or nolo contendere, the court must address the defendant personally in open court and determine that the plea is voluntary and did not result from force, threats, or promises (other than promises in a plea agreement).

(3) *Determining the Factual Basis for a Plea.* Before entering judgment on a guilty plea, the court must determine that there is a factual basis for the plea.

(c) Plea Agreement Procedure.

(1) *In General.* An attorney for the government and the defendant's attorney, or the defendant when proceeding pro se, may discuss and reach a plea agreement. The court must not participate in these discussions. If the defendant pleads guilty or nolo contendere to either a charged offense or a lesser or related offense, the plea agreement may specify that an attorney for the government will:

(A) not bring, or will move to dismiss, other charges;

(B) recommend, or agree not to oppose the defendant's request, that a particular sentence or sentencing range is appropriate or that a particular provision of the Sentencing Guidelines, or policy statement, or sentencing factor does or does not apply (such a recommendation or request does not bind the court); or

(C) agree that a specific sentence or sentencing range is the appropriate disposition of the case, or that a particular provision of the Sentencing Guidelines, or policy statement, or sentencing factor does or does not apply (such a recommendation or request binds the court once the court accepts the plea agreement).

(2) *Disclosing a Plea Agreement.* The parties must disclose the plea agreement in open court when the plea is offered, unless the court for good cause allows the parties to disclose the plea agreement in camera.

(3) *Judicial Consideration of a Plea Agreement.*

(A) To the extent the plea agreement is of the type specified in Rule 11(c)(1)(A) or (C), the court may accept the agreement, reject it, or defer a decision until the court has reviewed the presentence report.

(B) To the extent the plea agreement is of the type specified in Rule 11(c)(1)(B), the court must advise the defendant that the defendant has no right to withdraw the plea if the court does not follow the recommendation or request.

(4) *Accepting a Plea Agreement.* If the court accepts the plea agreement, it must inform the defendant that to the extent the plea agreement is of the type specified in Rule 11(c)(1)(A) or (C), the agreed disposition will be included in the judgment.

(5) *Rejecting a Plea Agreement.* If the court rejects a plea agreement containing provisions of the type specified in Rule

11(c)(1)(A) or (C), the court must do the following on the record and in open court (or, for good cause, in camera):

> (A) inform the parties that the court rejects the plea agreement;

> (B) advise the defendant personally that the court is not required to follow the plea agreement and give the defendant an opportunity to withdraw the plea; and

> (C) advise the defendant personally that if the plea is not withdrawn, the court may dispose of the case less favorably toward the defendant than the plea agreement contemplated.

(d) Withdrawing a Guilty or Nolo Contendere Plea. A defendant may withdraw a plea of guilty or nolo contendere:

> **(1)** before the court accepts the plea, for any reason or no reason; or

> **(2)** after the court accepts the plea, but before it imposes sentence if:

>> (A) the court rejects a plea agreement under Rule 11(c)(5); or

>> (B) the defendant can show a fair and just reason for requesting the withdrawal.

(e) Finality of a Guilty or Nolo Contendere Plea. After the court imposes sentence, the defendant may not withdraw a plea of guilty or nolo contendere, and the plea may be set aside only on direct appeal or collateral attack.

(f) Admissibility or Inadmissibility of a Plea, Plea Discussions, and Related Statements. The admissibility or inadmissibility of a plea, a plea discussion, and any related statement is governed by Federal Rule of Evidence 410.

(g) Recording the Proceedings. The proceedings during which the defendant enters a plea must be recorded by a court reporter or by a suitable recording device. If there is a guilty plea or a nolo contendere plea, the record must include the inquiries and advice to the defendant required under Rule 11(b) and (c).

(h) Harmless Error. A variance from the requirements of this rule is harmless error if it does not affect substantial rights.

Rule 12. Pleadings and Pretrial Motions

(a) Pleadings. The pleadings in a criminal proceeding are the indictment, the information, and the pleas of not guilty, guilty, and nolo contendere.

(b) Pretrial Motions.

(1) *In General.* A party may raise by pretrial motion any defense, objection, or request that the court can determine without a trial on the merits. Rule 47 applies to a pretrial motion.

(2) *Motions That May Be Made at Any Time.* A motion that the court lacks jurisdiction may be made at any time while the case is pending.

(3) *Motions That Must Be Made Before Trial.* The following defenses, objections, and requests must be must be raised by pretrial motion if the basis for the motion is then reasonably available and the motion can be determined without a trial on the merits:

(A) a defect in instituting the prosecution, including

(i)   improper venue;

(ii)   preindictment delay;

(iii) a violation of the constitutional right to a speedy trial;

(iv) selective or vindictive prosecution; and

(v)   an error in the grand-jury proceeding or preliminary hearing;

(B) a defect in the indictment or information, including;

(i)   joining two or more offense in the same count (duplicity);

(ii) charging the same offense in more than one count (multiplicity);

(iii) lack of specificity;

(iv) improper joinder; and

(v)   failure to state an offense;

(C) suppression of evidence;

(D) severance of charges or defendants under Rule 14; and

(E) discovery under Rule 16.

(4) *Notice of the Government's Intent to Use Evidence.*

(A) *At the Government's Discretion.* At the arraignment or as soon afterward as practicable, the government may notify the defendant of its intent to use specified evidence at trial in order to afford the defendant an opportunity to object before trial under Rule 12(b)(3)(C).

(B) *At the Defendant's Request.* At the arraignment or as soon afterward as practicable, the defendant may, in order to have an opportunity to move to suppress evidence under Rule 12(b)(3)(C), request notice of the government's intent to use (in its evidence-in-chief at trial) any evidence that the defendant may be entitled to discover under Rule 16.

(c) Deadline for a Pretrial Motion; Consequences of Not Making a Timely Motion.

(1) *Setting the Deadline.* The court may, at the arraignment or as soon afterward as practicable, set a deadline for the parties to make pretrial motions and may also schedule a motion hearing. If the court does not set one, the deadline is the start of trial.

(2) *Extending or Resetting the Deadline.* At any time before trial, the court may extend or reset the deadline for pretrial motions.

(3) *Consequences of Not Making a Timely Motion Under Rule 12(b)(3).* If a party does not meet the deadline for making a Rule 12(b)(3) motion, the motion is untimely. But a court may consider the defense, objection, or request if the party shows good cause.

(d) Ruling on a Motion. The court must decide every pretrial motion before trial unless it finds good cause to defer a ruling. The court must not defer ruling on a pretrial motion if the deferral will adversely affect a party's right to appeal. When factual issues are involved in deciding a motion, the court must state its essential findings on the record.

(e) [Reserved.]

(f) Recording the Proceedings. All proceedings at a motion hearing, including any findings of fact and conclusions of law made orally by the court, must be recorded by a court reporter or a suitable recording device.

(g) Defendant's Continued Custody or Release Status. If the court grants a motion to dismiss based on a defect in instituting the prosecution, in the indictment, or in the information, it may order the defendant to be released or detained under 18 U.S.C. § 3142 for a specified time until a new indictment or information is filed. This rule does not affect any federal statutory period of limitations.

(h) Producing Statements at a Suppression Hearing. Rule 26.2 applies at a suppression hearing under Rule 12(b)(3)(C). At a suppression hearing, a law enforcement officer is considered a government witness.

Rule 12.1. Notice of an Alibi Defense

(a) Government's Request for Notice and Defendant's Response.

(1) *Government's Request.* An attorney for the government may request in writing that the defendant notify an attorney for the government of any intended alibi defense. The request must state the time, date, and place of the alleged offense.

(2) *Defendant's Response.* Within 14 days after the request, or at some other time the court sets, the defendant must serve written notice on an attorney for the government of any intended alibi defense. The defendant's notice must state:

(A) each specific place where the defendant claims to have been at the time of the alleged offense; and

(B) the name, address, and telephone number of each alibi witness on whom the defendant intends to rely.

(b) Disclosing Government Witnesses.

(1) *Disclosure.*

(A) *In General.* If the defendant serves a Rule 12.1(a)(2) notice, an attorney for the government must disclose in writing to the defendant or the defendant's attorney:

(i) the name of each witness—and the address and telephone number of each witness other than a victim—that the government intends to rely on to establish that the defendant was present at the scene of the alleged offense; and

(ii) each government rebuttal witness to the defendant's alibi defense.

(B) *Victim's Address and Telephone Number.* If the government intends to rely on a victim's testimony to establish that the defendant was present at the scene of the alleged offense and the defendant establishes a need for the victim's address and telephone number, the court may:

(i) order the government to provide the information in writing to the defendant or the defendant's attorney; or

(ii) fashion a reasonable procedure that allows preparation of the defense and also protects the victim's interests.

(2) *Time to Disclose.* Unless the court directs otherwise, an attorney for the government must give its Rule 12.1(b)(1) disclosure within 14 days after the defendant serves notice of an intended alibi defense under Rule 12.1(a)(2), but no later than 14 days before trial.

(c) Continuing Duty to Disclose.

(1) *In General.* Both an attorney for the government and the defendant must promptly disclose in writing to the other party the name of each additional witness—and the address and telephone number of each additional witness other than a victim—if:

(A) the disclosing party learns of the witness before or during trial; and

(B) the witness should have been disclosed under Rule 12.1(a) or (b) if the disclosing party had known of the witness earlier.

(2) *Address and Telephone Number of an Additional Victim Witness.* The address and telephone number of an additional victim witness must not be disclosed except as provided in Rule 12.1(b)(1)(B).

(d) Exceptions. For good cause, the court may grant an exception to any requirement of Rule 12.1(a)–(c).

(e) Failure to Comply. If a party fails to comply with this rule, the court may exclude the testimony of any undisclosed witness regarding the defendant's alibi. This rule does not limit the defendant's right to testify.

(f) Inadmissibility of Withdrawn Intention. Evidence of an intention to rely on an alibi defense, later withdrawn, or of a statement made in connection with that intention, is not, in any civil or criminal proceeding, admissible against the person who gave notice of the intention.

Rule 12.2. Notice of an Insanity Defense; Mental Examination

(a) Notice of an Insanity Defense. A defendant who intends to assert a defense of insanity at the time of the alleged offense must so notify an attorney for the government in writing within the time provided for filing a pretrial motion, or at any later time the court sets, and file a copy of the notice with the clerk. A defendant who fails to do so cannot rely on an insanity defense. The court may, for good cause, allow the defendant to file the notice late, grant additional trial-preparation time, or make other appropriate orders.

(b) Notice of Expert Evidence of a Mental Condition. If a defendant intends to introduce expert evidence relating to a mental disease or defect or any other mental condition of the defendant bearing on either (1) the issue of guilt or (2) the issue of punishment in a capital case, the defendant must—within the time provided for filing a pretrial motion or at any later time the court sets—notify an attorney for the government in writing of this intention and file a copy of the notice with the clerk. The court may, for good cause, allow the defendant to file the notice late, grant the parties additional trial-preparation time, or make other appropriate orders.

(c) Mental Examination.

(1) *Authority to Order an Examination; Procedures.*

(A) The court may order the defendant to submit to a competency examination under 18 U.S.C. § 4241.

(B) If the defendant provides notice under Rule 12.2(a), the court must, upon the government's motion, order the defendant to be examined under 18 U.S.C. § 4242. If the defendant provides notice under Rule 12.2(b) the court may, upon the government's motion, order the defendant to be examined under procedures ordered by the court.

(2) *Disclosing Results and Reports of Capital Sentencing Examination.* The results and reports of any examination conducted solely under Rule 12.2(c)(1) after notice under Rule 12.2(b)(2) must be sealed and must not be disclosed to any attorney for the government or the defendant unless the defendant is found guilty of one or more capital crimes and the defendant confirms an intent to offer during sentencing proceedings expert evidence on mental condition.

(3) *Disclosing Results and Reports of the Defendant's Expert Examination.* After disclosure under Rule 12.2(c)(2) of the results and reports of the government's examination, the defendant must disclose to the government the results and reports of any examination on mental condition conducted by the defendant's expert about which the defendant intends to introduce expert evidence.

(4) *Inadmissibility of a Defendant's Statements.* No statement made by a defendant in the course of any examination conducted under this rule (whether conducted with or without the defendant's consent), no testimony by the expert based on the statement, and no other fruits of the statement may be admitted into evidence against the defendant in any criminal proceeding except on an issue regarding mental condition on which the defendant:

(A) has introduced evidence of incompetency or evidence requiring notice under Rule 12.2(a) or (b)(1), or

(B) has introduced expert evidence in a capital sentencing proceeding requiring notice under Rule 12.2(b)(2).

(d) Failure to Comply.

(1) *Failure to Give Notice or to Submit to Examination.* The court may exclude any expert evidence from the defendant on the issue of the defendant's mental disease, mental defect, or any other mental condition bearing on the defendant's guilt or the issue of punishment in a capital case if the defendant fails to:

(A) give notice under Rule 12.2(b); or

(B) submit to an examination when ordered under Rule 12.2(c).

(2) *Failure to Disclose.* The court may exclude any expert evidence for which the defendant has failed to comply with the disclosure requirement of Rule 12.2(c)(3).

(e) Inadmissibility of Withdrawn Intention. Evidence of an intention as to which notice was given under Rule 12.2(a) or (b), later withdrawn, is not, in any civil or criminal proceeding, admissible against the person who gave notice of the intention.

Rule 12.3. Notice of a Public-Authority Defense

(a) Notice of the Defense and Disclosure of Witnesses.

(1) *Notice in General.* If a defendant intends to assert a defense of actual or believed exercise of public authority on behalf of a law enforcement agency or federal intelligence agency at the time of the alleged offense, the defendant must so notify an attorney for the government in writing and must file a copy of the notice with the clerk within the time provided for filing a pretrial motion, or at any later time the court sets. The notice filed with the clerk must be under seal if the notice identifies a federal intelligence agency as the source of public authority.

(2) *Contents of Notice.* The notice must contain the following information:

(A) the law enforcement agency or federal intelligence agency involved;

(B) the agency member on whose behalf the defendant claims to have acted; and

(C) the time during which the defendant claims to have acted with public authority.

(3) *Response to the Notice.* An attorney for the government must serve a written response on the defendant or the defendant's attorney within 14 days after receiving the defendant's notice, but no later than 21 days before trial. The response must admit or deny that the defendant exercised the public authority identified in the defendant's notice.

(4) *Disclosing Witnesses.*

(A) *Government's Request.* An attorney for the government may request in writing that the defendant disclose the name, address, and telephone number of each witness the defendant intends to rely on to establish a public-authority defense. An attorney for the government may serve the request when the government serves its response to the defendant's notice under Rule 12.3(a)(3), or later, but must serve the request no later than 21 days before trial.

(B) *Defendant's Response.* Within 14 days after receiving the government's request, the defendant must serve on an attorney for the government a written statement of the name, address, and telephone number of each witness.

(C) *Government's Reply.* Within 14 days after receiving the defendant's statement, an attorney for the government must serve on the defendant or the defendant's attorney a written statement of the name of each witness—and the address and telephone number of each witness other than a victim—that the government intends to rely on to oppose the defendant's public-authority defense.

(D) *Victim's Address and Telephone Number.* If the government intends to rely on a victim's testimony to oppose the defendant's public-authority defense and the defendant establishes a need for the victim's address and telephone number, the court may:

(i)   order the government to provide the information in writing to the defendant or the defendant's attorney; or

(ii) fashion a reasonable procedure that allows for preparing the defense and also protects the victim's interests.

(5) *Additional Time.* The court may, for good cause, allow a party additional time to comply with this rule.

(b) Continuing Duty to Disclose.

(1) *In General.* Both an attorney for the government and the defendant must promptly disclose in writing to the other party the name of any additional witness—and the address, and telephone number of any additional witness other than a victim—if:

> (A) the disclosing party learns of the witness before or during trial; and

> (B) the witness should have been disclosed under Rule 12.3(a)(4) if the disclosing party had known of the witness earlier.

(2) *Address and Telephone Number of an Additional Victim-Witness.* The address and telephone number of an additional victim-witness must not be disclosed except as provided in Rule 12.3(a)(4)(D).

(c) Failure to Comply. If a party fails to comply with this rule, the court may exclude the testimony of any undisclosed witness regarding the public-authority defense. This rule does not limit the defendant's right to testify.

(d) Protective Procedures Unaffected. This rule does not limit the court's authority to issue appropriate protective orders or to order that any filings be under seal.

(e) Inadmissibility of Withdrawn Intention. Evidence of an intention as to which notice was given under Rule 12.3(a), later withdrawn, is not, in any civil or criminal proceeding, admissible against the person who gave notice of the intention.

Rule 12.4. Disclosure Statement

(a) Who Must File.

(1) *Nongovernmental   Corporate   Party.*   Any nongovernmental corporate party to a proceeding in a district court must file a statement that identifies any parent corporation and any publicly held corporation that owns 10% or more of its stock or states that there is no such corporation.

(2) *Organizational Victim.* If an organization is a victim of the alleged criminal activity, the government must file a statement identifying the victim. If the organizational victim is a corporation, the statement must also disclose the information required by Rule 12.4(a)(1) to the extent it can be obtained through due diligence.

(b) Time for Filing; Supplemental Filing. A party must:

(1) file the Rule 12.4(a) statement upon the defendant's initial appearance; and

(2) promptly file a supplemental statement upon any change in the information that the statement requires.

Rule 13. Joint Trial of Separate Cases

The court may order that separate cases be tried together as though brought in a single indictment or information if all offenses and all defendants could have been joined in a single indictment or information.

Rule 14. Relief from Prejudicial Joinder

(a) Relief. If the joinder of offenses or defendants in an indictment, an information, or a consolidation for trial appears to prejudice a defendant or the government, the court may order separate trials of counts, sever the defendants' trials, or provide any other relief that justice requires.

(b) Defendant's Statements. Before ruling on a defendant's motion to sever, the court may order an attorney for the government to deliver to the court for in camera inspection any defendant's statement that the government intends to use as evidence.

Rule 15. Depositions

(a) When Taken.

(1) *In General.* A party may move that a prospective witness be deposed in order to preserve testimony for trial. The court may grant the motion because of exceptional circumstances and in the interest of justice. If the court orders the deposition to be taken, it may also require the deponent to produce at the deposition any designated material that is not privileged, including any book, paper, document, record, recording, or data.

(2) *Detained Material Witness.* A witness who is detained under 18 U.S.C. § 3144 may request to be deposed by filing a written motion and giving notice to the parties. The court may then order that the deposition be taken and may discharge the witness after the witness has signed under oath the deposition transcript.

(b) Notice.

(1) *In General.* A party seeking to take a deposition must give every other party reasonable written notice of the deposition's date and location. The notice must state the name and address of each deponent. If requested by a party receiving the notice, the court may, for good cause, change the deposition's date or location.

(2) *To the Custodial Officer.* A party seeking to take the deposition must also notify the officer who has custody of the defendant of the scheduled date and location.

(c) Defendant's Presence.

(1) *Defendant in Custody.* Except as authorized by Rule 15(c)(3), the officer who has custody of the defendant must produce the defendant at the deposition and keep the defendant in the witness's presence during the examination, unless the defendant:

(A) waives in writing the right to be present; or

(B) persists in disruptive conduct justifying exclusion after being warned by the court that disruptive conduct will result in the defendant's exclusion.

(2) *Defendant Not in Custody.* Except as authorized by Rule 15(c)(3), a defendant who is not in custody has the right upon request to be present at the deposition, subject to any conditions imposed by the court. If the government tenders the defendant's expenses as provided in Rule 15(d) but the defendant still fails to appear, the defendant—absent good cause—waives both the right to appear and any objection to the taking and use of the deposition based on that right.

(3) *Taking Depositions Outside the United States Without the Defendant's Presence.* The deposition of a witness who is outside the United States may be taken without the defendant's presence if the court makes case-specific findings of all the following:

(A) the witness's testimony could provide substantial proof of a material fact in a felony prosecution;

(B) there is a substantial likelihood that the witness's attendance at trial cannot be obtained;

(C) the witness's presence for a deposition in the United States cannot be obtained;

(D) the defendant cannot be present because:

(i) the country where the witness is located will not permit the defendant to attend the deposition;

(ii) for an in-custody defendant, secure transportation and continuing custody cannot be assured at the witness's location; or

(iii) for an out-of-custody defendant, no reasonable conditions will assure an appearance at the deposition or at trial or sentencing; and

(E) the defendant can meaningfully participate in the deposition through reasonable means.

(d) Expenses. If the deposition was requested by the government, the court may—or if the defendant is unable to bear the deposition expenses, the court must—order the government to pay:

(1) any reasonable travel and subsistence expenses of the defendant and the defendant's attorney to attend the deposition; and

(2) the costs of the deposition transcript.

(e) Manner of Taking. Unless these rules or a court order provides otherwise, a deposition must be taken and filed in the same manner as a deposition in a civil action, except that:

(1) A defendant may not be deposed without that defendant's consent.

(2) The scope and manner of the deposition examination and cross-examination must be the same as would be allowed during trial.

(3) The government must provide to the defendant or the defendant's attorney, for use at the deposition, any statement of the deponent in the government's possession to which the defendant would be entitled at trial.

(f) Admissibility and Use as Evidence. An order authorizing a deposition to be taken under this rule does not determine its admissibility. A party may use all or part of a deposition as provided by the Federal Rules of Evidence.

(g) Objections. A party objecting to deposition testimony or evidence must state the grounds for the objection during the deposition.

(h) Depositions by Agreement Permitted. The parties may by agreement take and use a deposition with the court's consent.

Rule 16. Discovery and Inspection

(a) Government's Disclosure.

(1) *Information Subject to Disclosure.*

(A) *Defendant's Oral Statement.* Upon a defendant's request, the government must disclose to the defendant the substance of any relevant oral statement made by the defendant, before or after arrest, in response to interrogation by a person the defendant knew was a government agent if the government intends to use the statement at trial.

(B) *Defendant's Written or Recorded Statement.* Upon a defendant's request, the government must disclose to the defendant, and make available for inspection, copying, or photographing, all of the following:

(i) any relevant written or recorded statement by the defendant if:

- the statement is within the government's possession, custody, or control; and

- the attorney for the government knows—or through due diligence could know—that the statement exists;

(ii) the portion of any written record containing the substance of any relevant oral statement made before or after arrest if the defendant made the statement in response to interrogation by a person the defendant knew was a government agent; and

(iii) the defendant's recorded testimony before a grand jury relating to the charged offense.

(C) *Organizational Defendant.* Upon a defendant's request, if the defendant is an organization, the government must disclose to the defendant any statement described in Rule 16(a)(1)(A) and (B) if the government contends that the person making the statement:

(i) was legally able to bind the defendant regarding the subject of the statement because of that person's position as the defendant's director, officer, employee, or agent; or

(ii) was personally involved in the alleged conduct constituting the offense and was legally able to bind the defendant regarding that conduct because of that person's position as the defendant's director, officer, employee, or agent.

(D) *Defendant's Prior Record.* Upon a defendant's request, the government must furnish the defendant with a copy of the defendant's prior criminal record that is within the government's possession, custody, or control if the attorney for the government knows—or through due diligence could know—that the record exists.

(E) *Documents and Objects.* Upon a defendant's request, the government must permit the defendant to inspect and to copy or photograph books, papers, documents, data, photographs, tangible objects, buildings or places, or copies or portions of any of these items, if the item is within the government's possession, custody, or control and:

(i) the item is material to preparing the defense;

(ii) the government intends to use the item in its case-in-chief at trial; or

(iii) the item was obtained from or belongs to the defendant.

(F) *Reports of Examinations and Tests.* Upon a defendant's request, the government must permit a defendant to inspect and to copy or photograph the results or reports of any physical or mental examination and of any scientific test or experiment if:

(i) the item is within the government's possession, custody, or control;

(ii) the attorney for the government knows—or through due diligence could know—that the item exists; and

(iii) the item is material to preparing the defense or the government intends to use the item in its case-in-chief at trial.

(G) *Expert Witnesses.* At the defendant's request, the government must give to the defendant a written summary of any testimony that the government intends to use under Rules 702, 703, or 705 of the Federal Rules of Evidence during its case-in-chief at trial. If the government requests discovery under subdivision (b)(1)(C)(ii) and the defendant complies, the government must, at the defendant's request, give to the defendant a written summary of testimony that the government intends to use under Rules 702, 703, or 705 of the Federal Rules of Evidence as evidence at trial on the issue of the defendant's mental condition. The summary provided under this subparagraph must describe the witness's opinions, the bases and reasons for those opinions, and the witness's qualifications.

(2) *Information Not Subject to Disclosure.* Except as permitted by Rule 16(a)(1)(A)–(D), (F), and (G), this rule does not authorize the discovery or inspection of reports, memoranda, or other internal government documents made by an attorney for the government or other government agent in connection with investigating or prosecuting the case. Nor does this rule authorize the discovery or inspection of statements made by prospective government witnesses except as provided in 18 U.S.C. § 3500.

(3) *Grand Jury Transcripts.* This rule does not apply to the discovery or inspection of a grand jury's recorded proceedings, except as provided in Rules 6, 12(h), 16(a)(1), and 26.2.

(b) Defendant's Disclosure.

(1) *Information Subject to Disclosure.*

(A) *Documents and Objects.* If a defendant requests disclosure under Rule 16(a)(1)(E) and the government complies, then the defendant must permit the government, upon request, to inspect and to copy or photograph books, papers, documents, data, photographs, tangible objects, buildings or places, or copies or portions of any of these items if:

(i) the item is within the defendant's possession, custody, or control; and

(ii) the defendant intends to use the item in the defendant's case-in-chief at trial.

(B) *Reports of Examinations and Tests.* If a defendant requests disclosure under Rule 16(a)(1)(F) and the government complies, the defendant must permit the government, upon request, to inspect and to copy or photograph the results or reports of any physical or mental examination and of any scientific test or experiment if:

(i) the item is within the defendant's possession, custody, or control; and

(ii) the defendant intends to use the item in the defendant's case-in-chief at trial, or intends to call the witness who prepared the report and the report relates to the witness's testimony.

(C) *Expert Witnesses.* The defendant must, at the government's request, give to the government a written summary of any testimony that the defendant intends to use under Rules 702, 703, or 705 of the Federal Rules of Evidence as evidence at trial, if—

(i) the defendant requests disclosure under subdivision (a)(1)(G) and the government complies; or

(ii) the defendant has given notice under Rule 12.2(b) of an intent to present expert testimony on the defendant's mental condition.

This summary must describe the witness's opinions, the bases and reasons for those opinions, and the witness's qualifications.

(2) *Information Not Subject to Disclosure.* Except for scientific or medical reports, Rule 16(b)(1) does not authorize discovery or inspection of:

(A) reports, memoranda, or other documents made by the defendant, or the defendant's attorney or agent, during the case's investigation or defense; or

(B) a statement made to the defendant, or the defendant's attorney or agent, by:

(i) the defendant;

(ii) a government or defense witness; or

(iii) a prospective government or defense witness.

(c) Continuing Duty to Disclose. A party who discovers additional evidence or material before or during trial must promptly disclose its existence to the other party or the court if:

(1) the evidence or material is subject to discovery or inspection under this rule; and

(2) the other party previously requested, or the court ordered, its production.

(d) Regulating Discovery.

(1) *Protective and Modifying Orders.* At any time the court may, for good cause, deny, restrict, or defer discovery or inspection, or grant other appropriate relief. The court may permit a party to show good cause by a written statement that the court will inspect ex parte. If relief is granted, the court must preserve the entire text of the party's statement under seal.

(2) *Failure to Comply.* If a party fails to comply with this rule, the court may:

(A) order that party to permit the discovery or inspection; specify its time, place, and manner; and prescribe other just terms and conditions;

(B) grant a continuance;

(C) prohibit that party from introducing the undisclosed evidence; or

(D) enter any other order that is just under the circumstances.

Rule 17. Subpoena

(a) Content. A subpoena must state the court's name and the title of the proceeding, include the seal of the court, and command the witness to attend and testify at the time and place the subpoena specifies. The clerk must issue a blank subpoena—signed and sealed—to the party requesting it, and that party must fill in the blanks before the subpoena is served.

(b) Defendant Unable to Pay. Upon a defendant's ex parte application, the court must order that a subpoena be issued for a named witness if the defendant shows an inability to pay the witness's fees and the necessity of the witness's presence for an adequate defense. If the court orders a subpoena to be issued, the process costs and witness fees will be paid in the same manner as those paid for witnesses the government subpoenas.

(c) Producing Documents and Objects.

(1) *In General.* A subpoena may order the witness to produce any books, papers, documents, data, or other objects the subpoena designates. The court may direct the witness to produce the designated items in court before trial or before they are to be offered in evidence. When the items arrive, the court may permit the parties and their attorneys to inspect all or part of them.

(2) *Quashing or Modifying the Subpoena.* On motion made promptly, the court may quash or modify the subpoena if compliance would be unreasonable or oppressive.

(3) *Subpoena for Personal or Confidential Information About a Victim.* After a complaint, indictment, or information is filed, a subpoena requiring the production of personal or confidential information about a victim may be served on a third party only by court order. Before entering the order and unless there are exceptional circumstances, the court must require giving notice to the victim so that the victim can move to quash or modify the subpoena or otherwise object.

(d) Service. A marshal, a deputy marshal, or any nonparty who is at least 18 years old may serve a subpoena. The server must deliver a copy of the subpoena to the witness and must tender to the witness one day's witness-attendance fee and the legal mileage allowance. The server need not tender the attendance fee or mileage allowance when the United States, a federal officer, or a federal agency has requested the subpoena.

(e) Place of Service.

(1) *In the United States.* A subpoena requiring a witness to attend a hearing or trial may be served at any place within the United States.

(2) *In a Foreign Country.* If the witness is in a foreign country, 28 U.S.C. § 1783 governs the subpoena's service.

(f) Issuing a Deposition Subpoena.

(1) *Issuance.* A court order to take a deposition authorizes the clerk in the district where the deposition is to be taken to issue a subpoena for any witness named or described in the order.

(2) *Place.* After considering the convenience of the witness and the parties, the court may order—and the subpoena may require—the witness to appear anywhere the court designates.

(g) Contempt. The court (other than a magistrate judge) may hold in contempt a witness who, without adequate excuse, disobeys a subpoena issued by a federal court in that district. A magistrate judge may hold in contempt a witness who, without adequate excuse, disobeys a subpoena issued by that magistrate judge as provided in 28 U.S.C. § 636(e).

(h) Information Not Subject to a Subpoena. No party may subpoena a statement of a witness or of a prospective witness under this rule. Rule 26.2 governs the production of the statement.

Rule 17.1. Pretrial Conference

On its own, or on a party's motion, the court may hold one or more pretrial conferences to promote a fair and expeditious trial. When a conference ends, the court must prepare and file a memorandum of any matters agreed to during the conference. The government may not use any statement made during the conference by the defendant or the defendant's attorney unless it is in writing and is signed by the defendant and the defendant's attorney.

TITLE V. VENUE

Rule 18. Place of Prosecution and Trial

Unless a statute or these rules permit otherwise, the government must prosecute an offense in a district where the offense was committed. The court must set the place of trial within the district with due regard for the convenience of the defendant, any victim, and the witnesses, and the prompt administration of justice.

Rule 19. [Reserved]

Rule 20. Transfer for Plea and Sentence

(a) Consent to Transfer. A prosecution may be transferred from the district where the indictment or information is pending, or from which a warrant on a complaint has been issued, to the district where the defendant is arrested, held, or present if:

> **(1)** the defendant states in writing a wish to plead guilty or nolo contendere and to waive trial in the district where the indictment, information, or complaint is pending, consents in writing to the court's

disposing of the case in the transferee district, and files the statement in the transferee district; and

(2) the United States attorneys in both districts approve the transfer in writing.

(b) Clerk's Duties. After receiving the defendant's statement and the required approvals, the clerk where the indictment, information, or complaint is pending must send the file, or a certified copy, to the clerk in the transferee district.

(c) Effect of a Not Guilty Plea. If the defendant pleads not guilty after the case has been transferred under Rule 20(a), the clerk must return the papers to the court where the prosecution began, and that court must restore the proceeding to its docket. The defendant's statement that the defendant wished to plead guilty or nolo contendere is not, in any civil or criminal proceeding, admissible against the defendant.

(d) Juveniles.

(1) *Consent to Transfer.* A juvenile, as defined in 18 U.S.C. § 5031, may be proceeded against as a juvenile delinquent in the district where the juvenile is arrested, held, or present if:

(A) the alleged offense that occurred in the other district is not punishable by death or life imprisonment;

(B) an attorney has advised the juvenile;

(C) the court has informed the juvenile of the juvenile's rights—including the right to be returned to the district where the offense allegedly occurred—and the consequences of waiving those rights;

(D) the juvenile, after receiving the court's information about rights, consents in writing to be proceeded against in the transferee district, and files the consent in the transferee district;

(E) the United States attorneys for both districts approve the transfer in writing; and

(F) the transferee court approves the transfer.

(2) *Clerk's Duties.* After receiving the juvenile's written consent and the required approvals, the clerk where the indictment, information, or complaint is pending or where the alleged offense occurred must send the file, or a certified copy, to the clerk in the transferee district.

Rule 21. Transfer for Trial

(a) For Prejudice. Upon the defendant's motion, the court must transfer the proceeding against that defendant to another district if the court is satisfied that so great a prejudice against the defendant exists in the transferring district that the defendant cannot obtain a fair and impartial trial there.

(b) For Convenience. Upon the defendant's motion, the court may transfer the proceeding, or one or more counts, against that defendant to another district for the convenience of the parties, any victim, and the witnesses, and in the interest of justice.

(c) Proceedings on Transfer. When the court orders a transfer, the clerk must send to the transferee district the file, or a certified copy, and any bail taken. The prosecution will then continue in the transferee district.

(d) Time to File a Motion to Transfer. A motion to transfer may be made at or before arraignment or at any other time the court or these rules prescribe.

Rule 22. [Transferred]

TITLE VI. TRIAL

Rule 23. Jury or Nonjury Trial

(a) Jury Trial. If the defendant is entitled to a jury trial, the trial must be by jury unless:

(1) the defendant waives a jury trial in writing;

(2) the government consents; and

(3) the court approves.

(b) Jury Size.

(1) *In General.* A jury consists of 12 persons unless this rule provides otherwise.

(2) *Stipulation for a Smaller Jury.* At any time before the verdict, the parties may, with the court's approval, stipulate in writing that:

(A) the jury may consist of fewer than 12 persons; or

(B) a jury of fewer than 12 persons may return a verdict if the court finds it necessary to excuse a juror for good cause after the trial begins.

(3) *Court Order for a Jury of 11.* After the jury has retired to deliberate, the court may permit a jury of 11 persons to return a verdict, even without a stipulation by the parties, if the court finds good cause to excuse a juror.

(c) **Nonjury Trial.** In a case tried without a jury, the court must find the defendant guilty or not guilty. If a party requests before the finding of guilty or not guilty, the court must state its specific findings of fact in open court or in a written decision or opinion.

Rule 24. Trial Jurors

(a) **Examination.**

(1) *In General.* The court may examine prospective jurors or may permit the attorneys for the parties to do so.

(2) *Court Examination.* If the court examines the jurors, it must permit the attorneys for the parties to:

(A) ask further questions that the court considers proper; or

(B) submit further questions that the court may ask if it considers them proper.

(b) **Peremptory Challenges.** Each side is entitled to the number of peremptory challenges to prospective jurors specified below. The court may allow additional peremptory challenges to multiple defendants, and may allow the defendants to exercise those challenges separately or jointly.

(1) *Capital Case.* Each side has 20 peremptory challenges when the government seeks the death penalty.

(2) *Other Felony Case.* The government has 6 peremptory challenges and the defendant or defendants jointly have 10 peremptory challenges when the defendant is charged with a crime punishable by imprisonment of more than one year.

(3) *Misdemeanor Case.* Each side has 3 peremptory challenges when the defendant is charged with a crime punishable by fine, imprisonment of one year or less, or both.

(c) **Alternate Jurors.**

(1) *In General.* The court may impanel up to 6 alternate jurors to replace any jurors who are unable to perform or who are disqualified from performing their duties.

(2) *Procedure.*

(A) Alternate jurors must have the same qualifications and be selected and sworn in the same manner as any other juror.

(B) Alternate jurors replace jurors in the same sequence in which the alternates were selected. An alternate juror who replaces a juror has the same authority as the other jurors.

(3) *Retaining Alternate Jurors.* The court may retain alternate jurors after the jury retires to deliberate. The court must ensure that a retained alternate does not discuss the case with anyone until that alternate replaces a juror or is discharged. If an alternate replaces a juror after deliberations have begun, the court must instruct the jury to begin its deliberations anew.

(4) *Peremptory Challenges.* Each side is entitled to the number of additional peremptory challenges to prospective alternate jurors specified below. These additional challenges may be used only to remove alternate jurors.

(A) *One or Two Alternates.* One additional peremptory challenge is permitted when one or two alternates are impaneled.

(B) *Three or Four Alternates.* Two additional peremptory challenges are permitted when three or four alternates are impaneled.

(C) *Five or Six Alternates.* Three additional peremptory challenges are permitted when five or six alternates are impaneled.

Rule 25. Judge's Disability

(a) During Trial. Any judge regularly sitting in or assigned to the court may complete a jury trial if:

(1) the judge before whom the trial began cannot proceed because of death, sickness, or other disability; and

(2) the judge completing the trial certifies familiarity with the trial record.

(b) After a Verdict or Finding of Guilty.

(1) *In General.* After a verdict or finding of guilty, any judge regularly sitting in or assigned to a court may complete the court's duties if the judge who presided at trial cannot perform those duties because of absence, death, sickness, or other disability.

(2) *Granting a New Trial.* The successor judge may grant a new trial if satisfied that:

(A) a judge other than the one who presided at the trial cannot perform the post-trial duties; or

(B) a new trial is necessary for some other reason.

Rule 26. Taking Testimony

In every trial the testimony of witnesses must be taken in open court, unless otherwise provided by a statute or by rules adopted under 28 U.S.C. §§ 2072–2077.

Rule 26.1. Foreign Law Determination

A party intending to raise an issue of foreign law must provide the court and all parties with reasonable written notice. Issues of foreign law are questions of law, but in deciding such issues a court may consider any relevant material or source—including testimony—without regard to the Federal Rules of Evidence.

Rule 26.2. Producing a Witness's Statement

(a) Motion to Produce. After a witness other than the defendant has testified on direct examination, the court, on motion of a party who did not call the witness, must order an attorney for the government or the defendant and the defendant's attorney to produce, for the examination and use of the moving party, any statement of the witness that is in their possession and that relates to the subject matter of the witness's testimony.

(b) Producing the Entire Statement. If the entire statement relates to the subject matter of the witness's testimony, the court must order that the statement be delivered to the moving party.

(c) Producing a Redacted Statement. If the party who called the witness claims that the statement contains information that is privileged or does not relate to the subject matter of the witness's testimony, the court must inspect the statement in camera. After excising any privileged or unrelated portions, the court must order delivery of the redacted statement to the moving party. If the defendant objects to an excision, the court must preserve the entire statement with the excised portion indicated, under seal, as part of the record.

(d) Recess to Examine a Statement. The court may recess the proceedings to allow time for a party to examine the statement and prepare for its use.

(e) Sanction for Failure to Produce or Deliver a Statement. If the party who called the witness disobeys an order to produce or deliver a statement, the court must strike the witness's testimony from the record. If an attorney for the government disobeys the order, the court must declare a mistrial if justice so requires.

(f) "Statement" Defined. As used in this rule, a witness's "statement" means:

(1) a written statement that the witness makes and signs, or otherwise adopts or approves;

(2) a substantially verbatim, contemporaneously recorded recital of the witness's oral statement that is contained in any recording or any transcription of a recording; or

(3) the witness's statement to a grand jury, however taken or recorded, or a transcription of such a statement.

(g) Scope. This rule applies at trial, at a suppression hearing under Rule 12, and to the extent specified in the following rules:

(1) Rule 5.1(h) (preliminary hearing);

(2) Rule 32(i)(2) (sentencing);

(3) Rule 32.1(e) (hearing to revoke or modify probation or supervised release);

(4) Rule 46(j) (detention hearing); and

(5) Rule 8 of the Rules Governing Proceedings under 28 U.S.C. § 2255.

Rule 26.3. Mistrial

Before ordering a mistrial, the court must give each defendant and the government an opportunity to comment on the propriety of the order, to state whether that party consents or objects, and to suggest alternatives.

Rule 27. Proving an Official Record

A party may prove an official record, an entry in such a record, or the lack of a record or entry in the same manner as in a civil action.

Rule 28. Interpreters

The court may select, appoint, and set the reasonable compensation for an interpreter. The compensation must be paid from funds provided by law or by the government, as the court may direct.

Rule 29. Motion for a Judgment of Acquittal

(a) Before Submission to the Jury. After the government closes its evidence or after the close of all the evidence, the court on the defendant's motion must enter a judgment of acquittal of any offense for which the evidence is insufficient to sustain a conviction. The court may on its own consider whether the evidence is insufficient to sustain a conviction. If the court denies a motion for a judgment of acquittal at the close of the government's evidence, the defendant may offer evidence without having reserved the right to do so.

(b) Reserving Decision. The court may reserve decision on the motion, proceed with the trial (where the motion is made before the close of all the evidence), submit the case to the jury, and decide the motion either before the jury returns a verdict or after it returns a verdict of guilty or is discharged without having returned a verdict. If the court reserves decision, it must decide the motion on the basis of the evidence at the time the ruling was reserved.

(c) After Jury Verdict or Discharge.

(1) *Time for a Motion.* A defendant may move for a judgment of acquittal, or renew such a motion, within 14 days after a guilty verdict or after the court discharges the jury, whichever is later.

(2) *Ruling on the Motion.* If the jury has returned a guilty verdict, the court may set aside the verdict and enter an acquittal. If the jury has failed to return a verdict, the court may enter a judgment of acquittal.

(3) *No Prior Motion Required.* A defendant is not required to move for a judgment of acquittal before the court submits the case to the jury as a prerequisite for making such a motion after jury discharge.

(d) Conditional Ruling on a Motion for a New Trial.

(1) *Motion for a New Trial.* If the court enters a judgment of acquittal after a guilty verdict, the court must also conditionally determine whether any motion for a new trial should be granted if the judgment of acquittal is later vacated or reversed. The court must specify the reasons for that determination.

(2) *Finality.* The court's order conditionally granting a motion for a new trial does not affect the finality of the judgment of acquittal.

(3) *Appeal.*

(A) *Grant of a Motion for a New Trial.* If the court conditionally grants a motion for a new trial and an appellate court later reverses the judgment of acquittal, the trial court must proceed with the new trial unless the appellate court orders otherwise.

(B) *Denial of a Motion for a New* Trial. If the court conditionally denies a motion for a new trial, an appellee may assert that the denial was erroneous. If the appellate court later reverses the judgment of acquittal, the trial court must proceed as the appellate court directs.

Rule 29.1. Closing Argument

Closing arguments proceed in the following order:

(a) the government argues;

(b) the defense argues; and

(c) the government rebuts.

Rule 30. Jury Instructions

(a) In General. Any party may request in writing that the court instruct the jury on the law as specified in the request. The request must be made at the close of the evidence or at any earlier time that the court reasonably sets. When the request is made, the requesting party must furnish a copy to every other party.

(b) Ruling on a Request. The court must inform the parties before closing arguments how it intends to rule on the requested instructions.

(c) Time for Giving Instructions. The court may instruct the jury before or after the arguments are completed, or at both times.

(d) Objections to Instructions. A party who objects to any portion of the instructions or to a failure to give a requested instruction must inform the court of the specific objection and the grounds for the objection before the jury retires to deliberate. An opportunity must be given to object out of the jury's hearing and, on request, out of the jury's presence. Failure to object in accordance with this rule precludes appellate review, except as permitted under Rule 52(b).

Rule 31. Jury Verdict

(a) Return. The jury must return its verdict to a judge in open court. The verdict must be unanimous.

(b) Partial Verdicts, Mistrial, and Retrial.

(1) *Multiple Defendants.* If there are multiple defendants, the jury may return a verdict at any time during its deliberations as to any defendant about whom it has agreed.

(2) *Multiple Counts.* If the jury cannot agree on all counts as to any defendant, the jury may return a verdict on those counts on which it has agreed.

(3) *Mistrial and Retrial.* If the jury cannot agree on a verdict on one or more counts, the court may declare a mistrial on those counts. The government may retry any defendant on any count on which the jury could not agree.

(c) Lesser Offense or Attempt. A defendant may be found guilty of any of the following:

    (1) an offense necessarily included in the offense charged;

    (2) an attempt to commit the offense charged; or

    (3) an attempt to commit an offense necessarily included in the offense charged, if the attempt is an offense in its own right.

(d) Jury Poll. After a verdict is returned but before the jury is discharged, the court must on a party's request, or may on its own, poll the jurors individually. If the poll reveals a lack of unanimity, the court may direct the jury to deliberate further or may declare a mistrial and discharge the jury.

TITLE VII. POST-CONVICTION PROCEDURES

Rule 32. Sentencing and Judgment

(a) [Reserved.]

(b) Time of Sentencing.

    (1) *In General.* The court must impose sentence without unnecessary delay.

    (2) *Changing Time Limits.* The court may, for good cause, change any time limits prescribed in this rule.

(c) Presentence Investigation.

    (1) *Required Investigation.*

        (A) *In General.* The probation officer must conduct a presentence investigation and submit a report to the court before it imposes sentence unless:

            (i) 18 U.S.C. § 3593(c) or another statute requires otherwise; or

            (ii) the court finds that the information in the record enables it to meaningfully exercise its sentencing authority under 18 U.S.C. § 3553, and the court explains its finding on the record.

        (B) *Restitution.* If the law permits restitution, the probation officer must conduct an investigation and submit a report that contains sufficient information for the court to order restitution.

    (2) *Interviewing the Defendant.* The probation officer who interviews a defendant as part of a presentence investigation must, on request, give the defendant's attorney notice and a reasonable opportunity to attend the interview.

(d) Presentence Report.

(1) *Applying the Advisory Sentencing Guidelines.* The presentence report must:

(A) identify all applicable guidelines and policy statements of the Sentencing Commission;

(B) calculate the defendant's offense level and criminal history category;

(C) state the resulting sentencing range and kinds of sentences available;

(D) identify any factor relevant to:

(i)   the appropriate kind of sentence, or

(ii) the appropriate sentence within the applicable sentencing range; and

(E) identify any basis for departing from the applicable sentencing range.

(2) *Additional Information.* The presentence report must also contain the following:

(A) the defendant's history and characteristics, including:

(i)   any prior criminal record;

(ii) the defendant's financial condition; and

(iii) any circumstances affecting the defendant's behavior that may be helpful in imposing sentence or in correctional treatment;

(B) information that assesses any financial, social, psychological, and medical impact on any victim;

(C) when appropriate, the nature and extent of nonprison programs and resources available to the defendant;

(D) when the law provides for restitution, information sufficient for a restitution order;

(E) if the court orders a study under 18 U.S.C. § 3552(b), any resulting report and recommendation;

(F) a statement of whether the government seeks forfeiture under Rule 32.2 and any other law; and

(G) any other information that the court requires, including information relevant to the factors under 18 U.S.C. § 3553(a).

(3) *Exclusions.* The presentence report must exclude the following:

(A) any diagnoses that, if disclosed, might seriously disrupt a rehabilitation program;

(B) any sources of information obtained upon a promise of confidentiality; and

(C) any other information that, if disclosed, might result in physical or other harm to the defendant or others.

(e) Disclosing the Report and Recommendation.

(1) *Time to Disclose.* Unless the defendant has consented in writing, the probation officer must not submit a presentence report to the court or disclose its contents to anyone until the defendant has pleaded guilty or nolo contendere, or has been found guilty.

(2) *Minimum Required Notice.* The probation officer must give the presentence report to the defendant, the defendant's attorney, and an attorney for the government at least 35 days before sentencing unless the defendant waives this minimum period.

(3) *Sentence Recommendation.* By local rule or by order in a case, the court may direct the probation officer not to disclose to anyone other than the court the officer's recommendation on the sentence.

(f) Objecting to the Report.

(1) *Time to Object.* Within 14 days after receiving the presentence report, the parties must state in writing any objections, including objections to material information, sentencing guideline ranges, and policy statements contained in or omitted from the report.

(2) *Serving Objections.* An objecting party must provide a copy of its objections to the opposing party and to the probation officer.

(3) *Action on Objections.* After receiving objections, the probation officer may meet with the parties to discuss the objections. The probation officer may then investigate further and revise the presentence report as appropriate.

(g) Submitting the Report. At least 7 days before sentencing, the probation officer must submit to the court and to the parties the presentence report and an addendum containing any unresolved objections, the grounds for those objections, and the probation officer's comments on them.

(h) Notice of Possible Departure from Sentencing Guidelines. Before the court may depart from the applicable sentencing range on a ground not identified for departure either in the presentence report or in a party's prehearing submission, the court must give the parties reasonable notice that it is contemplating such a departure. The notice must specify any ground on which the court is contemplating a departure.

(i) Sentencing.

> **(1) *In General.*** At sentencing, the court:

>> (A) must verify that the defendant and the defendant's attorney have read and discussed the presentence report and any addendum to the report;

>> (B) must give to the defendant and an attorney for the government a written summary of—or summarize in camera— any information excluded from the presentence report under Rule 32(d)(3) on which the court will rely in sentencing, and give them a reasonable opportunity to comment on that information;

>> (C) must allow the parties' attorneys to comment on the probation officer's determinations and other matters relating to an appropriate sentence; and

>> (D) may, for good cause, allow a party to make a new objection at any time before sentence is imposed.

> **(2) *Introducing Evidence; Producing a Statement.*** The court may permit the parties to introduce evidence on the objections. If a witness testifies at sentencing, Rule 26.2(a)–(d) and (f) applies. If a party fails to comply with a Rule 26.2 order to produce a witness's statement, the court must not consider that witness's testimony.

> **(3) *Court Determinations.*** At sentencing, the court:

>> (A) may accept any undisputed portion of the presentence report as a finding of fact;

>> (B) must—for any disputed portion of the presentence report or other controverted matter—rule on the dispute or determine that a ruling is unnecessary either because the matter will not affect sentencing, or because the court will not consider the matter in sentencing; and

>> (C) must append a copy of the court's determinations under this rule to any copy of the presentence report made available to the Bureau of Prisons.

> **(4) *Opportunity to Speak.***

>> (A) *By a Party*. Before imposing sentence, the court must:

>>> (i) provide the defendant's attorney an opportunity to speak on the defendant's behalf;

(ii) address the defendant personally in order to permit the defendant to speak or present any information to mitigate the sentence; and

(iii) provide an attorney for the government an opportunity to speak equivalent to that of the defendant's attorney.

(B) *By a Victim.* Before imposing sentence, the court must address any victim of the crime who is present at sentencing and must permit the victim to be reasonably heard.

(C) *In Camera Proceedings.* Upon a party's motion and for good cause, the court may hear in camera any statement made under Rule 32(i)(4).

(j) Defendant's Right to Appeal.

(1) *Advice of a Right to Appeal.*

(A) *Appealing a Conviction.* If the defendant pleaded not guilty and was convicted, after sentencing the court must advise the defendant of the right to appeal the conviction.

(B) *Appealing a Sentence.* After sentencing—regardless of the defendant's plea—the court must advise the defendant of any right to appeal the sentence.

(C) *Appeal Costs.* The court must advise a defendant who is unable to pay appeal costs of the right to ask for permission to appeal in forma pauperis.

(2) *Clerk's Filing of Notice.* If the defendant so requests, the clerk must immediately prepare and file a notice of appeal on the defendant's behalf.

(k) Judgment.

(1) *In General.* In the judgment of conviction, the court must set forth the plea, the jury verdict or the court's findings, the adjudication, and the sentence. If the defendant is found not guilty or is otherwise entitled to be discharged, the court must so order. The judge must sign the judgment, and the clerk must enter it.

(2) *Criminal Forfeiture.* Forfeiture procedures are governed by Rule 32.2.

Rule 32.1. Revoking or Modifying Probation or Supervised Release

(a) Initial Appearance.

(1) *Person In Custody.* A person held in custody for violating probation or supervised release must be taken without unnecessary delay before a magistrate judge.

(A) If the person is held in custody in the district where an alleged violation occurred, the initial appearance must be in that district.

(B) If the person is held in custody in a district other than where an alleged violation occurred, the initial appearance must be in that district, or in an adjacent district if the appearance can occur more promptly there.

(2) *Upon a Summons.* When a person appears in response to a summons for violating probation or supervised release, a magistrate judge must proceed under this rule.

(3) *Advice.* The judge must inform the person of the following:

(A) the alleged violation of probation or supervised release;

(B) the person's right to retain counsel or to request that counsel be appointed if the person cannot obtain counsel; and

(C) the person's right, if held in custody, to a preliminary hearing under Rule 32.1(b)(1).

(4) *Appearance in the District With Jurisdiction.* If the person is arrested or appears in the district that has jurisdiction to conduct a revocation hearing—either originally or by transfer of jurisdiction—the court must proceed under Rule 32.1(b)–(e).

(5) *Appearance in a District Lacking Jurisdiction.* If the person is arrested or appears in a district that does not have jurisdiction to conduct a revocation hearing, the magistrate judge must:

(A) if the alleged violation occurred in the district of arrest, conduct a preliminary hearing under Rule 32.1(b) and either:

(i) transfer the person to the district that has jurisdiction, if the judge finds probable cause to believe that a violation occurred; or

(ii) dismiss the proceedings and so notify the court that has jurisdiction, if the judge finds no probable cause to believe that a violation occurred; or

(B) if the alleged violation did not occur in the district of arrest, transfer the person to the district that has jurisdiction if:

(i) the government produces certified copies of the judgment, warrant, and warrant application, or produces copies of those certified documents by reliable electronic means; and

(ii) the judge finds that the person is the same person named in the warrant.

(6) *Release or Detention.* The magistrate judge may release or detain the person under 18 U.S.C. § 3143(a)(1) pending further proceedings. The burden of establishing by clear and convincing evidence that the person will not flee or pose a danger to any other person or to the community rests with the person.

(b) Revocation.

(1) *Preliminary Hearing.*

(A) *In General.* If a person is in custody for violating a condition of probation or supervised release, a magistrate judge must promptly conduct a hearing to determine whether there is probable cause to believe that a violation occurred. The person may waive the hearing.

(B) *Requirements.* The hearing must be recorded by a court reporter or by a suitable recording device. The judge must give the person:

(i) notice of the hearing and its purpose, the alleged violation, and the person's right to retain counsel or to request that counsel be appointed if the person cannot obtain counsel;

(ii) an opportunity to appear at the hearing and present evidence; and

(iii) upon request, an opportunity to question any adverse witness, unless the judge determines that the interest of justice does not require the witness to appear.

(C) *Referral.* If the judge finds probable cause, the judge must conduct a revocation hearing. If the judge does not find probable cause, the judge must dismiss the proceeding.

(2) *Revocation Hearing.* Unless waived by the person, the court must hold the revocation hearing within a reasonable time in the district having jurisdiction. The person is entitled to:

(A) written notice of the alleged violation;

(B) disclosure of the evidence against the person;

(C) an opportunity to appear, present evidence, and question any adverse witness unless the court determines that the interest of justice does not require the witness to appear;

(D) notice of the person's right to retain counsel or to request that counsel be appointed if the person cannot obtain counsel; and

(E) an opportunity to make a statement and present any information in mitigation.

(c) Modification.

(1) *In General.* Before modifying the conditions of probation or supervised release, the court must hold a hearing, at which the person has the right to counsel and an opportunity to make a statement and present any information in mitigation.

(2) *Exceptions.* A hearing is not required if:

(A) the person waives the hearing; or

(B) the relief sought is favorable to the person and does not extend the term of probation or of supervised release; and

(C) an attorney for the government has received notice of the relief sought, has had a reasonable opportunity to object, and has not done so.

(d) Disposition of the Case. The court's disposition of the case is governed by 18 U.S.C. § 3563 and § 3565 (probation) and § 3583 (supervised release).

(e) Producing a Statement. Rule 26.2(a)–(d) and (f) applies at a hearing under this rule. If a party fails to comply with a Rule 26.2 order to produce a witness's statement, the court must not consider that witness's testimony.

Rule 32.2. Criminal Forfeiture

(a) Notice to the Defendant. A court must not enter a judgment of forfeiture in a criminal proceeding unless the indictment or information contains notice to the defendant that the government will seek the forfeiture of property as part of any sentence in accordance with the applicable statute. The notice should not be designated as a count of the indictment or information. The indictment or information need not identify the property subject to forfeiture or specify the amount of any forfeiture money judgment that the government seeks.

(b) Entering a Preliminary Order of Forfeiture.

(1) *Forfeiture Phase of the Trial.*

(A) *Forfeiture Determinations.* As soon as practical after a verdict or finding of guilty, or after a plea of guilty or nolo contendere is accepted, on any count in an indictment or information regarding which criminal forfeiture is sought, the court must determine what property is subject to forfeiture under the applicable statute. If the government seeks forfeiture of specific property, the court must determine whether the government has established the requisite nexus between the property and the offense. If the government seeks a personal money judgment, the court must determine the amount of money that the defendant will be ordered to pay.

(B) *Evidence and Hearing.* The court's determination may be based on evidence already in the record, including any written plea agreement, and on any additional evidence or information submitted by the parties and accepted by the court as relevant and reliable. If the forfeiture is contested, on either party's request the court must conduct a hearing after the verdict or finding of guilty.

(2) *Preliminary Order.*

(A) *Contents of a Specific Order.* If the court finds that property is subject to forfeiture, it must promptly enter a preliminary order of forfeiture setting forth the amount of any money judgment, directing the forfeiture of specific property, and directing the forfeiture of any substitute property if the government has met the statutory criteria. The court must enter the order without regard to any third party's interest in the property. Determining whether a third party has such an interest must be deferred until any third party files a claim in an ancillary proceeding under Rule 32.2(c).

(B) *Timing.* Unless doing so is impractical, the court must enter the preliminary order sufficiently in advance of sentencing to allow the parties to suggest revisions or modifications before the order becomes final as to the defendant under Rule 32.2(b)(4).

(C) *General Order.* If, before sentencing, the court cannot identify all the specific property subject to forfeiture or calculate the total amount of the money judgment, the court may enter a forfeiture order that:

    (i)   lists any identified property;

    (ii) describes other property in general terms; and

(iii) states that the order will be amended under Rule 32.2(e)(1) when additional specific property is identified or the amount of the money judgment has been calculated.

(3) Seizing Property. The entry of a preliminary order of forfeiture authorizes the Attorney General (or a designee) to seize the specific property subject to forfeiture; to conduct any discovery the court considers proper in identifying, locating, or disposing of the property; and to commence proceedings that comply with any statutes governing third-party rights. The court may include in the order of forfeiture conditions reasonably necessary to preserve the property's value pending any appeal.

(4) Sentence and Judgment.

(A) *When Final.* At sentencing—or at any time before sentencing if the defendant consents—the preliminary forfeiture order becomes final as to the defendant. If the order directs the defendant to forfeit specific property, it remains preliminary as to third parties until the ancillary proceeding is concluded under Rule 32.2(c).

(B) *Notice and Inclusion in the Judgment.* The court must include the forfeiture when orally announcing the sentence or must otherwise ensure that the defendant knows of the forfeiture at sentencing. The court must also include the forfeiture order, directly or by reference, in the judgment, but the court's failure to do so may be corrected at any time under Rule 36.

(C) *Time to Appeal.* The time for the defendant or the government to file an appeal from the forfeiture order, or from the court's failure to enter an order, begins to run when judgment is entered. If the court later amends or declines to amend a forfeiture order to include additional property under Rule 32.2(e), the defendant or the government may file an appeal regarding that property under Federal Rule of Appellate Procedure 4(b). The time for that appeal runs from the date when the order granting or denying the amendment becomes final.

(5) Jury Determination.

(A) *Retaining the Jury.* In any case tried before a jury, if the indictment or information states that the government is seeking forfeiture, the court must determine before the jury begins deliberating whether either party requests that the jury be retained to determine the forfeitability of specific property if it returns a guilty verdict.

(B) *Special Verdict Form.* If a party timely requests to have the jury determine forfeiture, the government must submit a proposed Special Verdict Form listing each property subject to forfeiture and asking the jury to determine whether the government has established the requisite nexus between the property and the offense committed by the defendant.

(6) *Notice of the Forfeiture Order.*

(A) *Publishing and Sending Notice.* If the court orders the forfeiture of specific property, the government must publish notice of the order and send notice to any person who reasonably appears to be a potential claimant with standing to contest the forfeiture in the ancillary proceeding.

(B) *Content of the Notice.* The notice must describe the forfeited property, state the times under the applicable statute when a petition contesting the forfeiture must be filed, and state the name and contact information for the government attorney to be served with the petition.

(C) *Means of Publication; Exceptions to Publication Requirement.* Publication must take place as described in Supplemental Rule G(4)(a)(iii) of the Federal Rules of Civil Procedure, and may be by any means described in Supplemental Rule G(4)(a)(iv). Publication is unnecessary if any exception in Supplemental Rule G(4)(a)(i) applies.

(D) *Means of Sending the Notice.* The notice may be sent in accordance with Supplemental Rules G(4)(b)(iii)–(v) of the Federal Rules of Civil Procedure.

(7) *Interlocutory Sale.* At any time before entry of a final forfeiture order, the court, in accordance with Supplemental Rule G(7) of the Federal Rules of Civil Procedure, may order the interlocutory sale of property alleged to be forfeitable.

(c) Ancillary Proceeding; Entering a Final Order of Forfeiture.

(1) *In General.* If, as prescribed by statute, a third party files a petition asserting an interest in the property to be forfeited, the court must conduct an ancillary proceeding, but no ancillary proceeding is required to the extent that the forfeiture consists of a money judgment.

(A) In the ancillary proceeding, the court may, on motion, dismiss the petition for lack of standing, for failure to state a claim, or for any other lawful reason. For purposes of the motion, the facts set forth in the petition are assumed to be true.

(B) After disposing of any motion filed under Rule 32.2(c)(1)(A) and before conducting a hearing on the petition, the court may permit the parties to conduct discovery in accordance with the Federal Rules of Civil Procedure if the court determines that discovery is necessary or desirable to resolve factual issues. When discovery ends, a party may move for summary judgment under Federal Rule of Civil Procedure 56.

(2) *Entering a Final Order.* When the ancillary proceeding ends, the court must enter a final order of forfeiture by amending the preliminary order as necessary to account for any third-party rights. If no third party files a timely petition, the preliminary order becomes the final order of forfeiture if the court finds that the defendant (or any combination of defendants convicted in the case) had an interest in the property that is forfeitable under the applicable statute. The defendant may not object to the entry of the final order on the ground that the property belongs, in whole or in part, to a codefendant or third party; nor may a third party object to the final order on the ground that the third party had an interest in the property.

(3) *Multiple Petitions.* If multiple third-party petitions are filed in the same case, an order dismissing or granting one petition is not appealable until rulings are made on all the petitions, unless the court determines that there is no just reason for delay.

(4) *Ancillary Proceeding Not Part of Sentencing.* An ancillary proceeding is not part of sentencing.

(d) Stay Pending Appeal. If a defendant appeals from a conviction or an order of forfeiture, the court may stay the order of forfeiture on terms appropriate to ensure that the property remains available pending appellate review. A stay does not delay the ancillary proceeding or the determination of a third party's rights or interests. If the court rules in favor of any third party while an appeal is pending, the court may amend the order of forfeiture but must not transfer any property interest to a third party until the decision on appeal becomes final, unless the defendant consents in writing or on the record.

(e) Subsequently Located Property; Substitute Property.

(1) *In General.* On the government's motion, the court may at any time enter an order of forfeiture or amend an existing order of forfeiture to include property that:

(A) is subject to forfeiture under an existing order of forfeiture but was located and identified after that order was entered; or

(B) is substitute property that qualifies for forfeiture under an applicable statute.

(2) *Procedure.* If the government shows that the property is subject to forfeiture under Rule 32.2(e)(1), the court must:

(A) enter an order forfeiting that property, or amend an existing preliminary or final order to include it; and

(B) if a third party files a petition claiming an interest in the property, conduct an ancillary proceeding under Rule 32.2(c).

(3) *Jury Trial Limited.* There is no right to a jury trial under Rule 32.2(e).

Rule 33. New Trial

(a) Defendant's Motion. Upon the defendant's motion, the court may vacate any judgment and grant a new trial if the interest of justice so requires. If the case was tried without a jury, the court may take additional testimony and enter a new judgment.

(b) Time to File.

(1) *Newly Discovered Evidence.* Any motion for a new trial grounded on newly discovered evidence must be filed within 3 years after the verdict or finding of guilty. If an appeal is pending, the court may not grant a motion for a new trial until the appellate court remands the case.

(2) *Other Grounds.* Any motion for a new trial grounded on any reason other than newly discovered evidence must be filed within 14 days after the verdict or finding of guilty.

Rule 34. Arresting Judgment

(a) In General. Upon the defendant's motion or on its own, the court must arrest judgment if the court does not have jurisdiction of the charged offense.

(b) Time to File. The defendant must move to arrest judgment within 14 days after the court accepts a verdict or finding of guilty, or after a plea of guilty or nolo contendere.

Rule 35. Correcting or Reducing a Sentence

(a) Correcting Clear Error. Within 14 days after sentencing, the court may correct a sentence that resulted from arithmetical, technical, or other clear error.

(b) Reducing a Sentence for Substantial Assistance.

(1) *In General.* Upon the government's motion made within one year of sentencing, the court may reduce a sentence if the defendant, after sentencing, provided substantial assistance in investigating or prosecuting another person.

(2) *Later Motion.* Upon the government's motion made more than one year after sentencing, the court may reduce a sentence if the defendant's substantial assistance involved:

> (A) information not known to the defendant until one year or more after sentencing;

> (B) information provided by the defendant to the government within one year of sentencing, but which did not become useful to the government until more than one year after sentencing; or

> (C) information the usefulness of which could not reasonably have been anticipated by the defendant until more than one year after sentencing and which was promptly provided to the government after its usefulness was reasonably apparent to the defendant.

(3) *Evaluating Substantial Assistance.* In evaluating whether the defendant has provided substantial assistance, the court may consider the defendant's presentence assistance.

(4) *Below Statutory Minimum.* When acting under Rule 35(b), the court may reduce the sentence to a level below the minimum sentence established by statute.

(c) "Sentencing" Defined. As used in this rule, "sentencing" means the oral announcement of the sentence.

Rule 36. Clerical Error

After giving any notice it considers appropriate, the court may at any time correct a clerical error in a judgment, order, or other part of the record, or correct an error in the record arising from oversight or omission.

Rule 37. Ruling on a Motion for Relief That Is Barred by a Pending Appeal

(a) Relief Pending Appeal. If a timely motion is made for relief that the court lacks authority to grant because of an appeal that has been docketed and is pending, the court may:

> **(1)** defer considering the motion;

> **(2)** deny the motion; or

(3) state either that it would grant the motion if the court of appeals remands for that purpose or that the motion raises a substantial issue.

(b) Notice to the Court of Appeals. The movant must promptly notify the circuit clerk under Federal Rule of Appellate Procedure 12.1 if the district court states that it would grant the motion or that the motion raises a substantial issue.

(c) Remand. The district court may decide the motion if the court of appeals remands for that purpose.

Rule 38. Staying a Sentence or a Disability

(a) Death Sentence. The court must stay a death sentence if the defendant appeals the conviction or sentence.

(b) Imprisonment.

(1) *Stay Granted.* If the defendant is released pending appeal, the court must stay a sentence of imprisonment.

(2) *Stay Denied; Place of Confinement.* If the defendant is not released pending appeal, the court may recommend to the Attorney General that the defendant be confined near the place of the trial or appeal for a period reasonably necessary to permit the defendant to assist in preparing the appeal.

(c) Fine. If the defendant appeals, the district court, or the court of appeals under Federal Rule of Appellate Procedure 8, may stay a sentence to pay a fine or a fine and costs. The court may stay the sentence on any terms considered appropriate and may require the defendant to:

(1) deposit all or part of the fine and costs into the district court's registry pending appeal;

(2) post a bond to pay the fine and costs; or

(3) submit to an examination concerning the defendant's assets and, if appropriate, order the defendant to refrain from dissipating assets.

(d) Probation. If the defendant appeals, the court may stay a sentence of probation. The court must set the terms of any stay.

(e) Restitution and Notice to Victims.

(1) *In General.* If the defendant appeals, the district court, or the court of appeals under Federal Rule of Appellate Procedure 8, may stay—on any terms considered appropriate—any sentence providing for restitution under 18 U.S.C. § 3556 or notice under 18 U.S.C. § 3555.

(2) *Ensuring Compliance.* The court may issue any order reasonably necessary to ensure compliance with a restitution order or a notice order after disposition of an appeal, including:

(A) a restraining order;

(B) an injunction;

(C) an order requiring the defendant to deposit all or part of any monetary restitution into the district court's registry; or

(D) an order requiring the defendant to post a bond.

(f) Forfeiture. A stay of a forfeiture order is governed by Rule 32.2(d).

(g) Disability. If the defendant's conviction or sentence creates a civil or employment disability under federal law, the district court, or the court of appeals under Federal Rule of Appellate Procedure 8, may stay the disability pending appeal on any terms considered appropriate. The court may issue any order reasonably necessary to protect the interest represented by the disability pending appeal, including a restraining order or an injunction.

Rule 39. [Reserved]

TITLE VIII. SUPPLEMENTARY AND SPECIAL PROCEEDINGS

Rule 40. Arrest for Failing to Appear in Another District or for Violating Conditions of Release Set in Another District

(a) In General. A person must be taken without unnecessary delay before a magistrate judge in the district of arrest if the person has been arrested under a warrant issued in another district for:

(i)   failing to appear as required by the terms of that person's release under 18 U.S.C. §§ 3141–3156 or by a subpoena; or

(ii) violating conditions of release set in another district.

(b) Proceedings. The judge must proceed under Rule 5(c)(3) as applicable.

(c) Release or Detention Order. The judge may modify any previous release or detention order issued in another district, but must state in writing the reasons for doing so.

(d) Video Teleconferencing. Video teleconferencing may be used to conduct an appearance under this rule if the defendant consents.

Rule 41. Search and Seizure

(a) Scope and Definitions.

(1) *Scope.* This rule does not modify any statute regulating search or seizure, or the issuance and execution of a search warrant in special circumstances.

(2) *Definitions.* The following definitions apply under this rule:

(A) "Property" includes documents, books, papers, any other tangible objects, and information.

(B) "Daytime" means the hours between 6:00 a.m. and 10:00 p.m. according to local time.

(C) "Federal law enforcement officer" means a government agent (other than an attorney for the government) who is engaged in enforcing the criminal laws and is within any category of officers authorized by the Attorney General to request a search warrant.

(D) "Domestic terrorism" and "international terrorism" have the meanings set out in 18 U.S.C. § 2331.

(E) "Tracking device" has the meaning set out in 18 U.S.C. § 3117(b).

(b) Venue for a Warrant Application.

At the request of a federal law enforcement officer or an attorney for the government:

(1) a magistrate judge with authority in the district—or if none is reasonably available, a judge of a state court of record in the district—has authority to issue a warrant to search for and seize a person or property located within the district;

(2) a magistrate judge with authority in the district has authority to issue a warrant for a person or property outside the district if the person or property is located within the district when the warrant is issued but might move or be moved outside the district before the warrant is executed;

(3) a magistrate judge—in an investigation of domestic terrorism or international terrorism—with authority in any district in which activities related to the terrorism may have occurred has authority to issue a warrant for a person or property within or outside that district;

(4) a magistrate judge with authority in the district has authority to issue a warrant to install within the district a tracking device; the warrant may authorize use of the device to track the movement of a person or property located within the district, outside the district, or both; and

(5) a magistrate judge having authority in any district where activities related to the crime may have occurred, or in the District of Columbia, may issue a warrant for property that is located outside the jurisdiction of any state or district, but within any of the following:

> **(A)** a United States territory, possession, or commonwealth;

> **(B)** the premises—no matter who owns them—of a United States diplomatic or consular mission in a foreign state, including any appurtenant building, part of a building, or land used for the mission's purposes; or

> **(C)** a residence and any appurtenant land owned or leased by the United States and used by United States personnel assigned to a United States diplomatic or consular mission in a foreign state.

(6) a magistrate judge with authority in any district where activities related to a crime may have occurred has authority to issue a warrant to use remote access to search electronic storage media and to seize or copy electronically stored information located within or outside that district if:

> **(A)** the district where the media or information is located has been concealed through technological means; or

> **(B)** in an investigation of a violation of 18 U.S.C. § 1030(a)(5), the media are protected computers that have been damaged without authorization and are located in five or more districts.

(c) Persons or Property Subject to Search or Seizure. A warrant may be issued for any of the following:

> **(1)** evidence of a crime;

> **(2)** contraband, fruits of crime, or other items illegally possessed;

> **(3)** property designed for use, intended for use, or used in committing a crime; or

> **(4)** a person to be arrested or a person who is unlawfully restrained.

(d) Obtaining a Warrant.

> **(1)** *In General.* After receiving an affidavit or other information, a magistrate judge—or if authorized by Rule 41(b), a judge of a state court of record—must issue the warrant if there is probable cause to search for and seize a person or property or to install and use a tracking device.

(2) *Requesting a Warrant in the Presence of a Judge.*

(A) *Warrant on an Affidavit.* When a federal law enforcement officer or an attorney for the government presents an affidavit in support of a warrant, the judge may require the affiant to appear personally and may examine under oath the affiant and any witness the affiant produces.

(B) *Warrant on Sworn Testimony.* The judge may wholly or partially dispense with a written affidavit and base a warrant on sworn testimony if doing so is reasonable under the circumstances.

(C) *Recording Testimony.* Testimony taken in support of a warrant must be recorded by a court reporter or by a suitable recording device, and the judge must file the transcript or recording with the clerk, along with any affidavit.

(3) *Requesting a Warrant by Telephonic or Other Reliable Electronic Means.* In accordance with Rule 4.1, a magistrate judge may issue a warrant based on information communicated by telephone or other reliable electronic means.

(e) **Issuing the Warrant.**

(1) *In General.* The magistrate judge or a judge of a state court of record must issue the warrant to an officer authorized to execute it.

(2) *Contents of the Warrant.*

(A) *Warrant to Search for and Seize a Person or Property.* Except for a tracking-device warrant, the warrant must identify the person or property to be searched, identify any person or property to be seized, and designate the magistrate judge to whom it must be returned. The warrant must command the officer to:

(i) execute the warrant within a specified time no longer than 14 days;

(ii) execute the warrant during the daytime, unless the judge for good cause expressly authorizes execution at another time; and

(iii) return the warrant to the magistrate judge designated in the warrant.

(B) *Warrant Seeking Electronically Stored Information.* A warrant under Rule 41(e)(2)(A) may authorize the seizure of electronic storage media or the seizure or copying of electronically stored information. Unless otherwise specified, the warrant authorizes a later review of the media or information consistent with the warrant. The time for executing the warrant in Rule

41(e)(2)(A) and (f)(1)(A) refers to the seizure or on-site copying of the media or information, and not to any later off-site copying or review.

(C) *Warrant for a Tracking Device.* A tracking-device warrant must identify the person or property to be tracked, designate the magistrate judge to whom it must be returned, and specify a reasonable length of time that the device may be used. The time must not exceed 45 days from the date the warrant was issued. The court may, for good cause, grant one or more extensions for a reasonable period not to exceed 45 days each. The warrant must command the officer to:

(i)   complete any installation authorized by the warrant within a specified time no longer than 10 days;

(ii)   perform any installation authorized by the warrant during the daytime, unless the judge for good cause expressly authorizes installation at another time; and

(iii)   return the warrant to the judge designated in the warrant.

(f)   Executing and Returning the Warrant.

(1)   *Warrant to Search for and Seize a Person or Property.*

(A) *Noting the Time.* The officer executing the warrant must enter on it the exact date and time it was executed.

(B) *Inventory.* An officer present during the execution of the warrant must prepare and verify an inventory of any property seized. The officer must do so in the presence of another officer and the person from whom, or from whose premises, the property was taken. If either one is not present, the officer must prepare and verify the inventory in the presence of at least one other credible person. In a case involving the seizure of electronic storage media or the seizure or copying of electronically stored information, the inventory may be limited to describing the physical storage media that were seized or copied. The officer may retain a copy of the electronically stored information that was seized or copied.

(C) *Receipt.* The officer executing the warrant must give a copy of the warrant and a receipt for the property taken to the person from whom, or from whose premises, the property was taken or leave a copy of the warrant and receipt at the place where the officer took the property. For a warrant to use remote access to search electronic storage media and seize or copy electronically stored information, the officer must make reasonable efforts to serve a copy of the warrant and receipt on the person whose property was searched or who possessed the information that was seized or copied. Service may be accomplished by any means, including electronic means, reasonably calculated to reach that person.

(D) *Return.* The officer executing the warrant must promptly return it—together with a copy of the inventory—to the magistrate judge designated on the warrant. The officer may do so by reliable electronic means. The judge must, on request, give a copy of the inventory to the person from whom, or from whose premises, the property was taken and to the applicant for the warrant.

(2) *Warrant for a Tracking Device.*

(A) *Noting the Time.* The officer executing a tracking-device warrant must enter on it the exact date and time the device was installed and the period during which it was used.

(B) *Return.* Within 10 days after the use of the tracking device has ended, the officer executing the warrant must return it to the judge designated in the warrant. The officer may do so by reliable electronic means.

(C) *Service.* Within 10 days after the use of the tracking device has ended, the officer executing a tracking-device warrant must serve a copy of the warrant on the person who was tracked or whose property was tracked. Service may be accomplished by delivering a copy to the person who, or whose property, was tracked; or by leaving a copy at the person's residence or usual place of abode with an individual of suitable age and discretion who resides at that location and by mailing a copy to the person's last known address. Upon request of the government, the judge may delay notice as provided in Rule 41(f)(3).

(3) *Delayed Notice.* Upon the government's request, a magistrate judge—or if authorized by Rule 41(b), a judge of a state court of record—may delay any notice required by this rule if the delay is authorized by statute.

(g) Motion to Return Property. A person aggrieved by an unlawful search and seizure of property or by the deprivation of property may move for the property's return. The motion must be filed in the district where the property was seized. The court must receive evidence on any factual issue necessary to decide the motion. If it grants the motion, the court must return the property to the movant, but may impose reasonable conditions to protect access to the property and its use in later proceedings.

(h) Motion to Suppress. A defendant may move to suppress evidence in the court where the trial will occur, as Rule 12 provides.

(i) Forwarding Papers to the Clerk. The magistrate judge to whom the warrant is returned must attach to the warrant a copy of the return, of the inventory, and of all other related papers and must deliver them to the clerk in the district where the property was seized.

Rule 42. Criminal Contempt

(a) Disposition After Notice. Any person who commits criminal contempt may be punished for that contempt after prosecution on notice.

(1) *Notice.* The court must give the person notice in open court, in an order to show cause, or in an arrest order. The notice must:

(A) state the time and place of the trial;

(B) allow the defendant a reasonable time to prepare a defense; and

(C) state the essential facts constituting the charged criminal contempt and describe it as such.

(2) *Appointing a Prosecutor.* The court must request that the contempt be prosecuted by an attorney for the government, unless the interest of justice requires the appointment of another attorney. If the government declines the request, the court must appoint another attorney to prosecute the contempt.

(3) *Trial and Disposition.* A person being prosecuted for criminal contempt is entitled to a jury trial in any case in which federal law so provides and must be released or detained as Rule 46 provides. If the criminal contempt involves disrespect toward or criticism of a judge, that judge is disqualified from presiding at the contempt trial or hearing unless the defendant consents. Upon a finding or verdict of guilty, the court must impose the punishment.

(b) Summary Disposition. Notwithstanding any other provision of these rules, the court (other than a magistrate judge) may summarily punish a person who commits criminal contempt in its presence if the judge saw or heard the contemptuous conduct and so certifies; a magistrate judge may summarily punish a person as provided in 28 U.S.C. § 636(e). The contempt order must recite the facts, be signed by the judge, and be filed with the clerk.

TITLE IX. GENERAL PROVISIONS

Rule 43. Defendant's Presence

(a) When Required. Unless this rule, Rule 5, or Rule 10 provides otherwise, the defendant must be present at:

(1) the initial appearance, the initial arraignment, and the plea;

(2) every trial stage, including jury impanelment and the return of the verdict; and

(3) sentencing.

(b) When Not Required. A defendant need not be present under any of the following circumstances:

(1) *Organizational Defendant.* The defendant is an organization represented by counsel who is present.

(2) *Misdemeanor Offense.* The offense is punishable by fine or by imprisonment for not more than one year, or both, and with the defendant's written consent, the court permits arraignment, plea, trial, and sentencing to occur by video teleconferencing or in the defendant's absence.

(3) *Conference or Hearing on a Legal Question.* The proceeding involves only a conference or hearing on a question of law.

(4) *Sentence Correction.* The proceeding involves the correction or reduction of sentence under Rule 35 or 18 U.S.C. § 3582(c).

(c) Waiving Continued Presence.

(1) *In General.* A defendant who was initially present at trial, or who had pleaded guilty or nolo contendere, waives the right to be present under the following circumstances:

(A) when the defendant is voluntarily absent after the trial has begun, regardless of whether the court informed the defendant of an obligation to remain during trial;

(B) in a noncapital case, when the defendant is voluntarily absent during sentencing; or

(C) when the court warns the defendant that it will remove the defendant from the courtroom for disruptive behavior, but the defendant persists in conduct that justifies removal from the courtroom.

(2) *Waiver's Effect.* If the defendant waives the right to be present, the trial may proceed to completion, including the verdict's return and sentencing, during the defendant's absence.

Rule 44. Right to and Appointment of Counsel

(a) Right to Appointed Counsel. A defendant who is unable to obtain counsel is entitled to have counsel appointed to represent the defendant at every stage of the proceeding from initial appearance through appeal, unless the defendant waives this right.

(b) Appointment Procedure. Federal law and local court rules govern the procedure for implementing the right to counsel.

(c) Inquiry Into Joint Representation.

(1) *Joint Representation.* Joint representation occurs when:

(A) two or more defendants have been charged jointly under Rule 8(b) or have been joined for trial under Rule 13; and

(B) the defendants are represented by the same counsel, or counsel who are associated in law practice.

(2) *Court's Responsibilities in Cases of Joint Representation.* The court must promptly inquire about the propriety of joint representation and must personally advise each defendant of the right to the effective assistance of counsel, including separate representation. Unless there is good cause to believe that no conflict of interest is likely to arise, the court must take appropriate measures to protect each defendant's right to counsel.

Rule 45. Computing and Extending Time

(a) Computing Time. The following rules apply in computing any time period specified in these rules, in any local rule or court order, or in any statute that does not specify a method of computing time.

(1) *Period Stated in Days or a Longer Unit.* When the period is stated in days or a longer unit of time:

(A) exclude the day of the event that triggers the period;

(B) count every day, including intermediate Saturdays, Sundays, and legal holidays; and

(C) include the last day of the period, but if the last day is a Saturday, Sunday, or legal holiday, the period continues to run until the end of the next day that is not a Saturday, Sunday, or legal holiday.

(2) *Period Stated in Hours.* When the period is stated in hours:

(A) begin counting immediately on the occurrence of the event that triggers the period;

(B) count every hour, including hours during intermediate Saturdays, Sundays, and legal holidays; and

(C) if the period would end on a Saturday, Sunday, or legal holiday, the period continues to run until the same time on the next day that is not a Saturday, Sunday, or legal holiday.

(3) *Inaccessibility of the Clerk's Office.* Unless the court orders otherwise, if the clerk's office is inaccessible:

(A) on the last day for filing under Rule 45(a)(1), then the time for filing is extended to the first accessible day that is not a Saturday, Sunday, or legal holiday; or

(B) during the last hour for filing under Rule 45(a)(2), then the time for filing is extended to the same time on the first accessible day that is not a Saturday, Sunday, or legal holiday.

(4) *"Last Day" Defined.* Unless a different time is set by a statute, local rule, or court order, the last day ends:

(A) for electronic filing, at midnight in the court's time zone; and

(B) for filing by other means, when the clerk's office is scheduled to close.

(5) *"Next Day" Defined.* The "next day" is determined by continuing to count forward when the period is measured after an event and backward when measured before an event.

(6) *"Legal Holiday" Defined.* "Legal holiday" means:

(A) the day set aside by statute for observing New Year's Day, Martin Luther King Jr.'s Birthday, Washington's Birthday, Memorial Day, Independence Day, Labor Day, Columbus Day, Veterans' Day, Thanksgiving Day, or Christmas Day;

(B) any day declared a holiday by the President or Congress; and

(C) for periods that are measured after an event, any other day declared a holiday by the state where the district court is located.

(b) Extending Time.

(1) *In General.* When an act must or may be done within a specified period, the court on its own may extend the time, or for good cause may do so on a party's motion made:

(A) before the originally prescribed or previously extended time expires; or

(B) after the time expires if the party failed to act because of excusable neglect.

(2) *Exception.* The court may not extend the time to take any action under Rule 35, except as stated in that rule.

(c) Additional Time After Certain Kinds of Service. Whenever a party must or may act within a specified time after being served and service is made under Federal Rule of Civil Procedure 5(b)(2)(C) (mailing), (D) (leaving with the clerk), or (F) (other means consented to), 3 days are added after the period would otherwise expire under subdivision (a).

Rule 46. Release from Custody; Supervising Detention

(a) Before Trial. The provisions of 18 U.S.C. §§ 3142 and 3144 govern pretrial release.

(b) During Trial. A person released before trial continues on release during trial under the same terms and conditions. But the court may order different terms and conditions or terminate the release if necessary to ensure that the person will be present during trial or that the person's conduct will not obstruct the orderly and expeditious progress of the trial.

(c) Pending Sentencing or Appeal. The provisions of 18 U.S.C. § 3143 govern release pending sentencing or appeal. The burden of establishing that the defendant will not flee or pose a danger to any other person or to the community rests with the defendant.

(d) Pending Hearing on a Violation of Probation or Supervised Release. Rule 32.1(a)(6) governs release pending a hearing on a violation of probation or supervised release.

(e) Surety. The court must not approve a bond unless any surety appears to be qualified. Every surety, except a legally approved corporate surety, must demonstrate by affidavit that its assets are adequate. The court may require the affidavit to describe the following:

(1) the property that the surety proposes to use as security;

(2) any encumbrance on that property;

(3) the number and amount of any other undischarged bonds and bail undertakings the surety has issued; and

(4) any other liability of the surety.

(f) Bail Forfeiture.

(1) *Declaration.* The court must declare the bail forfeited if a condition of the bond is breached.

(2) *Setting Aside.* The court may set aside in whole or in part a bail forfeiture upon any condition the court may impose if:

(A) the surety later surrenders into custody the person released on the surety's appearance bond; or

(B) it appears that justice does not require bail forfeiture.

(3) *Enforcement.*

(A) *Default Judgment and Execution.* If it does not set aside a bail forfeiture, the court must, upon the government's motion, enter a default judgment.

(B) *Jurisdiction and Service.* By entering into a bond, each surety submits to the district court's jurisdiction and irrevocably appoints the district clerk as its agent to receive service of any filings affecting its liability.

(C) *Motion to Enforce.* The court may, upon the government's motion, enforce the surety's liability without an independent action. The government must serve any motion, and notice as the court prescribes, on the district clerk. If so served, the clerk must promptly mail a copy to the surety at its last known address.

(4) *Remission.* After entering a judgment under Rule 46(f)(3), the court may remit in whole or in part the judgment under the same conditions specified in Rule 46(f)(2).

(g) Exoneration. The court must exonerate the surety and release any bail when a bond condition has been satisfied or when the court has set aside or remitted the forfeiture. The court must exonerate a surety who deposits cash in the amount of the bond or timely surrenders the defendant into custody.

(h) Supervising Detention Pending Trial.

(1) *In General.* To eliminate unnecessary detention, the court must supervise the detention within the district of any defendants awaiting trial and of any persons held as material witnesses.

(2) *Reports.* An attorney for the government must report biweekly to the court, listing each material witness held in custody for more than 10 days pending indictment, arraignment, or trial. For each material witness listed in the report, an attorney for the government must state why the witness should not be released with or without a deposition being taken under Rule 15(a).

(i) Forfeiture of Property. The court may dispose of a charged offense by ordering the forfeiture of 18 U.S.C. § 3142(c)(1)(B)(xi) property under 18 U.S.C. § 3146(d), if a fine in the amount of the property's value would be an appropriate sentence for the charged offense.

(j) Producing a Statement.

(1) *In General.* Rule 26.2(a)–(d) and (f) applies at a detention hearing under 18 U.S.C. § 3142, unless the court for good cause rules otherwise.

(2) *Sanctions for Not Producing a Statement.* If a party disobeys a Rule 26.2 order to produce a witness's statement, the court must not consider that witness's testimony at the detention hearing.

Rule 47. Motions and Supporting Affidavits

(a) In General. A party applying to the court for an order must do so by motion.

(b) Form and Content of a Motion. A motion—except when made during a trial or hearing—must be in writing, unless the court permits the party to make the motion by other means. A motion must state the grounds on which it is based and the relief or order sought. A motion may be supported by affidavit.

(c) Timing of a Motion. A party must serve a written motion—other than one that the court may hear ex parte—and any hearing notice at least 7 days before the hearing date, unless a rule or court order sets a different period. For good cause, the court may set a different period upon ex parte application.

(d) Affidavit Supporting a Motion. The moving party must serve any supporting affidavit with the motion. A responding party must serve any opposing affidavit at least one day before the hearing, unless the court permits later service.

Rule 48. Dismissal

(a) By the Government. The government may, with leave of court, dismiss an indictment, information, or complaint. The government may not dismiss the prosecution during trial without the defendant's consent.

(b) By the Court. The court may dismiss an indictment, information, or complaint if unnecessary delay occurs in:

(1) presenting a charge to a grand jury;

(2) filing an information against a defendant; or

(3) bringing a defendant to trial.

Rule 49. Serving and Filing Papers

(a) When Required. A party must serve on every other party any written motion (other than one to be heard ex parte), written notice, designation of the record on appeal, or similar paper.

(b) How Made. Service must be made in the manner provided for a civil action. When these rules or a court order requires or permits service on a party represented by an attorney, service must be made on the attorney instead of the party, unless the court orders otherwise.

(c) Notice of a Court Order. When the court issues an order on any post-arraignment motion, the clerk must provide notice in a manner provided for in a civil action. Except as Federal Rule of Appellate Procedure 4(b) provides otherwise, the clerk's failure to give notice does not affect the time to appeal, or relieve—or authorize the court to relieve—a party's failure to appeal within the allowed time.

(d) Filing. A party must file with the court a copy of any paper the party is required to serve. A paper must be filed in a manner provided for in a civil action.

(e) Electronic Service and Filing. A court may, by local rule, allow papers to be filed, signed, or verified by electronic means that are consistent with any technical standards established by the Judicial Conference of the United States. A local rule may require electronic filing only if reasonable exceptions are allowed. A paper filed electronically in compliance with a local rule is written or in writing under these rules.

Rule 49.1. Privacy Protection for Filings Made with the Court

(a) Redacted Filings. Unless the court orders otherwise, in an electronic or paper filing with the court that contains an individual's social-security number, taxpayer-identification number, or birth date, the name of an individual known to be a minor, a financial-account number, or the home address of an individual, a party or nonparty making the filing may include only:

>   **(1)** the last four digits of the social-security number and taxpayer-identification number;

>   **(2)** the year of the individual's birth;

>   **(3)** the minor's initials;

>   **(4)** the last four digits of the financial-account number; and

>   **(5)** the city and state of the home address.

(b) Exemptions from the Redaction Requirement. The redaction requirement does not apply to the following:

>   **(1)** a financial-account number or real property address that identifies the property allegedly subject to forfeiture in a forfeiture proceeding;

>   **(2)** the record of an administrative or agency proceeding;

>   **(3)** the official record of a state-court proceeding;

(4) the record of a court or tribunal, if that record was not subject to the redaction requirement when originally filed;

(5) a filing covered by Rule 49.1(d);

(6) a pro se filing in an action brought under 28 U.S.C. §§ 2241, 2254, or 2255;

(7) a court filing that is related to a criminal matter or investigation and that is prepared before the filing of a criminal charge or is not filed as part of any docketed criminal case;

(8) an arrest or search warrant; and

(9) a charging document and an affidavit filed in support of any charging document.

(c) Immigration Cases. A filing in an action brought under 28 U.S.C. § 2241 that relates to the petitioner's immigration rights is governed by Federal Rule of Civil Procedure 5.2.

(d) Filings Made Under Seal. The court may order that a filing be made under seal without redaction. The court may later unseal the filing or order the person who made the filing to file a redacted version for the public record.

(e) Protective Orders. For good cause, the court may by order in a case:

(1) require redaction of additional information; or

(2) limit or prohibit a nonparty's remote electronic access to a document filed with the court.

(f) Option for Additional Unredacted Filing Under Seal. A person making a redacted filing may also file an unredacted copy under seal. The court must retain the unredacted copy as part of the record.

(g) Option for Filing a Reference List. A filing that contains redacted information may be filed together with a reference list that identifies each item of redacted information and specifies an appropriate identifier that uniquely corresponds to each item listed. The list must be filed under seal and may be amended as of right. Any reference in the case to a listed identifier will be construed to refer to the corresponding item of information.

(h) Waiver of Protection of Identifiers. A person waives the protection of Rule 49.1(a) as to the person's own information by filing it without redaction and not under seal.

Rule 50. Prompt Disposition

Scheduling preference must be given to criminal proceedings as far as practicable.

Rule 51. Preserving Claimed Error

(a) Exceptions Unnecessary. Exceptions to rulings or orders of the court are unnecessary.

(b) Preserving a Claim of Error. A party may preserve a claim of error by informing the court—when the court ruling or order is made or sought—of the action the party wishes the court to take, or the party's objection to the court's action and the grounds for that objection. If a party does not have an opportunity to object to a ruling or order, the absence of an objection does not later prejudice that party. A ruling or order that admits or excludes evidence is governed by Federal Rule of Evidence 103.

Rule 52. Harmless and Plain Error

(a) Harmless Error. Any error, defect, irregularity, or variance that does not affect substantial rights must be disregarded.

(b) Plain Error. A plain error that affects substantial rights may be considered even though it was not brought to the court's attention.

Rule 53. Courtroom Photographing and Broadcasting Prohibited

Except as otherwise provided by a statute or these rules, the court must not permit the taking of photographs in the courtroom during judicial proceedings or the broadcasting of judicial proceedings from the courtroom.

Rule 54. [Transferred]

[Editor's Note: In the 2002 restyling of the Criminal Rules, all of Rule 54 was transferred to Rule 1.]

Rule 55. Records

The clerk of the district court must keep records of criminal proceedings in the form prescribed by the Director of the Administrative Office of the United States courts. The clerk must enter in the records every court order or judgment and the date of entry.

Rule 56. When Court is Open

(a) In General. A district court is considered always open for any filing, and for issuing and returning process, making a motion, or entering an order.

(b) Office Hours. The clerk's office—with the clerk or a deputy in attendance—must be open during business hours on all days except Saturdays, Sundays, and legal holidays.

(c) Special Hours. A court may provide by local rule or order that its clerk's office will be open for specified hours on Saturdays or legal holidays other than those set aside by statute for observing New Year's Day, Martin Luther King, Jr.'s Birthday, Washington's Birthday, Memorial Day, Independence Day, Labor Day, Columbus Day, Veterans' Day, Thanksgiving Day, and Christmas Day.

Rule 57. District Court Rules

(a) In General.

(1) *Adopting Local Rules.* Each district court acting by a majority of its district judges may, after giving appropriate public notice and an opportunity to comment, make and amend rules governing its practice. A local rule must be consistent with—but not duplicative of—federal statutes and rules adopted under 28 U.S.C. § 2072 and must conform to any uniform numbering system prescribed by the Judicial Conference of the United States.

(2) *Limiting Enforcement.* A local rule imposing a requirement of form must not be enforced in a manner that causes a party to lose rights because of an unintentional failure to comply with the requirement.

(b) Procedure When There Is No Controlling Law. A judge may regulate practice in any manner consistent with federal law, these rules, and the local rules of the district. No sanction or other disadvantage may be imposed for noncompliance with any requirement not in federal law, federal rules, or the local district rules unless the alleged violator was furnished with actual notice of the requirement before the noncompliance.

(c) Effective Date and Notice. A local rule adopted under this rule takes effect on the date specified by the district court and remains in effect unless amended by the district court or abrogated by the judicial council of the circuit in which the district is located. Copies of local rules and their amendments, when promulgated, must be furnished to the judicial council and the Administrative Office of the United States Courts and must be made available to the public.

Rule 58. Petty Offenses and Other Misdemeanors

(a) Scope.

(1) *In General.* These rules apply in petty offense and other misdemeanor cases and on appeal to a district judge in a case tried by a magistrate judge, unless this rule provides otherwise.

(2) *Petty Offense Case Without Imprisonment.* In a case involving a petty offense for which no sentence of imprisonment will be imposed, the court may follow any provision of these rules that is not inconsistent with this rule and that the court considers appropriate.

(3) *Definition.* As used in this rule, the term "petty offense for which no sentence of imprisonment will be imposed" means a petty offense for which the court determines that, in the event of conviction, no sentence of imprisonment will be imposed.

(b) Pretrial Procedure.

(1) *Charging Document.* The trial of a misdemeanor may proceed on an indictment, information, or complaint. The trial of a petty offense may also proceed on a citation or violation notice.

(2) *Initial Appearance.* At the defendant's initial appearance on a petty offense or other misdemeanor charge, the magistrate judge must inform the defendant of the following:

(A) the charge, and the minimum and maximum penalties, including imprisonment, fines, any special assessment under 18 U.S.C. § 3013, and restitution under 18 U.S.C. § 3556;

(B) the right to retain counsel;

(C) the right to request the appointment of counsel if the defendant is unable to retain counsel—unless the charge is a petty offense for which the appointment of counsel is not required;

(D) the defendant's right not to make a statement, and that any statement made may be used against the defendant;

(E) the right to trial, judgment, and sentencing before a district judge—unless:

(i)   the charge is a petty offense; or

(ii) the defendant consents to trial, judgment, and sentencing before a magistrate judge;

(F) the right to a jury trial before either a magistrate judge or a district judge—unless the charge is a petty offense;

(G) any right to a preliminary hearing under Rule 5.1, and the general circumstances, if any, under which the defendant may secure pretrial release; and

(H) that a defendant who is not a United States citizen may request that an attorney for the government or a federal law enforcement official notify a consular officer from the defendant's country of nationality that the defendant has been arrested—but that even without the defendant's request, a treaty or other international agreement may require consular notification.

(3) *Arraignment.*

(A) *Plea Before a Magistrate Judge.* A magistrate judge may take the defendant's plea in a petty offense case. In every other misdemeanor case, a magistrate judge may take the plea only if the defendant consents either in writing or on the record to be tried before a magistrate judge and specifically waives trial before a district judge. The defendant may plead not guilty, guilty, or (with the consent of the magistrate judge) nolo contendere.

(B) *Failure to Consent.* Except in a petty offense case, the magistrate judge must order a defendant who does not consent to trial before a magistrate judge to appear before a district judge for further proceedings.

(c) Additional Procedures in Certain Petty Offense Cases. The following procedures also apply in a case involving a petty offense for which no sentence of imprisonment will be imposed:

(1) *Guilty or Nolo Contendere Plea.* The court must not accept a guilty or nolo contendere plea unless satisfied that the defendant understands the nature of the charge and the maximum possible penalty.

(2) *Waiving Venue.*

(A) *Conditions of Waiving Venue.* If a defendant is arrested, held, or present in a district different from the one where the indictment, information, complaint, citation, or violation notice is pending, the defendant may state in writing a desire to plead guilty or nolo contendere; to waive venue and trial in the district where the proceeding is pending; and to consent to the court's disposing of the case in the district where the defendant was arrested, is held, or is present.

(B) *Effect of Waiving Venue.* Unless the defendant later pleads not guilty, the prosecution will proceed in the district where the defendant was arrested, is held, or is present. The district clerk must notify the clerk in the original district of the defendant's waiver of venue. The defendant's statement of a desire to plead guilty or nolo contendere is not admissible against the defendant.

(3) *Sentencing.* The court must give the defendant an opportunity to be heard in mitigation and then proceed immediately to sentencing. The court may, however, postpone sentencing to allow the probation service to investigate or to permit either party to submit additional information.

(4) *Notice of a Right to Appeal.* After imposing sentence in a case tried on a not-guilty plea, the court must advise the defendant of a right to appeal the conviction and of any right to appeal the sentence. If the defendant was convicted on a plea of guilty or nolo contendere, the court must advise the defendant of any right to appeal the sentence.

(d) Paying a Fixed Sum in Lieu of Appearance.

(1) *In General.* If the court has a local rule governing forfeiture of collateral, the court may accept a fixed-sum payment in lieu of the defendant's appearance and end the case, but the fixed sum may not exceed the maximum fine allowed by law.

(2) *Notice to Appear.* If the defendant fails to pay a fixed sum, request a hearing, or appear in response to a citation or violation notice, the district clerk or a magistrate judge may issue a notice for the defendant to appear before the court on a date certain. The notice may give the defendant an additional opportunity to pay a fixed sum in lieu of appearance. The district clerk must serve the notice on the defendant by mailing a copy to the defendant's last known address.

(3) *Summons or Warrant.* Upon an indictment, or upon a showing by one of the other charging documents specified in Rule 58(b)(1) of probable cause to believe that an offense has been committed and that the defendant has committed it, the court may issue an arrest warrant or, if no warrant is requested by an attorney for the government, a summons. The showing of probable cause must be made under oath or under penalty of perjury, but the affiant need not appear before the court. If the defendant fails to appear before the court in response to a summons, the court may summarily issue a warrant for the defendant's arrest.

(e) Recording the Proceedings. The court must record any proceedings under this rule by using a court reporter or a suitable recording device.

(f) New Trial. Rule 33 applies to a motion for a new trial.

(g) Appeal.

(1) *From a District Judge's Order or Judgment.* The Federal Rules of Appellate Procedure govern an appeal from a district judge's order or a judgment of conviction or sentence.

(2) *From a Magistrate Judge's Order or Judgment.*

(A) *Interlocutory Appeal.* Either party may appeal an order of a magistrate judge to a district judge within 14 days of its entry if a district judge's order could similarly be appealed. The party appealing must file a notice with the clerk specifying the order being appealed and must serve a copy on the adverse party.

(B) *Appeal from a Conviction or Sentence.* A defendant may appeal a magistrate judge's judgment of conviction or sentence to a district judge within 14 days of its entry. To appeal, the defendant must file a notice with the clerk specifying the judgment being appealed and must serve a copy on an attorney for the government.

(C) *Record.* The record consists of the original papers and exhibits in the case; any transcript, tape, or other recording of the proceedings; and a certified copy of the docket entries. For purposes of the appeal, a copy of the record of the proceedings must be made available to a defendant who establishes by affidavit an inability to pay or give security for the record. The Director of the Administrative Office of the United States Courts must pay for those copies.

(D) *Scope of Appeal.* The defendant is not entitled to a trial de novo by a district judge. The scope of the appeal is the same as in an appeal to the court of appeals from a judgment entered by a district judge.

(3) *Stay of Execution and Release Pending Appeal.* Rule 38 applies to a stay of a judgment of conviction or sentence. The court may release the defendant pending appeal under the law relating to release pending appeal from a district court to a court of appeals.

Rule 59. Matters Before a Magistrate Judge

(a) Nondispositive Matters. A district judge may refer to a magistrate judge for determination any matter that does not dispose of a charge or defense. The magistrate judge must promptly conduct the required proceedings and, when appropriate, enter on the record an oral or written order stating the determination. A party may serve and file objections to the order within 14 days after being served with a copy of a written order or after the oral order is stated on the record, or at some other time the court sets. The district judge must consider timely objections and modify or set aside any part of the order that is contrary to law or clearly erroneous. Failure to object in accordance with this rule waives a party's right to review.

(b) Dispositive Matters.

(1) *Referral to Magistrate Judge.* A district judge may refer to a magistrate judge for recommendation a defendant's motion to dismiss or quash an indictment or information, a motion to suppress evidence, or any matter that may dispose of a charge or defense. The magistrate judge must promptly conduct the required proceedings. A record must be made of any evidentiary proceeding and of any other proceeding if the magistrate judge considers it necessary. The magistrate judge must enter on the record a recommendation for disposing of the matter, including any proposed findings of fact. The clerk must immediately serve copies on all parties.

(2) *Objections to Findings and Recommendations.* Within 14 days after being served with a copy of the recommended disposition, or at some other time the court sets, a party may serve and file specific written objections to the proposed findings and recommendations. Unless the district judge directs otherwise, the objecting party must promptly arrange for transcribing the record, or whatever portions of it the parties agree to or the magistrate judge considers sufficient. Failure to object in accordance with this rule waives a party's right to review.

(3) *De Novo Review of Recommendations.* The district judge must consider de novo any objection to the magistrate judge's recommendation. The district judge may accept, reject, or modify the recommendation, receive further evidence, or resubmit the matter to the magistrate judge with instructions.

Rule 60. Victim's Rights

(a) In General.

(1) *Notice of a Proceeding.* The government must use its best efforts to give the victim reasonable, accurate, and timely notice of any public court proceeding involving the crime.

(2) *Attending the Proceeding.* The court must not exclude a victim from a public court proceeding involving the crime, unless the court determines by clear and convincing evidence that the victim's testimony would be materially altered if the victim heard other testimony at that proceeding. In determining whether to exclude a victim, the court must make every effort to permit the fullest attendance possible by the victim and must consider reasonable

alternatives to exclusion. The reasons for any exclusion must be clearly stated on the record.

(3) *Right to Be Heard on Release, a Plea, or Sentencing.* The court must permit a victim to be reasonably heard at any public proceeding in the district court concerning release, plea, or sentencing involving the crime.

(b) Enforcement and Limitations.

(1) *Time for Deciding a Motion.* The court must promptly decide any motion asserting a victim's rights described in these rules.

(2) *Who May Assert the Rights.* A victim's rights described in these rules may be asserted by the victim, the victim's lawful representative, the attorney for the government, or any other person as authorized by 18 U.S.C. § 3771(d) and (e).

(3) *Multiple Victims.* If the court finds that the number of victims makes it impracticable to accord all of them their rights described in these rules, the court must fashion a reasonable procedure that gives effect to these rights without unduly complicating or prolonging the proceedings.

(4) *Where Rights May Be Asserted.* A victim's rights described in these rules must be asserted in the district where a defendant is being prosecuted for the crime.

(5) *Limitations on Relief.* A victim may move to reopen a plea or sentence only if:

(A) the victim asked to be heard before or during the proceeding at issue, and the request was denied;

(B) the victim petitions the court of appeals for a writ of mandamus within 10 days after the denial, and the writ is granted; and

(C) in the case of a plea, the accused has not pleaded to the highest offense charged.

(6) *No New Trial.* A failure to afford a victim any right described in these rules is not grounds for a new trial.

Rule 61. Title

These rules may be known and cited as the Federal Rules of Criminal Procedure.